The New Testament as True Fiction

Playing the Texts, 3

Series Editor
George Aichele

Author of

Re-exploring Paul's Imagination: A Cynical Laywoman's Guide to Paul of Tarsus

The New Testament as True Fiction

Literature, Literary Criticism, Aesthetics

Douglas A. Templeton

Sheffield
Academic Press

BS2361.2
.T46
1999x

Copyright © 1999 Sheffield Academic Press

Published by Sheffield Academic Press Ltd
Mansion House
19 Kingfield Road
Sheffield S11 9AS
England

Printed on acid-free paper in Great Britain
by Bookcraft Ltd
Midsomer Norton, Bath

British Library Cataloguing in Publication Data

A catalogue record for this book is available
from the British Library

ISBN 1-85075-945-6
ISBN 1-85075-950-2 pbk

ἴσκε ψεύδεα πολλὰ λέγων ἐτύμοισιν ὁμοῖα...

[So he told many a false tale in the likeness of truth...]
Homer, *Odyssey*

MAR 0 8 2000

ROBERT LOWTH, *D.D.*
Bifhop of London.

Drawn & Engraved by H.Cook. ———— Published Nov.10. 1787. by W.Bent.

Robert Lowth (1710–87), author of *De sacra poesi Hebraeorum* [*On the Sacred Poetry of the Hebrews*] (1753) (portrait, by T. Cook, published in *Memoirs*... [1787]) (reproduced by courtesy of New College Library, University of Edinburgh)

Extract from a Sermon: At the visitation of the Bishop (1758)

By Robert Lowth (1710-87)

Christianity was published to the world in the most enlightened age; it invited and challenged the examination of the ablest judges, and stood the test of the severest scrutiny: the more it is brought to the light, to the greater advantage will it appear. When, on the other hand, the dark ages of barbarism came on, as every art and science was almost extinguished, so was christianity in proportion oppressed and overwhelmed by error and superstition: and they that pretended to defend it from the assaults of its enemies, by prohibiting examination and free enquiry, took the surest method of cutting off all hopes of its recovery. Again, when letters revived, and reason regained her liberty; when a spirit of inquiry began to prevail, and was kept up and promoted by a happy invention, by which the communication of knowledge was wonderfully facilitated; christianity immediately emerged out of darkness, and was in a manner re-published to the world in its native simplicity. It has always flourished or decayed together with learning and liberty: it will ever stand or fall with them. It is therefore of the utmost importance to the cause of true religion, that it be submitted to an open and impartial examination: that every disquisition concerning it be allowed its free course; that even the malice of its enemies should have its full scope, and try its utmost strength of argument against it. Let no man be alarmed at the attempts of Atheists or Infidels: let them produce their cause; let them bring forth their strong reasons to their own confusion: afford them not the advantage of restraint, the only advantage which their cause admits of: let them not boast the false credit of supposed arguments and pretended demonstrations, which they are forced to suppress. What has been the consequence of all that licentious contradiction, with which the gospel has been received in these our times and in this nation? Hath it not given birth to such irrefragable apologies and convincing illustrations of our most holy religion, as no other age or nation ever produced? What in particular has been the effect of unrestrained opposition in a very recent instance, prepared with much labour and study, and supported with all the art and eloquence of late celebrated genius? Hath not the very weakness and impotence of the assault given the most signal and decisive victory to the cause of truth? And do not the arms of this mighty champion of infidelity stand as a trophy erected by himself to display and to perpetuate the triumph? Let no one lightly entertain suspicions of any serious proposal for the advancement of religious knowledge, nor out of unreasonable prejudice endeavour to obstruct any inquiry, that professes to aim at the farther illustration of the great scheme of the gospel in general, or the removal of error in any part, in faith, in doctrine, in practice, or in worship. An opinion is not therefore false, because it contradicts received notions: but whether true or false, let it be submitted to a fair examination; truth must in the end be a gainer by it, and appear with the greater evidence. Where freedom of enquiry is maintained and exercised under the direction of the sincere word of God, falsehood may perhaps triumph for a day, but tomorrow truth will certainly prevail, and every succeeding day will confirm her superiority.

Dedication

Elizabethae
uxori meae
a deo dilectae
et a viro quodammodo
5   *(secundum hominem dico)*
a deo dilectus
dat donum dat
qualecunque
et virgini puerisque
10   *quotquot sunt*
Kirstenae et Alano necnon Calumo
calamo conatus honoratis omnibus
immo oneratis
non sine fele cum cane
15   †††††††††††††††††††††††††††††
ultima in epula convivioque
esurienter cum pane
panem comedentes
tubarum in sonitu
20   *nunc simul requiescentes*
tunc requiescent
animae eorum
ibi ubi nec tumultus in ululatu
nec/non Culicoides latebit/patebit in herba
25   *impunctatus/pulicaris coelestis/infernalis*
nec silentium
aequalis sed musica una

paeninsularum insularumque ocello:
Gigha
30   *Earaghàidheal*

MDCCCCXCV

To my wife, Elizabeth,
Loved by God,
And loved in his fashion by her husband
(I speak after human fashion),
5   A husband, loved, too, by God,
Offers this gift,
Such as it is;
And to the young men and maiden,
As many as they are,
10   Kirsten and Alan and Calum, too;
All of whom, without calumny,
I have tried to honour with my pen,
Though I have laid great burdens on them;
Not without the [late] cat, too, and the dog,
15   [1]

            Convives at the last banquet,
            A company dining eagerly
            On substantial fare,
            To the sound of trumpets,
20   Their selves, at the present time now resting,
            Then shall take their rest there,
            Where there will be neither noise, nor sorrow,

25   †Nor/not† the Highland Midge
            †Shall lie hidden/lie open†
            In the grass,
            That Midge †Celestial/Infernal†,[2]
            Nor silence, but
30   One Equal Music.

                  Of isles and almost islands
                  The apple of the eye:
                  Gigha
                  Argyll
                       1995

1.   This line cannot be translated.
2.   This passage is hopelessly corrupt. There seems to be a disjunction, antinomy even, between two textual traditions, one of which seems to be asserting and the other denying the after-life of the Highland Midge, or *Culicoides impunctatus* or *pulicaris* (which has the authority of Darling [1937: 145]). Difficulties with the sequence of thought suggest that the lines are an interpolation.

Contents

List of Illustrations

Preface

There is no more time to lick this whelp. *Tempus erat...*, it is high
time, and more than high time, that it should be in the hands of the
Editor.

I should warn my reader that I have been unable to convince
myself that I have been able to make use of the same edition of
Diels, *Fragmente der Vorsokratiker*, as was made in Harvard,
Oxford or Kensington by T.S. Eliot, but I have tried to make this
plain, when Diels has been cited.

I should apologize also for the brackets by which the name of
Hamann is surrounded. This is partly because I did not discover
that his *Aesthetica in nuce* had appeared in English in 1985
(Nisbet), until writing was well advanced. There is, moreover, in
the useful work of Lumpp (1970), a *facsimile* of the original
publication, which appeared in 1762. And this must be a delight to
every bibliophile. The *A.i.n.* (as Mr Wooster would no doubt term
it) appears in the splendid edition of the collected works by Nadler
in the 1950 volume. There is finally what is perhaps the best
introduction to Hamann in English by Gregor Smith (1960), which
contains some brief extracts from this perplexing work. These
various contributions provide some explanation for the forest of
parentheses that surround Hamann's name.

If, finally, the piety of an Aeneas be permitted, or of a Lorenzo, to
turn to 'a seminal work in a secular cult of sepulchral melancholy'
(Cornford, in Young 1989: ix), I cannot do better than cite Thomas
(1971), from the initial 'Author's Note'—No. Thomas's words are
too good to be removed from their place (where the persevering
can find them). I will cite only, with some, small modifications:

> [This book], with all [its] crudities, doubts, and confusions, is writ-
> ten for the love of Man [and Woman] and in praise of God, and I'd
> be a damn' fool if [it wasn't].

It is with similar sentiments that this work is put before my reader.

The Mound, Edinburgh
27 September 1996

Acknowledgments

von unten kristallisiert das Werk niemals
(the work never crystallizes from below)
H.U. von Balthasar, *Herrlichkeit: Eine
theologische Ästhetik*

'From Myth to Plot' (Chapter 2) is the acorn from which this thistle sprang. I would like to thank David Jasper, of the Centre for the Study of Literature and Theology, in the University of Glasgow, for the opportunity of giving an early version of it to one of the Centre Conferences, and Gregory Salyer and Robert Detweiler for including it in *Literature and Theology at Century's End* (Atlanta: Scholars Press, 1995).

I would like to thank also Graeme Auld (1993), of New College, Edinburgh, who first evoked, in honour of George Anderson (here Chapter 3), 'The Pauline Epistles as Border Ballads: Truth and Fiction in the *Carmen Christi*', in the volume edited by him, *Understanding Poets and Prophets* (Sheffield: JSOT Press). The dedicatory poem to George Anderson, doctored by Ms Kirsteen Moir (her help is more fully recognized at the end of that chapter), has been not excluded here, for, after all, our trade is song.

An early word, too, should be spoken on behalf of the Editor of the Series, Professor George Aichele (Adrian College), who, having grown accustomed to framing (1996), is now growing accustomed to being framed. In his endeavours to save my reader from the worst he is to be congratulated on showing what St Paul calls 'patience' (Rom. 5.3) and W.S. Gilbert calls 'Patience' (1923).

If what the writer has has been gained by theft, it is only right that this criminal, where his memory still serves him, should make some show of acknowledging the guilt of theft, distortion and generally wanton damage. I have some fear that I do not agree with me, but I would not wish those who have assisted me in any way to fear that I am expecting them, or expecting others to expect them, to do so. Sins of omission here may be put down to incipient encephalopathy, if the epithet may be allowed to stand.

Thanks are due to Fr Käthe Gregor Smith, the Queen of the King of Chapter 12.

Help and encouragement have been received from my friends: John Ashton (eponymous studies), of Wolfson College, Oxford; Ian Mackenzie, (late) of Religious Broadcasting (BBC Scotland); Robert Morgan (biblical interpretation), of Linacre College, Oxford; Richard Proudfoot (English Literature), of King's College, London; John Rowlands (art history) (very late) of the British Museum (Prints and Drawings); Roland Walls (history, literature, philosophy) (together with Brother John, no tyro on *An Teallach* gneiss, and Sister Patty), of the Community of the Transfiguration, Roslin (Midlothian); and Tony Weir (Grotius studies, tort), of Trinity College, Cambridge.

Dr Eberhard Bethge (Bonhoeffer studies), of Wachtberg, Professor Henry Chadwick (Church History) (late) of Christchurch, Oxford, and Professor Oliver O'Donovan (Moral and Pastoral Theology) (early) of the same place; Professor Ernst Feil (Bonhoeffer studies), Munich; and Professor John Riches (von Balthasar), University of Glasgow, have responded with celerity to my queries. Professor Charles Davis, Emeritus of Toronto and Practitioner of Christian Thought, assisted with acumen.

Professor Geoffrey Barrow (Albanian Studies), Professor Alec Cheyne ([late] Church History: Walter Scott studies) of Peebles, Professor Tony Cohen (Social Anthropology), Dr George Davie (Scottish Common and Uncommon Sense), Professor Ronald Hepburn (Aesthetics), Professor Peter Higgs (Small Particle Physics), Professor Timothy Sprigge (Spinoza) and Professor John Richardson (Classics, Law, Fiction), all of the University of Edinburgh, have proffered advice, manuscripts, articles and books. Professor Ian Parsons (Geology and Geophysics) and Mr Peder Aspen, Curator of the Departmental Collections, kindly supplied Brother John Halsey with an empirically fitting hammer for examining the physical aspects (petrified) of the metaphysics (petrified, but none the worse for that) of *An Teallach*. I would also like to thank, from an impertinent distance, Christoph von Dohnányi (Conductor of the Cleveland Orchestra) for a performance at the 1996 Edinburgh Festival of Brahms's Symphony No. 1 in C Minor, for the last movement in particular, preceded, I should perhaps add, by Charles Ives's 'The Unanswered Question'.

And a special note of thanks is due to Professor Dan Jacobson, Emeritus of University College, London, novelist and critic, for his kind encouragement at more than one crucial point—and for his sometimes salutary warnings, ignored at all points.

Canine drafts (breakfasts!) have been read by some of the above and by Mr Peter Gowans (Edinburgh). M. and Mme Alastair J.M. Hulbert, of Brussels, have kept me in touch with the 'soul and body of Europe'. Mr Niall Campbell has fulfilled the good Scottish offices of supplying me with information on Corrag Buidhe, Sgurr Fiona (Fheoin, 'The peaked, rocky hill of wine') and Lord Berkeley's Seat (*An Teallach*) and Mrs Campbell with information on the higher echelons of the Church of Scotland and the thinking, and imagining, there. Thanks, too, to Ms David Beckett, surprised, in the School of Scottish Studies, into producing the etymology of Cara, Craro, Gigalum and Gigha.

The local long-suffering of colleagues: staff, students, administration, support, and those who have dusted piles of books (Ms Wilma Gray and Ms Effie Haston), should not go unmentioned; and I hope it will not be invidious if I give especial thanks to Mr David Wright (Church History), Dr A.C. Ross (History of the Church), Dr Iain W. Provan (Old Testament) and Dr Nicholas Wyatt (Theology and Religious Studies/Hebrew and Old Testament Studies). And Ms Christine Brown (undergraduate) ran down for me Eliot's dove/ *Taube* ('Little Gidding' II [= 1944: 38]). Ms Hocking, ably assisted by Ms Rankin, offered me coffee, counsel and correspondence; and burnt Goverment circulars. Dr Ronald Seiler and Mr Ronald Beasley gave generously of their time during the gestation of these pages and Ms Anne Stewart, *inter alia* also, provisioned kind access to the music of the '45.

Acknowledgment, too, is due to the stirling efforts of Dr Simpson (now ably replaced by Ms P.M. Gilchrist) and the New College Library Staff, the *norma normans* by which other libraries are *normatae* (Jdt 2, Paul *passim*). Ms Eileen Dickson pursued my 'running head' (Black 1963: 438, 440) and conducted signal searches on what follows; but I forbear to mention that Paul tried to lock me up for the weekend with St Bonaventura (1754) and his *Itinerarium mentis in deum*.

My wife, my family, and other animals, are recognized in another place, but I should say, here, that my wife has told me what all this looks like from Djakarta, Kirsten (16) has kept me abreast with Suffragette studies, Alan (14) with architecture and Calum (12) with Jerome and, for Extreme Skiing and ski jumps, the Swedish *friktionskoefficient för skida mot snö* (μ).

And to all those others, whose help has been gratefully received, but under the conditions of existence have here remained nameless, much thanks.

Note

The word, 'late', as perhaps idiosyncratically used above, means only that the scholars, to whom that epithet is applied, are, having retired, now *late to work* and that their colleagues do not see them so often—except (so far as I know) in the case of the late and much lamented, Peter Gowans, esq., who struggled so valiantly with his last illness.

Addendum

Now that this beast is lurching to Sheffield to be born (another mis-allusion, I am afraid), one does have the impression that Horace's *dictum* on the deferring of texts for a decade (just about) is too sanguine. It is only the author of the fairy-tale, perhaps, who has the power to convert a toad into a prince, even if it may and perhaps must also be said that even the humble toad has its place. But before this lurching takes place, there are some final, but necessary, additions.

Only Mr John Ashton, a considerable scholar and theologian, and, still more, friend and counsellor, knows how much he has contributed to these pages. The Canon, our Brother, and, with him, the Brother's Brother, Mr John Halsey, has his tribute in the Coda—let that suffice. But, above all, a tribute is due to the patience, macrothymy even (if Murray will permit) of my wife, Elizabeth, and then to the rest of the family—Donald, the dog (to name only one [before naming Kirsten, Alan and Calum]), has been short on pheasants and peasants and has had only the sporadic compensation of the systematic persecution of the urban cat (if, and only if, as must be admitted, the urban cat is already in flight).

But once this has been said, I am bound to acknowledge the magnificent aid of Ms Mandy Marks of the National Gallery, London, of a concatenation of researchers in the Bridgeman Art

Library, the generous help of the Tate Gallery, London, and the National Gallery of Scotland, Herr Rohlfing of the Niedersächsische Staats- und Universitätsbibliotek, Göttingen, the energetic Dr Norman Reid, Keeper of Manuscripts and Muniments in the St Andrews University Library and his rapid assistant, Ms Cilla Jackson, for R.M. Adam (Mr Niall Campbell's genial suggestion), and (nearer home) from the University of Edinburgh, Dr Joe Rock, Photographer of the Department of Fine Art, Mr Goddard, Photographer of the University Library, and Mr Kevin Hicks of the Centre for Field Archaeology for his skill in dictating to his computer Piero della Francesca's employment, for the Baptism of Jesus, of a refinement of Euclid's sixteenth Proposition of the fourth of Euclid's 13 books of *Elements*.

Not every one knows that, as the archaeologist's field notes on the Phigaleian Frieze of the Temple of Bassae were thrown overboard in a storm (without the archaeologist), it has been a standing challenge to scholarship to arrive at the right arrangement; and that to this challenge, over time, the scholarly world has risen magnificently. Dinsmoor (*q.v.*) had provided me with the six right arrangements that are listed in Chapter 5, and had produced another two (2) right arrangements of his own (with the earlier disowned). I have to thank Mr B.A. Jackson (for the Keeper) of the Department of Greek and Roman Antiquities, British Museum, for providing me with a ninth (Corbett) and with two superb photographs.

Thanks, too, must go to Mr Colin Kerr for the apospasm from 'The Ripening Seed' in Chapter 8 and to the Gairm Press, Glaschu and Mr Maoilios M. Caimbeul for their permission to include the Gaelic poem in Chapter 9.

The College computing team, Mr N. Timmins and Ms G. McKinnon, condescended with a good deal of cheerfulness from their electronic universe into a corner of the Gutenberg galaxy. If we fall short of the Bletchley Enigma, the Age of Swift is at any rate an achievement. And the late arrival of Ms C. Webster, with a manual solution when the ends were upon us of the ages this has all taken, was quite beyond praise.

But a special note is due, first to my Desk Editor, Mrs V. Acklam, for her invariable cheerfulness and resourcefulness under onslaught, to the producers of Proof 1 and Proof 2, and to all those at Sheffield Academic Press, who have taken time and trouble, and especially, more recently, to the Managing Editor, Mr Steve Barganski, who showed great openness to an experimental text, despite the great labour, not Sisyphean, it seems, but certainly Herculean, that that would involve. And, second, to the meticulous proof-reading and infinite indexing of Ms Christine Brown. And I would that the word 'meticulous' had not universally been so appropriate, as Ms Brown had the temerity (and this is only one instance) to point out that the 'axe' that ensured the death of Agamemnon was not, in point of fact, what Aeschylus had actually said. For any other blunders, beyond those she has scried, that have escaped her accipitrine scrutiny, or have been obdurately retained by the author in the face of all evidence to the contrary, the devils must take some responsibility and myself some more.

And there *is* more!

There is much in this essay that would need a real philosophical head. And I should here confess (acknowledge?) that what I say about Anselm in Chapter 12 is said or implied by Anselm himself, as I have subsequently discovered from Anthony Kenny, in 'Anselm on the Conceivability of God', in *What is Faith? Essays in the Philosophy of Religion* (Oxford: Oxford University Press, 1992 [Ch. 8, pp. 110-21]), if I am understanding either. In Chapter 12 I make the matter formulaic and there, I am afraid, for the moment is where it *lies*. But my thanks to Mr Philip Newell for enabling me to become acquainted with the poetry of Mr Maoilios M. Caimbeul.

Let others, then, do better, but let *this* now lurch.

New College
2 October 1998

Albanaich!

H.M. Lynch, *Scotland: A New History*

Albani! Albani!

Henrici Archidiaconi Huntindoniensis Historiarum lib. VIII[1]

Albania,[2]
(Late) Cenozoic/(Early) Ecozoic

1.   *Exclamavit simul exercitus Scottorum insigne patrium, et ascendit clamor usque in coelum, Albani, Albani* ('At the same moment the Scots raised their country's war-cry, Alban! Alban! till it reached the clouds' [Henry of Huntingdon 1596: 223 (The Battle of the Standard [1138])]).

2.   *Illa regio, que nunc corrupte vocatur Scotia, antiquitus appellabatur Albania...* ('That region, which is now called Scotland, was in ancient times called Albania...' [?Ailred of Rievaulx? 1165: fol. 26 verso]).

1

Porridge in my Salt: The Plot of This Book

Oats

Is defined by the learned Doctor (Samuel Johnson 1805 *s.v.*) as 'a grain, which in England is generally given to horses, but in Scotland supports the people'. And, after: 'The oats have eaten the horses' (from [the better known] Shakespeare) a certain person, called Miller, in a quotation below the entry, ends with the words: 'The meal makes tolerable good bread.' Oats are substantial.

Well, the 'substance' (Aristotle and my Editor want to know) of what follows is as follows:

Chapter 3 says that the Hymn to Christ in Paul's letter to the Philippians (2.6-11) is what, in a parliamentary democracy, like Scotland, is called an 'auld sang', or, as my children put it (but not their mother), is a 'poyyum'. The question is: How much does, or does not, follow from saying this?

The insight that generated what follows comes in Chapter 2 and is introduced by this one (Chapter 1) and derives from the fact, nowadays presupposed by most thinking scholars, that John, the Fourth Gospel, hardly represents, if it represents at all, what Jesus actually said. And this fact suggests the response, Well, dammit (German: *damit* [Walls]), it's all just a fiction.

'Do you mean', asked a late colleague (O'Neill n.d.), 'that it's all like P.D. James?' Barbara Cartland, better known to the present writer, is the answer given here. I am thinking of Cartland and all her works, but it is *Love and the Marquis* that is in question here. Something also on the Gospels of Mark and John is included also.

Chapter 4 then goes to the classical place, or topos, in the New Testament, to the Parables of Jesus, where fiction is to be expected and can be found. Here, if anywhere, the word, 'fiction', needs no defence, at least in those regions where a philosophy of common sense receives no attack.

The next two chapters (6 and 7) return to Mark and John and try to give more detail and more detailed reflection in relation to some questions that appear and persistently reappear throughout the book. What is the pigeon doing in Mark (1.11)? In what sense is the word, in John, a person?

And what about Paul? Is there more to say about him than was said in Chapter 2—in meeting Jesus on a cloud (1 Thess. 4.17), in the 'resurrection' passage in 1 Cor. 15 (both of these in Chapter 5), or in a dazzling display of coruscating metaphors in 2 Corinthians 3 (Chapter 8)? But metaphors are non-literal, are they not? Where do we touch solid ground? Does the theologian touch solid ground in the sky? But the sky is full of holes, surely? Is there more in all this than meets the eye?

But what about the 'Fool's Speech' in 2 Corinthians 11 and 12 (Chapter 9)? That looks frankly autobiographical. But what kind of an autobiography is the autobiography of someone who has travelled to outer space, to the 'third heaven' (2 Cor. 12.2)? And what about the voice that breaks in just below (2 Cor. 12.9) and says,

> My grace is sufficient for thee:
> for my strength is made perfect in weakness?

And why does the voice speak in an almost perfect chiasmus? Could the voice, one feels, not have done a little better? But, of course, we cannot all be perfect.

But the beginning of the end sets in with T.S. Eliot and Wallace Stevens (Chapters 10 and 11, respectively). Two very different kinds of post-scriptural scripture are looked at here. Their writing is instructively useful in interestingly different ways, the relation between history and something else in Eliot and the relation between theology as it is usually done and how it *is* done by Wallace Stevens. These two chapters are written with the seriousness proper to scripture of this kind (there being only one rather jejune joke).

All this means that we are dealing in some measure (but *what* measure?) in all of this with fiction, poetry and story. And Chapter 12, a response to the seminal reflections of Gregor Smith, endeavours to draw some conclusions. A Coda forms an end-piece, unless the Index (*mot juste!*), or Indexes, and Bibliography (where the wise will begin and end) more properly should fill that role.

But whose job is it to look at fiction, poetry and story? It is the job of the literary critic, the looking at form and content, at narrative techniques, at figures and tropes, *et hoc genus omne*, as Dennis Nineham might put it (1967: 199-222). But literary criticism is a very young discipline in the universities, though, of course, we have had literary criticism since the beginning of literature, or almost. Aristotle, anyway, and Horace.

And what is the difference between merely producing a lot of interesting (and usually desiccated) information and showing real insight and the kind of sensibility that allows you to see inside the poetry and climb inside the story?

And lastly: What is the *philosophy* of literature? Are we to say that fiction is false? Or are we to say that, while it is, or may be, in some ways false, nevertheless it may be, or maybe *is*, true in some other way. But in what way, or ways?

The reader must frankly be warned that there are some places, perhaps many, in what follows, that are clearly obscure. And other places, I am afraid, that are frankly obscure to the author. And there are some places (Chapter 8 on 2 Cor. 3), where the bored reader, or the irritated reader, would be well advised to skip to pastures new in the search of something more jocund. There are some chapters that should not be missed. This one should be. Though I am bound, in defence of what stands written and has not been erased, to say that dimly through the rant, or obscurity, or apparent (or real?) repetition, or the intermittent absence of obvious advance, there may still be important questions at stake, such as (in Chapter 3) the question of the relation between criticism and scholarship and the question whether 'incarnation' only happened once and, if so, in what sense.

I hope that some of the things that follows are clear, since I am clear that not all of them are. At least there are many quotations that deserve a hearing. But the pusillanimous reader should give up here.

But the less pusillanimous and more intrepid should perhaps, and perhaps will, leave a decade between chapters. But what is my Publisher to make of that? Is it a selling point? But each chapter (the faint-hearted reader may be happy to hear) is preceded by some five lines of readable prose. The reader may be less happy to hear that these five lines are succeeded by a great many more that are less readable. They can, however, quite easily be made quite illegible. The useful highlighter has its correlative.

The rest is noise. It does not last long.

But some of it is silence. R.G. Collingwood says,

> Work ceases upon the picture or manuscript, not because it is
> finished, but because sending-in day is at hand, or because the
> printer is clamorous for copy, or because 'I am sick of working at
> this thing' or 'I can't see what more I can do to it' (1939: 2).

What he omitted to say, but what he said by implication, is that some books are unready and others will remain so. But there is this to be said to the reader of this one, that the present author has been working on the texts that are here considered, the Gospels, the Hymn to Christ and the rest, on and off for some 38 years and longer. And that, even though the present author may be thought an irrelevant critic and blundering philosopher, the texts considered are such as sustained Dietrich Bonhoeffer as he knelt in prayer before the Nazis took his life and Johann Georg Hamann living with his wife quietly unmarried (Smith 1960: 34-35). The reader should at least pose the question, Why are these texts such that such men have been able to live by them?

If all else fails, the reader should *work* on the texts. That is certainly necessary for the comprehension even partially of what in what follows is partially comprehensible. If *laborare est orare*, 'to work is to pray', it is equally true that *laborare est laborare*, that by the sweat of one's brow one must eat this bread. The texts repay.

And yet even this is not the *unum necessarium*, the 'one thing necessary' of the Gospel tradition (Lk. 10.42). And what is *that*? In New Testament terms (not the only ones), it is God. It is love. In one set of other terms, it is that which may be 'absolutely presupposed' (Collingwood 1940). It is (again) love.

But: 'No word is so full of lies [fiction?] as the little word, "love"' (Ibsen [no ref.], cit. Henderson *obiter dictum*). Love is usually a sin, that covers a multitude of others. It is the *Inbegriff*, the 'covering concept', of much evil. But love means also 'being there for others' (Bonhoeffer 1971: 381), means love consciously willed, not just the knowledge that one is willing the good and willing it well, but that one is willing so to will it, in Gnostic Jonas's terms, not *cogito me velle*, but *volo me velle* (1971: 337).

Porridge in my Salt

Well.

Well, this book is an essay, to lick, like a dog, one of the sores of theology. And the sore is prose. And the cure poetry, poetry and song. It might be described as a study in spiration: of breath, of wind, of air, of spirit. It attempts to say what the New Testament is, but succeeds only, in so far as it does succeed, in saying what it is like. What is offered is not the truth, but, in intention at any rate, a contribution to it.

To write fiction, to engage in poetics, is to fashion, to make out of thin air, or ether (αἰθήρ: *aither*). To write religious fiction, engage in religious poetics, is to fashion and make out of thick air, or *pneuma*. And *pneuma* is more than you thought. The former is hot. The latter is hotter.

Fiction is as wide as poetry; more true than history. Fiction is one mode of doing something about something and the something, about which it is, is reality. Fiction and reality are, or are here taken to be, correlative concepts. If fiction is one mode of approaching reality, of doing something about what is real, history is another. And reality, whatever is real, may sometimes be approached by the one, sometimes by the other and sometimes by both together.

This book is primarily concerned with fiction. It is also concerned with the mixture of fiction and history. It is concerned only secondarily with history alone. The finding of history is an aid to the finding of what is either not history, or is a mixture of history with something else, a mixture of history with fiction. If you can convincingly show, or if it has been convincingly shown, what something is not, you are left with the problem of showing what it is. It is with history in its negative aspect that this book is concerned. History, here, to put it so, is the 'control' discipline. For when you have talked about history in the New Testament, there remains, over and above, something other, something more.

The word 'fiction' I believe to be a good word. For what do we find in the Gospels? We find The Good Samaritan and The Prodigal Son. And who told those stories?

If Jesus of Nazareth could do it, then why should not the Early Christians do it? And if the Early Christians could do it, why should not the Late Christians do it? And if the Late Christians can do it, why should not the Late Presbyterians do it? And if the Late Presbyterians can do it, why not the True Church of Scotland? (Connoisseurs of literature will recall here that Book III, 3, of Fielding's novel, *The History of Tom Jones* [1959: 60 (*'History'*[!]— and what is Fielding calling 'history'?)], includes a similar catena, or series.) And if there were nothing in fiction, if fiction were about nothing at all, then not so many of us would spend time on the quadrature of the eyes, the quadrature of their round pupils, fixed on, affixed on, transfixed by, a quadrated box.

The debate is only about how far the word, 'fiction', is useful. And it is the kind of debate that is already raging. It is not only in the ancient Near East that ancient Near Eastern carpets were chewed. And to this debate this (blessedly quite short) book is intended as a contribution.

It is not intended to produce answers. The intention is to wrestle with the questions, though the reader may find that some answers to some of the questions involved are suggested and even stated. But I expect the reader to make up their own mind. And, even more importantly, the reader should muse (the Scots' word 'dwam' [sc. some kind of suspension of animation, suspension of intellection], or any other ethnic equivalent, is one that should not be forgotten).

But what does it matter? Are there not more important things to do than read books? Or write them? Compare and contrast inscription on the page and on the heart.

But most words that have some value are double-edged. And so too the word 'fiction'. But then so are most scissors, if you want to cut cloth. And if Jesus of Nazareth found it worth his while to tell stories, it is also a fact that some people found it worth their while that he should stop telling them and that it is a fact that he was killed. And that, for very many reasons, is regarded by very many as an important fact—one that belongs to Bonhoeffer's three fundamentals: 'incarnate, crucified and risen' (1992: 78 [= 1955: 16]).

It is also, or may also be a fact that Jesus *is*, though there may be, quite properly, very great perplexity about what can be meant by 'is' and about what sort of a fact such a fact may be, and about how the histories, or stories, that recount that fact, or imply that fact, are to be taken. And if I were tiresome, I would probably say that such facts are meant to be taken 'lambitively', are meant to be 'licked up', like some medicines. And this may well, in fact (!), *be* part, at least, of an answer. But it would, here at least, be the wrong answer, because too quick an answer, and, though this book is only in spurts philosophical, it would be improper to resist a quoting of Wittgenstein here: 'In philosophy the winner of the race is the one who can run most slowly. Or: the one who gets there last'[1] (1980: 34c). But let that 'fact' stand, or try to stagger to its feet, that Jesus 'is', or may, for the nonce, be taken, or claimed, to be.

And let another fact stand, too, whatever it means, or whatever it should be taken to mean, that '[w]hatever is, is in God'[2] (Spinoza 1843: I, 197 [= *Ethica* I, prop. xv]), if 'whatever is' may be taken to mean (as why should it not?) our literature, too, and our language, though there are other ways, I think, even atheistic ones, of saying these things—just as there are theistic ways of denying them. But some word, or some equivalent gesture, or grimace, has to be found.

'Fiction', the word, 'fiction', brings in its trail other terms. And these will be met with along the way. So, first, a word, or words, on 'imagination', derived from Collingwood, on 'the historical imagination' (1946: 231-48, and *passim*) and McIntyre, who made the word more recently central, in *Faith, Theology and Imagination* (1987), for the exegete, interpreter, theologian and philosopher, this being re-taken up by Mackey (1986) in *Religious Imagination*.

On 'imagination' I will say only here (the examples are Collingwood's), that, when one sees a matchbox (1938: 137) on a desk, one can also 'see', that is: imagine, the underside of it; that when one sits on a shore and sees a ship at point A, and then 'take[s] down a book and slowly read[s]' (Yeats 1950: 46), and then looks again and sees a ship at point B, one can 'see', that is: imagine, the passage between the two points (Collingwood 1946: 241)—and, to add this to Collingwood, that, when one, like Wordsworth, is lying on one's pensive 'couch' and is, as one sometimes is, 'In vacant... mood', one can 'see', that is: imagine, 'A host of golden daffodils', even in the case where one has not seen the daffodils oneself,

1. 'Im Rennen der Philosophie gewinnt, wer am langsamsten laufen kann. Oder: der, der das Ziel zuletzt erreicht.'
2. 'Quicquid est in Deo est.'

but has been told that they were seen by another (it was not Wordsworth; it was his sister). And, in a sort of similar fashion, one can 'see', imagine, a chrysoprase city, one can 'see', that is: imagine, the New Jerusalem. What rocks! What rocks?

And, second, along with, aligned with 'imagination', is the word 'reality'. Some of Wallace Stevens's excursions in prose, entitled *The Necessary Angel* (1960), are subtitled: *Essays on Reality and the Imagination*. The collocation of these two words is, with Stevens, a favoured one. And he holds on to 'reality', when it is easy on summer days and in winter, too, when it is difficult, when the imagination is thinned and sometimes thinned to nothing. There are times when the life of the imagination has to move through, or into, or apparently into, annihilation, into nothing at all.

But 'reality', like 'fiction', is a useful word, which has every chance of covering all that there is and, in this respect, has the opportunity (I think) of being wider than 'history', which deals better with pastness, than with presentness, or with (horrible locution) 'futureness', or futurity, or (simply) the future (see Oakeshott 1983).

And with 'imagination' and 'reality' comes 'truth'. In the 'old and happy, far-off days' of Rudolf Bultmann (to garble, this time, the Wordsworth of 'The Solitary Reaper') and of 'The New Testament and Mythology' (1953 [= 1960a, 1988]), one (this is the débutante's use of 'one': 'one goes to Scotland in August') discussed the truth of myth. This book is concerned with the truth of fiction.

Let me first cite Santayana, the student of Spinoza (Sprigge 1993: 1) and the 'master' of Stevens (Kermode 1960: 33) (the sentence that matters here is Santayana's last, but I give the context, for one is travelling, too, to Scotland and the Heavenly City):

> The traveller must be somebody and come from somewhere, so that his definite character and moral traditions may supply an organ and a point of comparison for his observations. He must not go nosing about like a pedlar for profit or like an emigrant for a vacant lot. Everywhere he should show the discretion and maintain the dignity of a guest. Everywhere he should remain a stranger no matter how benevolent, and a critic no matter how appreciative. Were he a mere sensorium, without his own purposes, moral categories and points of reference, he might as well have left those variegated natives to lead their lives undisturbed and unvisited. They would

have gone on the more comfortably without him, and he the more inexpensively without them, at home. The traveller should be an artist recomposing what he sees; then he can carry away the picture and add it to a transmissible fund of wisdom, not as further miscellaneous experience but as a corrected view of the truth (1953: 46).

And, again:

[Hellas must remain for me an ideal, a thing to recompose,] as the Evangelists recomposed their idea of Jesus, so as to individualise and replenish their ideal of Christ (1953: 72).

The word to be fastened on is 'recompose'.

Fiction is not, like the historian, concerned, or only concerned with the reproductive, but with the productive imagination. The historian and the philosopher (or the scientist) do not have a monopoly of truth-telling. Fiction, while it does not state, nevertheless embodies truth. If Sir Walter Scott was not wasting his time, or Sophocles, or, to change horses, Ovid, neither was John wasting his. This book (it was said) is an essay, a *Guide to the Classics*, a guide to the poetics of the classics of the New Testament and two more recent classics of the mid-twentieth century, T.S. Eliot and Wallace Stevens. Griffith and Oakeshott, who in dealing with the classics must be our guides, put the matter with characteristic insight (1936: 9):

Nearly 2,000 years ago the poet Ovid wrote: *Nec te nobilium fugiat certamen equorum*—Never miss a good race meeting; and Ovid, like most poets, knew what was what (*Ars amatoria* 1.135).

It is this 'knowing what's what' that most poets, most creative writers, most writers of fiction (Welsh 1995) have at their command, or are commanded by reality to have. And to Oakeshott, Ovid and Griffith add (before re-adding—they will reappear) these fecund words of a critic familiar with Wallace Stevens: 'the opposite of "fiction" is not "truth", but "fact"' (Pack 1958: 122).

Fiction and truth, imagination and reality will be themes here.

But, to return to the 'fiction' of the title, something like the following may, perhaps, be said, or, as the early Plato would say, 'so it seems to me, at any rate'.

Fiction, the term 'fiction', is wider than fact, because it can include fact. And can affirm what it includes. But together with the actual, it can include the possible; and, with the merely possible, the possible that will some day, or later today, become actual. In other words, fiction is (I am supposing), for the writers of the New Testament, a superordinate concept, a concept superior to fact. The facts are plastic to its touch. The fiction-writer, for instance, can compose eschatologies, Utopias. But (and this is the aspect that the cautious 'even-Christian', or 'evyncristene' [Julian 1950: 15; Beer 1978: 46] finds difficult) fiction can also be opposed to fact, as the Cheshire cat of *Alice's Adventures in Wonderland* (Carroll 1929: 56) is opposed to my family's (late) cat. Her tail was bent, by a farmyard door. All tales are bent by the artist's mind. The relation between the bent tail of the (late) cat and the farmyard door is a historical fact (somebody left the door open, or never shut it) to be inferred from the tail's (late) shape. But what is to be inferred from a tale about a cat that was tail-less, and more?

Fiction, to use a technical term for a relation that is at once affirmative and negative, 'sublates' fact, or, in Collingwood's terminology (1933), 'overlaps' with fact. And this relation will be further touched on below, in Chapter 8, where Paul of Tarsus, the Jew, has the brass neck, like the Jews, to 'sublate' the law of the Jews, a law that 'overlaps' with 'grace', or 'spirit' or 'beauty'.

If '[w]hat I tell you three times is true' (Carroll 1929: 233), let me cite now, before citing and re-citing the quotation again, Paton, in *The Categorical Imperative* (1965). (The words that count are the words that occur in parentheses; the music is 'between the bars' [Swann 1968].) Paton, in speaking of the philosopher, the mathematician and the physicist, speaks also '(if we may regard as also a thinker him who is so much more) [of] the artist' (1965: 19).

The poet, the painter, the sculptor, the novelist is, in a word, speaking the language of the heart, is speaking from the heart. And a great deal of thinking may be required, before the heart can be rightly interpreted. The early Christians did metaphysics by telling stories, writing poems; by finding metaphors, symbols, images. For them, fiction is more important than fact. For them, fiction is to fact as metaphysics is to history. All that they said implies a metaphysic, that they did not, or could not, state. A metaphysic is not what they said, but is instantiated in, or embodied in, what they said.

The author of fiction is best placed, or well placed, to introduce 'the new' into history. And this is a point made by Kant, when he writes about originality and genius (1914: 188-206). An account of what Kant is saying there is offered by Kemal (1992: 136):

> Kant's emphasis on originality suggests that genius is a matter of producing new rules...
>
> In talking of producing rules Kant is taking a step beyond the strictly classical account of genius. The latter supposes that the rules by which we assess a work are given and have authority. We try to attain them in our works because those standards are valuable. The form of a sonnet, for example, is given once and for all, and serves as a standard which we try to attain in the particular works we create. But by pointing to our production of rules, Kant denies the simple authority of given models, and allows for us to generate new values in producing new objects. By producing new rules we develop new standards and forms of poetry or art, and do not merely seek to fulfil the given standards in newly interesting ways.

There are no rules for the productions of genius, but rules may be derived from them. And, if it was Kant's (revised) view, that the artist of genius is operating, not by the application of no concepts to sensibility, but by the application of an indeterminate, and not a determinate concept, or concepts, and that it is on this situation, on which the interpreter is called to operate, then how much more mysterious must the productions of genius be, and how much more difficult must the interpretation be, when the genius is an artist of *religion*, when the genius is a *religious* genius and the interpreter in question has been compelled or encouraged by the use of the speculative reason to construct a supersensible object.

But if Kant is too difficult and should more safely be left in the hands of his disciples—to Fries (1805), to de Wette (1821, 1831) and (more recently) Davidovich (1993), then at least this can be said, that, if the writers of the New Testament do not contain thought, as Plato, Aristotle, Spinoza and Wittgenstein may be said to contain it and do not contain it, until what is implied by what they say has been made explicit by such a subtle thinker as John Duns Scotus, because he has transformed them, then if they are thinking at all, their thought is loose, not to say 'arbitrary' (Paton 1965: 100). They give rise to the thought that they do not themselves think. What we find are intelligent images, new ones, old ones engaged to new purposes. What we find is genius; homely, perhaps, but genius all the same.

Thus new works (the Synoptists—Matthew, Mark and Luke? Paul? John?) somehow spring up, without our being able adequately to give a genetic account. And it may be that we can then go on to speak both about new reality creatively occurring in history and about new writing creating new reality.

But how can such things be said clearly? Can they be said clearly at all?

Fiction, the writer of fiction, may be more capable than the historian of dealing with the intervention of 'the new'. The novelist has more freedom than the historian. The Genesis myth is a *fiction* about God's *fiction* (making, fashioning) of Adam. Just as the resurrection stories are fictions about God's fiction of Jesus, a new fashioning of a new Adam? Just as, though we are not all yet dead, at least not in all senses, we are the fictional characters that God is in the process of writing? Of what will the Great Authour think next?

But I outrun reason.

The themes and questions, stated and implied above, are the themes and questions with which I obscurely struggle in the pages that follow. Anyone who is impatient of where this all leads to, or of how far it leads anywhere, and who is chary of labouring through too many pages of subfusc prose, should turn immediately to the Conclusion (Chapter 12), where all that can be made plain will be made plain, even if this should turn out to be only the extent of the obfuscation, that, having persisted from the beginning, persists in remaining at the end. For if the reader wants to know more and does not want to know how the processor of the word got there (which was sometimes the [late] cat, White and Brown Sugar, on the keys), as the 'Auroras of Autumn' (Stevens 1955: 411-21) moved from the 'green' and 'fluent mundo' (Stevens 1955: 407) of summer towards the 'winter' (Stevens 1955: 9) of sublatable fact, then recourse should immediately be made to that chapter, where the closure demands (and finds) an open-ended supplement. Green students of the domestic animal should give thanks, though they may be surprised to learn, that the cat's procedure was not also adopted by the dog.

But I *want* to say that fiction has the power to illuminate fact. For, if you have any of these (facts), how are they to be explained? What is to be made of the fact that there are facts to be explained?

If there is a fact, or facts, to explain that there are facts, is that fact to be factually, or fictionally explained? Wittgenstein, in the *Tractatus*, in a much-quoted passage (1960: 81), first makes this observation:

> 6.44   Not *how* the world is, is the mystical, but *that* it is.[3]

and then goes on to say (1960: 82):

> 6.45   The view of the world as a limited whole is the mystical.[4]

The world is a pen, a reed shaped for the writing of a story. The world is a story written with a pen, which has a beginning, a middle and an end. It is not unfair to say that the writer of fiction can deal with the world better by holding to Aristotle's 'beginning, middle and end' than can the writer who writes facts, though the factual story (!) of *The Universe Story* of Swimme and Berry (1992) may be an exception. Both sorts of writers, however, must remain indifferently embarrassed by either fact or fiction and their occurrence.

The notion of reality (though not realism) is wider than fact and fiction combined. But we must do what we can, if we ought not to do what we cannot. But what we can, we need not do without merriment.

Hilaritas is one of the great Bonhoeffer (and Bethge) words (1971: 229, 232, 243). And of Spinoza, too (1843: I, 361 [= *Ethica* IV, *prop*. XLII]). Had Paul been a better Latinist, it would have fitted well into the *catena* of 'fruits of the spirit': 'Love, joy, peace…' in Gal. 5.22, where Jerome has: *caritas, gaudium, pax…* And then one could say with Ecclesiastes:

> Hilarity of hilarities
> everything is hilarity.[5]

The Idea of Fiction

We shall never know what Paul of Tarsus thought or imagined when he was halfway through a letter. More on circumcision here?

---

3.   'Nicht *wie* die Welt ist, ist das Mystische, sondern *dass* sie ist.'
4.   'Die Anschauung der Welt sub specie aeterni ist ihre Anschauung als—begrenztes—Ganzes. Das Gefühl der Welt als begrenztes Ganzes ist das Mystische.'
5.   'Hilaritas hilaritatum omnia hilaritas.'

What time does the trireme go?

Whatever ran through the mind and imagination of Paul, when his *calamus* (reed-pen) was raised above his *papyrus* (reed-paper), it seems to be appropriate here to say, that three questions are going to be asked in the following pages:

1. How did certain writers feel about things?
2. How is the reader to get inside what they felt?
3. What is the reader to think about this?

In different words:

1. What sort of literary expression is this?
2. What is the literary critic to make of all this?
3. To what sort of a philosophy does it add up?

And it all adds up, no doubt, to something 'through a glass, in a riddle' (1 Cor. 13.12). It is like code-breaking (Wiles 1993), like can-opening (Jerome 1889). When a can is to be opened by the *Three Men in a Boat* (Jerome 1889: 195), a stone has to be placed on the can and a stick has to be found which will strike the stone: 'It was George's straw hat that saved his life that day' (Jerome 1889: 196). (It is better for the exegete that another exegete should lose his life.) If one is not vainly to repeat one's primary text, a key is required for the code, a can-opener for the can. If there is text-level and interpretation-level, the languages of the levels will differ. What is sought here is: (a) the language of literary criticism and (b) the language of philosophy to probe the postulates of the literary critic.

Thus the topics are three: literature, literary criticism and philosophy.

This book will have no chance at all of being misunderstood unless the reader knows out of what stable it is coming. Ideas have a history. What is the history of the idea of fiction?

That history might be said to begin with the history of the idea of history. But, if the 'theocratic history and myth' (Collingwood 1946: 14-17) of the Sumerians and Babylonians may be (here) safely left with them, we can begin this history of fiction nearer the end of it by starting with Reimarus. In other words, if we ask how the question of fiction arises within New Testament scholarship, we must begin with the history of non-fiction; we must begin with an inquiry into the period, at which people began to ask the question, 'Yes, but what actually happened?' Now if you marry Rodin's *Age of Bronze* to *Le Penseur* and then ask the Bronze Age thinker whether he was asking the historical question, whether he was worried, body and mind, about the distinction between history and fiction, my guess is that he would reply: 'The question is as old as, is co-eval with man.'

To begin with Reimarus is merely a *faute de mieux*, for we could start anywhere—with the Canaanites, with the pre-Socratics, with Origen... But, for immediate purposes, Reimarus is a good place to start, not least because that is where the Alsatian, Albert Schweitzer, began his 'matchless critical review of a century and a half of engagements of varying quality to infer an historical situation from what has survived in record' (Oakeshott 1983: 56-57 n. 14). But what Ian Henderson calls the 'nuttiness coefficient' (1969: 97) was in Reimarus peculiarly well developed: the disciples of Jesus stole the body of Jesus. Very few have been persuaded by this hypothesis. But Reimarus had the acumen to spot that there was a problem, the guts to offer an answer and the caution to keep his mouth shut (his work was never published in his lifetime). As is known to every citizen that knows it, as is known to the citizen of the home of Hume, the Enlightenment was an axial period.

The story (here) now turns to de Wette, but not to re-tell what Rogerson (1992) has told, nor to tell all that might be told. Much of de Wette remains untranslated and uneasily available. He is adduced here, on the basis of Rogerson, an ancillary account by Smend (1958), the exemplary monograph of Hartlich and Sachs (1952), the introductory section of de Wette's *Biblische Dogmatik*, supplemented by his *Ueber Religion und Theologie* (this latter a discussion of the former) and Davidovich's contribution (1993) to hitherto unexplored possibilities of Kant's investigations into aesthetics:

> My study offers a radical interpretation of Kant's *Third Critique* and demonstrates that the book's central argument that reflective judgment bridges the gap between nature and freedom, led Kant to a contemplative conception of religion that differs significantly from the conception of religion of the first two *Critiques* (1993: xi-xii).

Some smatterings of de Wette's views will, intermittently, surface in what follows, but the word to fasten on is *Ahnung* (de Wette), or *Ahndung* (Fries 1805), which means a *sense* or intimation of things, that finds literary expression in story and poem, in metaphor and symbol, in the seminal image. De Wette knew that, in reading the Old Testament, or the Hebrew Bible (call it what you will), he was reading something that differed from the (admittedly sesquipedalian) sentences of Immanuel Kant. De Wette was reading the deliverances of artists, poets and story-tellers. Of the somewhat later patristic dogma of the divinity of Christ, for example, a dogma derived by reflection on these deliverances, he says that it 'cannot be a concept, but must be an *aesthetic* idea'[6] (1821: 251). An aesthetic idea is the fruit of reflection on literature.

But where do Hartlich and Sachs begin? They begin with Lowth and his *De Sacra Poesi Hebraeorum Praelectiones Academicae* (*Lectures on the Sacred Poesy of the Hebrews*) (1770 [1st edn 1758]). All this non-history, in a word, this non-history bound up, sometimes more, sometimes less, sometimes not at all, with history (*Ineinanderverflochtenheit*, inextricable co-implication!) is sacred poetry, is metaphor, personification, artistic form, poetic imagery. The book of Job is a drama, the *Look Back in Anger* of its day (if greater may be compared with lesser). Lowth was pointing to the mythopoeic talents of the ancient Hebrews, but saw, as a poet himself (Hunt 1893: 214), no need to demythologize what the mythmakers had made. Lowth was a literary critic and fooled himself into thinking, or had the good sense to see, that he was dealing with literature. Göttingen gave him a doctorate and then 'Herder and Eichhorn carried Lowth's work further' (Shaffer 1975: 21).

But if Lowth and de Wette were pioneers of the Old, it is with Strauss that fiction enters the New. A waiting world was struck with a dull thud. Was one not now after all, in the vestibules of secluded chapels up and down the land, to 'hang up one's brains with one's cloak', as one does when one goes to the opera? Strauss's term was 'myth'. What we are now pleased to call 'pericopes', the stories, into which we can easily segment the Gospels, Strauss, or his translator, Ms Eliot, calls '*mythi*'. The 'generative grammar' (so to speak) of the discourse of the New was the Old: if Elijah had a feeding, so should Jesus. So should Jesus, if Moses had a Sermon on the Mount. If Elijah could awaken another from the

6.   'Es soll diese Lehre...auch kein Begriff, sondern eine ästhetische Idee seyn.'

sleep of death (1 Kgs 17.22), and could depart (without going to sleep; 2 Kgs 2.11), so could Jesus, too (though having been to sleep). But in Martin Noth's acidulous *History of Israel*, Elijah is given, perhaps too generously, only two half-lines (1960: 242). In other words, the writers of the Gospels were not following the necessities of history, the critical examination of evidence, the sifting, the winnowing, the interrogation, the torture of witnesses. They were following the necessities of the religious imagination, as that imagination had been trained by a millennium of poetry to imagine.

Wallace Stevens well puts the plain man's point (he has been reading Dante's *Vita Nuova*, the 'New Life', 'one of the great documents of Christianity'; then he goes on):

> It is very strange to read, as I am reading now, the *chief* document— the New Testament—and to consider the growth of our Western religion. St. Matthew opens with a list of the families from which Jesus descended as if to impress the fact of his humanity. And then follows, as I said the other night, a narration of the most incredible adventures that ever befell a human being. The Catholic church, for reasons of its own, has made much of the Virgin, and when I have finished my reading, I must meditate on it and try to find the reason (Stevens, in Stevens H. 1977: 223-24)

Is not, indeed, the modern reader of the Lukan prologue incorrigibly reminded of a certain Mr Espinasse (at the end of the eighteenth century), of whom 'it is said that he only heard half of what went on and reported the other half' (D. Pannick, *The Times*, 10 October 1995). But is the historically implausible not plausible in literature? If so, *what* account can be given of literary plausibility? Is there an account that does not resile from literature and turn to philosophy, but stays with it, enjoys it and, pursuing the truth embedded in it, tries then, and only then, to give an account of *that*?

For Bultmann shows his literary sensitivity in every line he writes, even if only in the succinctness with which he does so; but too easily, especially on cursory reading, or, worse, on no reading at all, leaves the impression of what Spinoza calls, in his 'Definition of the Emotions', 'irrision' (1843: I, 319 [= *Ethica* III, *Affectuum Definitiones* XI: *irrisio*]), followed by an irritable reaching after philosophy. But to think of Bultmann in this way as an exponent of irrision is to short-circuit the complex wiring of his mind and conscience. He is not deriding Scripture; he is using his head. He is using what is one (if only one) twentieth-century philosophy (Existentialism) to express what is expressed otherwise by the writers of the New Testament. He is using a philosophy to make sense of literature.

These four figures, at any rate, Lowth, de Wette, Strauss and Bultmann, stand behind every line, some of them, of the present piece. But anyone who thinks that these questions can be easily solved has got another think, has got another imagine coming. Anyone, indeed, who thinks that, in the end, they are soluble at all, or more than in a modest measure, has no idea, or no adequate image, of either metaphysics or theology. 'When Mr. so-and-so deals with a theological problem', said Gregor Smith (*obiter dictum*), 'he solves it'. This was irrision.

But though these figures stand behind every line, they do not improve them. The obscurity, that will follow here, is sometimes wanton, often failure, but always struggle. Accordingly, a measure of empathy and cooperation will be demanded from the reader. As Wittgenstein says, and I feel before him, as he felt with Sraffa, 'like a tree from which all branches had been cut' (von Wright, in Malcolm 1967: 15-16, cited in Potier 1991: 48): 'This book is written for those who are in sympathy with the spirit in which it is written...' (Wittgenstein 1980: 6).[7]

Such philosophical structure as this book has depends, more than on any other, on a reading of, an employment of the work of R.G. Collingwood, a philosopher, who was concerned to be understood by those interested in philosophy, who were not themselves by profession philosophers.

Collingwood (1924) believes, or began by believing, and continued, I think, to believe, that there were five ways of knowing: art, religion, science, history and philosophy. Religion is like art, but differs from it, not in what it says, but in its attitude to what is said: religion asserts that to be true, what the artist imagines (cf. Paton 1922: 255-82). And this is an error. It is an error that can be corrected by the philosophy of religion, by religion, not only asserted, but thought about. If we may ignore the chemical composition of the atmosphere of Venus and the oxygen content

---

7. 'Dieses Buch ist für diejenigen geschrieben, die dem Geist in dem es geschrieben ist, freundlich gegenüberstehen...'

of the thigh-muscles of the *anopheles* mosquito, if, that is, we may ignore science, we find that what religion produces by way of history is not history, but 'theocratic history', or the amalgam of 'theocratic history and myth' (Collingwood 1946: 14-17), which the historian, if he is so inclined, may investigate and from which, if lucky, some historical and other inferences may sometimes be drawn.

But, if religion is like art, then we need some account of art. And this Collingwood provides, not only in the early version found in *Speculum Mentis* (1924), and shortly afterwards in *Outlines of a Philosophy of Art* (1925a), but later in *The Principles of Art* (1938).

Art (so Collingwood) differs from a craft, like shoe-making, or cabinet-making, in that the artist does not know what he is going to say, or she is going to paint, or they are going to chisel, until their chisels, her brush and his pen have told them what to do. These express what they mean, if and only if the expression *is* the meaning. The meaning, and the truth, is embedded, embodied, instantiated in what is done, in the thing made, the *poiema* of the *poietes*, in what is constructed, in the work. Thus what is made is peculiarly pregnant, but it takes (both the art critic and) the philosophical midwife, or metaphysical mid-person, to bring it to bed and to birth. Art needs to be, can be, thought about.

Mutatis mutandis, the documents of the New Testament, if these are works of art, or like works of art, need a 'hermeneutic'. Thought is required. A stick and a stone are required for the tin and a key for the code: literary criticism and an aesthetic philosophy. The meaning and the truth are *in* there, but have to be got *out of* there. For the artist is operating at a level where the animal spirits are groping for language.

Thus, if there is any history in there (and there is, or there is sometimes), the historian has to work at it. And this is what has been going on, in the modern period, in a modern way, since Reimarus (say).

But if there is any art in there, and artistic meaning and artistic truth, this is what we are *now* trying to get out of there. And many are the monographs that are making the attempt. This one is another.

But if the documents of the New Testament, if the works of the

New Testament, the *opera* (John, Paul, the synoptists), the *opuscula* (Jude, and the 'straw'-opuscle, James), are not works of art *tout court*, but only like them, if, to take de Wette's epithet, they are not 'aesthetic' simply, but 'aesthetic-*religious*' (*ästhetisch-religiös* [1817: 218 (= 1821: 254)], cit. Hartlich and Sachs 1952: 115), how are we to give *full value to both halves of the epithet*?

Aristotle's artists (Aristotle 1909, 1925b, 1980), the Greek tragedians, were feeling their way with theocratic plots (the prophet, Teiresias, in Sophocles's *Oedipus Tyrannus*, is under instruction, the instruction of Apollo). As the stories came to them, so they used them, re-working and re-shaping. What people said (φασι, *phasi*: 'this is what is said', 'this is how men say the thing is' [Aristotle, *Po.* 1460b36, 1461a1]) is what people say, and re-say. But what they say, and re-say, is 'more philosophical than history' (1451b5). And is 'more philosophical', in that what is said by the poet can be analysed by the philosopher into statements that are 'universal', statements that are about 'how a person of a certain type will on occasion speak or act, according to the law of probability or necessity' (Aristotle, *Po.* 1451b5-10). Truth may be hard to get at here, but truth is there for the finding. But what is truth, when the question is asked of works, that are not aesthetic merely, but are 'aesthetic-*religious*'? The gods, or god, or 'God', or God, may be part of an answer, Jesus of Nazareth another.

But thinking is a process and definitions cohere ill with dialectic. And definitions properly belong at the beginning in order to be decisively proved wrong at the end. And the present task is to enter the process, without 'conduct to the prejudice of good order and military discipline'. It is 'sitting well in order', that we are to 'smite the sounding furrows' (Tennyson, 'Ulysses'). But, in order that nothing should not be said, let this, at least, at this juncture, be said, that, when I write fiction, what I do is *fingo*; that is, I fashion something that may be related to the historical, but need not be. And when I 'imaginatively express emotion' (to summarize Collingwood on art), I express something that I must express, for that is how I feel; that is how I feel as a person of 'senses and passions' (Hamann 1950: 197 [= Lumpp 1970: 205], trans. Crick, in Nisbet 1985: 141). And an expression is right, when the words said say it, as other words would not. There is a specific accuracy that is peculiar to poetry. What validity my senses and passions have is something about which I shall have to expend some thought. For how is the artist's 'opinion' (δόξα, *doxa*) to be related to the thinker's 'knowledge' (ἐπιστήμη, *episteme*)? How is Plato's 'Divided Line', the line that divides picture-thinking and conviction from understanding and reason (*Republic* 509d5–511e6), to be seen from both ends (Paton 1951: 255-82)? How is the thinker's knowledge to be related to the artist's imagination? If the poet is a thinker, what is it that is being thought? If the poet is not, how is thinking to be done about what is not thought?

But thought (or something like it) is here in this essay being expended on art, on religious art, that is 20 centuries old. And our plight would only be a millennium worse, if we had to include Homer and the Pentateuch, the Hebrew epic with the Greek. But if we can as little do without Homer and with J, D, E and P, we can, by the argument 'from the older to the newer' (*a seniore ad juvenilius*), even less do without the New Testament. That without which we can even less do has a date; there are styles, conventions and fashions to be learnt. The unchanging gospel has devilishly changed over time.

But (and this is the Montanist moment) we can never be content with it, the New Testament, or them, the New Testament writers, unless writing should have ended there and God had hung up his boots with his pen. A church that is not (human beings that are not) busied in writing scripture is a dead thing. Inquiry, that is, is being made into documents in the context of an inquiry into documents that do not yet exist at all. And for an inquiry into a new New Testament new New Labour is mandatory. Or to put the matter less wilfully, it is a fact, whether the historian will or no, that 'the organization of the totality of experience *sub specie prae-teritorum*' (Oakeshott 1933: 111) is an abstraction from its organization *sub specie futurorum*. More briefly, and thinking of *rerum scribendarum*, of what is to be written: *Scribendumst*, we must write.

If none of these can be ignored, we must see what we can do. And should thought here be primarily concerned with documents, it cannot be forgotten that documents are (still) written by persons and that if persons matter more than texts (the Corinthians are Paul's letter [2 Cor. 3.2]), still the authors of texts were persons. And if living persons are persons, dead persons were persons, too;

and even dead authors, to boot (this sometimes the *mot juste*).

But what sort of documents? What sort of texts? There are books worth reading (and we call them 'classics'). And if they are worth reading, then they are worth interpreting. But not all artists, and not all religious artists, belong to the first century AD ('after the Lord'), or CE ('the era that is common to a number of groups'). And artists need to write, not only to have written. Artists need to go on writing, and interpreters to go on interpreting, interpreting not only what has been, but what is being written.

The study of the New Testament is only part of a larger picture; is only like one of those immediately puzzling details, from some picture or other, provided for competition by a newspaper. A location on a map may be the centre of the map, but is not all the map. Jerusalem need not erase Capernaum, Corinth, Joppa, nor Portobello. Paul, John and the rest are only doing what Eliot and Stevens are taking further, are taking forward.

Signal resources, moreover, are derived from Gregor Smith. But his work will be more thoroughly discussed, even parried with, when the Gordian knots are undone in the Conclusion (in Chapter 12). But, if more will be said later, something can also be said now. And together with Gregor Smith comes Hamann, evangelist of poetry, protagonist with Kant: the Enlightenment can handle 'problems', but how well does it handle 'mystery' (Foster's distinction [1957: 18])?

Longinus, or 'Longinus' (say it how you will) becomes lyrical over a Homeric comparison:

> And far as a man with his eyes through the sea-line haze may
>   discern,
> On a cliff as he sitteth and gazeth away o'er the wine-dark deep,
> So far at a bound do the loud-neighing steeds of the Deathless leap.[8]
>   (*Il.* 5.770-72, cit. Longinus 1899: 9.5)

This is not, in a secular world, how we speak. To speak this way would be to 'pass beyond the confines of the world' (οὐκέθ' εὑρήσουσιν ἐν κόσμῳ τόπον, *ouketh' heuresousin en kosmo[i] topon*: Longinus 1899: 9.5), the world, that is, as we have come to understand it. 'Transcendent…images' (ὑπερφυᾶ…φαντάσματα,

---

8.   ὅσσον δ' ἠεροειδὲς ἀνὴρ ἴνηρ ἴδεν ὀφθαλμοῖσιν,
     ἥμενος ἐν σκοπιῇ, λεύσσων ἐπὶ οἴνοπα πόντον·
     τόσσον ἐπιθρώσκουσι θεῶν ὑψηχέες ἵπποι.

huperphua...phantasmata: Longinus 1899: 9.5) these may be, but
this is not how nowadays, in a brave, new world, we deal linguistically with transcendence. The present-day poet, literary critic,
historian, philosopher would now write otherwise about the
Trojan War. But how otherwise? If Bonhoeffer wrestled with these
questions in Berlin, Gregor Smith wrestled with them, in a (somewhat) less apocalyptic Glasgow.

But Hamann wrestled with them, too, in their Enlightenment
form. And Gregor Smith tried a throw with Hamann (Gregor Smith
1960). The present essay does no more than merely re-ask what
Gregor Smith re-asked of the question Hamann asked and answered
by speaking (I will say this again) of '[p]oetry as the mother-tongue
of the human race' (Hamann 1950: 197). But poetry, in this book,
as, too, in Hamann's *Aesthetica in nuce*, is placed more promi-
nently in the foreground than I dare to think it was by Gregor
Smith (see Chapter 12).

In what ways is poetry *fictive*? How is *poetry* rooted in *ontology*,
does *fiction* relate to *fact*—and to that, by which a fact is one (is a
fact, that is)? How, by telling lies, can one tell the truth?

The anthropologist, it may be, may prescind from these questions, from the 'discussion of the content of belief and of the
rationality or otherwise of that content', and hold that '[m]ost such
arguments seem...to be scholastic nonsense' (Leach 1954: 13). But
what of the literary critic and the aesthetic philosopher, the
metaphysician and theologian? Can *they* prescind from these
questions? And can they not ask, what it is that, for the
functionalist (Leach), has a function?

Thus, if the word 'literature', under which the word 'poetry' is
subsumed, is central to this book, in a fashion that diverges from
Gregor Smith, from whom the word is not absent, and out of
whom these contingent developments come, the 'depth-structure'
of the whole (so to speak), as any 'mereological' analysis, namely,
'study of parts' (Scaltsas 1990: 583) would make plain (contra Lk.
1.26-38 in Chapter 4 below), rests on a passacaglia, a 'ground-bass',
a *cantus firmus* (the words are Bonhoeffer's, when he speaks of
'joy' [1971: 295] and 'love...to which the other melodies of life
provide the counterpoint' [1971: 303]). This depth-structure is
constituted by what (after de Wette 1821: 251) might be called

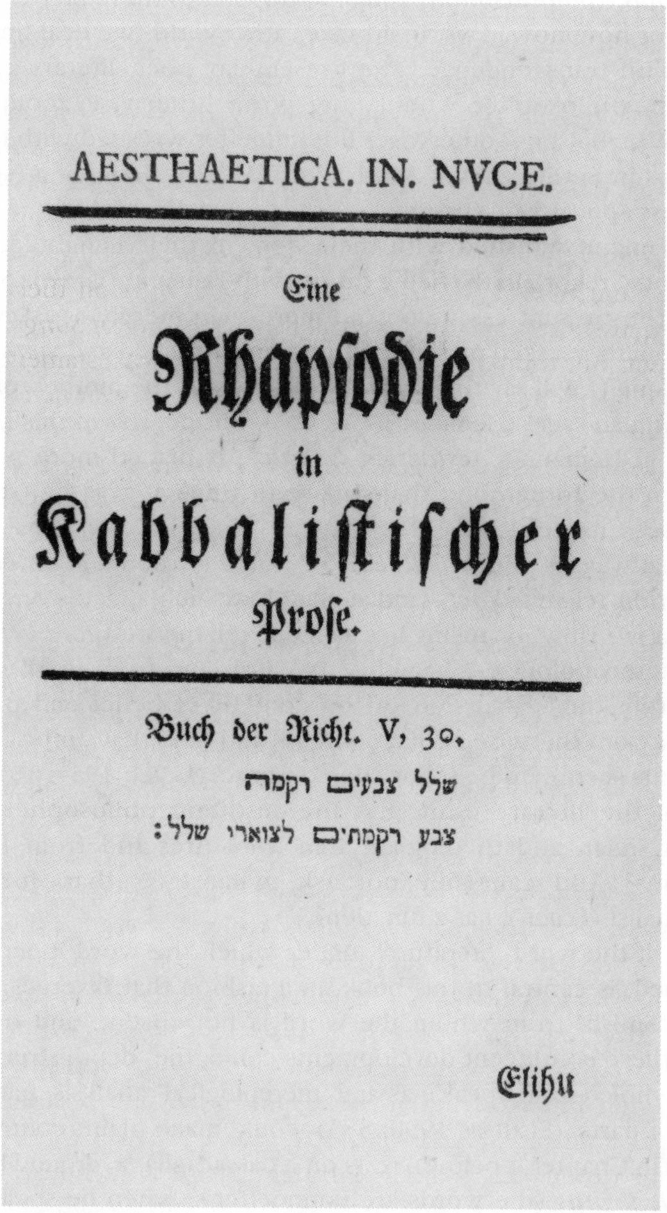

AESTHAETICA. IN. NVCE.

Eine

Rhapsodie

in

Kabbalistischer

Prose.

Buch der Richt. V, 30.

שלל צבעים רקמה

צבע רקמתים לצוארי שלל׃

Elihu

Figure 1. *Aesthaetica in nuce*, 1762 [Aesthetics in a Nutshell] (title page), by J.G. Hamann (1730–88) (reproduced by courtesy of the Niedersächsische Staats- und Universitätsbibliotek, Göttingen)

Bonhoeffer's three 'aesthetic ideas': 'incarnation', 'crucifixion' and 'resurrection'; and further by a little list of what nowadays, in anxious, academic committees, are usually called 'comparators': the *Oedipus Tyrannus*, *Macbeth*, *Waverley*, *Her Story* by the novelist Dan Jacobson (1987), Douglas Adams's *Hitch-Hiker's Guide to the Galaxy* (and the whole of his 'trilogy in four parts' [1992]), Eliot's *Four Quartets*, Wallace Stevens's 'Notes towards a Supreme Fiction', together with the poems of Hopkins, D.H. Lawrence's *Rainbow* and those songs sung by the young men on their way back to their short home, that we call now *The Song of Songs*. And I take them up, though I am aware that the New Testament is a much more democratic entity, is less élitist, is vernacular fiction.

And if literature, then literary criticism. Some attention is given here to Aristotle's *Poetics* and, more cursorily, to Horace's *Ars Poetica*. And, if we have, with Horace, one who was not only a poet, but a poet-critic, we have this with Eliot, too, as *both* critic *and* poet. And to these three there is added also Kermode, who takes, or was sometime taking, a biblical turn. And R.P. Blackmur is important (*inter alios*) for pointing out the difference between scholarship and literary criticism (1954: 394-96), though I am damned (I think) if I know what to do with his distinction. But his distinction, whatever it is, may have implications for the way exegetes should be doing exegesis, when the exegete is one with a literary bent, or has been blest with a knowledge of what *he* is doing, or *she* is being done by.

And should we ask F.R. Leavis's 'Yes, but...?' question (1969: 139) and ask, 'Yes, but what *is* literary criticism?' we are then led on (by the serpent that deceived Eve [2 Cor. 11.3]) to philosophy, a philosophy of literary criticism and a philosophy of art. But, if a philosophy of art means above all in this essay Collingwood (1925), Collingwood (1925b) and Collingwood (1938, etc.), though what Collingwood thinks of literary criticism has to be 'jaloused', or guessed at, it also means Aristotle (1925, etc.).

And, for various reasons (e.g. Pirbright, *apud* Wodehouse 1957: 121), it also means Spinoza, *Tractatus* (1862)[9] and *Ethics* (1959).[10]

And it also means, by reason of de Wette (1821, 1831) and

9. 1843: II.
10. 1843: I.

Hamann (1950: 195-217),[11] the beginnings, no bigger than 'a man's hand' (1 Kgs 18.44), of a look at the philosophy of Kant (1915 [ET 1914]).

And, if 'literature' is central, then 'history' is not, though it has been. And, while it has been for some, for some it still is. History is used here as the 'control' discipline, to warn the reader what this book is *not* doing, or, perhaps better, trying not to do, though when the two, 'literature' and 'history', are so *ineinanderverflochten*, so 'involved, the one with the other', it is very hard to separate what the scholars have joined—for so long. But, at any rate, it should be clear that *fides historica* is a thing, but not *the* thing (Bultmann 1984: 130). Convictions about historical facts, such as they are, do not exhaustively account for what Jesus started.

But the matter is not to be solved by a sound-bite, but only by a multiple. And yet not solved. A direction only is being indicated, a cynosure pointed at. If Lowth 'considered the Old Testament simply as literature and Oriental literature' (Shaffer 1975: 20), the task is to do for the New Testament what Lowth did for the Old. If there is a difference between using *Macbeth* for the quest of the historical Macbeth and contemplating the play as the work of a poet, then so too with the New Testament. (We do not find Macbeth?) But, where much (but how much?) of the New Testament is not fiction *tout court*, but is *historical* fiction, is a mixed form (Ashton 1994: 165); and where fiction *tout court* is still, if elliptically (but what ellipse?), related to history, the task assigned, here, is not so much to disjoin, as to distinguish, where distinction is possible, but all the time to concentrate, where dissipation permits, more fully on fiction.

Must this result in distortion, in an imbalance?

Balance is the refuge of the scoundrel.

Take (again) *The Political Systems of Highland Burma*:

> When the anthropologist attempts to describe a social system he necessarily describes only a model of the social reality. This model represents in effect the anthropologist's hypothesis about 'how the social system works'. The different parts of the model system therefore necessarily form a coherent whole—it is part of a system in equilibrium. But this does not imply that the social reality forms a

11. ET 1985: 139-50.

coherent whole; on the contrary the reality situation is in most cases full of inconsistencies; and it is precisely these inconsistencies which can provide us with an understanding of the processes of social change (Leach 1954: 8).

And, if the society, then the academy. And, if the academy, then the church. Rest and movement are dialectical concepts. Pedestrian advance, locomotion by walking, is achieved by a dynamic sequence of imbalances. Falstaff, thou shouldst be living at this hour!

The mind should be changing gear here.

What is it, one is asking, gives us access to the poetry of it all? And not only to the poetry as there, but to the poetry as it was coming to be? And here we can turn to other makers and to what others have made of their making: to the painters, for instance, and to the art historians. For both of these are capable of the kind of utterance or delineation, that is requisite, when dealing with the expression of an infinite object and its finite counterparts, *capax* (each of them) *infiniti*, 'capable of the infinite'. And we can have recourse, too, to the makers of musical tunes and to the intrepid among the critics, who open their mouths about notes and keys, and are eloquent about the shift from noise to sound and the palmary importance of silence.

Analogues, that is, can help, analogues of words in paint and notes. For is not the New Testament more like the stuff of celebration and festival than like the sobrieties of prose and no less capable than painting or music of including depth with height? Should we not be alert to the fact that it, whatever it is, the *je ne sais quoi* with which the New Testament is concerned, has caught the imagination of the artists of the West (Brahms's *Four Serious Songs*, say)? And does it not all encourage its readers, with its writers, to be themselves (to say it with the linguistic ghetto) 'incarnate', 'crucified' and 'raised'? For the speech of such as these is contiguous with body and anchored in sensibility and sense: Piero della Francesca and Turner, Brahms and Handel, Berenson and Tovey.

Meta-Epiprologue to the Uncultured among the Despisers of Academic Prose

Dear Lady Holland,

I take the liberty to send you two brace of grouse, curious, because killed by a Scotch metaphysician; in other and better language they are mere ideas, shot by other ideas, out of a pure intellectual notion called a gun. yrs ever very truely

Sydney Smith

I will do myself the pleasure of dining with you on Saturday next— tomorrow evening I am engaged. The modification of matter called Grouse which accompanies this note is not in the common apprehension of Edinburgh considered to be dependant upon a first cause, but to have existed from All Eternity. Allen will explain (6 October 1808 [Smith 1953: 143]).

I doubt whether this book can be read fast. I doubt whether it can be read at all. It could hardly be written. 'Rapid reading', however, should be reserved for works like the *Tractatus* of Wittgenstein and the Sermon on the Mount.

The title of the book has gone through various redactions. Earlier forms of it contained an allusion to de Wette's *Beiträge zur Einführung in das AT* (*Contributions to the Introduction to the Old Testament*) (1806–1807) and to the *Essays and Addresses* of Baron von Hügel (1921, 1926). The first of these was a pioneer in drawing attention to the aesthetic qualities of the Old Testament, the second in drawing a distinction between 'perpetual incomprehensibility' and 'infinite apprehensibility'. The concentration here is on the former of von Hügel's pairs.

The final form alludes to Bultmann's essay, 'The New Testament and Mythology' (1960 [ET 1957]), but with less caution than Bultmann: '*as*' is different from '*and*', but with more caution than Bultmann by the insertion of the little word 'TRUE'. The word 'FICTION' merely gives a new turn to an old debate. It gives a literary turn to the debate on 'mythology'. But, with Lowth in mind (*The Sacred Poesy of the Hebrews* [1770 (ET 1829)]), *The Secular Poesy of the Christians* would have done as well, the revised epithet emanating from and indicating the approach of Bonhoeffer, Bethge and Gregor Smith.

In a former subtitle THE NEW ALLIANCE referred by contrast to the Old Testament, but not to that relation between Scotland and

France, which is known as THE AULD ALLIANCE. The present sub-title might well have been *Salt in my Porridge*, but that has already been used by one properly called the 'Local Bard' (MacVicar 1971), local, that is, to the region which is south of the Island of Gigha, north of the Glens of Antrim, west of the Island of Arran and east of Long Island, namely, the Mull of Kintyre, but whose real ubiety is more ubiquitous. *Lumps in my Porridge* would have served as well, *Lumps without Porridge* better still and, best of all, simply *Lumps*. But I have tried to make amends for this omission in the title of this chapter.

In the hope of offering my reader some further assistance, it should be added that the book makes the following Propositions:

1. The New Testament is a work of art. If it is anything else, we cannot say what it is.
2. History is not the subject of investigation here. History is the 'control' discipline.
3. The Gospels are not biographies, nor histories, but historical novels.
4. A metaphor is a historical novel, only shorter.
5. The parables of Jesus are short stories.
6. The Philippians hymn (2.6-11) is a poem.
5. If God is the next stage above mind, there is not much the mind can do, except send up a few metaphors, for after all we are dealing neither with life, nor with death, but with something stranger than either (Mackenzie 1995).
6. We have, then, in the New Testament, primarily to do with literature.
7. If the 'mythology…is the thing itself' (Bonhoeffer 1971: 329), and mythology is fiction, then a defence of the truth of fiction is a defence of the thing itself.
8. 'What about thing [itself], then?' (Walls 1995: *passim* [see Chapter 12, in the CODA]).

'Historical novels' (Prop. 3 above)?

Without more exaggeration than will be found to be customary in these pages, the equation of the Gospels with historical novels was a seed from which this book grew, an *idée génératrice*, or 'generative idea'.

The nature of the allegation, that the Gospels are not histories, may be clarified by a comparison, that was introduced above and will be repeated below: out of the whole Elijah cycle the historian Martin Noth derives two half-lines of history (1960: 242). A not wholly dissimilar result, I think, follows from a historical treatment of the Gospels.

What we find with these is a series of impossible stories (micro-stories) in the context of an impossible story (the macro-story). They are stories told by poets in a context of poetry. Just round the corners of their minds the old cycles—of Elijah, of Moses—are revolving. The miraculous, what Aristotle calls the 'wonderful' (*to thaumaston* [*Po*. 1460a11-27]), is not peripheral, but of the essence. But, at the same time, the larger story and the stories embraced by it bear sufficient relation to actual events to allow historians, not always (or not ever) without difficulty, to write a more or less possible, probable, even (at points) certain historical narrative. A whole and parts of a whole that are phantastic enough to persuade some of us that we are dealing with the fumes of a mushroom (Allegro 1970) are at the same time familiar enough and familiarly related enough to the otherwise familiar to persuade (perhaps) most of us that we are discerning something more than the coagulation of a mere miasma. These two aspects, the historical and the novelistic, are not found here together as oil and water, but as a compound solution, about the proportions of which men with women may legitimately disagree. Further generalities of this kind are protracted more extensively in Chapter 2 and some specification is aimed at in Chapter 6, on Mark, and Chapter 7, on John. Let so much, accordingly, suffice for now.

But if it is these Propositions (1–8 above), or something like them, that the book is propounding, it is also asking something like the following Questions:

1. How does literature relate to history on the one hand and philosophy on the other?
2. How does this theoretical inquiry relate to the practice of religion, that is, to ordinary life?
3. How can body (substance, tangibility [as it were]) best be given to a series of abstract propositions? Does the concreteness of poetry, that is, have some genuine advantages over philosophical expression?
4. Is there available to the critic some idea of literary criticism that is sufficiently determinate to get somewhere?

5. Would another way of looking at all this be to say that the subject of this essay is history, that is, precisely, a history of the symbolism of Jesus and of early Christianity; that is, art history, the history of the art of some of the words that have been spoken in the past?

6. If I knew the answers, would I be interested in the questions?

7. Should the inquiry be conducted, not in the *koine*, or 'common' dialect of the ancient Near East, but in the *kathareuousa*, or 'pure' dialect of modern Athens: ἀποκύημα, *apokuema* (birth of a swelling in the womb [?]), πλάσμα τῆς φαντασίας, *plasma tes phantasias* (plasma of phantasy), μυθιστόρημα, *muth-historema* (myth-history), μυθιστόρημα ἐπιστημονικῆς φαντασίας ('myth-story of epistemic phantasy'—this the modern Greek for Science Fiction)?

8. Can any of this be done at all without 'the light of the early Plato and the whole Montaigne' (Blackmur 1954: 375)?

The style, with which the following pages are written, leaves before the reader little to be desired. Their idiom fails to come within measurable distance even of pre-postmodernism, but occasionally, by way of compensation, attains the pre-posterous.

Moreover, I was brought up to rule the British Empire, which, in those days, meant translating Tennyson's 'Ulysses' into Latin, Arnold's 'Merope' into Greek and pupils into Purgatory. This means that, although, to all intents and purposes, the British Empire has disappeared, my Greek and Latin, no doubt to the regret of some and the incomprehension of others, has (as theologians say) 'not yet' disappeared. But I have tried (by giving translations) to make what remains of these more or less accessible.

But it may nevertheless still be said of me, as Housman says of Scaliger (1903: I, xiv), that

> he will often propound interpretations which have no bearing either on his own text of Manilius or on any other, but pertain to things which he has read elsewhere, and which like mists in his memory veil from his eyes the verses which he thinks he is explaining.

The book makes the attempt to avoid the jargon of the schools and aims at 'the non-religious interpretation of religious concepts' (Bonhoeffer 1971: 344), or at 'the radical application of the doctrine of justification by faith to the sphere of knowledge and thought' (Bultmann 1960a: 84). But not here rather to the sphere of knowledge and thought, but to the sphere of the imagination and the expression of emotion. It attempts to insert the language of the New Testament into the world, where it belongs, and to withdraw it from the ghetto, where it does not. It is an attempt to show that the New Testament texts tie in quite well with quite a lot that is going on there, though I do wish sometimes that they would tie up the children.

The poet, Horace, the critic, Horace, exhorts the writer to suppress his work for nine years (*A.P.* 388: *nonumque prematur in annum*), as 'there is no possibility of revoking an emitted voice' (*A.P.* 390: *nescit vox missa reverti*), but, without wishing to pay tribute to the British Government (writing in 1996), whose estimate of family values depends on a perspectival viewing of the cinematographic film *Spartacus*, this longer view is not nowadays encouraged. And it is certainly not possible. Some of the repetitions in a less-than-nine-year-edited text may be put down to the near-expectation of the professional eschatologist, some to the (late) cat (*vide supra*) and some to the influence of Richard Wagner: the *Leitmotiv* has its place. Some things are too important *not* to be repeated.

'In my end is my beginning', writes Eliot ('East Coker' V [= 1944: 23]): the puzzled reader, or the baffled reviewer, who has not followed Sydney Smith's advice ('I never read a book before reviewing it—it prejudices one so'), should turn over a new leaf and turn to the end of Chapter 12 and the Bibliography. But for the rest:

Legendum est tibi: here is a legend for you:

2

From Myth to Plot: Adumbrations on the Logic of Evangelical Propositions (Mark and John)

Earlier generations (and it continues [Wyatt 1996a]) have done their time on 'myth'. Hartlich and Sachs (1952) provide the history and Bultmann provides the end of that history (2001). It is now time (and few there be, that are not now doing it) to turn to inquiries that are more literary. And time to reflect, that is, find an aesthetic philosophy for what the literary critics are doing. And here von Balthasar is a major figure (1961–88). For what is the meaning of what the writers of literature have said and are saying? And what they will be saying?

If a myth is a story, then a proper story should have a plot. But what is it that is plotted? How do plots relate to reality? To your reality and mine?

'In general', says Aristotle (*Po.* 1461b 9-10), 'the impossible must be justified by reference to artistic requirements…' This stuff, the *Gospels*, is impossible, impossible in Aristotle's sense and in many others. How can grown men deal with it? Fairy-tales, merely.

But there is a world, or at least what Joyce calls a 'chaosmos'. Or there is a *deus sive natura*, what Spinoza would call a 'substance' (*Ethica* I, *def.* III: *substantia*). There is a substance, with the attributes of thought and extension. And there are finite modes of infinite substance.

In this area of inquiry, it may be suggested that three disciplines are mainly involved: philosophy, history and literature, with literary criticism parasitic on the latter; that history has *had* a run for its money, from Hermann Samuel Reimarus to Ed Parrish Sanders, and that literature is *having* a run for its money.

If we need philosophy, there is the question of *what* philosophy we need. But, leaving out Rudolf Bultmann's 'right philosophy' (1965: 169) and 'right' philosopher, Martin Heidegger, let us take Spinoza. Let us suppose, or let Spinoza prove, *more geometrico,* that we and Jesus of Nazareth are finite modes of infinite substance, extended for a while and thinking a little. And free a little, if also in some servitude to the bestialities of ourselves and our governments. If Spinoza is right to say that 'a free man thinks of nothing less than of death' (*Ethica* IV, *prop.* LXVII), it follows, as the day the night, or as the sum of the square on the hypotenuse to the sum of the squares on the other two sides, that the wise man does not think about death, but only of the death of his passions and his politicians. 'Hilarity' (*hilaritas*) names the game, the game of *homo ludens* or *animal risibilis* (*Ethica* II, *prop.* XL, *schol.* I), the sporting, or laughing animal.

History has had its day and its say and found only little bits of Jesus and those little bits of not much interest (Trocmé 1992: 321). And has shown that in interpreting the New Testament, 'one is in the same position as a person who tries to understand the histories of Denmark and Scotland by reading *Hamlet* and *Macbeth*' (so Whitehead, according to Johnson [1962: 59]).[1] To be compared also is Arthur, whose 'name in later ages was a magnet drawing to itself all manner of folk-lore and fable', about whom 'an Arthurian cycle grew up composed partly of events transferred from other contexts' (Collingwood, in Collingwood and Myres 1937: 321).

But not only, nevertheless, does a remarkable character obtrude sufficiently for the historian to mark it, but also an idea of incarnation, that while it appears only once *expressis verbis* (*verbum caro*, 'the word became flesh' [Jn 1.14]) appears there with such force and clarity as to shed light on many like instances, which it assembles and collects, as a Secretary assembles a Senate, or a Stentor an army of Argives. For God is extended in his modes. God is extended in his christs: '...who, being in the form of God, thought it not robbery to become equal with God...' This famous, Philippian song (2.5-11) is one suchlike instance. And another is like it, if the reader may infer what Paul must imply, when, in declaring that God has 'anointed' (the active verb: χρίσας, *chrisas* [2 Cor. 1.21]), he is declaring his reader 'anointed' (the passive adjective: 'christ' [χριστός, *christos*]).

History has had its day and such little bits of history as there are come wrapped in the integument, trapped in the net of myth,

---

1. And cf. Alter 1981: 35, cit. Prickett 1986: 204.

Figure 2. *Macbeth*, 1820, by John Martin (1789–1854) (reproduced by courtesy of the Trustees, The National Gallery, Edinburgh)

through the 'interstitial vacuities' (Johnson 1786, s.v. 'net') of which all little fish fall. And the Jesus of history slips through this net, texture, text, this net that is cast for the redeeming fish, the bronto-ichthyan form, the ΊΧΘΥΣ (*ichthus*) that demands an 'ichtheology' (Tindall 1959: 156), that storied acrostic (*I*[*esous*] *Ch*[*ristos*] *Th*[*eou*] *U*[*ios*] *S*[*oter*], 'Jesus Christ, Son of God, Saviour'), not beast of abyss (or 666), but man from the height (or 888 [so *Iesous*, by gematria]).

And why should we not go for the 'bronto-ichthyan form', the 'thunder-fish'? Why should we not go, not for the historical, but for the mythical Jesus? And, if 'myth' is plot and plot is story and story is literature, why should we not go for the literary Jesus, the Jesus of narrative fiction? Art can catch fish that escape the net of history.

Oh, yes, you can do history with this stuff, if you want. As Ashton vulgarly puts it in *Understanding the Fourth Gospel* (1991), 'You can use a table-cloth as a bath-towel, but it won't do the job very well, because that is not what it is designed for' (Ashton 1991: 430). Oh, yes, you can do history all right, if you are really convinced that a table-cloth is as good as a bath-towel. But Jesus of Nazareth is more successfully concealed than revealed by the New Testament myth, by the plot of the New Testament story. But what do we have on our hands, when we do not have history on our hands? We have literature. Folk-literature for the most part, but literature all the same. The New Testament is a table-cloth on which a literary banquet is spread, but not a bath-towel with which the historian can dry himself.

We have fairy-tales, fairy-tales about feeding 5000, fairy-tales about butcher meat in Corinth, or the Sunday joint of the Christian housewife. But Paul's Sunday joint is something of a red herring, so it is better to take Paul's trumpetology, the *tuba mirum spargens sonum*, 'the trumpet scattering its marvellous sound'. For Paul's butcher meat is, at the plain historical level, plain butcher meat, but the meat comes wrapped in pagan and Christian story—there are tables of Demeter and Asclepius, or tables of demons, on the one hand, and tables, on the other, proleptic of the end of the story. But Paul's Christian story surfaces more obviously with his trumpet. Even the most obviously, plainly historical material, not only in the Gospels, but in the Epistles, in the New Testament as a whole, occurs in the context of myth, of story, of story-world and plot. Even where there are facts, the problem of fiction arises, the problem of fiction *and its truth*.

But Ashton's term, 'fairy-tales', or rather my use of it, for Ashton, more strictly, speaks of 'the fairy-tale atmosphere of the resurrection stories', deserves an apology. Somewhat extravagantly, the phrase is being used here to cover loosely all that in the New Testament is not historical, an 'all' that includes a scale, a gamut of writing, that runs from Jesus saying soberly what he did not say in the Fourth Gospel to the fantastic geology of Jerusalem New Town in the book of Revelation. The term 'literature' is wider and will do as a covering concept, that covers also fairy-tales, but not fairy-tales only.

In the '50s and '60s, in New Testament study, the word we wanted was 'myth' (and if it was not the word we wanted, it was the word we got!). What we want now is 'plot' and Aristotle shows us the way, for if *muthos* is the word he uses, 'myth' is not the only translation. The story of Jesus, Aristotle would say, and say perspicaciously, has 'a beginning, a middle and an end' (*Po.* 1450b27f.), followed by what, in Greek, he would call a περιπέτεια ('peripety' [*Po.* 1452a22f.]) and, in German, *das happy end*. Then to that story (sc. the story of Jesus) add first the story of the early church, then Paul's correspondence about both stories and add finally the chrysoprase, jacinth and jasper 'sci-fi' of St John the Divine; and set those three stories within an overarching story, or story-world, that runs from Eden to the Heavenly City, that begins in a garden susceptible to thistles and ends in a garden, where the only thistle is the spiritual body of John Knox.

This literature can be used for historical purposes, can be used to answer the question, What actually happened? But to do this is to use it for a purpose for which it was not written. And literature anyway (Aristotle again [*Po.* 1451b5]) is 'more philosophical than history', in part, at least, because it offers the reader possibilities: the story of Jesus is the reader's autobiography. But if the story is to be used for the purpose for which it *was* written, to provide, namely, a folk-novel for folk, a number, not a finite, but an indeterminate number of questions arises.

But before touching on one or two of these, something may be said about *John*. For nobody nowadays needs to be persuaded that what Jesus said in *John* is what Jesus did not say. And that what Jesus did, he did not. The omniscience of Jesus slides into and is swallowed up (much as death by victory) by the omniscience of the author. Jesus of Nazareth is omniscient in the Fourth Gospel, because the author of the *Gospel* is an omniscient author. Nor does the picture substantially alter when the necessary qualifications are made, such as that, for example, Jesus really, historically, was put under arrest. For that fact, too, is incapsulated within John's fiction, that makes the arresters the 'arrestees', the biters bit ('they went backward, and fell to the ground' [18.6]). The *Grundkonzeption*, moreover, the central motif of the work, is the notion of Jesus as the alien from outer space (Meeks 1972), a space into which the reader too is shoe-horned, or transposed, or made to rise: in the café at the corner of the universe, the father sends the son on a mission to go, with fortitude, to earth, to get the synagogue off the back of the infant church in Ephesus (to assume this provenance for the work). What is *not* an assumption, but plainly demonstrable, is that, while *formally* the Gospel of John is the history, or 'history', of Jesus, it is, as far as *content* is concerned, a history, or 'history' of the church life of its author (Martyn 1979; Ashton 1991). Put all this together and what we have is as near as dammit (the *mot juste*, perhaps) a historical novel in a fantastic framework of pre-, or proto-gothic, or gothicizing 'sci-fi', though the epithet 'astringent' would be juster, as John's apocalyptic crotchets are 'reduced' (in comparison, or contrast, with the book of Revelation). The son is sent, but little is said on the geology, or uranology, of where he starts from. On jasper and jacinth, chrysoprase and amethyst, we have aposiopesis.

What is the logic of evangelical propositions? What is the logic of *these* evangelical propositions? John's propositions are literary propositions and relate to reality as fiction does; relate to what is the case and to what the case could be; relate to reality 'more philosophically than history'.

If we are going to have commerce with the New Testament, it is with literature, rather than either philosophy or history, with which we have to do. Nor need such an approach hinder anyone who wishes to use a table-cloth for his bath-towel, should the wish, the desiderating wish, be to fill in the back of a picture postcard with cautious assertions about the historical consumption of historical wine by the historical Jesus (Bultmann 1967: 451-52) You *can* ask historical questions of the Gospels. It is more promising to ask literary ones. And the discipline that puts these questions is literary criticism.

For parasitic on the body of literature is literary criticism, which occupies the no-man's-land between philosophy on the one hand and history on the other, a discipline that overlaps with both. With philosophy literary criticism overlaps in two ways, the one in tension with the other: first, literature is bad philosophy, but, second, literature provides the philosopher with accurate evidence, evidence which he can obtain more accurately nowhere else.

In the hierarchy of knowledge, according to Spinoza, the imaginative knowledge, that finds expression in literature, occupies the lowest rank, below both scientific (or rational) and intuitive knowledge. In the hierarchy of knowledge, sc. imagination, reason and intuition, imagination is the lowest form of animal. The New Testament (so Spinoza) is confused cognition (*confusa cognitio*).

Take Mark's voice at the baptism. A voice from the sky does not cohere with what we otherwise know of voices, unless we are bound to think of Winnie the Pooh at the end of a balloon. And why a dove, or dove-like descent? Mark does not tell us—though we may not be doing wrong to tell him that he is drawing an ornithological inference from a Hebrew participle in the feminine ('brooding over', 'moving over': Gen. 1.2), an inference to which Luke in his turn makes his own substantial contribution: the dove is 'in bodily form' (Lk. 3.22). It is true that (according to Spinoza) God's infinite thought is accessible to the finite thought of human beings. But Mark's story is a mess of anthropomorphism, jejune chronology and spatial location. The father opens his mouth in the sky and speaks to his son on the ground. 'We find', writes Hampshire on Spinoza (1988: 154), 'that (sc. the old Jewish prophets)…were ignorant men brilliantly gifted to instil faith and obedience in an ignorant society by myth and story'. This is, I think, as true of Mark as of 'the old Jewish prophets'. They belong in one bag.

And yet, and yet… For not only did Mark (to take only him) produce something that was more philosophical than history, but also something that was, or may be claimed to be, more philosophical than philosophy. For does not the literary imagination that produces 'myth and story' produce better what the philosopher produces worse? Take Spinoza's definition of ambition: 'Ambition', he says, 'is the immoderate desire of glory or honour' (*Ethica* III, *def*. XLIV: *ambitio est immodica gloriae cupiditas*). But the question arises whether Macbeth does not define ambition as well as, or better than, Spinoza. For is not our idea of ambition clearer and distincter after five acts of *Macbeth* than after five words of Spinoza? Or is Spinoza speaking five words with his mind against Shakespeare's ten thousand in a tongue? Spinoza has ground a lens, Shakespeare painted a picture. What is clear is that Mark had read neither Heidegger nor Spinoza. Mark 'with his many miracle stories shows the secret epiphany of the one who achieves his full glory at Easter' (Käsemann 1964: 96 [= 1960: 215]). Mark, telling stories within an overarching story, depicts the free and finite mode of infinite substance, which cannot be grasped by those who are in servitude to their passions, for Mark, or the kingdom of God, is a mystery to outsiders (Kermode 1979). Secrecy has here a genesis. Mark produces in his Gospel a secret epiphany, not in the philosophical, but in the literary mode, a mode (why not?) more philosophical than philosophy.

'Whatever is is in God', says Spinoza (*Ethica* I, *prop*. XV: *quicquid est, in Deo est*). To be 'in God', says Mark, is to be sitting *in* a nest and *under* a pigeon, if and only if the pigeon is broody. Which is to be preferred, the artist or the philosopher?

The problem is to begin where Strauss, in his *Leben* (1840), leaves off. As he puts it (or Ms Eliot [see Strauss 1970: 867]),

> The boundless store of truth and life which for eighteen centuries has been the aliment of humanity, seems irretrievably dissipated; the most sublime levelled with the dust, God divested of his grace, man of his dignity and the tie between heaven and earth broken.

The problem is to begin where Bultmann's negative programme of *de*-mythologizing leaves off and to move forward, not into, or not straight into philosophy, but into the *Zwielicht*, chiaroscuro, or clear-obscurities of literary criticism.

It makes much more sense to say that these authors did what they did than to say that they knew what they were doing when they did it, though again it is probable that they were here much wiser than we often think them. John, certainly, has at least the rudiments of overt reflection and many of our more flat-footed

fundamentalisms, what Northrop Frye might have called 'imaginative illiteracy' (1964), the authors of the New Testament would all
regard with a wild surmise. Folk-literature may be folk-literature,
but folk are not all that dumb. Folk-literature can be little less
Proustian than Proust. Farrer's *Mark* (1951) is no Boeotian pig, or,
if Boeotian (the proverbial fool), then still no pig.

The Fourth Gospel can be compared with the historical novel,
for instance *Waverley*: 'There are mists too', thinks our hero,
Waverley, as he looks back on Flora and Glennaquoich (1972: 226),
'in the mental as well as the natural horizon... and there are happy
lights to stream in full glory upon those points which can profit by
brilliant illumination'. As the sun of John's imagination rises, the
early-born Jesus is shadowed by the light of John's rosy-fingered
pen. But, moreover, the Fourth Gospel can also be compared with
'sci-fi', with, for instance, *A Hitch-Hiker's Guide to the Galaxy*
(Adams 1979). Both of these comparisons say something, I believe,
about the Fourth Gospel. But if the Fourth Gospel is really a work
of genius, it is not likely that *Waverley* and the *Hitch-Hiker's Guide*
will exhaust the possibilities of comparison and evaluation. For the
Fourth Gospel is also a symbolist work, in which the writer spins a
diaphanous web of such symbols as bread and water—and other
prison fare devised by one of the more creative in-dwellers in 'the
prison-house of language'. In a lapidary style 'that is distinctive to
the point of monotony' (Ashton 1986a: 16), these symbols are also
themes around which the writer revolves, in a retreating and
returning dialectic: vine, wine, light and life: abide in these.

But apart from telling us that Judaism is a watery religion and not
the real McKay, or Daniels, a drink for no real man; apart from
telling us that Jesus is the best thing before sliced bread, who sheds
light on God the gardener, as he grafts or prunes with a will, John
does something even more important, something already adum-
brated in the adjective of 'historical novel' and in the name 'Jesus'.
For his book, or booklet, takes the form of a biography, even if that
biography is constructed out of only loosely concatenated—and
indeed *non*-biographical—scenes.

Since Ashton, Martyn, Strauss and others, we have learned, it
is true, to read the Fourth Gospel as a thinly disguised history of
the church in Ephesus, with its insiders, outsiders and boundary
Nicodemuses, the prudential visitors under the cover of the dark.

But it is plain fact that the writer has disguised his history of the church as the history of Jesus, his history of Ephesus and Asia Minor as the history of Palestine. And John can do this, because there is a similarity between the history of his own time and the history of Jesus (*that* is at least *part* of what is meant by calling his work classical). Both Jesus and John's church had problems with the Jews. Why Jesus, why the *historical* Jesus, was at odds with the authorities John's *fiction* does not tell us, but that he was he strongly implies. That skeletal plot of Jesus' life, of opposition and defeat, successful defeat (for the way up and the way down are one and the same), is a myth, is a plot that eternally returns, that must 'ever anew' (*je und je* [Bultmann *passim*]) be recapitulated in the life of human beings: *tua res, nostra res agitur*, 'it is you, it is we, who are in question here'. The pattern of opposition, defeat and victory is a myth, a pattern, a structure that recurs, eternally returns. John is 'more philosophical than history'. In this novel, in other words, two histories, two sociologies, two biographies, constitute a structural component.

To concede this much to the historian is to concede to him *only* so much. For by and large these writers are not operating under the constraints of history, but under the constraints of literature. Jesus is being measured not by historical, but by literary criteria. Anything, Mark tells us, Moses or Elijah could do, Jesus could do better. Anything, John tells us, Moses or Elijah could do, *I* could do better. Jesus, that is, is beyond measure, beyond *that* measure. He out-Moseses Moses and out-Elijahs Elijah. Jesus in the Gospels is dressed in borrowed plumes. It is not John's text that is the problem, but his intertextuality. Jesus is a stick dipped into the stream of Old Testament thought and only seen as refracted.

Strauss and Bultmann have said it all. But our task is not to turn with them from their *muthos* (Bultmann 1960a) or *mythi* (Strauss 1840) to philosophy, be it sub-Hegelian or super-Heideggerian and transposed; not to turn from the discomforts of myth to the rationality of philosophy, not to turn *from*, but to turn *to*, or *remain with* the enjoyment of literature. For 'there can never be too much merriment' (Spinoza *Ethica* IV, *prop.* XLII [= Boyle 1959: 171]). The task is thus to assume uninhibitedly the critical vocabulary not of evidence, fact, eye-witness testimony, authority and the like, but of imagery, metaphor, style, characterization, plot, narrative-world and the like, spiced, if you must, with words like 'foregrounding', 'sub-text', and (but not too often) 'hetero-', 'homo-', 'hyper-' or 'hypo-diegetic analepsis' (Funk 1988: 304).

But not one, but two responses are possible to the enjoyment of the text: (1) writing literary criticism, and (2) writing literature. For a movement of man that is not writing words about the Word is as little a movement as one that is not singing *Lieder*, hymns or songs. There are movements and there are 'stopments', the 'rush of the sap in spring' (Lawrence 1949: 8) and sheer petrefaction. But *however* we write, we cannot write like them. For one thing, it has been done before. And for another, it cannot be done again. Take Joyce and Kazantzakis: however hard they tried, what came out was not the *Odyssey*, but *Ulysses* (1922) or the *Odyssey—A Modern Sequel* (1958). The best tribute we can pay to the New Testament is by writing something else, much as John did something else with the Synoptic Gospels. What John does with Jesus is what *Ulysses* does to the *Odyssey*.

The energy with which Strauss seeks to demolish the New Testament as history (with such cautious caveats as that phrase deserves) serves no purpose so well as to establish the New Testament as literature. History expelled with Strauss's pitchfork returns as literature. But what is it to return as literature, to establish as literature? Strauss establishes, of course, that the astonishing brevity, lithic lapidarity (to be, for a moment, perhaps properly tautologous) of the evangelical style is dependent on literary models from the Old Testament. But what is the relation between style and truth? What is the truth of fiction? What is the truth of *this* fiction? Not, here, what relation is borne by Dickens's London to London, but what relation is borne by the portrait of Jesus to Jesus?

In losing, or prescinding from, history, we gain literature. But, in gaining literature, do we lose the truth? No, we gain *literary* truth. And what is literary truth? Take Mark. What is Mark's literary truth? Would it be right to say that Mark, the poet, makes the historical claim, 'Jesus was like that', but supports that claim, not by (or, on the whole, not by) history, but by story? But his stories are not there so much to support his claim, as to explain what his claim was, namely, that Jesus was like (but more than like) the Moses that we find in Exodus and the Elijah that we find in Kings.

Mark makes a claim, then, but does not provide us with the

evidence that would allow us to make up our minds whether his claim is true. Intertextuality, as it is called, here raises its ugly head: the Jesus of popular fancy Mark creates on the model of the popular fancy that created Moses and Elijah. Jesus of Nazareth provides food for thought, for thousands, for nine thousand (for five and four are nine), and is anxious to relax some of the legal restrictions to which extended substance is prone where an Antipas or a Pilate extends his sway. And, as the ravens 'forget their natural voracity' (Addis 1914: col. 1271) and feed Elijah, so the angels forget their supernatural voracity and feed the Messiah in the wilderness, as he journeys through a new wilderness on a new exodus without the γογγυσμός, *gongusmos*, or 'grumbling', of the first. Texts here are redolent of texts. The imagery occurs and recurs in a hall of mirrors.

The critics agree that the historical novel begins with Scott, with *Waverley*. But need we agree with the critics? May we not, with pleasure and instruction, antedate the emergence of the genre to the Gospels, and antedate, in turn, that antedating to the Court Narrative of King David (2 Sam. 9-20; 1 Kgs 1-2). For is Dan Jacobson, with his *Rape of Tamar* (1970), doing something so very different by writing a novel from the novel on the basis of which he writes it, or, advancing to the Gospels again, by writing *Her Story* (1987), and not *His*? Is there an analogue between Waverley's backward look at heathery Glennaquoich and clarsach-clutching Flora and the backward look, the ideological retrospection, as Lukács (1989) might call it, of Mark and the early Christians at the metaphysically laundered Jesus, in 'raiment...shining, exceeding white as snow; so as no fuller on earth can white them' (Mk 9.3), the one who out-glowed at once both Moses and Elijah? For 'All that was common-place—all that belonged to the every-day world—was melted away and obliterated in those dreams of imagination, which only remembered with advantage the points of grace and dignity that distinguished...' (Scott 1972: 226)—that distinguished whom? 'Flora from the generality of her sex'? That is Scott on Waverley. It might as well have been either Mark or John on Jesus. 'What must the truth have been and be if men who thought and spoke as they did saw it and spoke of it like that?' (Hodgson 1957: 5)—Hodgson's question stands, but any answer to it, that in its remit seriously includes 'thought and wrote like that', must transcend (must it not?) the bounds of historiography. Any answer must be more novel.

As the year 2000 approaches, it may be that the question of the presence and extent, the meaning and the truth, of the fiction in the New Testament will return and keep returning. That meaning, it may be, will lie not far either from Shelley's assertion, that he falls 'upon the thorns of life and bleeds', or from Paul's ontologically vehement fiction (Ricoeur 1978: 249) that he has been 'crucified with Christ', as a letter-writer patently cannot be, for you cannot write letters with your hands spread out to a rebellious people, even if, at the same time, you cannot nail creativity down.

We may broadly agree with Strauss and Bultmann, with the *mythi* of the former and the latter's myth. We may broadly agree that it is legitimate to turn to philosophy for the rational expression of the content of the Gospels. But it is also legitimate to turn to literary criticism, to Kermode (for example) from outside theology and Farrer (for example) within it. The peculiar blend of history and fiction in the Gospels makes it reasonable to turn away from the Gospels to history, but also reasonable to stay with, to perdure with their peculiar blend of history and fiction and regard them as what we would nowadays call 'historical novels', of the kind of Tamar and *Her Story*'s heroine, a heroine who does not appear in the Gospels, but whose existence may reasonably be implied there. Particular stress here has been laid on the Moses–Elijah typology in Mark; and John may not be altogether dissimilar. But to take the Gospels in this way, as narrative fiction, raises with some urgency the question of the truth of fiction, a matter on which Hepburn (1990, cf. 1984 *passim*) makes pertinent comments: To what extent, one wonders, is the 'optative' (1990: 189) a feature of Mark's amalgam? To what extent do the evangelical assertions, or quasi-assertions, exhibit 'the power of art both to modify our grasp of the real and even partly to *constitute* it?' (1990: 188). If we do not read, or watch, Shakespeare for nothing, it follows that it is not for nothing that we read the Gospels.

Mark's hero is not Waverley, but a *Firmley*, who makes us firm. *Tua res, nostra res agitur*: the reader is in question here.

3

A Poem Plotted: *The Carmen Christi* as Border Ballad (Philippians 2.6-11)

Georgicon*

(For Professor Emeritus George W. Anderson)

Scripta virumque cano carmenque georgicon uror   1
E corde eructans, salit et fons laeta canendi.
Felix qui potuit verbi cognoscere formas
Materiamque dei divinam inflataque fata.
Laudabunt alios alii bene dicta probantes   5
Doctaque clarorum. Stat praeclarissimus iste,
Soracte niveo stat non nive candidus exstans
Superior. Floruit sapiens sapiensque florebit.
O fortunatos nimium sua si bona nossent
Emeritos; ficus sub tegmine quisque, sub umbra   10
Quisque sedet vitis. Ridet rubicunda senectus,
Ridet amans conjunx, sub eodem tegmine tecta;
Dum balant olim comites, dum tota facultas
Mugitus circum mensam dat; vana vacat vox.
At nunc laudantes, at tu laudate, canorae   15
Suspensam citharae deferte salice rapinam:
Primum hominem vacuum ipse pater jactavit in orbem,
Ultimus advenit jactatus filius ipse—
Christi grande meo canto tibi carmine carmen.

D. Templetoni Moronis

---

*   A translation is appended to this chapter, together with a copy of Paul's song.

Is Phil. 2.6-11 a poem? Are there poems like it? And what got into this poem? Can we move behind the 'certainties' of dogma to that pre-dogmatic moment, before the poet got his poem onto paper? Leave the theologians on one side, for a moment or two, and let us give the literary a chance, before we accumulate that silt, that sometimes passes for that science (*scientia*), that is called 'theology'. Theology, and metaphysical thinking, is a vital task. At its best it is heuristic, but not obfuscatory. And Genesis, the myth of Genesis, is, if very deep, very clear.

In Genesis 2–3, George, Farmer George Adam (for smiths are not invented till Gen. 4), in dire circumstances (he is married), eats an apple. In Philippians 2, George Adam eats no apple. He is, in a word, amelophagous. He is George Adam (Mark II [the later and superior model])—and flying, on one reading (what may be called 'the catabatic-anabatic'), at high Mach numbers. In Philippians 2, Paul sings a song (*carmen canit*) and, in singing a song, rewrites a story. He rewrites a piece of narrative fiction, by writing out, erasing, an apple. In addition, he re-sings a song: Isaiah's dumb lamb is a re-sung lamb, glossed (they say) by Paul, as a slaughtered lamb (...*mortem autem crucis!*). If a 'Hebrew of the Hebrews' is thus parasitic on Hebrew song and story, if Paul is imagining among imaginers, literary criticism *s'impose*.

The *Carmen Christi* looks unlike 'The Economic Influence of the Developments in Shipbuilding Techniques, 1450 to 1485' (Amis 1961: 15). What we require here, desiderate, perhaps, is not the historical method, but an ontology of fiction. In *Hamlet and the Philosophy of Literary Criticism*, Weitz (1965) first recommends to the critic 'non-trivial description'. I attempt to offer here only some ante-prolegomena to trivial description.

All run the race and all win prizes. Philippians 2 cannot be said to suffer from a paucity either of attention or of readings of what has been attended to. The Adamic line, following Grotius's *tanquam Adam* ('as Adam', sc. Jesus did not rob, as Adam did),[1] will

---

1. Grotius 1646 Phil. 2.7 *ad loc.* (cit. Henry 1950: 43; cit. Martin 1967: 161): 'ὡς ἄνθρωπος *kᵉādām, tanquam Adam, qui* ὁ πρῶτος ἄνθρωπος. *Dignitate talis apparuit qualis Adam, id est, dominio in omnes creaturas, in mare, ventos, panes, aquam. ob quam causam id quod de Adamo dictum fuerat in* Ps. VIII *Christo* μυστικῶς *applicatur.*' Grotius's Ps. 8 also produces

be followed here: Adam made a pretty kettle of fish, Jesus not; or
Adam erred, Jesus not. And an appropriate debt will be paid to
Herrick ('Gather ye rosebuds...') and Murphy-O'Connor (1976),
who with a well-armed missile from the Ecole Biblique holes pre-
existence below the water-line, when it had already anyway, since
Reimarus, been sailing in the wrong direction. For Herrick and
Murphy-O'Connor concentrate also on the fate, or destiny, of the
good man in Wisdom, who is compassed about by a cloud of
perfumes and bad men wreathed in roses:

> Let us take our fill of costly wine and perfumes,
>   and let no flower of spring pass by us.
> Let us crown ourselves with rosebuds before they wither...
>
> Let us lie in wait for the righteous man... (Wis. 2.7-8, 12).

Adam in the Genesis story, we are sometimes told, was in the
'image' or 'form' of God. And we need not be surprised that
according to this early story an anthropomorphic god should have
fashioned a theomorphic man. Everything in the garden was
lovely—lots of fruit, no death, no thistles (though the Scot may be
permitted the question whether Paradise can be complete without
them). Everything in the garden was lovely, except for one real
snake. And though, according to the myth, there were no signs
with the legend, *Das Betreten ist verboten*, 'Do Not Walk on the
Grass', there was one tree and one prohibition promulgated by the
anthropomorphic pedestrian (it was, we remember, the 'cool of
the day').

In some of the best stories animals talk. And this one is no
exception. And the talking snake very soon makes clear what is in
the wind: 'Here's a pretty kettle of fruit' (Joyce), he says, 'and if
you eat it you will be like God. You too will be pedestrians on an
equal footing with Capability Jehovah.' Then, without so much as a
'by your leave', Adam's early feminist hinder-meet 'took of its fruit'.

Like θανάτου δὲ σταυροῦ, *thanatou de staurou* (even death on a
cross) *HARPAGMOS* (robbery: Phil. 2.6) is a crux, that, taken by
Grotius, remains, it seems, a prize for the taking. There are many
more positive and more negative ways of tying, re-tying and

(v. 7) *tᵉaṭṭᵉrēbû* (MT), ἐστεφάνωσας (LXX), *coronasti* (nov. vg.), which accord
well with Käsemann's form-critical remarks, based on Peterson (1926), on
Akklamation (re Phil. 2.11).

severing the Gordian nots (*sic*) here (for example O'Neill [1988] [one of our negatives is missing]: '...thought it not robbery not to be equal with God').

> Let us drink and be merry, dance, joke, and rejoice,
> With claret and sherry, theorbo and voice...
>
> (Thomas Jordan).

Coronemus nos rosis antequam marcescant, 'let us crown ourselves with roses, before they fade'. A man who is going to crown himself with what Mimnermus (fr.1.4, cit. Burton 1962: 12) calls ἥβης ἄνθεα...ἁρπαλέα, *hebes anthea...harpalea*: 'flowers of youth for the picking', must pick them first (Mimnermus, we may be relieved to hear [Bowra 1949: s.v. 'Mimnermus'], also 'tempers his hedonism with a respect for truth [fr. 8]'—it is, he says there, if not quite in these words, a *sine qua non* of the inter-personal). If Hedea at Isthmia is to win the race for war chariots (she won [Dittenberger no. 802, cit. Murphy-O'Connor 1983: 16]), she must get it straight (if a woman of that sort [four victories], with those sisters [two sisters, four victories], needs the telling) that the gift of athletic success is ἁρπαλέα δόσις, *harpalea dosis* (Pindar, *Pythians* 8.65, cit. Burton 1962: 12), 'a gift to be snatched eagerly'. The word 'take' has some force in the context of flowers, but still more elsewhere, as we see from 2 Cor. 11.20, where RSV translates with 'takes advantage of', NEB with 'gets...in his clutches' and Lorimer with 'taks ye in his girns' (sc. 'noose', 'snares'). Nor is there more rapacity and rapine in the Greek than in the Hebrew *lāqaḥ* (BDB, s.v. 9: 'take = carry off: a. as booty...b. as prisoners'), while the cognate noun *malqôaḥ* can mean, indifferently, the 'booty' taken and the 'jaw' that takes it. Nor is the violence diminished by either the English or the German of Bonhoeffer's ex-, or eisegesis, of Adam's 'Nazi' *Apfelergreifung* ('apple-seizure'—Bonhoeffer gave these lectures in Berlin, in the Winter Semester 1932, and wrote the introduction to their publication when 1933 was sufficiently well advanced to draw the exegete's attention to the more sinister aspects of the semantic range of this one Hebrew word [Bethge 1967: 260-63])—'snatch', 'violate', *rauben*, 'rob', *an sich reissen*, 'wrest to oneself' (Bonhoeffer 1955: 90-97 and 1959: 73-78). The apple, the *res rapienda*, 'the thing to be snatched', rapidly became a *res rapta*, 'a thing snatched'. And then not a *res retinenda*, 'a thing to be retained', for the forbidden fruit, understood by Eve as a *res donanda*, 'a thing to be given', rapidly (again) became *donata*, 'given' (Adam an early Donatist?). There is good and there is evil and there is knowing and there is mis-knowing. Only recently introduced to one another, Adam and Eve knew evil. And we know the result: thistles (in the English sense) and labour pains.

Suppose you do retell the story, with Jesus taking the place of Adam, with Jesus taking the place of Man, with a man, the man Jesus, taking the place of Man, with Adam (Mark II) taking the place of Adam (Mark I), then you do not aim upwards at the knowledge of good and evil, you do not aim to know too much, or at 'equality with God', at *sicut deus*, or τὸ εἶναι ἴσα θεῷ, *to einai isa theo(i)*, but downwards at the knowledge of the good, the knowledge of one thing only, for the gravest problems are only to be dealt with by a 'deeper immersion in existence' (Kierkegaard [no ref.], cit. Robinson 1963: 47). While the sluggard must go to the ant and the Samaritan to the ditch, the good man must go early to his long home. You aim at obedience to the prohibition, you aim to respond to God and man. You are an earthen pot full of coins and you pour out your treasure. You are a pitcher and you pour out water, not on to the thirsty ground, but into thirsty mouths, to slake the heart: ἑαυτὸν ἐκένωσεν, *heauton ekenosen* (Phil. 2.7: he 'emptied himself').

'What is man?' you might ask. Supremely memorable? Master of fish and fowl? Lord of creation? What do you make of this one, the one of whom I sing? Supremely forgettable. Contemptible, a mere nothing—and 'contempt is the imagination of anything which touches the mind so little that the mind is moved by the presence of that thing to think rather of things which are not contained in the thing than those which are contained in it' (Spinoza 1843: III, 318 [= *Ethica* III, *def.* V^2]). When a man is born, something is born; when this man was born, nothing was born. A silhouette without substance. Form without content:

> his appearance was so marred,
> beyond human semblance,
> and his form beyond that of the sons of men (Isa. 52.14).

2.　Contemtus est rei alicuius imaginatio, quae mentem adeo parum tangit, ut ipsa mens ex rei praesentia magis moveatur ad ea imaginandum, quae in ipsa re non sunt, quam quae in ipsa sunt.

Crowned less with honour than with the absence of honour. Born like others, become less than others. 'Jesus of Nazareth? I don't seem to remember the name' (France 1891: *Jésus de Nazareth? Je ne me rappelle pas*). But his distinctness from those who did not honour him both brings to light and by bringing to light brings about the discomfort of those who are now conscious of *their* distinctness from *him*:

> the very sight of him is a burden to us,
> because his manner of life is unlike that of others,
> and his ways are strange (Wis. 2.15).

Lest his name should be only too well remembered, erase the written discomfort and liquidate the man.

Once this biography, compressed into these three verbs, 'emptied...humbled...became obedient', has been thrown as a supposititious sop to the historian, less substantial, less extended, less discursive, than one day in Dublin for Joyce's Bloom, this poem, this social lyric, this song for society, introduces, with 'Therefore...', a caesura. Isaiah's dumb dulocrat, 'master-slave', Genesis's theomorphic master of fish, fowl and fauna, the Genesis might-have-been, finds himself the occasion of the 'acclamation' (Peterson 1926: 317, cit. Käsemann 1960: 87): 'Jesus Christ is Lord', from the lips of multiple (and beyond necessity multiplied) entities, astral, terrestrial and chthonic, with whom Jesus joins in genuflection. As tongue acknowledges a coronation, the coronation of a regent (Jesus), so knee acknowledges the hand (God's) that bestows the crown. When what has been named has been named, but Jesus remains unnamed, you have not named the highest under the Most High.

Subordinationist texts invite subordinationist reading.

It is unlikely that 'the handling of a medium' (sc. words) 'that facilitates the simultaneous achievement of numerous effects' (Hepburn 1984: 4) can be exhausted by one brief reading. Nor is it exhaustive to claim that the poem, as a whole, is refracted through Genesis, Isaiah and Wisdom as the leading texts of the linguistic universe in which this poet has his being.

For some aesthetic theorists

> the more aesthetically valuable is to be distinguished from the less
> valuable by reference to the concept of form. They argue that both

mimetic and creative activity may result in ill-formed objects which
offer no reward to contemplation; but it is by reason of their form
that other objects do reward and inexhaustibly sustain contemplation (Hepburn 1984: 3).

Critics, at least since Lohmeyer (1928), have been easily persuaded that we have to do here with formal excellence, but have
not been able so easily to persuade one another to agree on
what that form precisely is: three four-line strophes? Six two-line
strophes? Six three-line strophes? This last version (Lohmeyer's
[1928: 5-6]) has much to be said for it. It requires only the omission
of 'even death on a cross' as metrically redundant and a Pauline
cliché, or rather *theologoumenon* (Paul never *has* clichés). Now
the song, the poem (what is the right word here?), is very widely
thought to be of non-Pauline authorship, but it may surely be asked
whether the man who was capable of the rhythmic, artistic prose
(*Kunstprosa*) of 1 Corinthians 13 could not also have been capable
of creating this *carmen* himself. But whether Paul is providing a
gloss to what someone else wrote, or to what he wrote himself
(the word is in process for Paul, too), these words of the gloss are,
if any words are, the words most likely to 'speak themselves', to
have spoken themselves, in Paul's own mind.

The triple division, then, of reality, of 'that which is', into astral,
terrestrial and chthonic, is replicated in two groups of six three-line
stanzas, many of them of triple ictus, or 'three-beat tristichs', a
form that Burney (1925: 30) finds, for example, in Ps. 24.7-10. And
9 of the 18 lines of Levertoff and Martin's retro-translation of
Philippians 2 into Aramaic (Levertoff [no ref.], in Clarke 1929: 148;
cit. Martin 1967: 40-41) consist of no more than three Aramaic
words (with the wrong word for 'robbery' [*šālālā*]).

'The peculiarity of this psalm', writes Lohmeyer (1928: 10),
'consists in this, that it narrates, as it were, in ballad-like tones
[...*dass er wie in balladenartigem Tone erzählt*...], that it, so to
say, crystallizes around verbs'. But Lohmeyer's comparison with
the ballad has wider relevance. There is the same conciseness,
concision even (κατατομή, *katatome*[!]: Phil. 3.2). We may compare:

> She sought to bind his many wounds,
> But he lay dead on Yarrow...

with:

> ...and became obedient unto death...

And compare:

> And he's stayed for seven lang years and a day,
> And the birk and broom blooms bonnie:
>
> Seven lang years by land and sea...

Here in neighbouring stanzas (7-8) of 'Hynd Horn' (Allingham 1865: 6-7) 'seven lang years' is resumed, much as 'in human likeness', the last line of stanza 2, is resumed by 'in human shape', the first line of stanza 3 (NEB, which here more accurately replicates the form of the Greek). Or compare how 'the name which is above every name' (the last line of stanza 4) is picked up by 'that at the name of Jesus...' (the first line of stanza 5). 'Form of God', moreover, clashes antithetically and anaphorically with 'form of a servant', while the 'humbled himself' of stanza 3 and the 'highly exalted' of stanza 4 form a closely conjoined contrast within the over all architectonic contrast between 'servant' or 'slave' (stanza 2) and 'master' or 'lord' (stanza 6). And add to all this the list of bewildering near-synonyms: 'form', 'likeness' and 'shape' (stanza 3 for this last, where RSV translates [again] by 'form').

Matthew 23.12 summarizes well: '...whoever humbles himself will be exalted.'

So much for some observations on the song's artistic form. But what of the *content* thus formed? What can the literary critic say of this, without turning like Strauss to Hegel, like George Eliot to Feuerbach, or like Bultmann to Heidegger? The epic sweep of *Paradise Lost* and *Regained* is here contracted into a lyrical encomium of 18 lines. And to contract is not to narrate, is to abbreviate, is to allude to. Milton was a long-distance runner, but what we have here is something more like the valetudinarian primary school 20-yard dash. Our author's breath is briefer. 'An apple a day', he says, 'keeps the doctor on the way; but doctors should keep off apples and this doctor did'.

There is a double allusion here (to leave Isaiah and Wisdom out of account for the moment), (1) a literary and (2) a historical, to the life of Adam and the life of Jesus, neither of these being narrated, though both narratives are presupposed. And these presuppositions, the literary and the historical, make a double appeal to the imagination, the literary imagination and the historical. A story (Gen. 2–3) is alluded to; it is not narrated. A history (the history of Jesus) is alluded to; it is presupposed.

But this word 'historical' does not tell the whole truth, because the history of Jesus that is alluded to and that we find in the Synoptics, is rather more like the 'history' of Tom Jones and rather less like 'Developments in Shipbuilding'. It is storied history, history and story fused; historical sense combined with historical nonsense. It is fictionalized history, or 'faction'; not the facts of the matter, but, to put it that way, the 'ficts'. It is a character assessment ('he humbled himself'), but without the facts on which such an assessment should be based. We are offered the banality that Jesus did not know everything and did not try to know more than men can. He knew his limits and he knew his limits, as Adam in the story did not know his. And 'hybris breeds the tyrant' (Sophocles, *Oedipus Tyrannus* 873: ὕβρις φυτεύει τύραννον, *hubris phuteuei turannon*), for aiming at too much makes too much of a man. Adam's trouble was 'titanism' (von Rad 1949: 72), Jesus' trouble was humanism.

Paul of Tarsus, to judge by his non-practice, malpractice even, cannot tell a story for a sweetmeat from the souk. *Ab abesse ad non posse consequentia valet*, from the absence of something to the impossibility of something the conclusion is valid enough for my purposes: Paul does not tell stories, so he cannot. But he stands to the biblical tradition, the one, that is, that was written, not the one he was writing, much as Mark, in Augustine's view, stands to Matthew: *tanquam pedisequus et breviator*, as following in the footsteps of the tradition and abbreviating it. 'Jesus ate no apple', he tells us. By contrast with Jesus, Adam, lord of hens and hamsters, did eat the apple and, doubtless to the playing of the first trump, is rapidly sent out of the park.

Paul's song now turns from paradise-park to Isaiah's famous image (52–53) of the pariah and to 'the righteous man' of Wisdom (2): ἑαυτὸν ἐκένωσεν...ἐταπείνωσεν ἑαυτόν, *heauton ekenosen... etapeinosen heauton* (chiasmus[!]: 'himself he emptied...he humbled himself'). To turn aside Spinoza's critique of 'humility' as the tactic of self-destruction, or, at any rate, as giving rise to self-despising (1843: I, 323 [= *Ethica* III, *def*. XXVIII, *explic.*: *abjectio*]), humility and self-emptying in Philippians 2 are to be understood,

not as under-estimation, but as adequate, not exaggerated, estima-
tion; and as the kind of generosity (*generositas*) towards others
that does not preclude 'animosity' (*animositas*) or 'spiritedness
towards oneself'. Christ acts in a societal context where virtue, or
manliness, is not prized highly by the vicious. It is not Jesus' fault,
if the endeavours wherewith he endeavoured, combining *generositas* and *animositas*, to persist in his own being were annihilated,
deed and doer, by the pride and contempt to which risible man is
prone. It was by external causes that he was overcome and those
contrary to his nature (cf. Spinoza 1843: I, 345 [= *Ethica* IV, *prop.*
XX *schol.*]). Spinoza's hilarity, his *hilaritas*, Nietsche's *fröhliche
Wissenschaft*, his 'gay science', are banished by loathèd melancholy
to Erebus; the happy man by the unhappy, the just by the unjust.

But 'But...', or 'Therefore...', for διό (Phil. 2.9) inserts a caesura
into the song. For 'Then they blew the trumpet; and the people
said, "Long live King Jesus!" And all the people went up after him,
playing on pipes, and rejoicing with great joy, so that the earth was
split by their noise' (1 Kgs 1.39-40 [my emendation]). These verses
belong, of course, not to the song in Philippians 2, but to the
narrative of Zadok and Nathan and the anointing of Solomon as
king. The 'account', in Philippians, of Jesus' coronation is Scottish
and spare. Thus subject becomes monarch and high is related to
low by what we might call 'executive antithesis', the antithesis
being 'executive', God being God (to use a 'significant tautology'
[Ramsey 1967: 40]). When God is in question, 'low' is made 'high'.
The making is by the kind of executive *fiat* that makes, if two
nouns may be juxtaposed, for Quality Assurance.

One of the constituents, or apanages, of this poem is a historical
fact, namely, that there was once a man, Jesus. And he died;
perhaps, was executed. We could not be sure from the poem alone
that this was a historical fact, but we can be pretty sure, when we
correlate with this poem written evidence that we find elsewhere.
We are, moreover, offered a character assessment, a 'mere how'
added to a 'mere that': Jesus' actions warrant the judgment that he
was humble and prepared to expend himself, that indeed he
expended himself. But much the larger part of the poem is concerned with the explanation and understanding of the fact, impli-
cating the warp of fact in the woof of story and song.

Jesus is understood in terms of a story, a piece of narrative fiction about hanky-panky in the rose garden. Further, Jesus is understood in terms of two poems about recurrent features of human behaviour (Aristotle's τὰ καθόλου, *ta katholou* [*Po.* 1451b7: 'the universal']), on how the pariah is cast out, or how the gadfly comes to hemlock (Isa. 53; Wis. 2). And finally he is understood in terms of imagery that Feuerbach would derive from the Hebrew monarchy, the *vivat rex* motif, which calls into question the evaluations of the despisers.

Paul's readers, then and now, are invited to rehearse this movement in themselves, for 'each of us has been the Adam of his own soul' (*2 Bar.* 54.19). And each of us can be the second Adam of his own soul. Though each can fall like that Adam, each too can fail to fall, can rise like this one. Particularity and generality are paradoxically combined by the artists here: garden and snake, leaves and thistles, dumb sheep and rose garland. But *their* stories, *their* songs and stories, of Adam, of the Servant, of the Righteous One, is *our* story, is our song. Hepburn (1984: 128) thus puts Baruch's point:

> In watching a drama we are often—even typically—aware both of a character in his particularity and of the general insights he yields about humanity-at-large (Hamlet the man, for instance, and the Hamlet in men).

Humanity-at-large is offered possibilities by the particularities of Paul's poem. The poem is formally a wrought gem, a miniature of major content, an intaglio, a seal that stamps, that impresses the impressionable reader. It is a classic.

But what of the ontology of the poem? Shall we say that we have here *tout court* the ontology of fiction, a poetic ontology? Shall we say that what we have here is the product of an *ars adulterina*, an adulterous art, a mixed form, a fusion of history and fiction? Or a fusion of time and eternity fictionally expressed? Is the poem autonomous? Does the history belong to the poem as Lady Macbeth's children to the play? Is the history extra-textual? Not quite, surely. The aorists, not in themselves decisive, have a historical smell and so strike the sense. It is the Jesus, who was (*der Dagewesene*, 'the one who was there'), who has taught the poet to sing, though it is the Jesus, no less certainly, of the poet's experience. Most men, like most women, can wear different hats. The combined office of poet and historian belongs to humankind as such. And yet the question remains here: What hat was the poet wearing? For the *Iliad* does not make Homer a historian of the Trojan War. Or if the *Carmen Christi* is not the *Iliad* and if the author was wearing two hats, which hat is the top hat?

The question arises whether, rather, the hats are collateral, whether the ontology of fiction and the ontology of history have here equivalent weighting, whether each is making an equally substantial contribution, whether the truth of the one is not less true than the truth of the other, or whether poetry is substituting the vacuous for the substantial, the would-be real for the really real.

Not so, at least Aristotle. Fact cannot thus be contrasted with fiction, for 'poetry is more philosophical than history' (*Po.* 1451b5-6). And, it may be contended (against Spinoza), no less philosophical than philosophy. For what is more philosophical than history and no less philosophical than philosophy can be set by the poet 'before the eyes' (Aristotle *Rh.* 1405b12), '[i]n this way, seeing everything with the utmost vividness, as if he were a spectator of the action' (Aristotle, *Po.* 1455a23-25: οὕτω γὰρ ἂν ἐναργέστατα [ὁ] ὁρῶν ὥσπερ παρ' αὐτοῖς γιγνόμενος τοῖς πραττομένοις, *houto gar an enargestata* [*ho*] *horon hosper par' autois gignomenos tois prattomenois*), in such a way that it commands our assent. The rhythm of the poem itself convinces, sets its truth within the ear. And the textual background (Genesis, Isaiah, Wisdom) supplies density of meaning. 'Knee' and 'tongue', for instance, the tree of knowledge, provide concretion. And 'God', the presiding term, the term that presides over the whole, begins to provide an ontological argument and supply a reference for the sense.

To turn from the Peloponnesian War, the history of the Papacy, 'The Economic Influence of Developments in Shipbuilding Techniques 1450-1485' is to turn from history. It is not to turn from reality. To touch on these and turn to other things and grasp them is not to turn from history, but to do other things as well and more importantly. To touch on the Jesus of history and turn to Hebrew song and story on the one hand and the God and the Christ of the poet's experience on the other is to turn not from the real to the imaginary, but to the imagined.

In this ballad-like lyric, in this ballad-like ballad, the historical Jesus plays the part that Moscow plays in *War and Peace*. Had Moscow, however, been different, *War and Peace* would have been otherwise. In this lyric, in that novel, the sentences do not have the assertorial quality of a historical narrative. They are, Ingarden (1985: 133-62) tells us, 'quasi-assertive': Jesus is Adam, Jesus is a lamb, Jesus is a king and wears a crown. It is only by delicate inference from such plainly metaphorical predications that we arrive at the history that Paul's song plainly presupposes and that is plainly present, though not as incision, but as striation. But behind these quasi-assertive sentences lie non-quasi-assertive ones, such as (1) that Jesus was a man, was a good man; and as good men go, he went; and (2) that *sub specie aeternitatis* Jesus *is* a man and a good one; and (3) that the reader may be so also, in Paul's antinomian sense.

This is a *mode* of saying it (in Eliot's and Spinoza's sense), but not, George, very satisfactory, not to be preferred before Paul's, or A.N. Thropostis's, George Adam. The song is better than what is said about it. It might be regretted that it is not Alcaics that we have here, not Sapphics, not Glyconics, nor even the iambic tetrameter catalectic (Griffith, in Hammond and Griffith 1979: 605). For what Spinoza says is true of John is no less true of Paul's *carmen grande*: *quamvis...Graece scripserit, hebraizat tamen* (though he has written...in Greek, he hebraizes nonetheless 1843: II, 200 [= *Epistola* XXIII]). But that for a Hebraist is all to the good.

1
ὃς ἐν μορφῇ Θεοῦ ὑπάρχων
who, though he was in the form of God,
οὐχ ἁρπαγμὸν ἡγήσατο
did not count a thing to be grasped
τὸ εἶναι ἴσα Θεῷ,
[equality] with God,

2
ἀλλ' ἑαυτὸν ἐκένωσεν,
but emptied himself
μορφὴν δούλου λαβών,
taking the form of a servant,
ἐν ὁμοιώματι ἀνθρώπων γενόμενος·
being born in the likeness of men.

3
καὶ σχήματι εὑρεθεὶς ὡς ἄνθρωπος
and being found in human form
ἐταπείνωσεν ἑαυτὸν
he humbled himself
γενόμενος ὑπήκοος μέχρι θανάτου.
and became obedient unto death.

4
διὸ καὶ ὁ Θεὸς αὐτὸν ὑπερύψωσεν
Therefore God has highly exalted him
καὶ ἐχαρίσατο αὐτῷ
and bestowed on him
τὸ ὄνομα τὸ ὑπὲρ πᾶν ὄνομα,
the name which is above every name,

5
ἵνα ἐν τῷ ὀνόματι Ἰησοῦ
that at the name of Jesus
πᾶν γόνυ κάμψῃ
every knee should bow,
ἐπουρανίων καὶ ἐπιγείων καὶ καταχθονίων
in heaven and on earth and under the earth,

6
καὶ πᾶσα γλῶσσα ἐξομολογήσηται
and every tongue confess
ὅτι κύριος Ἰησοῦς Χριστὸς
that Jesus Christ is lord,
εἰς δόξαν Θεοῦ πατρός.
to the glory of God the father.

The Song (Phil. 2)

Appendix

Translation of the dedicatory poem, 'Georgicon': 'Writings and the man I sing and I am consumed with passion as I bubble forth from the heart a song for George, and there leaps up a fountain of singing joyful things. Happy is he who is able to know the forms of the word and the divine content of God and the sayings he has in(suf)flated. Let others praise others, (testing and) approving what they have said well and the learned (utterances) of famous men. But that man stands supremely famous, stands, white not with snow, standing out higher than snowy Soracte. He has flourished, a wise man, and, a wise man, he will flourish. O happy, more than happy are the Emeriti, were they but knowing it; each one under the covering of his fig-tree, each one under the shadow of his vine. Ruddy old-age smiles, there smiles the loving wife, protected under the same covering, †while the former colleagues bleat, while the whole Faculty (Ability?) moos around the table; their vain voice is vacant (sc. of sense)†. But now you, who praise, but now you, who are praised, take down from the willow-tree the suspended robbery of your canorous harp: the first man the father himself threw into the empty world, the last man, thrown, the son himself, has arrived—Christ's great song in my song I sing to you.'

Acknowledgment

I am very grateful to Ms K. Moir for corrections, help and advice for these vv. To put it another way, apotropaic of *Robigus* (the god of rust), she engen-*der*ed help in *quantities*: *laeta* will have to do what it can with *canendi*, not with *fons*, and *Soracte*, whatever else it can be, *cannot* be *nivea* (found in the autograph). *Facultas*, if it is to mean here what it must, is first (Murray thinks) found in this sense in 1255 (in the *Chartularium* of the University of Paris). But this is a little late. The best defence of what remains may be found in Ps. 44.2 (*Nova Vulgata* MCMLXXXVI): *Lingua mea calamus scribae velociter scribentis* (if *velociter* [= KJV Ps. 45.1: 'my tongue is the pen of a ready writer'] is allowed sufficient force).

4

Samaritan and Prodigal as Nonentities: Jesus of Nazareth as Author of Narrative Fiction

What is the status of fictional entities? We spend enough time on them, do we not? Do not the *media*, radio and television, does not the artist, the painter, the poet, the storyteller supply us with an abundance? Can we not give Jesus his due? He was a dab hand at storytelling, even his most benighted followers would agree. There are other ways, surely, of telling the truth, than supplying information, writing history and compiling birth registers.

While from the standpoint of the calf the story of the Prodigal Son is undoubtedly a tragedy, the following remarks prescind both from this and from the doubtless valuable observation that the Latin 'running head' (Black [with acknowledgments to Ms Eileen Dickson] 1963: 438, 440) for 'prodigal' (*prodigus*) and the Vulgate version of 'fatted' (*saginatus*) occur together in Tacitus's *History* (1.62), where he has occasion, or takes occasion, to describe the dining indiscretions of the not yet imperial Vitellius. They attempt rather to come to terms with the idea of fiction in the New Testament and with the question in what sense, or senses, fiction is, or may be, true. The present writer has probably bitten off more than he can chew, but at least this is unlike Henry James, of whom it has been said (by someone) that 'he has chewed more than he has bitten off'.

Fiction in the New Testament is a complex area, but the author of fiction, who is not the author of a history, or, at least, plain history, takes us, I believe, into an area where we find ourselves confronted both by actualities and possibilities—and even, in the case of *Alice and Wonderland* and the Gospels, by impossibilities, in both of these works, or groups of works, perhaps *plausible* impossibilities (the notion is Aristotle's [πιθανὸν ἀδύνατον, *pithanon adunaton* (*Po.* 1461b11)]). But the author of fiction has a sharper grasp of these actualities, possibilities and impossibilities than most other authors. He, or she, it might be said, has a true grasp. The significance of the question is not far to seek, for if the idea of fiction can be validated in stories *by*, or often thought to be *by* Jesus, then the idea may be more easily validated in stories *about* him also.

These two Parables of Jesus, or two Parables of which there is no good reason to doubt the authenticity, the Prodigal Son and the Good Samaritan are 'unusually well crafted' (Funk 1988: 177). They are examples of narrative fiction, though if anyone were to ask whether they are not rather examples of narrative history (to speak tautologously), one would hardly know how to answer. Certainly, we only have L. There is no other corroborative evidence that these two stories are historically true, if no cogent inference on historicity can be drawn, for example, from such a localization as ' "the Ascent of Adummim" (Josh. 18.17)' (Fitzmyer 1985: 886, cf. 888).

The topics envisaged here are the idea of fiction and the ontology of art. But before some remarks are offered on these, with the help of Aristotle's *Poetics* (1909, 1925b, 1968), Collingwood's *Principles of Art* (1938) and Isenberg's *Aesthetics and the Theory of Criticism* (1973), an attempt will first be made to say what these parables are *about*, to speak about their *content*, to offer on this question some platitudes without longitude.

Categories may be arranged in a hierarchy. The Prodigal Son is making, or allows one to make, such an arrangement. Of the two categories, 'mercy' and 'judgment', 'mercy' stands higher, overrides 'judgment', though, no doubt, there is more to be said. To put it, for example, with Manson:

> The religious authorities were horrified by the freedom with which He criticised doctrines and practices hallowed by centuries of pious observance. Yet He was wont to go to the Synagogue on the Sabbath; and he enjoined the healed leper to do what Moses commanded in the matter of his healing. The explanation of this seeming inconsistency lies in the fact that the claims of the kingdom of God take precedence over the requirements of the Law (1949: 344).

The point, or a point, of the Good Samaritan is that the word 'neighbour' is indefinable, or, more cautiously, cannot be defined in terms of nationhood, or social rôle. No doubt (again), there is more to be said.

Mercy, then, stands higher than judgment; the word 'neighbour' is indefinable.

These two assertions, on the content, or point, or meaning, of the two parables are by way of orientation, though the question may immediately be raised, whether Jesus does not say it better, whether what is said in these two propositions about precedence and indefinability respectively has not already been said better in the story (but say *what* better?). For does a story not make a point better than a point is made by stating the point? Is it not better to make a point by telling a story than to make a point by stating a point?

Now one or two literary-critical remarks—by which is *not* meant the question whether we are not here dealing with 2 parables, but with 28, because there are 28 verses in the 2 parables and therefore (as some might say) 28 different sources. The concern here is *not* with literary criticism in *that* sense, but rather with questions of character, scene and style of narration; and so must even prescind from the really burning question about the Prodigal Son, the question whether at any point for any reason we are dealing with bagpipes or not, the question how ἤκουσεν συμφωνίας, *ekousen sumphonias* ('he heard music': Lk. 15.25) is to be translated. Leaving that question to Tovey (Wittgenstein 1980: 81e) and the historians of music on the one hand and to the cacophonous contest of Barry (1904: 180-90) and Moore (1905: 166-75) on the other, one may merely re-observe what Funk has already observed (1988: 202-203), that the Younger Son's prepared lecture, 'I will arise and go to my father...' (Lk. 15.18), is interrupted by the Father. The Younger Son never gets as far as 'Make me as one of your hired servants' (Lk. 15.19—omitted 15.21). Not only does mercy override; it is impetuous. Secondly, when the Elder Son comes along and asks, 'Why the bagpipes [or 'symphony']?' (15.26), the Servant does not say, as the Father had said (15.24), 'Your brother was dead and is alive'. He is not quite so *bouleversé*, he is underwhelmed, for he will have to tidy the house and dispose of the bones. He simply says that the Younger Brother is alive and well, or 'safe and sound' (15.27). And, thirdly, the Christian reader knows what in the 'far country' the Younger Son has been up to—he has been visiting, perhaps too frequently, The Old Bull and Beef (or The Young Calf and Veal). The Elder Son, however, knows better:

his brother (so Lorimer 1983: 137; Lk.15.30 *ad loc.*) 'hes gane throu your haill haudin wi hures' (sc. 'has gone through your whole holding [sc. ὁ καταφαγών σου τὸν βίον, *ho kataphagon sou ton bion*] with whores').

As regards the Good Samaritan story (Lk. 10.30-35), Funk makes the point (1988: 184) that, before the eponymous hero arrives, there are the two scenes of the Priest and the Levite. Now as Aristotle has astutely pointed out (*Po.* 1450b27-28), every good drama, every well-constructed plot has a 'beginning, a middle and an end' (ἀρχὴν καὶ μέσον καὶ τελευτήν, *archen kai meson kai teleuten*). And what goes for a drama as a whole may be said to go also for its parts, for the whole of each part: every scene, we may say, has a beginning, a middle and an end, or (alternatively, with Funk [1988: 62-63]) an 'introduction, a nucleus and a conclusion'. But what we have in these two scenes is the first and the third of these without the second, a beginning and an end, but no middle— one may compare the story (in Lee 1955: 39 n. 1, here abbreviated) about the mother who had occasion to explain to her child, 'You see, dear...God doesn't eat anything because He hasn't got a body like you and me'. 'Oh', said the little girl, 'you mean his legs go right up to his neck.'

There is being explored here the assumption that in these two stories Jesus is not doing historiography, that he is not talking about what actually happened, about τὰ γενόμενα (*ta genomena*, 'what happened' [Aristotle *Po.* 1451a36]), about *wie es eigentlich gewesen* ('how it actually was', 'how it actually happened': 'People have assigned to history the task of judging the past, of teaching those of the present day for the benefit of the time to come; the present essay dispenses with such high tasks: it attempts only to show how it actually was' [von Ranke 1874: xxxiii-xxxiv, vii]).

We are dealing here, on Collingwoodian *Principles* (cf. 1938: 128-35), with Jesus as creator, as creator in (at least) two senses: (1) creator of a nuisance and (2) creator of two works of art.

First, then, in Shakespeare's *Hamlet*, at III.iv.24, Polonius gets Hamlet's point. In this case, the sword is mightier than the pen. In other cases, the pen is mightier than the sword (an Act of Parliament, say, for the deform of the English university). You can 'do things with words' (so Austin 1962). Sarcasm can skin people. Language is a mode of action, is 'dramatistic' (so Burke 1970: 38-39, cf. 1945: xv-xxiii; 1966: *passim*, esp. 419-68). A parable is a sword, one might say—much as one might say that it is not; for despite what 'the old hermit of Prague, that never saw pen and ink, very wittily said to the niece of King Gorboduc, That, that is, is: for what is that, but that? and is, but is?' (Shakespeare, *Twelfth Night* IV.ii.14, cit. Collingwood 1939: 99), that which is sometimes both is and is not. One of the Arabic cognates of the Hebrew, *bārā*, means to '…pare a reed for writing, a stick for an arrow' (BDB, s.v.). Hence one might say that in creating a parable Jesus creates an arrow, which strikes the reader, or which the reader finds striking. He 'gets the point' (we say). Or one might say that a parable is a 'rod and staff' (Ps. 23.4), a rod for smiting wolves and a staff for supporting sheep.

In The Good Samaritan, the aristocrats of Hebrew society, the priests and Levites, are palpably hit. In The Prodigal Son, law is distinguished from mercy and opposed to it. We have here (do we not?) an antinomian thrust. Caiaphas and Pilate have been warned. If tragedy (after Aristotle [*Po.* 1449b27]) is the katharsis of 'pity and fear', 'effecting [so Butcher, in Aristotle 1907b: 23] the proper purgation of these emotions' (τραγῳδία δι᾽ ἐλέου καὶ φόβου περαίνουσα τὴν τῶν τοιούτων παθημάτων κάθαρσιν, *trago(i)dia… di'eleou kai phobou perainousa ten ton toiouton pathematon katharsin*), if art (so Collingwood 1938: *passim*) is 'imagination' and 'expression', and the expression of 'emotions', of which Aristotle's 'pity and fear' are two, but only two, we are offered here, in these two stories, a felt critique of Palestinian society: '…his word was in mine heart as a burning fire shut up in my bones, and I was weary with forbearing and I could not stay' (Jer. 20.9). The very bones orate. A nuisance is created.

Secondly, with these two parables Jesus creates two works of art. If literary criticism is thinking about works of art, it tends to overlap with and then, by leading to, to coincide with aesthetics, or the philosophy of art. What is disastrous, if the word, 'disastrous', is strong enough, is the confusion of art with history. At the very least it is clear that time spent in searching through the registraries of Jerusalem, Jericho and Samaria for the birth certificates of the Samaritan and Prodigal is time ill-spent. An expert in 'folk-literature' here (so Funk 1988: 7), Jesus, is setting forth simple models to enable himself and his hearers to come to terms with certain features of the society of his day, believing as he did that the relation between infinite and finite has implications for the relation between finite and finite. In the only way he could, for this was how he felt, he is setting before himself and his hearers certain possibilities of acting; and is evaluating one of these possibilities (sc. mercy) more highly than the other (sc. judgment). Moreover, it is the inveterate temptation of the human animal to narrow the possibilities of what, or who, is to be found acceptable (as for example, 'only nationals are neighbours—perhaps, too, foreigners, but if, and only if, they are permanent residents'). But constriction follows narrowing and strangulation follows both. That, or the like, situation arises, in other words, in which the Corinthians stand (so Paul) and in which Paul (so Paul) does not: 'Our mouth is open to you, Corinthians; our heart is wide [πεπλάτυνται, peplatuntai]. You are not restricted by us, but you are restricted in your own affections' (στενοχωρεῖσθε δὲ ἐν τοῖς σπλάγχνοις ὑμῶν, steno-choreisthe de en tois splangchnois humon: 2 Cor. 11-12). They are, not in one word, but in three, and not in Paul's words, but in Macbeth's (III.iv.24), 'cabin'd, cribb'd, confin'd'. Authenticity, authentic life, is compromised. The implicate of infinity is unending neighbours and innumerable calves.

And Jesus (if it is he) generalizes, typifies. In dealing with the particular, with 'a certain man', he deals with Everyman, with 'the general', or 'the universal', with τὰ καθόλου, ta katholou—ἔστιν δὲ καθόλου… τῷ ποίῳ τὰ ποῖα ἄττα συμβαίνει λέγειν ἢ πράττειν κατὰ τὸ εἰκὸς ἢ τὸ ἀναγκαῖον, estin de katholou…to(i) poio(i) ta poia atta sumbainei legein e prattein kata to eikos e to anang-kaion ('By the universal I mean how a person of a certain type will on occasion speak or act, according to the law of probability or necessity' [Aristotle Po. 1451b8-9]). We are not just dealing with the Elder Brother here, but with Legal Man and Legal Woman, with the Place of Law in Society; much as Shakespeare in Macbeth is not only dealing with a man who ensures that his guests sleep soundly (Duncan) and has an interest in sectarian cooking ('liver of blaspheming Jew' [IV.i.26]), but with the Ambitious Man as such and the Ambitious Man's Wife. Shakespeare is dealing, if you like, with Ambition tout court, though, of course, this generality is 'embodied' (to use Halliwell's word (1986: 22, cit. Heath 1991: 390]) in the particularities of the poet's drama, for Shakespeare says more, or says differently, than that 'the man who exceeds in his desires is called ambitious' (λέγεται...ὁ μὲν ὑπερβάλλων ταῖς ὀρέξεσι φιλότιμος, *legetai...ho men huperballon tais orexesi philotimos* [Aristotle *Ethica Nicomachea* 1107b28]).

So far Aristotle, his τὰ καθόλου, *ta katholou* (the general, the universal) and not his τὰ γενόμενα (*ta genomena*, what has happened), but οἷα ἂν γένοιτο (*hoia an genoito*, what may happen), modestly refracted through Collingwood's *Principles of Art*. But how is one to come to terms with the fact that the artist 'tells it slant' (Dickinson 1955: No. 1129, cit. Tinsley 1983, cit. Jasper 1989: 32). Why does it seem natural to think of the artist as a kind of liar? Why does the artist, why does Jesus use 'is not' to tell us what 'is', the dialectic denoted by Plantinga's title: 'Possible But Unactual Objects: On What There Isn't' (in Margolis 1978: 438), and pursued by Ricoeur (1978: 248)?

But no declining academic who has succeeded in living through the years of the current (British Thatcherite) régime and the years of her *diadochi* can doubt that Clytaemnestra (Aeschylus, *Agamemnon, passim*, but esp. 1343) had an axe to grind or at least a blade to sharpen (1351). Nor must it be doubted (but that is another topic) that the nearest modern analogue to the Gospels is the historical novel, so that thus John is aligned with Scott, *Waverley* (1972 [1st edn 1814]) with *The Gospel*. Nor is the syllogism necessarily to be doubted, that Jesus of Nazareth always told the truth, that Jesus of Nazareth told stories and that therefore stories are true. But if 'reason is faith cultivating itself' (Collingwood 1927b: 3-14), how does one reason out these *credenda*?

There is a story, not well verified, related to the Mariological verses (Lk. 1.26-38), that St Luke was once enrolled for the Masters/Diploma degree in Near Eastern Cultural Values at Antioch University, where he produced, for an outside, post-ancientist course in the Reproductive Biology Unit (it was an inter-disciplinary, or, perhaps, multi-disciplinary course), an essay (3000 words) on the Virgin Birth: 'Parthenogenesis: Some Observations by an Eyewitness: Angels and Chromosomes Compared'. The Examining Board refused to award more than 49 per cent (fail): 'a section on "Contrasted" was to seek', a mark commuted on appeal (and after re-submission of the essay [not normally permitted in that Centre of Excellence]) to 50 per cent, on the grounds that the first Examiner to read his Paper (an over-worked man [AHEFC]) had mislaid the Appendix, a very full one, on the natal (and pre-natal) circumstances and birth-story of 'Augustus, Alexander, Plato, and every pharaoh of Egypt since, at latest, the beginning of the Fifth Dynasty' (Toynbee 1956: 280). He was allowed to proceed to the Diploma, which he failed (despite an appeal to Caesar) on the grounds of 'persistent chronological weakness', and, in pique, turned to narrative fiction, with a historical element.

The later career of the Evangelist has been very variously esti-mated, and Rome, at any rate, took a very dim view of the well-known M. Loisy, who was sufficiently temerarious to speak of *la banalité coutumière du rédacteur* (the customary banality of the redactor). But the French have perhaps always been somewhat unreliable on these (as on other) matters, witness the more recent remark of M. Trocmé, who avers, in one manuscript (1957: 145) and in despite of Geneva, that St Luke *n'avait pas la tête très théologique* (lit. 'did not have the head very theological') and, in another manuscript, *n'avait pas la tête* (lit. 'did not have the head').

For a surer guide to the evaluation of a writer, whose story-telling powers have enabled him almost single-handedly to hijack the litur-gical calendar of the Christian church and its concomitant pressure groups, we must turn to one of the Greek Fathers of the Church, Origen (c. 185–c. 254), who said of St Luke, as of all the Evange-lists, that it was their purpose 'to give the truth where possible at once spiritually and corporeally [or outwardly], but where this was not possible, to prefer the spiritual to the corporeal, the true spir-itual meaning being often preserved in what at the corporeal level might be called a falsehood' (*comm. in Jn*, x.4, cit. Nineham 1958: 248 n. 2).

What and why, we might ask, is a good story? Are *War and Peace* and *Neighbours* for nothing—to say nothing of the Scottish play? But if stories are better remembered than scientific papers (most), that does not, for all that, and all that, make stories sci-entific. But a more important question for the present, than either science or scientific history, may very well be whether, seeing that Paul of Tarsus, some time ago now, managed successfully to democratize the death of Jesus ('I have been crucified with Christ'), it is not now high time to democratize, in its Lukan and Matthaean form, his birth; in Scotland especially so (Davie 1964).

In telling the story of the Virgin Birth, Luke is not giving us a scientific paper. Is he then giving us a rattling good yarn? Is he here 'telling it slant' and giving us not a paper on exceptional and non-paradigmatic reproduction, but an essay on the relation between substance and its modes, between finite and infinite, but giving that essay in the expressive language of the imagination?

Jesus of Nazareth was not a member of Plato's Academy and though he was a peripatetic, itinerantly speaking, he did not walk about, intellectually speaking, with Aristotle. He belonged to an expressive tradition (one recalls again here Aristotle's φασί, *phasi*: 'this is what is said', 'this is how men say the thing is' [*Po.* 1461a1, cf. 1460b36]), within which telling stories was a dominant convention. In telling stories he was only doing what came naturally within the context in which he was doing it.

Then why did his tradition 'tell it slant'? Why did it come naturally to the tradition to tell stories, to refer to the real by referring to it by the medium of a 'constructed referent', 'a focus [as Faust—and the Elder and Younger Brothers and the Good Samaritan] for an amalgam of certain features of human experience' (Martin 1975: 89)?[1] One answer, certainly, is that it is easier, for some, to get the point of a story, to understand an 'example', or *exemplum* (Fitzmyer 1985: 883), than to take the force of a philosophical proposition, to answer, respond to the force of poetry than of philosophy.

Artists, among other things, do two things. They ask: Have you tried looking at it this way? And: Have you tried looking at it at all?

Have you tried looking over the edges of the problem? If you place the Younger Brother on the margins, are you going to leave him there? You ask, *To whom* should I be a neighbour? But have you asked, For whom am I a neighbour, who is a neighbour to *me*? What if the neighbour to me is someone whom I have myself put on the margins? You assume (do you not?) in your question that the concept, 'neighbour', has limits. Does it?

Why not take a concrete instance, an *exemplum*, a παράδειγμα (*paradeigma*)? That's not 'telling it slant' (—and yet it is telling it not historically). That's getting down to brass tacks (—and yet the

---

1.   Citing (so n. 88) an *obiter dictum* of Paul van Buren (of Utrecht).

tacks are fictional). That's getting down to the details, to application; the example is a *worked* example. A problem seen is a problem created (sc. expressed and expressed in the *right* language); and a problem created is a problem solved—by oil, by wine, by the delivery of healthcare at the point of need. Or, more cautiously we should say that a problem created is a problem on the way to solution, give or take 'the morose dynamics of our dumb friend, Jehovah' (Fry 1950: 33)—'Let us hope…that a kind Providence will put a speedy end to the acts of God under which we have been laboring' (de Vries 1958: 28). The mind, that is, has the capacity to come up with worked examples, examples not quite from nowhere, if not quite from somewhere. Here is imaginative grasp, imaginative and emotional grasp, like the grasp of a father for a son.

In these two stories, we are very far from the atmosphere of the *Posterior Analytics* and very far from historiography. It is, of course, not *impossible* that these two stories are drawn from history, that they recount actual incidents. But if to write fiction is to form and shape, we might say that both stories are too well shaped, too tidy to be history, even if we have to concede, with Kermode (1990), that between poetry and history the boundaries are porous. So on the assumption that the word, 'fiction', is the one we want, and if fiction (to speak negatively) is by definition that which is not historically true, is there any other sense of the word 'true' that can be brought into play here? Does the Prodigal Son story not exhibit a good logical grasp of the concept 'mercy'? Does The Good Samaritan not exhibit a good grasp of the logical difficulties raised by the word 'neighbour'?

But are stories logical? Is there a 'logic' of the imagination? Is the collocation, 'logic and imagination', a proper and tolerable collocation of words? How do reason and logic relate to imagination and logic? According to Collingwood, at any rate, the task of the artistic imagination is to grasp particulars truly, to create a problem by specifying what it is, while the task of intellect (or reason) is to relate particulars to one another. It is the task of literary criticism, we might say, to talk about the meaning of stories, or, to put the matter in slightly more logical form, to relate the example to the proposition it exemplifies. This might mean that Jesus, while capable of speech, was incapable of criticizing what he had spoken;

that while he was capable of (oral) literature, he was incapable of literary criticism. But that is perhaps too strong. All we should perhaps say is that at least he does not do so here, for he does say elsewhere, in scornful irony, that 'it is easier for heaven and earth to pass away than for one tittle of the law to fall' (Lk. 16.17), which is as much as to say (so Manson 1949: 25) that to hold to a tittle is no better than tittle-tattle, for there are limits to the rule of law, where the infinite and the unbounded are in question. And to grasp a particular truly, whether the particular be mercy, or a prodigal son, is different from not grasping it at all, as the Elder Son fails to grasp his brother. But you may never know in advance either what is to be grasped by you, or by what you are going to be grasped.

These two fictions, the Samaritan and the Prodigal, are fictions in the service of a fiction. They are parables of the kingdom. They are stories in the service of a metaphor, stories in the service of a story *in nuce* (sc. 'kingdom'). For the kingdom of God, too, is a fiction, if one is speaking literally when one speaks of the kingdom of David, or Herod, but using a metaphor, or model, when one speaks of the kingdom of God. The kingdom of God is not a category that belongs to philosophical theology, but a metaphor that belongs to the history of Christian art. For 'metaphors are strokes, if not always works, of art' (Isenberg 1973: 115).

That is as much as to say that the Samaritan and the Prodigal, those two personages alike, are historical nonentities. Historical entities are what they are not. What they are, however, is linguistic entities, phenomena of language. They are expressions, imaginative expressions, of a highly emotional kind—if bowels in both stories are mightily moved, how are we (historically?) to imagine the emotions of the stories' creator? They are, if you like, textual entities, or, in their oral form, verbal entities. But there is not only here a 'what-they-are', there is a 'what-they-are-*about*'. And the 'about-what' here we could say, very crudely, is the proper conduct of human relations—or the subversion of the improper conduct of human relations by the adducing of conduct in its proper form, for 'parable subverts world... As subversive stories, reversing our priorities, upsetting our expectations, shattering the world in which we enclose ourselves, parables have a permanent function' (Davis 1986: 85-86).[2] But if Jesus had said as much, the crowd

2.   Referring (n. 90) to Crossan 1975.

would have disappeared. Stories can do what propositions do not.

The present chapter is continuing the attempt to come to terms with the New Testament as fiction, by taking a look at the most obvious place, the parables, two parables, of Jesus. But where we are dealing with fiction, some questions are appropriate, others not. 'What really happened' is not. The question that *does* arise is the question of the *meaning* of the story, while the question of the craft of the storyteller is subsidiary. The difficulty of the enterprise is that sensibility changes over time, as the man on the Jericho road found to his cost! For one has, with these stories, to learn a language, not so difficult in these two pellucid cases, though particular questions about the particular context in which the particular language of these two particular parables arose are always there, like Circe, beckoning real men to become academic swine: if one sees the trees, if one sees a tree, if one sees the bark of a tree, can one ever see the wood? The tithing of 'mint and anise and cummin' (Mt. 23.23) remains the 'ownmost' propensity of the critic. But the fundamental question is to decide what it is with which the critic has to deal, with history, or fiction, or some mixture of both. What is fundamental, one fundamental question at least, is the question of genre.

However things may stand with that whole work of fiction, the New Testament, with these two small parts of it, Samaritan and Prodigal, things stand thus: Aristotle is right to say that in entering sympathetically into the story-world, one is entering not the world of actuality, of what actually happened, but the world of possibility, of οἷα ἂν γένοιτο, *hoia an genoito*. And that world, in these two stories, was created by a man of faith, or axioms, or implicit axioms, or religious passion, or human passion, who was cultivating his faith by his imagination, or implicit reason. For if there is that than which nothing greater can be thought, then it follows that there is not what is less than the greatest that cannot be altered. There is, in a word, an alternative. The force of these two stories is to introduce something of the possible into the actual world, fortifying the hope of action even there, where in the actual world the possibilities of action seem to cease. Faith in God means that you can imagine and that you can think that things can be changed. It is possible to be convinced (perhaps falsely, of course) that that can become otherwise which might have been otherwise.

Aristotle is, I think, right to describe the world of story as a possible world. Good Samaritan and Prodigal Son are historical nonentities. But they are, by the rules of poetics and by the judgment of the critic, possible entities. But that is not all, for *from the standpoint of the author* they are necessary entities, that compel, or rather invite, the reader to decide what kind of an entity it is necessary that he the reader, or she the reader, should become: Prodigal Son, or Father prodigal of mercy? Unsuccouring Priest, or Certain Man succoured, of all people, by a Samaritan?

Creativity and revelation are synonyms. For the artist, this artist (the pre-Raphaelites have proved that he had long hair) invents as he finds and finds as he invents (or invents [so modern usage], as he invents [so etymology: *invenire*—this is somewhere, I think, Ricoeur's point]). What Jesus is doing here (if it is not just Luke) is expressing a felt reaction to the situation in which he found himself and, standing in the kind of imaginative tradition and narrative conventions that from varying perspectives men like Alter (1981) and Jacobson (1987, 1989) explore, he is using his own imagination and finding his own language to express it. The story is truthful in that it gives necessary expression to what Jesus actually felt and thought about the predicament, or some aspects of the predicament, of existence in pre-modern Palestine. A sentence, or two, of Collingwood, will make the point better (he is criticizing the view that the artist's job is to imagine possible worlds):

> An imagination which contented itself with constructing possible worlds could never be at the same time an expression of emotion. For an imaginative construction which expresses a given emotion is not merely possible, it is necessary. It is necessitated by that emotion; for it is the only one which will express it (1938: 286).

In this sense of the word 'necessary', Jesus necessarily created, and goes on creating, the world. *Sua res agebatur* (lit. 'his thing was being done'). *Tua res agitur* (lit. 'your thing is being done'). But, if the history of European thought is only a footnote to Aristotle, this yoking of possibility with necessity is only to put the two halves of Aristotle together, (1) his theory of poetry as possibility over against history as actuality and (2) his view that poetry effects the *katharsis* of pity and fear.

In sum, then, in these two stories Jesus puts forward two possibilities; it was necessary that he should put them forward, because that was truly how he thought and felt; if it is asked why he put them forward in the way he did, in the form of stories, the answer is only to be found by leaving the world of imaginative thinking and entering the world of reason or intellect, of literary criticism or philosophy.

The historian, when he looks at an aesthetic text, will conclude that the events recounted were not actual, but possible, while the literary critic, when he looks at the same text, will conclude that the events were not possible, but necessary: at this stage of his artistic development, this is what the writer had to say. In that sense, his fiction (or fictions) was true. His emotions are truly expressed. The word, 'truth', it is not unfair to say, is not out of order here, for 'the opposite of "fiction" is not "truth" but "fact"' (Pack 1958: 122).

5

From Myth to Myth: Staying Happy with the Uncommon Nonsense of the Ancient Near East (Jesus the General: 1 Corinthians 15.20-28)

Modern theology has been much influenced by Rudolf Bultmann's 'Demythologizing' controversy (1960a, 1988). That essay of Bultmann is axial. How is such a controversy to be understood and to be continued? Is it to be taken up, as Bultmann took it up, by the existentialist philosophy of Martin Heidegger? Is that what we should be doing with this passage of St Paul? Or should we delay before taking up philosophy and look first more slowly and carefully at Paul's texts? For here is a wealth of imagery, in particular, the metaphor of sleeping and waking, fighting a war and winning it.

In 'History, Truth and Narrative', Sutherland asks (1990: 105): 'What is the nature of the text or texts we are considering? What sorts of texts are they?' The question is plain and platypod (broad-footed), but not platitudinous. It is 'central' (Stevens 1955: 380). It is the 'ephebe's' question (Stevens 1955: 380, cf. 1960: 39-67), 'ephebe' and 'central' being central, for Stevens, too (Walsh 1963, s.v.). It is the kind of question that the virile poet should importantly ask. It is the kind of question with which, in a virist context, the feminist poetess should put.

Sutherland's question licences the formulation of the following Law:

> If you are going to interpret a document, you must at some point decide *what kind* of document you are interpreting.

This point, for preference, should not coincide with any point before the point at which the reader begins to read. This Law, in order to allude to the title of a recent television series, which was made by the surviving, but decimated, Scottish maniple of the British Broadcasting Corporation and represented episodes in the fictional life of an Oban solicitor (and *senkrecht* [straight down] von Oban the series came), may accordingly be eponymously so called: sc. 'Sutherland's Law'. The following discussion, unlike the theology of Karl Barth, which came *senkrecht von oben*, 'straight down from above', will come *senkrecht von unten*, or straight from underneath the centre of the earth.

Television is a more multimedia medium than a book and this television film, this far-seeing series, was no exception: it was introduced by the Overture, 'The Land of the Mountain and the Flood' by Hamish MacCunn, a composer, to lower a spate of inter-rogative surmising, not nowadays otherwise known, perhaps unde-servedly, than for this piece, but in the present political, sc. devolutionary, or revolutionary, crisis, deservedly known for this. His notes should here be overheard.

To formulate the same Law in the Aristotelian terms of the *De Anima*, you, the interpreter, must decide at some relevant point, or go on deciding at some relevant points, on the τὸ τί ἦν εἶναι, *to ti en einai* (412b11, etc. and Aristotle *passim*) of the text. You must decide, that is, on the 'yes-so-that's-what-it-was-all-along-and-I-didn't-realize-it', or on 'the-what-it-is-to-be-that-thing' (Guthrie 1981: 147), or on 'the quiddity' (so Hicks, in Aristotle 1907: 51), or on 'its being what it was all along' (315).

What is the nature of the text we are dealing with here? What sort of text are we dealing with here? What text is *this one* that we are dealing with here?

In dealing with 1 Cor. 15.20-28, we are dealing (or so it seems to me, at any rate), not with philosophy, nor with history, but with art, or literature; with poetry and story—with sleeping and waking, with lying down and standing up, with a military victory, in which the Messiah has his feet on the necks of his enemies, on the necks of 'the principals and powers' (1 Cor. 15.24), and on the personi-fication of 'Death'. The phrase 'God shall be all in all' provides the end of the passage with a terminal incoherence, in which all but one, God, disappears into a cosmic soup, a view that Paul here shares with the Huichol Indians of the Sierra Madre Occidental in north-central Mexico, who 'experience a total fusion of man and nature and a perfect unity among all the elements of life. The boundaries which, in the mundane world [*sic*], divide people and separate them from nature and the gods, are ecstatically diffused' (Cohen 1985: 51).

The *Resurrection* of Piero della Francesca shows in paint what Paul shows in words. As regards Piero's central image (it is [again] an 'ephebe'), Lightbrown (1992: 201) aptly cites Isa. 63.1-6:

Figure 3. *The Resurrection*, c. 1463 (fresco) by Piero della Francesca (c. 1419/21-92) Pinacoteca, Sansepolcro, Italy/Bridgeman Art Library, London/ New York

Who is this that cometh from Edom,
with dyed garments from Bosra,
this beautiful one in his robe,
walking in the greatness of his strength?

'I that speak justice and am a defender to save.'
Wherefore then is thine apparel red
and thy garments like theirs that tread in the wine-press?

and one might add Ps. 110.3:

From the womb of the morning
like dew your youth will come to you...

Arguing on the basis of the picture as argument (cf. Hess 1975) and guided by Lightbrown's close exegesis, we find ourselves before a picture of 'the firstfruits of them that sleep', before an ear of orient wheat. As is the normal stance of the theologian, when he is not in outer space (2 Cor. 12.2-4), the perspective is *di sotto in su* (from below, looking upward). Miraculously, or at any rate pictorially, the row of trees on the left are leafless (it is still winter), while the trees on the right are in leaf (it is spring, and it is wonderful). This is the juncture of winter and spring, the juncture of death and life.

Piero's picture has formal, structural excellence. And we shall learn more of Piero's structural excellence, when we turn to his *Baptism*, below in Chapter 8. But here, confronted by his *Resurrection*, the viewer's mind can reconstruct Piero's constructing mind by noting the triangle that culminates in the navel of the awakened sleeper, the triad of horizontals and triple segmentation, formed by the upper edge of the tomb, the (admittedly somewhat un-horizontal) line of hills (we have variety here), with the head of the resurrected figure set against the v-shaped depression of a valley, and the top edge of the picture. The viewer may note also the contrapuntal symphony of smooth and rumpled in the soldiers' clothes and armour.

The shroud of the charnel house has been transfigured into a royal robe of pinkish-red, 'the habit of a victor' (so Anton Maria Graziani, a sixteenth-century bishop of the town, for which the picture was painted [sc. Borgo San Sepolcro]); 'unaided...he (sc. Christ) has trodden down his enemies and it is their blood that has made his garments red'; the wounds are rather 'ensigns of victory than stigmata of sorrow', not intended to excite our grief, but our rejoicing in his triumph over 'sin, the world [the *world*? What's wrong with the world? Or by world do you mean 'world'?] and death' (Lightbrown 1992: 201).

Two further art-historical observations may be mentioned, first: 'This country god, who rises in the grey light while human beings are still asleep, has been worshipped ever since man first knew that seed is not dead in the winter earth, but will force its way upwards through an iron crust' (Clark 1969: 57); and, second:

> He [sc. Jesus] is at once man and God in an image that, in its combined naturalism and ideal beauty, reconciles orthodox theology—in which man is the image of God and Christ has two natures, one human and one divine—with the fifteenth century conception of art as the imitation of nature and humanist reverence for classical sculpture as the perfection of human form (Lightbrown 1992: 202).

But 'go to Bassae' (Collingwood 1940b: 61)—there is another analogue of this Pauline passage, a military and mythical analogue, in the Phigaleian Frieze of the Temple of Bassae, a temple dedicated to Apollo Epikourios, 'Apollo who comes to give aid and assistance'. The Frieze depicts (and we are taking the segments of that Frieze, of course, not in the order of Stackelberg, or Cockerell, or Ivanoff, or Lange, or Murray and Smith, or Dinsmoor [1], but in the order of Dinsmoor [2] [Dinsmoor 1956: 403]), a Kentauro-machy and an Amazonomachy, a battle between Lapiths and Centaurs and a battle between Greeks and Amazons. The subject of the Frieze tells us, not only of *homo homini lupus*, 'man is a wolf to man', but, as we have been more recently taught to say this, of *homo homini lupa*, '*woman* is a *she-wolf* to man'.

Thus Yahweh as Hebrew war god, Yahweh Soterios, 'Yahweh who brings salvation, Yahweh who rescues', is paralleled by Apollo Epikourios,

> Apollo who lends his assistance. Find the right room in the British Museum and you will find what the French architect, Bocher, found after sixteen hundred years, in 1765, and, in 1811, what an international society of antiquaries, of whom Charles R. Cockerell and Haller von Hallerstein were the leaders, purchased from the Turkish governor of the Peloponnese for £750 and sold to the British Museum for 60,000 Spanish dollars (Dinsmoor 1933: 204-27).

(a) Battle of Lapiths and Centaurs (detail)

(b) Battle of Greeks and Amazons (detail)

Figure 4. *The Phigaleian Frieze* (details) c. 480 BCE, Temple of Apollo at Bassae, by Ictinus (*fl*. after 450 BCE) (reproduced by courtesy of the Trustees, The British Museum, London)

Conflict can be set forth, as well in stone, as in word. The eye of the archaeologist has scried, or her foot exhumed, numerous ancient Near Eastern examples of this kind of thing. Particular reference in his commentary on 'mak[ing] your enemies your footstool' (Ps. 110.1 [= 1 Cor. 15.25]) is made by Dahood (1970: 114) to a relief from the palace of Sennacherib (705–681 BCE), on the (visible) side of whose throne are depicted 12 Israelite captives from the siege of Lachish (illustrated in Pritchard 1954: 129, no. 371 and Wiseman [1958] Plate 57).

No one who has struggled through Dahood's impeccable Ugaritic can remain unaware that Hebrew and ANE (sc. ancient Near Eastern) artistry is, in Psalms 8 and 110, and in the Sennacherib relief and in 1 Corinthians 15, at its apogee, the whole weave, in the latter of these texts, being articulated in Paul's characteristically angular antitheses:

> As in Adam all die,
> Even so in Christ shall all be made alive (v. 22).

And the music of the phrase was no stranger to Handel, for art calls unto art.

To set the interpretation of these pictorial parallels, from sculpture and painting and word, in the context of the history of thought, it is here being presupposed:

(1) that the Enlightenment inheritance, the work of Lowth, de Wette, Strauss and Bultmann is broadly speaking valid; and that Bonhoeffer's dictum about truth is true, namely that: 'Intellectual honesty in all things, including questions of belief, was the great achievement of emancipated reason and it has ever since been one of the indispensable moral requirements of western man' (1955a: 34 [=1992: 106]);[1]

(2) that secular theology, or secularity, as expounded (among others) by Bonhoeffer and Ronald Gregor Smith, and thinking, or imagining, *etsi deus non daretur*, 'as though God were not being given', is a possible theological option; that 'there is no specifically religious language' (Davis 1994: 115),

---

1. 'Intellektuelle Redlichkeit in allen Dingen, auch in den Fragen des Glaubens, war das hohe Gut der befreiten ratio und gehört seitdem zu den unaufgebbaren sittlichen Forderungen des abendländischen Menschen.'

but only, to take the example we have here in 1 Corinthians 15, the language of agriculture ('first fruits'), of military operations ('enemies under the feet'), of politics and government (the 'king' and his appointee, or anointee, the 'christ'); and that the 'demythologizing' debate of the 1940s, 1950s and 1960s, is a stable, out of which Stephen Leacock's horse may gallop off in all directions: a mythical has given rise to a literary debate;

(3) that what Paul is doing here is more like art, or literature, than history and that de Wette's adjective, *ästhetisch-religiös*, 'aesthetic-religious' (1817: 219, cit. Hartlich and Sachs 1952: 115) is running on the right lines; and that the right way of interpreting this passage is by doing literary, not historical, criticism (as Kermode, Ricks, Helen Gardner and Kenneth Muir, not to mention Aristotle, Longinus, Horace, Sydney, Johnson, Coleridge and T.S. Eliot [to name a few]; and

(4) that literature, poetry and story may be held to more lightly than dogma, for other formulations are possible, other stories may be told, other poems may be made—the way in which literature is held to be true and the way in which dogmas are held to be true are distinguishable and distinct; that the flexibility of literature is more appropriate than the fixity of dogma to the mobility of an entity, who may be defined as 'the one who is going to be what he will be': God is the carrot the donkey does not catch.

In the view of de Wette: the Pentateuch bears the same kind of relation to the Hebrews as Homer's *Odyssey* and *Iliad* to the Greeks and Virgil's *Aeneid* to the Romans.

It is an epic.

It is a myth—a myth, which, if it is combined with history at all, is inextricably combined with it, in such a way that it is, on the whole, no longer possible to extricate the history. Disambiguation is, on the whole, no longer possible.

But (so Bultmann) 'modern man' (or, now, 'postmodern woman') can no longer be doing with myth—we must translate into philosophy. And what with Martin Heidegger being around in Marburg and doing time in Bultmann's seminar, we must translate the language of the myth into the almost-German language of *Being and Time*.

But if the move from myth to philosophy is legitimate (and why should it not be?), there are, I think, two prior moves: (1) the move from myth to myth, and (2) the move from myth to literary criticism.

By the (paradoxically formulated) 'move from myth to myth', I mean simply this, that one should stay with the myth long enough to understand, or begin to understand it, that one should stay with the story long enough to follow it. But there is more: Why irritably reach for fact when there is a myth, a story to enjoy?

Now 1 Cor. 15.20-28 is not the Hebrew epic, but is rather the sci-fi of (one of) the early Christians (after a bad night with Phoebe of Cenchreae).

This fiction, this sci-fi, is based on poetry (two psalms, two poems to string accompaniment) and story (the myth of Adam) and is itself poetic, sufficiently poetic to attract Handel's attention. The first of these psalms (Ps. 8) is a poem of two stanzas, each of 74 syllables; and the second (Ps. 110) is a paean on the coronation of the Hebrew monarch, for whom and with whom the warlord Yahweh will 'shatter kings on the day of his wrath'. And if 1 Cor. 15.20-28 is not the Hebrew epic, it is, at least to this extent, based on the Hebrew epic, in that Paul alludes to the story of how the first man forfeited immortality by a too conspicuous consumption. And de Wette himself, even if he is not getting very far as an interpreter of poetry, at least gets as far as observing (1855: 145) that in the verses, the stichs (1 Cor. 15.21-22 KJV):

> For since by man came death,
> > by man came also the resurrection of the dead.
> For as in Adam all die,
> > even so in Christ shall all be made alive

'we have two sentences that correspond to one another, in the first of which the parallelism is general and the concept "man", in the second individual, in Adam and Christ' (1855: 145). But this is less than Lowth. The door to poetry is not open, but is merely ajar. De Wette's insights into the nature of the Pentateuch have only just begun to prove fruitful for the interpretation of early Christian texts. They are not, in this New Testament commentary, carried through. 'Animal earnestness' (*tierische Ernst*) and 'consistency' (*Konsequenz*) are to seek. Does de Wette really do for the New what he did for the Old Testament?

Paul is drawing a map, or painting a picture, of the future and is doing so in terms of 'the rush of sap in spring' (Lawrence, 1949: 8, cf. 122-26), now culminating in the first heavy sheaf, so that by a kind of poetic iridescence spring and autumn co-incide. And he is doing so also in terms of the warlord, who proves himself the enemy of the enemy of all those who come within 'his bending sickle's compass'. And these two metaphors, sheaf and warlord, in a context of common places, are based on the 'root metaphor' (Tracy 1979: 89-104) of 'resurrection', of 'waking from sleep'.

De Wette (unwisely) speaks of Paul's 'axiom' here (1855: 145), for 'axiom' is much too logical a term for this kind of writing and the 'axioms' are not present in the discourse as *stated*, but present as *embodied*—we have the *exemplum*, but not the proposition that the *exemplum* exemplifies. Axioms are present only in so far as they can be inferred by the philosophical theologian, by the philosopher. Poetry (so Aristotle *Po.* 1451b5-6) is more philosophical than history, because poetry embodies, instantiates or exemplifies statements, of a necessary or probable sort, statements that are valid ὡς ἐπὶ τὸ πόλυ, *hos epi to polu*, 'for the most part' (de Ste Croix 1975: 45-58). Take for example *Oedipus*: the message of the play is not that wives (for the most part) should first test the ankles of their husbands, but rather that it is important, before asking of another, 'Are you the guilty man?' to make sure, first, that the question should not be addressed to oneself. Or take *Macbeth*: the message of this Scottish play is not so much that, when looking for overnight accommodation, it is first important to ascertain whether encephalopathy in the owner of the accommodation will now or in the future be the likely result of an ophite diet, but to ascertain, whether the owner, or the owner and his wife together constitute an ambitious team, for ambitious men, and women, are apt to be ruthless. On the philosophical proposition that might be said to be implied here in 1 Corinthians 15 it will be said (again) below, that something for the most part comes of nothing.

History is the 'control' discipline, of course, in this chapter as in this essay. But history is not much to the purpose here. The only relevant history here is (1) that Jesus was 'dead' (2) that he was 'buried' and (3) that, when he was dead, he was dead as a doornail. And, by historical inference, we might add a fourth, (4) that friends of Phoebe of Cenchreae, members of the Corinthian congregation, had just kicked the bucket and that this fact appeared to at least some of the Corinthians to be in tension with what Paul had said and was saying.

But what was he saying? He was doing aesthetic writing, combined with what is, or is very like, a line or two of literary criticism, for 'what is it to say "subjected", unless you are to exclude the subjector of the subjected...? (1 Cor. 15.27), for B subjects all except A, who enables B to subject all, before himself being subjected to A'. At this point Paul is not only using military imagery, but reflecting on the implications of the imagery he is using and of whom he is using it. Writing is here combined with reflection on writing.

And how was he saying it? In word-pictures. He sets a scene 'before our eyes' (Aristotle, *Po.* 1455a23).

Now Paul, while an angular writer, is a pictorial writer and is producing here not another Amazonomachy or Kentauromachy, but a Thanatomachy and Archontomachy, 'a battle with Death and with principalities and powers'. His theme is: 'The Messiah Goes to War'. And, to do this, Paul, parasitic on the tradition of Hebrew poesy, has combined the story of Adam in the garden with two Hebrew epinician odes, or songs of victory, Psalm 8 and Psalm 110. In order to understand *this* writer and *this* writer following *these* literary models, where the topic is resurrection, and where the coming of Jesus from the tomb is like the coming of the dew of youth from the womb of the morning, we must exercise what Gregor Smith calls our 'literary imagination' (1969: 134).

And when we do that, we see, or are invited to see, that there are grounds, Paul and Gregor Smith are saying, for 'joy and assurance' (1969: 132)—and that in a context where the temper of the empiricist tells us to 'lie in cold obstruction and to rot'.

But how strong are these grounds? How strong are aesthetic objects? Is science fiction of this kind strong enough to do what we want here?

A lot depends on whether you think that Sophocles, Shakespeare, Tolstoy, Aristophanes, James Joyce and Jesus of Nazareth were trying to say anything; and, if so, to say it persuasively. And if Jesus could get away with naturalistic fiction in the Samaritan and Prodigal, why should not Paul get away with science fiction, especially if it is, like Samuel Butler's *Erewhon*, well written. And if

Aristophanes could get away with a Research Assessment Exercise in hell (instead of making hell by getting away with one)—weighing the comparative merits of Aeschylus and Euripides, why should not Paul get away with a war in heaven and the Messiah's contest with Death?

We are of course (says Isenberg 1973: 169) in 'the present stone age of aesthetic inquiry' and, in biblical study, in an age when the lava is still molten, in an age before petrifaction has settled down into something stable enough to be called a 'stone age'. But if it is true that artists are seriously saying something, why should it not be true that Paul, the artist, is saying something?

And here we must pay attention, again, to the latter half of de Wette's epithet: aesthetic-*religious*. For Paul's 'root metaphor', 'Resurrection', or 'Awakening', draws its nourishment from theological soil. But that theology is not Hegel, as for Strauss, nor Heidegger, as for Bultmann, nor even the *deus sive natura*, 'God or Nature', or infinite substance of Spinoza. Paul's *theos* appears rather in the military dress of the old Hebrew war God. This is theology in a literary sense. It is not philosophical theology. And it could be said that literary theology is not theology at all. It is not theology, it is not philosophy, it is not thought. It is art. It is literature. It is imagination.

But as *religious* art, the necessary, or probable, statements embodied in it embody a truth, or truths, about reality, that are peculiarly important. And this truth, or these truths, endow the language that embodies it, or them, with a peculiar force, though because they are embodied in *art*, and not in philosophy, or theology, they are endowed with the plasticity and flexibility of poetry, not the fixity of dogma. Confronted by literature of this kind, it is the task of the critic first to make use of literary criticism and secondly to produce a philosophy of aesthetics, or aesthetic theology. Would it be going too far to say that we do not need to demythologize, but that all we need to do is to stay with the mythology and to think about it? Or is to think about it to depart from it?

For my contention here is that *this* theology is more like literature than it is like anything else. And these observations and these questions, and observations and questions like these, join together to drive us towards the question of art and truth, drive us first to literary criticism, and then to the philosophy of literary criticism and aesthetics.

Paul here is offering us truth, as he would say, 'in a mirror, in a riddle', δι' ἐσόπτρου ἐν αἰνίγματι, *di esoptrou en ainigmati, durch einen Spiegelglas in einem dunklen Worte,* 'through a mirror glass in a dark word' (1 Cor. 13.12), is offering us 'rubbings of a glass in which we peer' (Stevens 1955: 398 [= II, x]). It is truth refracted in the mirror of poetic language, truth (so Aristotle) embodied or instantiated, not in history, or philosophy, but in poetry; actual truth embodied in a possible world, the possible world of a text. It is truth (so Collingwood) imaginatively expressed, the emotional expression of the kind of optimism, which, on one definition of the optimist, is only accessible to someone who is 'in incomplete possession of the facts'. On another view, however, such a view is only possible to someone who is in complete possession of the facts, but these facts being such facts as can only, perhaps, be accessible in a supreme fiction. The possession is in the present only a possession complete enough for present purposes, enough to be going on with. That this 'supreme fiction' (Stevens 1955: 380-408 [see Chapter 10, below]) is based on fact is an axiom I am prepared to hazard. And if axioms are indemonstrable, they are also heuristic: they enable one to find one's way. Paul's fictions are stories, are poems, are metaphors we can live by. Or we have 'absolute presuppositions', that have 'logical efficacy' (Collingwood 1940a: 27), that raise the questions we are bold to answer.

Fiction differs from history as the possible differs from the actual—the historian (so Aristotle) is concerned with what actually happened, fiction with what might happen, as a man might marry his mother (*Oedipus*) and a rabbit *might* look at his watch (*Alice in Wonderland*). But Paul's fictions here are *religious* fictions, ontological or very important fictions. It was necessary that Paul should produce these possibilities, if he was going to comfort the bereaved Corinthians. Paul is half-conscious of the realities that shine through these fictions, the realities, namely, that God replaces nothing and Christ replaces death, but he has no other language at his disposal, with his training and tradition, than the metaphors of rising sap, winning war and waking from sleep. This poetry and story he is putting to religious, to 'important' use (Whitehead 1956: 1-27).

All art is implicitly assertoric, in so far as the assertions are embodied, or instantiated in the work; and religious art pre-eminently so and classical religious art super-pre-eminently so. But it is for the literary critic, or for the philosopher of literary criticism, not for the artist, or not for *this* artist, to say what these assertions are. Good reasons, that is, can be found for studying literature, for counting Hebrew syllables, for animadverting to antitheses, for pointing to those places where language collapses into everything. Had Paul read Aristotle, he might have told us more. But we do not need to point to the limitations of a writer, who pointed them out himself two chapters earlier: ἐκ μέρους γὰρ γινώσκομεν καὶ ἐκ μέρους προφητεύομεν, *ek merous gar ginoskomen kai ek merous propheteuomen*: 'for we know in part and we prophesy in part'. But if we can both live inside *and* talk about *Alice in Wonderland*, then we can move through the looking glass and live in these lines of Paul and then pass back through and talk about them.

These then are the limits of story, the limits of poetry. Whether there are analogous limits for the philosophical theologian and for the philosophical philosopher is for others to decide. But let no one say that there is any problem that cannot in principle by solved by any religion, of which the salt has not lost its savour. For the present let only this be said, that fiction here rules, and sets up here a possible alternative, and that we cannot be sure that there is no alternative.

In this passage Paul 'sets before the eyes' (Aristotle *Po.* 145522f.) some images from his imagination. He does not set before the mind an axiom, or axioms, of thought. 'It is the mundo of the imagination in which the imaginative man delights and not the gaunt world of reason...' (Stevens 1960: 57-58, cit. Kermode 1960: 89). Had Paul done so, or had he been able to do so, had he been a man of thought and had he inhabited the world of reason, he might have said that he was denying the jointly shared proposition of Germbergius (*Carminum Proverbialium*, 1583) and King Lear, that *ex nihilo nihil fit*, 'out of nothing nothing comes'. For something does come of nothing—patently, in the case of the universe, impatently, or 'through a glass darkly', in the case of dead men, and through a glass clearly, in the case of dead women.

Poetry, says Aristotle, is more philosophical than history. It is also more philosophical than philosophy, or so it seems to me at any rate. For (to re-cite) H.J. Paton, in speaking of the philosopher, the mathematician and the physicist, speaks also '(if we may regard as also a thinker him who is so much more) [of] the artist' (1965: 19). And Paul of Tarsus, far from being philosopher, mathematician, or physicist, is not being a historian here at any rate (is he anywhere?), for you cannot be a historian of the future. Nor is he guessing what the historical future will be, for the picture he paints is at the least historically improbable and historically is probably impossible. Nor is he being a philosopher of religion. He is an artist rather who, as artists do, is embodying a philosophy and embodying it in story and song, in image and metaphor. He is, in Aristotle's terms, embodying a possible world, a world, that is, that is possible for the artist, but not for the historian, to imagine as happening. Paul, of course, is convinced that this possible world will become actual, not in the sense that his images will become reality and his metaphors literal, but in the sense that the philosophy embodied in these will turn out to be true, the philosophical proposition, say, that *ex nihilo nihil fit* is false, *or*, the other way around, that *ex nihilo aliquid fit* is true, if this attempt to disambiguate Paul's confused cognition is right, or running along on the right lines.

These are Paul's fictions. Piero's *Resurrection* and the Phigaleian Frieze are analogues. The word, 'fiction', derives its force, in part, from what it is not. A fiction is not history. Of the history of the resurrection, there is no reason why we should not be content with Renan (n.d. 449 [= 1864: 295): 'The cry, "He is risen!" quickly spread amongst the disciples. Love caused it to find ready credence everywhere.'[2] And love includes the making of aesthetic judgments.

There is no point in the critic inserting his toe into the pool of criticism. 'Old men', Eliot said ('East Coker' V [= 1944: 22]), 'ought to be explorers'; old critics, Eliot might have gone on to say, ought to be swimmers. One cannot become bold about Elijah's axe-head and become craven about Jesus' resurrection. It is not that the point needs to be made, of course, for Reimarus has already shot ten torpedoes (1971: 177-97) through the narratives in the Gospels, though, misconceiving the nature of the narratives, as he did, he only destroyed a historical reading that was impossible, in order to

2. 'Le cri "Il est ressuscité!" courut parmi les disciples comme un éclair. L'amour lui fit trouver partout une créance facile.'

produce a historical reading that was improbable: 'the disciples',
he said, 'stole the body'.

But this particular move from the supernaturalist to the rationalist can hardly be said to have succeeded. This was only to move
from the impossible to the improbable. It was to jump from the
frying pan, if not into the fire, then into the tureen. Strauss joined
Reimarus in using his wits, but, abandoning the supernaturalist
view on the one hand and the naturalist, or rationalist, on the other
arrived at the right reading: *tertium dabatur*, 'there was a third
option', sc. the mythical.

Now all that is being attempted here by the substitution of the
word 'fiction' for the word 'mythical' is to give the mythical
reading a literary slant; or to confirm it. It is to shy more thoroughly
away than Strauss from what myth is not to what it is, to the
question how meaning is conveyed by it and whether and in what
sense that meaning is true. If we adopt the historical standpoint,
we are dealing with a legend. And legend, in current usage is
pejorative. But if we adopt, if we thorougly adopt the literary
standpoint, we are dealing with a story. And stories are what Jesus
told and what the early Christians told about him. And here four
lines of approach are possible, between which I am not much concerned to discriminate: we are dealing here with phantasy (Aichele,
were he to think otherwise, might follow this line [1992: 53-66,
etc.]), or with a fairy-tale (Ashton runs in this direction [1991:
511]), or with Utopianism (Sir Thomas More might do more here
[1895]), or with science fiction (about which more might be done
by those who, like God, or James Joyce, can do everything). It is,
however, clear, that the fact, that *3 Enoch* contains many angels,
the Gospels some and Paul in this passage none does not mean that
these three writings, or groups of writings, from the historian's
point of view, show continual improvement.

If we further adopt the Scottish, or philosophical point of view,
we ask further. We ask not only how the story runs and with what
art it is told, but we ask also what the story means. We ask what
the storyteller is after. We ask why he finds the story worth telling.

Now Reimarus and Strauss were not dealing with Paul, but with
the Gospel stories. But, while Paul was no storyteller, he was one
who made use of stories—in 1 Corinthians 15, of the story of
Adam. Whether or not, and, if so, in what form, stories, such as we

find in the Gospels, were already circulating in Paul's day and whether he is alluding to them here (which is very likely) does not much matter. If they were, he is alluding to them; he is abbreviating them. If they were not, he is continuing to transmit the punctiliar cry, 'he is risen'. And then the question, for the literary critic, for the aesthete, for the philosopher, is this: What kind of cry is that?

Take 'the one with the Gospels', Ludwig Wittgenstein, who, on the Austro-Hungarian front in the First World War, had purchased 'Tolstoy's *The Gospel in Brief...* in a small bookshop in Tarnow... "I say Tolstoy's words over and over again in my head: 'Man is powerless in the flesh but free because of the spirit'. May the spirit be in me!"' (McGuinness 1988: 220-21).

I cannot claim to have Wittgenstein entirely on my side, but I can claim that there is sufficient ambiguity in what he says to allow me to cite him. A decent treatment would require a decent book. And for a decent book we are allowed no time. But, on the one hand, he says this:

> What inclines even me to believe in Christ's resurrection? It is as though I play with the thought.—If he did not rise from the dead, then he decomposed in the grave like any other man. *He is dead and decomposed.* In that case he is a teacher like any other and can no longer *help*; and once more we are orphaned and alone. So we have to content ourselves with wisdom and speculation. We are in a sort of hell where we can do nothing but dream, roofed in, as it were, and cut off from heaven. But if I am to be REALLY saved,— what I need is *certainty*—not wisdom, dreams or speculation—and this certainty is faith. And faith is faith in what is needed by my *heart*, my *soul*, not my speculative intelligence. For it is my soul with its passions, as it were with its flesh and blood, that has to be saved, not my abstract mind. Perhaps we can say: Only *love* can believe the Resurrection. Or, it is *love* that believes the Resurrection. We might say: Redeeming love believes even in the Resurrection; holds fast even to the Resurrection. What combats doubt is, as it were, *redemption*. Holding fast to *this* must be holding fast to that belief. So what that means is: first you must be redeemed and hold on to your redemption (keep hold of your redemption)—then you will see that you are holding fast to this belief. So this can come about only if you no longer rest your weight on the earth but suspend yourself from heaven. Then *everything* will be different and it will be 'no wonder' if you can do things you cannot do now. (A man who is suspended looks the same as one who is standing,

but the interplay of forces within him is nevertheless quite different, so that he can act quite differently than can a standing man) (1980: 33e).[3]

Noting only in the above passage, first, the phrase: 'It is as though I play with the thought', and, then, the frequency, throughout the passage, of 'as though', one should go on to add the following:

> Christianity is not based on a historical truth; rather it offers us a (historical) narrative and says: now believe! But not, believe this narrative with the belief appropriate to a historical narrative, rather: believe, through thick and thin, which you can do only as the result of a life. *Here you have a narrative, don't take the same attitude to it as you take to other historical narratives!* Make a *quite different* place in your life for it.—There is nothing *paradoxical* about that! (1980: 32e).[4]

3. 'Was neigt auch mich zu dem Glauben an die Auferstehung Christi hin? Ich spiele gleichsam mit dem Gedanken.—Ist er nicht auferstanden, so ist er im Grab verwest, wie jeder Mensch. Er is tot und verwest. Dann ist er ein Lehrer, wie jeder andere und kann nicht mehr helfen; und wir sind wieder verwaist und allein. Und können uns mit der Weisheit und Spekulation begnügen. Wir sind gleichsam in einer Hölle, wo wir nur träumen können, und vom Himmel, durch eine Decke gleichsam, abgeschlossen. Wenn ich aber WIRKLICH erlöst werden soll—so brauche ich *Gewissheit*—nicht Weisheit, Träume, Spekulation—und diese Gewissheit ist der Glaube. Und der Glaube ist Glaube an das, was mein *Herz*, meine *Seele* braucht, nicht mein spekulierender Verstand. Denn meine Seele, mit ihren Leidenschaften, gleichsam mit ihrem Fleisch und Blut, muss erlöst werden, nicht mein abstrakter Geist. Man kann vielleicht sagen: Nur die *Liebe* kann die Auferstehung glauben. Oder: Es ist die *Liebe*, was die Auferstehung glaubt. Man könnte sagen: Die erlösende Liebe glaubt auch an die Auferstehung; hält auch an der Auferstehung fest. Was den Zweifel bekämpft, ist gleichsam die *Erlösung*. Das Festhalten an *ihr* muss das Festhalten an diesem Glauben sein. Das heisst also: sei erst erlöst und halte an Deiner Erlösung (halte Deine Erlösung) fest—dann wirst Du sehen, dass Du an diesem Glauben festhältst. Das kann also nur geschehen, wenn Du dich nicht mehr auf die Erde stützt, sondern am Himmel hängst. Dann ist alles anders und es ist 'kein Wunder', wenn Du dann kannst, was Du jetzt nicht kannst. (Anzusehen ist freilich der Hängende wie der Stehende, aber das Kräftespiel in ihm ist ja ein ganz anderes und er kann daher ganz anderes tun, als der Stehende.)'

4. 'Das Christentum gründet sich nicht auf eine historische Wahrheit, sondern es gibt uns ein (historische) Nachricht und sagt: jetzt glaube! Aber nicht, glaube diese Nachricht mit dem Glauben, der zu einer geschichtlichen Nachricht gehört,—sondern glaube, durch dick und dünn und das kannst Du

And the question to ask here is this: Why did Wittgenstein have the good sense to put the second occurrence of 'historical' in parentheses? And why did he have the good sense to omit the epithet, when he says, '...believe this narrative...*Here you have a narrative*...'?

Then, finally, add the following:

> Queer as it sounds: The historical accounts in the Gospels might, historically speaking, be demonstrably false and belief would lose nothing by this: *not*, however, because it concerns 'universal truths of reason'! Rather, because historical proof (the historical proof-game) is irrelevant to belief. This message (the Gospels) is seized on by men believingly (i.e. lovingly). *That* is the certainty characterizing this particular acceptance-as-true, not something *else*.
>
> A believer's relation to these narratives is *neither* the relation to historical truth (probability), *nor yet* that to a theory consisting of 'truths of reason'. There is such a thing.—(We have quite different attitudes even to different species of what we call fiction!) (1980: 32e).[5]

All I wish to add here is that there are narratives in the Gospels, which are fictional narratives. If these narratives are wrongly supposed to be historical narratives, they are, I think, demonstrably false. The problem is to determine to what 'species of what we call fiction' (*Dichtung*—from *dicto*, 'say often', the frequentative of *dico*, 'say') such narratives belong and by what 'logic of poetry' (*Dichtung*) they are to be called 'true'. I have tried to make it plain—and will go on, frequentatively, to insist—that Aristotle and Collingwood have something to contribute here. If one takes,

nur als Resultat eines Lebens. *Hier hast Du eine Nachricht,—verhalte Dich zu ihr nicht, wie zu einer anderen historischen Nachricht! Lass sie eine ganz andere* Stelle in Deinem Leben einnehmen.—Daran ist nichts *Paradoxes!*'

5. 'So sonderbar es klingt: Die historischen Berichte der Evangelien könnten, im historischen Sinn, erweislich falsch sein, und der Glaube verlöre doch nichts dadurch: aber *nicht*, weil er sich etwa auf "allgemeine Vernunft-wahrheiten" bezöge!, sondern, weil der historische Beweis (das historische Beweis-Spiel) den Glauben gar nichts angeht. Diese Nachricht (die Evangelien) wird glaubend (d.h. liebend) vom Menschen ergriffen. Das ist die Sicherheit dieses Für-wahr-haltens, nicht *Anderes*.'

'Der Glaubende hat zu diesen Nachrichten *weder* das Verhältnis zur historischen Wahrheit (Wahrscheinlichkeit), *noch* das zu einer Lehre von "Vernunftwahrheiten". Das gibt's.—(Man hat ja sogar zu verschiedenen Arten dessen, was man Dichtung nennt, ganz verschiedene Einstellungen!).'

finally, Wittgenstein's proposition, or 'proposition', from the *Tractatus* (6.45 [= 1960: 82]), that 'the feeling of the world as a limited whole is the mystical', and one were to go on to say that 'the feeling of the life of Jesus as a whole limited by death is the mystical', then one might ask whether 'the mystical' might be expanded from two words into more, by the poet, by the philosopher, by the literary critic, by the storyteller and, perhaps, even by the historian—and that in the classical light of such pioneering attempts as have been made by the Gospel writers, Paul and *3 Enoch*. What are the languages that are available, rightly available, to faith, hope and love? Or, lest that Pauline triad, hierarchically organized as it is, should seem too much like hortatory sleet, what language, or languages, is or are available to the metaphysician, who is engaged on 'a special study of the existential aspect of that same subject matter whose aspect as truth is studied by logic, and its aspect as goodness by ethics' (Collingwood 1933: 127)?

Once, in Cambridge, C.S. Lewis, to keep as close as possible to the sense of what was then actually said, invited me (and some 1500 others) to take the following three sentences:

> (1) The thermometer was reading seven degrees below on the Fahrenheit scale.
>
> (2) It was bloody cold.
>
> (3) St Agnes Eve—and bitter chill it was,
> The owl for all his feathers was a-cold;
> The hare limpd trembling through the frozen grass,
> And silent was the flock in woolly fold...(Keats).

Despite, or, perhaps, because of the curious construction of folds in Keats's day, it is to the third of these that the language of the New Testament conforms. Whether these texts are being read in Tegel (Bonhoeffer 1951, 1971; Bethge 1970: 703-95), or on the Austro-Hungarian front (as Wittgenstein [McGuinness 1990: 204-66]), or in that 'interval' (Oakeshott 1989: 101), which is 'the characteristic gift of a university', where the student may 'play the texts', it is to this third type, to which one should look, if one is concerned with the conformation of the human animal to incarnation, crucifixion and resurrection. For:

> what is said is never, in religion or elsewhere, what is meant: the language never is the meaning. This truth religion has not discovered, and it thinks that its symbolic imagery, blood and fire, sin and

redemption, prayer, grace, immortality, even God, is the literal
statement of its thought, whereas it is in reality a texture of metaphor through and through (Collingwood 1924: 130).

And:

[t]he task of theology is to convert the implicit thought of religion
into explicit thought, by disentangling the symbol from its meaning
and making clear the merely metaphorical character of religious
imagery (Collingwood 1924: 148).

The language of 1 Cor. 15.20-28 belongs to Lewis's third sort.
One is concerned with metaphor, image, symbol, story. One imagines, re-imagines; makes and re-makes; constructs: *fingo*, 'I fashion',
as God 'formed man' (Heb. *yātsār*; LXX ἔπλασεν, *eplasen*, vg.
formavit [Gen. 2.7]). One finds language to express one's religious
passion.

It is language like this that one is reading. This is what is being
read.

It is not the language of scientific history, when we say, 'The
evidence at our disposal obliges us to conclude that...'; nor even
do we quite have, 'The story says that...', or, 'Now the story goes
on to say that...' (Collingwood 1940a: 56). For 1 Cor. 15.20-28
offers only *fragments* of a longer story, which only archaeological
patience can reassemble—from what Paul says elsewhere, from
what others have said elsewhere and from what others will say
later. 'It is one of the peculiarities of the imagination', says Stevens
(1960: 22), 'that it is always at the end of an era'. 'Resurrection',
'awakening', is only one moment in the great change, in the Great
Change, the arrival of an epoch, when:

> on each vine there shall be a thousand branches,
>   and each branch shall produce a thousand clusters,
>   and each cluster produce a thousand grapes,
>   and each grape produce a cor[!] of wine (*2 Bar.* 29.5-8).

But leaving aside Daniel, the Apocalypse of St John the Divine
and its synoptic approximation, the 'Little Apocalypse' of Mark 13
and its parallels in Matthew and Luke; leaving aside the angels,
from 'Anaphiel H (sc. 'of Yahweh', 'Jehovah')[6] through Sammael to
Zi'iel and Ziqiel, and the winds, from the 'Brooding Wind' (Gen.

---

6. For, by convention, H = *Tetragrammaton* = the four Hebrew letters, of
which 'Yahweh' is composed.

1.2) through the 'Wind of Rain' (Prov. 25.23) to the 'Storm-Wind' (Ps. 148.8) of *3 Enoch* (Odeberg 1928); leaving aside the labour pains by which the new world comes to birth and what by that genesis comes to be; leaving aside, that is, all but one element of the whole elevenfold-sequence of 'Messianism', of which Schürer (1979: II, 514-47) gives a systematic account, let us animadvert only to the influence of Shakespeare on St Paul ('To die, to sleep' [*Hamlet* III.i.60]), *via* the Hebrew background of Eccl. 47.23 ('Solomon rested with his fathers'). And then we shall turn from there to the gradual complication of the elementary semantics of 'sleeping' and 'waking'; and then to notes on the preposition, 'up'.

To do this is to interpret literature in the context of literature, is to do comparative literature.

When, from 1896 onwards, Solomon Shechter (and others) exhumed from the Cairo Geniza some Hebrew portions of Ecclesiasticus, they found that where the Septuagint (LXX 47.23) had ἀνεπαύσατο (*anepausato*, 'rested'), the Hebrew had *shākābh* ('he lay down'). The verb, 'lie down', raises two questions: With whom are you lying down? And: Where are you lying down? You may find yourself lying down with your fathers, as Solomon. Or you may find yourself lying down with your mother, as Oedipus. If, like Oedipus, you are lying down in bed, it may be that you will wake up in the morning. Or you may find that you will be woken up in the morning, by the busy sun, or by a tuba (*mirum spargens sonum*, 'scattering a wondrous sound'), or by a brass band, or as in Gerald Hoffnung's concert,[7] by a number of brass bands, entering the concert hall by an equal number of doors, playing an equal number of national anthems, playing a penultimate trump.

The standard articulated sequence would then be: 'resting/ lying down', 'wake up', 'get up', 'stand up'. And the sequence might be further explicated thus: 'go up', and 'sit up' (on a seat). And this in turn might be succeeded by a 'going down' and a 'turning up'. The first two items of this sixfold sequence, 'wake up' and 'get up', would be covered by the Greek word ἐγείρω, *egeiro*, 'wake up', 'get up', or (in the passive), ἐγείρομαι, *egeiromai*, 'be woken up', 'be raised up'.

To use a word is to find yourself in a position to use other words.

---

7.   And *Hoffnung* (German) means 'hope' (cf. ἐλπίδα, *elpida*; cf. vg. spem [1 Thess. 4.13 *vide infra*]).

Words have 'articulation possibilities' (Ramsey 1964: 49) and what it is possible to articulate can be actually articulated. And, by theologians, will be: give them an inch, and they will give you all ell.

Where are you lying down? In a bed? In a grave? The metaphorical equation of 'grave' and 'bed' is very widespread in the ancient and post-ancient Near East. Take 'A New Epigram by Poseidippus on an Irritable Dead Cretan' (Dickie 1995: 5-12):

> Why have you stopped to look at me? Why haven't you let me sleep,
>> asking who I am, where I come from or to what people I
>>> belong?
> Go past my tomb! I am Menoitios, the son of Philarchos,
>> a Cretan, a man of few words as one would be in a foreign
>>> land.[8]

For '(a)t least from the time of Homer death is imagined as a sleep' (Dickie 1995: 7) and the κοιμάομαι (*koimaomai*: 'sleep', 'rest in sleep', 'lie down in sleep') of 1 Cor. 15.20 reappears in the *Iliad* (11.241), where Iphidamas, 'smote...on the neck' (trans. Hobbes 1844: 124), 'slept a bronze sleep' (κοιμήσατο χάλκεον ὕπνον, *koimesato chalkeon hupnon*), the sleeper as immobile as a bronze sword when no warrior is holding it.

And there the sequence may end—or rather may never begin, as Hamlet (III.i.60-61): 'To die, to sleep—No more'. Or there the sequence may start, as Hamlet (III.i.64-65): 'To die, to sleep; To sleep, perchance to dream...' But Hamlet's dreams are nightmares. And to the language of sleeping and waking, and the language of locomotion, interrupted by 'session on the right' (*sessio ad dextram* [Rom. 8.34]), there seems to be joined, in Hamlet's mind, intimations of judgment ('the dread of something after death': III.i.78).

Dread? But not so Paul (or not only so Paul), nor Gregor Smith neither, but 'joy and assurance' (1969: 132). Joy and assurance, in 1 Cor. 15.20-28, find their linguistic grounding, first, in the defeat of his enemies by the Messiah, and, secondly, in the terminal (and terminological) incoherence of God being 'all in all'. But the sixfold

---

8.   τί πρὸς ἐμ᾽ ὧδ᾽ ἔστητε; τί μ᾽ οὐκ ἤσατ᾽ ἰαύειν,
     εἰρόμενοι τίς ἐγὼ καὶ πόθεν ἢ ποδαπός;
     στεῖχε <τέ> μου παρὰ σῆμα· Μενοίτιός εἰμι Φιλάρχω
     Κρής, ὀλιγορρήμων ὡς ἂν ἐπὶ ξενίης.

locomotion, from waking up, getting up, standing up, going up, sitting up to coming down, has the last of these phrases ('coming down') most clearly expressed in 1 Thess. 4.17, where the dead and the living 'shall be caught up together...in the clouds to meet the Lord in the air'. There is ἀπάντησις, *apantesis*, 'meeting'. The absence of the word does not deny the fact of παρουσία, *parousia*, 'presence'.

The *passacaglia*, the ground-bass, the architecture of the language here is classically expounded by Bevan, in his *Symbolism and Belief* (1962) and more recently by Lakoff and Johnson, in *Metaphors We Live By* (1980). The key is 'height' (Bevan 1962: 25-72) and 'up' (Lakoff and Johnson 1980: 14-21): take, on the one side, 'Her face *fell*', 'He was *down* in the mouth', and, on the other, 'The Stock Exchange Index is going *up*', 'Things are looking *up*', 'They were *above* it all', and 'Lazarus *rose* from the grave'. The use of such language, and in particular, 'claucht up among cluds tae meet the Lord i the lift' (Lorimer 1983: 350, 1 Thess. 4.17 *ad loc.*: ἀρπαγησόμεθα ἐν νεφέλαις εἰς ἀπάντησιν τοῦ κυρίου εἰς ἀέρα, *harpagesometha en nephelais eis apantesis tou kuriou eis aera*) explains, or helps to explain, why hang-gliding is popular with the Theological Students Fellowship and the evangelical wing in general.

But whatever the height above ground, in what medium does the meeting take place? 'Air' is Paul's answer. If the expulsion of air, in the form of words, is to qualify as apostolic (or as academic for that matter), it must be sufficiently hot. The Greeks have three words for air: (1) ἀήρ, *aer*, or 'blowing air' (Eng. 'air'), (2) αἴθηρ, *aither*, or 'hot air' (Eng. 'ether') and πνεῦμα, *pneuma*, or 'breathing', or 'blowing air'. As one might expect of a subtle doctor of the calibre of St Paul, he permits himself to make use only of the first and third. But when, in 1 Thess. 4.17, he makes use of the first, one cannot discount the association of this one with the third: '"Man is powerless in the flesh but free because of the spirit" [Tolstoy]. May the spirit be in me!' (Wittgenstein, cit. McGuinness 1988: 220-21). The 'air' (ἀήρ, *aer*) of 1 Thess. 4.17 may reasonably be brought into conjunction with the 'air' (πνεῦμα, *pneuma*) of 1 Cor. 15.45: 'the last Adam became a life-giving spirit' (Gk πνεῦμα ζῳοποιοῦν, *pneuma zo(i)opoioun*). The medium, perhaps, is the message.

What the modern mind can make, or whether the modern mind

should be making anything of it at all, is another question. In *The Free Man* (1969: 117) Gregor Smith writes: 'The presence of the theological crisis means that faith has now no way of formulating itself, it has no unassailable model, and no certain assured style. Even the Bible as a model is on the run.' The science fiction, or Utopian parcel, in which the early Christian metaphysic comes swaddled, is not now, by the juncture we have reached, the only possible integument. And even in its own day and in our own day, Paul of Tarsus and Margaret Thatcher had severally to remind the church of God, that, while the first duty of man might be to love God and enjoy him for ever, the first duty of woman was to enjoy the Stock Exchange and live on it for ever, or (more cautiously formulated) that inferences from the understanding of the future to the activity of wealth creation should be drawn with care.

In a fine letter to the Editor of *Philosophy* in 1934, a letter imbued with the fervour of early Christian eschatology, Collingwood wrote of 'The Present Need of Philosophy'. The foundation for the triumphs that science was one day to achieve was laid at the beginning of the seventeenth century and

> was based on the belief that nature is a single system of things, controlled throughout its extent by a single system of laws

and that

> [t]his philosophical conception of nature has played the part, in relation to scientific research, of a constant stimulus to effort, a reasoned refutation of defeatism, a promise that all scientific problems are soluble (1934: 263).

The state of things in the modern world is one

> whose special problems are concerned with human relations. The solution of these must rest on two things: a conviction that the problems can be solved, and a determination that they shall be solved…[t]here is always a vast mass of opinion…in favour of allowing established institutions to stand firm for fear of worse to follow; there is always a dead weight of inclination, however bad things may be, to enjoy what good we can snatch for the short time allowed us; but, more dangerous than either of these, there is the defeatist spirit which fears that what we are aiming at what is no more than a Utopian dream… As the seventeenth century needed a reasoned conviction that nature is intelligible and problems of science in principle soluble, so the twentieth needs a reasoned

conviction that human progress is possible and that the problems of
moral and political life are in principle soluble... What would
correspond to the Renaissance conception of nature as a single
intelligible system would be a philosophy showing that the human
will is of a piece with nature in being genuinely creative, a *vera
causa*, though singular in being consciously creative; that social and
political institutions are creations of the human will, conserved by
the same power which created them, and essentially plastic to its
hand; and that therefore whatever evils they contain are in principle
remediable. In short, the help which philosophy might give to our
'dissatisfied, anxious, apprehensive generation' would lie in a reasoned statement of the principle that there can be no evils in any
human institution which human will cannot cure (1934: 264-65).

Then after a reference to Alexander's *Space, Time and Deity*,
Smuts's *Holism and Evolution*, and Whitehead's *Process and
Reality*, Collingwood concludes:

These, with others hardly less important, seem to me the firstfruits
of a new philosophical movement in which epistemological dis-
cussions and the old controversy between realism and idealism have
fallen...into the background; in which the central place is
taken...by the idea of development; in which philosophy feels itself
a collaborator with science... and in which man is conceived
neither as lifted clean out of nature nor yet as the plaything of
natural forces, but as sharing, and sharing to an eminent degree, in
the creative power which constitutes the inward essence of all
things.

From his 'juvenile studies in theology' of the First World War
(1916) to The *New Leviathan* of the Second (1942), Collingwood
was a hoper and a fighter: 'We asked, why does God permit evil?
He does not permit it. His omnipotence is not restricted by it. He
conquers it' (1916: 144).

Immortality is a harder nut to crack. It is hard both how to say
that the nut has been cracked, and how to live in recognition of
the fact that it has been. This is to ask (again) how Wittgenstein's
'mystical' is to be glossed, how Germbergius's *ex nihilo nihil fit*,
'nothing comes of nothing',[9] is to be refuted.

9.   Cf. Persius 3.83-84: *gigni de nihilo nihil*, cit. Muir in Shakespeare 1972:
9 (*King Lear* I.i.89: 'Nothing will come of nothing'); cf. Aristotle *Metaphysics*
1062b24-25: τὸ γὰρ μηδὲν ἐκ μὴ ὄντος γίγνεσθαι, *to gar meden ek me ontos
gignesthai*, 'nothing comes of non-being'.

But the language of the poets has not left us comfortless—Donne's 'Death, be not proud...' and Thomas's 'Heads of the characters hammer through daisies'. And the vulgar saws of the common man, that 'You can't keep a good man down', that 'You can't nail a good man down'. And all this within the brackets of 'esomenology', the study of what will be, and the Hebrew joke: *eheyeh asher eheyeh*: 'I will be what I will be' (Exod. 3.14).

But, on our side, too, we have Paul, the poet, in whose birth, and in the birth of the Christian religion, we are witnesses to the birth of an unstatable metaphysic; unstatable (but stated), because it is primarily concerned with what has not yet happened; a metaphysic that rises so close to the springs of thought, that it cannot qualify as thought at all, but as imagination, as fiction, as imaginative fiction.

Paul's metaphysic comes in the form of poetry, of metaphor—of growth, victory and awakening from sleep. But in so far as one can think about what is not thought and have convictions about what has not yet happened, this much at least can be said, that if, as can be supposed, all problems are soluble, if all problems can be, will be, or in principle have been solved, then death, too, is included.

6

A Pigeon and the Solidity of Thin Air:
πνέων τροπαίαν, *pneon tropaian*
('Blowing a Wind of Change')
(The Prologue of Mark: 1.1-15)

Before the Beginning

God, in the New Testament, is imagined as 'wind', or 'breath'. He is also imagined as a pigeon. What kind of effect does this have on those who imagine him as such? The effect is this: That there is not, ever, no alternative.

It is the view of J. Enoch Powell (1977: 112), as expressed to Gowans (see Acknowledgments), that Mark has not only a Lost Ending, but also a Lost Beginning (Mark's first sentence, according as it now stands, is hard to construe). It is also the view of most scholars that Mark has two Found Endings, a Shorter and a Longer, of which neither is genuine, in the sense that neither belongs to the earliest extant manuscripts.

This chapter accordingly will consist of:

A Shorter Beginning

A Longer Beginning

BEGINNING I

A Little Beginning

BEGINNING II

THE BEGINNING

A Short End of the Beginning

But (let the reader mark! [Mk 13.14]), this chapter will have no ENDING (will remain an *UNDING*, or 'No-Thing'). Should, however, the reader be sufficiently intrepid to set out, like Abraham, who did not know where he was going (Heb. 11.8 [and see

Chapter 12 below]), I can assure that person, that I am myself convinced, that what is not in this chapter disambiguated, has not been made sufficiently clear, is important and not much more difficult than Mark, when you come to think about him, when thought has been applied.

The main point is something like this, that it is easier boldly to go on triumphantly to show what Mark is not, than to show what he is. Plato is worried by what Mark is worried, that is, by poets in his republic, and says quite a lot about it; Aristotle is not, but says almost nothing—I can find, in Aristotle, four words only; and these words amount to two statements: (1) artists (he is thinking of Greek tragedians) are trying to tell the truth (λέγει τὰ καθόλου, *legei ta katholou*: '[poetry] tends to express the universal' [*Po.* 1451b6-7]), and (2) the truth poets are trying to tell comes in the form of stories that have been passed from mouth to ear (φασί, *phasi*: 'this is what is said' [*Po.* 1461a1]). And the academic world, and the Christian Church, or world *tout court*, has been revolving ever since.

Austin Farrer has an essay on 'The Mind of St Mark', in which he says:

> What did the author set himself to do? No doubt St Mark set himself to write a story of Christ; and so everything he does write has its meaning as contributory to that story. But a story can be written with different aims, all perhaps equally serious—historical, theological, hortatory; and the general purpose of a writer will not leave unaffected the meaning of what he writes in detail. It would be a simple misunderstanding of the author to take as historical information what was intended (let us say) as dramatized theology, or *vice versa* (1976: 14).

A Shorter Beginning

In his article, 'Plato's Philosophy of Art', Collingwood writes:

> [T]he phantasm indirectly symbolises truth... Symbolism, by its very nature, is the apprehension of truth veiled or disguised in an imaginative form; and truth so disguised is felt rather than thought, that is, it is present to the mind in the form of an emotional atmosphere clinging to the symbol. The symbol is heavy with an import which can only convey itself in the shape of a feeling of urgency, a feeling that there is something here which is of supreme value, a feeling

that we are in the presence of a mystery revealed and yet not revealed (1925b: 162).

Now Collingwood has said earlier in that article (1925b: 155), that the thesis that Plato is defending in the tenth book of the *Republic* is 'that poetry [ποίησις, *poiesis*] is an intellectual danger to everyone who is unprovided with an antidote in the shape of a knowledge of its real nature'.

It is this ignorance that has bedevilled (*au pied de la lettre*) the study of the Gospels, until de Wette and Strauss pulled the duck from the hat and persuaded it (the rabbit) to tell the time and place and real nature of the texts. Of de Wette it may, however, be said that, while he carried through (but how far?) his insights into the 'aesthetic-religious' character of the Pentateuch as 'the Hebrew epic' (de Wette 1807: 31), he did not consequently, and consistently, do the same for the four brief epics of Christian origins that are here being called 'historical novels'; and it may be said of Strauss that he was more successful in proving that story was not history than that history is not the only avenue to truth. In showing what the Gospels were not (sc. history), he almost inadvertently showed what they were (sc. story—or, as Ms Evans would say, 'mythi' [Strauss 1840 (= 1970) *passim*]) without at the same time being able to persuade the learned world of the worth of what they were. Where he *did* succeed was in persuading the learned world to dismiss him. But a story, is a story, is a story, after all; and stories have a point; and these stories are stories of the Christian religion, 'of which the substance...is identical with the highest philosophical truth' (Zeller 1874: 47). But are they philosophy?

Zeller, in *David Friedrich Strauss in his Life and Writings* (1874), declares there that Strauss believed

> that none of our Gospels can be proved as the work of a man, the period and circumstances of whose life would render impossible the assumption of incorrectness of statement; that consequently criticism was perfectly free to expunge from their narratives everything which carried with it the appearance of being untrue to history (1874: 42).

But why 'expunge'? If you are writing history, yes. But what if you are not? And what if they were not? What if the Gospel writers were not?

Strauss 'arrived at length at the result, that a great part, indeed, as regards its extent, the greater part of the Gospel records contained either no historical matter at all, or historical matter so disfigured that it was scarcely recognisable as such' (1874: 44). But what if the boot is put on the other foot? What if it is the historian who disfigures stories?

'Strauss [as I said above] adhered to the statement that the critic of the 19th century, differing from the free-thinker and the naturalist, is conscious of the substance of the Christian religion as identical with the highest philosophical truth' (1874: 47). Fair enough. But what if the Christian religion, in its first century form, is identical with the highest story? What if the story is more philosophical than philosophy?

But all honour is due to Strauss for what he did. For 'while many guard against [the collision between 'active representation' (sc. myth) and 'pure theory' (sc. philosophy)] by abstaining from study and thought, or even from freedom of speech and writing, there are others who, in spite of all opposition, freely confess what can no longer remain concealed' (Zeller 1874: 49). And yet why was Strauss himself so alarmed by what he had done, as to go cantering away from mythology into philosophy? He lost his job, of course. And that is hard enough, even if, which is perhaps too easy to say, it was less hard *sub specie aeternitatis*, for he did, after all, erect a monument more perennial than bronze. But, again it may be asked, why not *stay with mythology* and 'enjoy' it as such (Whitehead and Barthes [*jouïssance*])? Why not rejoice in it in that 'second naïveté', whereby the critical reader returns to his original delight (Ricoeur 1969: 351). Why do we not all 'become as children' and enjoy childrens' stories? Hamann says exactly this: '[V]erily, verily, we must become children, if we are to receive the spirit of truth' (1950: 202).[1]

And then (from 'the ample preface which [Strauss] affixed in

---

1.   Lumpp 1970: 213 (= Hamann 1762: 178). '[E]xactly' is an inadequate word to use of Hamann, when only the decent, biblical portion is being extracted from a sentence that contains, poised above a long footnote from Francis Bacon (*Augm. Scient.* 2.13 [= 1858: 535]) on Paracelsus and the Cabbalists, a reference to the *Orbis sensualium pictus*, a Latin picture book (1658), by J. Amos Comenius, and another to the *Exercitia*, a Latin exercise book, by Friedrich Muzelius (1684-1753).

May 1860 to his translation of the 'Discourses' [sc. of Ulrich von Hütten]' [so Zeller 1874: 108]):

> Why not mutually confess that we can perceive nothing in the Biblical stories but fiction and truth, and in the dogmas of the Church nothing but significant symbols; but that we remain attached with unalterable reverence to the moral value of Christianity, and to the character of its founder, so far as the human form is recognisable amid the accumulation of miracles in which its first biographers have enveloped it?

But why should we not also 'remain attached with unalterable reverence' to the *ontological* value of Christianity and to the accumulation of miracles in which that ontology is embodied, as ontology is embodied in *Oedipus*, *Macbeth*, *Waverley*? Was Leonardo doing nothing, when he did what he did? But Strauss (so Zeller) is already saying this, for he is not talking about perceiving 'nothing in the Biblical stories but fiction'. What he says is, 'fiction and truth'.

A Longer Beginning

All texts have a provenance and a milieu. So too all authors.

On the shoulders of Lowth stood Heyne, Eichhorn, Gabler and de Wette. And on their shoulders, in turn, Strauss and George Eliot. They based themselves, all of them, on the axiom that mythical and historical thinking were not one thing, but two.

It was this same view, that, launched as a missile at the Confessing Church, constituted one of Rudolf Bultmann's contributions to the Second World War. Bultmann's purport was this, that to counter the myth of Nazism by the New Testament is to counter a myth by a myth (Jüngel, in Bultmann 1988: 7). Among the other projectiles in the air at the time, Bultmann's essay passed relatively unnoticed. Much as Strauss had earlier launched a sequence of theses, antitheses and syntheses, a translation, that is, of Christianity into the terms of Hegel's philosophy, Bultmann's assault on New Testament myth was accompanied by the simultaneous launch of a translation of the myth into the terms of a *phänomenal-ontologische Analyse der Zeitlichkeit*, the phenomenological and ontological analysis of temporality of Martin Heidegger. The study of myth, that is, was complemented by the study of philosophy, or what one biblical author (not Paul) calls the study of 'philosophy and vain deceit' (Col. 2.8), on the grounds that, though the author was not thinking himself, or herself, someone else had had the impertinence to do so.

But seams get worked out and leave the enquirer with basalt, or oolite, or a residue of dross, but no more gold. Meanwhile, however, Thornton Wilder's brother, Amos, something of a solo climber at that time, instead of turning from myth to philosophy, stayed with it and pioneered the study of myth as a literary phenomenon: the word, 'oneiric' ('dream-like'), he said, characterizes much of the New Testament 'theopoetic' (1976). And now there is no one (worth noticing) who is not, like Dante, infernally havering, in a less specialist manner, on 'plot' and 'point of view', and, in a more specialist manner, on 'sub-text', 'foregrounding', 'privileging', 'sociolect', 'syllepsis', 'sememe' and 'squaring the semeiotic circle'.

If 'fiction' is to be added to this list, the question arises, what that word licenses us to do: if the word, 'fiction', is substituted for the word, 'myth', what do we see that we did not see before?

Now Goodspeed once said of Cadbury that 'the consciousness of even a single certainty would be an insupportable weight upon his mind'. It may be that in the present essay we shall see nothing, or see nothing clearly. But even if '[t]o ask questions which you see no prospect of answering is the fundamental sin in science' (Collingwood 1946: 281), in theology the fundamental task is to 'sin boldly' and, still better, to boldly sin. A question may be worth asking, even if it cannot decisively be answered. A question may be worth asking, even if it cannot be answered at all.

It is, however, clear that fiction is not fact, though it may overlap with fact. That there is *some* connection between fiction and fact is simply the point made by the man from Stagira (Aristotle), when he says that 'poetry tends to express the universal' (λέγει τὰ καθ-όλου, *legei ta katholou* [*Po.* 1451b6-7]) and when his commentator, Bywater (in Aristotle 1909: 188-89) cites Diderot (1821-34: III, 18):

> Oh Richardson! I would venture to say that the most true history is full of lies, and that your novel is full of truths. History paints certain individuals; you paint humankind; history attributes to certain persons what they have neither said, nor done; all that you attribute to man, he has said and done: history embraces only a portion of time, only one point on the surface of the globe; you have embraced

all places and all times. The human heart, which has been, is and and will be ever the same, is the model, after which you make your copy. Were one to subject to severe criticism the best historians, would any of them survive the test, as you would do? From this point of view, I would venture to say that history is often a bad novel; and that the novel, as you have fashioned it, is a good history. Oh painter of nature! It is you who never lie.[2]

Or, again, more briefly, Fielding:

The provision, then, which we have here made is no other than *Human Nature* (1959: 1).

In other words, the language of the imagination, at least on Aristotle's view of *typical* art, if not on Collingwood's of the 'individualization' of each work of art (1938: 111-15, esp. 114-15), permits, or licenses, the passage from particular images to general propositions, such as that 'it is a generally observed fact that ambitious men and women are ruthless'. Or there is a passage between *Vorstellung*, 'representation', on the one hand, to *Begriff*, 'concept', on the other.

Diderot on Richardson may be compared with James on James, with James on fiction. James says, in *The Art of the Novel*, that 'the fictive hero successfully appeals to us only as an eminent instance, as eminent as we like, of our own conscious kind' (James 1962: 12), that 'the province of art is all life, all feeling, all observation, all vision...it is all experience' (James 1962: 38). Now, then, would Mark be fairly summarized as saying that his 'fictive hero' is 'an eminent instance...of our own conscious kind', and, thus, that incarnation, crucifixion and resurrection, apply only to the hero, in so far as they apply to Mark himself and Mark's reader also?

2.   'O Richardson! j'oserai dire que l'histoire la plus vraie est pleine de mensonges, et que ton roman est plein de vérités. L'histoire peint quelques individus; tu peins l'espèce humaine: l'histoire attribue à quelques individus ce qu'ils n'ont ni dit, ni fait; tout ce que tu attribues à l'homme, il l'a dit et fait: l'histoire n'embrasse qu'une portion de la durée, qu'un point de la surface du globe; tu as embrassé tous les lieux et tous les temps. Le coeur humain, qui a été, est et sera toujours le même, est le modèle d'après lequel tu copies. Si l'on appliquait au meilleur historien une critique sévère, y en a-t-il qui la soutînt comme toi? Sous ce point de vue, j'oserai dire que souvent l'histoire est un mauvais roman; et que le roman, comme tu l'as fait, est une bonne histoire. O peintre de la nature! c'est toi qui ne mens jamais.'

'A classic', says Friedrich Schlegel (1956: 6), 'is a writing that is never fully understood. But those that are educated and educate themselves must always want to have more from it.'[3] Now then, is not Mark a classic of this kind and, prescinding from an exhaustive account of all those modes of thought by which we might 'want to get more from it', might we not here select the following three: metaphysics, history and literature?

First, the Gospel of Mark is a metaphysical essay. He is trying to give some account of how things are, in the community of his day, say, and of how things might be in the future that is implied by the sense of his ending. But we are bound to take note that how Mark does it, does his metaphysics, is to be distinguished from how Aristotle does it, in *Metaphysics Lambda* (say) and even from the more perspicuous parts of the *Posterior Analytics*. We find out what Mark is also by finding out what Mark is not.

But we cannot allow Mark to get away with throwing 'god', or 'God', at us and allow him to remain innocent of all metaphysical claims. But he has served up the word, not really in the lordly dish, that Aristotle provides (or Spinoza), but in the kind of earthen vessel used in humbler circles. But still Mark must answer for what he does say. As regards the making of metaphysical claims, if he is not guilty after the manner of Aristotle, he is not innocent either.

Secondly, the Gospel of Mark is a history. But, again, he is good at covering his tracks. Here is history, without the vestiges of it, one might say, but cannot get away with saying. For he has put evidence (dangerous word) at our disposal and that evidence allows us to conclude that, whatever else may or may not be true about Jesus, it is true that, in seeming to be a man, he was what he seemed; and that, for example, he began his career as a Baptist.

In the third place, which is the first place in importance, Mark has given us literature, though much less abstract than *The Wings of a Dove* (James). If Mark is more Cartland than Proust, he is more Hemingway than James. He is vernacular, staccato, of the people. His literature is the literature of a time and a place; not our place, not our time. We *cannot* ourselves write that way, unless we are to parody him. In *this* sense, literature is a *historical* phenomenon, a

3.   'Eine klassische Schrift muss nie ganz verstanden werden können. Aber die, welche gebildet sind und sich bilden, müssen immer mehr draus lernen wollen.'

phenomenon of changing styles and fashions, all of them radically contingent (Oakeshott, Collingwood, Gombrich—Piero is not Picasso).

These three elements are distinguishable, but not separable. Mark is a matrix. The peculiar quiddity of Mark is not a layer cake, not a liqueur drink of discrete segments. It is a unitary amalgam, all of a piece, a fusion. But we have a name for this kind of thing, or a name that covers history and literature: 'historical novel'. But we could call it a 'metaphysical-historical-novel'. And, then, in order to make clear that Markan metaphysics differs from the metaphysics of Spinoza and Aristotle, we need to introduce into the catena the notion of science fiction, of Utopia, in order to cover all the elements, components, features, facets. Like Hoyle's *Black Cloud*, Mark's colourless cloud is vocal; like *Hamlet*, is 'full of quotations': 'You are my beloved son...' (Mk 1.11), for Mark has density, intensity of reference to a variety of Old Testament locutions (Ps. 2.7; Gen. 22.2; Isa. 42.1).

The debate about *what* Mark is has got to be wider, needs the context of comparative literature. Unlike history, which is constrained by evidence, Mark is doing something that is more like mathematics, in its freedom (Waismann 1977: 120). His hold on history is tenuous. If his fingers are prised off, he will fall off.

Mark is setting out to tell the reader what he thinks to be the truth about Jesus. But there is more than one way of telling the truth and more than one way of establishing whether the truth has been told:

> Now the way in which truth is established... and whether it can be established at all, conclusively or not, has a bearing on the notion of truth itself, and changes and modifies it in ways which deeply colour its signification. Accordingly, the term 'truth' acquires a multiplicity of meaning... And the reason for this is...that only *part* of the full and rich content of [this notion] can be formalized, whereas the other one, the material, serves to *adjust* the abstract notion to the varying needs of reality (Waismann 1977: 120).

What Mark does, he uses the resources of fiction to do.

Take the temptation story (Mk 1.12-13). Here Mark is not so much setting out to tell us what happened in history, to one hero on one occasion, as setting out to tell the story about what happened once upon a time and what happens all the time; a story that delineates the determinants within which all heroes operate; and is telling us this from the resources at his disposal, from the resources that are provided by what Mack, standing on the shoulders of de Wette (*das Epos der hebräischen Poesie* [1807: 31]), calls 'the Hebrew epic' (1988: 30): tempted for 40 years in the desert— tempted for 40 days in the desert. The temptation is an epic *topos*, common place, *locus communis*, κοινὸς τόπος, *koinos topos* (we have rhetoric here): if anyone is going to get anywhere, it will be necessary to go 'through it' first, as Jesus went through it; as, once upon a time, according to the necessities of the religious imagination, he must have gone through it. And Mark, for double traditions are compatible, tells us this from the resources provided by the cycle of fictions that, like milk with rennet, have coagulated round the name of Elijah, that cycle, as we have seen above, reduced by historical-critical inquiry to two half-lines of Noth's laconic print (1960: 242). And add Elisha (Farrer 1976: 18).

In Edinburgh, the Jerusalem (or Babylon) of the North, the scientist Appleton is commemorated by a tower contingent with the eponymous layer. Some way above that, stably supported (according to the Free Church of Scotland) on cumulo-nimbus and fulmination, there lives Someone with alpha-omegaphone and doocot. He has won a prize for Scripture Knowledge (β, *befriedigend*, or 'adequate').

The point is put dissimilarly, but analogously:

> And under that almighty fin,
> The littlest fish may enter in.
>
> (Brooke, 'The Fish's Heaven')

Fictions are not history. That is the polemical point.

But what is the apologetic point?

The beginning of an apologia is this: Mark may be defended by the observation that the point is embedded in the target, but is beside the mark. It is true that, if Mark is setting out to write history, he is failing to do it. But what if he is setting out to do something else? What if he is following Hemingway, or James, or Cartland or Scott, or Horace, or Eliot, or Stevens? And this last, Stevens, says something about that 'something else', when he speaks of that 'more severe, More harassing master' who

> would extemporize
> Subtler, more urgent proof that the theory
> Of poetry is the theory of life
>
> As it is, in the intricate evasions of as,
> In things seen and unseen, created from nothingness,
> The heavens, the hells, the worlds, the longed-for lands.
>   (Stevens 1955: 486, cit. Kermode 1967:155)

That is the literary-critical point: Mark's 'intricate evasions' begin with a series of complicated simplicities.

His book begins. The world begins. A new world begins. Bibliogony is cosmogony is christogony: the birth of a book, of a world, of the 'christ'. A poet (Isaiah? Mark?) with experience of road building makes a poem for the mouth of his maker ('creativity is the real God of Whitehead's metaphysics': Macquarrie *obiter dictum*). The maker of the poet is the maker of a universe of poets, is a maker of the universe, his poem, is a maker of a universe of kings, is king of the universe, is king of kings. And as king he has servants who run his errands. He has messengers. And one of these is John, whom he sends, to make of Jesus a Baptist.

Mark, the poet (he has literary experience, he stands in a literary tradition) makes of Jesus an Elijah, makes of Jesus a son, and makes the son the mouthpiece of his father. And Jesus, a poet with experience of a kingdom, sets off to talk of another.

Now if all literary critical points are steered by metaphysical axioms, the axiom we want is the axiom of agreement. This agreement can be expressed in various ways:

> There is agreement between God and man.
> There is argument between God and woman.

Once the axiom has been stated, there imposes itself on the literary critic the question of the meaning of fiction and the question of the mode by which that meaning is conveyed. Take the pigeon fancier and the pigeon he fancies. Stories, Aristotle, brilliantly, coruscatingly even, tells us, have 'a beginning, a middle and an end' (*Po.* 1450b27-28). Like all good stories, this collection (the Bible) of 'one and a half million intemperate words' (Mitchison R.M. *obiter dictum*), itself takes the form of a story and begins with a beginning, which is not so much the beginning of a drama as the beginning of those conditions without which there could not be a drama: the Great Stentor's shout that brings the world into being

(Gen. 1–3). 'All the world's a stage', said Macbeth, anticipating von Balthasar (c. 1988). Yes, but no stage, no drama. If the world is to be a stage, there must be a world to stage it on. The beginning lies in ontological surprise, but one gets used to such things.

Mark, much as John ('In the beginning...': Jn 1.1), Mark, obedient to Aristotle's command, begins with a beginning. He begins with an intertextual beginning which *dovetails* with Genesis 1: 'And the spirit of God was *brooding* over the face of the waters.' By the combination of a rudimentary ornithology with Leviticus 11, one of the articulation possibilities of the metaphor 'brood', or one of its logical implicates, allows us to pass over the ossifrage and settle on the pigeon, a pigeon in Piero della Francesca's painting of the *Baptism* so nebulous (*stricto sensu*: Piero's pigeon is as cloud-shaped as Piero's Tuscan, not Torridonian clouds), as to be the pure embodiment of wind.

By such easy and wholly persuasive and almost geometrical steps (and I mean Riemann, not Euclid, thus transcending the limitations of a geometry that is based on the postulate of parallels) we arrive at the idea of creative agreement. But this is only to say more abstractly what Mark says more concretely. For whether is it easier to say, 'We have creative agreement', or to say, 'A pigeon has landed' (or is poised to land)? But Mark is creating an aesthetic object, not a geometrical theorem or a demonstration by a posterior analytic. As Eichhorn, or Gabler, would say, his is the mode of *Versinnlichung*, 'the making sensible of the insensible'. Mark, a child in the childhood of the human race, a lisping infant, a νήπιος, *nepios* (one without epic?), is making use of his five senses. He does not propound, he murmurs. And the force of saying it as he does, is not simply to call on an earlier text, Genesis, but to suggest that the creativity, of which the earlier text speaks, belongs not only, if to a lesser degree, to the earlier text, but to his own also, to a greater. Now the fishing season is open. The asylums of the demented are closed. Care in the Community can come into its own. The career of Jesus can begin.

Mark spins his web as a spider from its belly. And what he spins, Mark thinks, is not so much 'optative' (Hepburn 1990: 189), not so much something he wants, but may not get, as indicative, or on the way to being so, as something he *wants* and *will yet get* and (can this sensibly be said?) in some sense (but *what* sense?) *has*. What is not yet will be soon. But indicative, not as *thought*, but as *imagined*. Mark's is not Spinoza's rationality of substance and its modes, but the imagery (so Hamann 1950: 204)[4] of 'blood and fire and vapour of smoke', of paternity, filiation and filiality ('You are my son…'), and, by implication, of course also, of sorority and maternity—only a matripassian God can help.

Mark's language is molten. Why do we petrify him by cooling it?

Beginning I

I am taking as axiomatic that the art of St Mark is anchored in what Hamann calls his 'senses and passions' (1950: 197);[5] or is anchored in 'aesthetic-religious' feeling, or *Ahnung*, 'presentiment', or 'hunch' (following, responding to 'hint') (de Wette 1831: 6-12),[6] a feeling that is analysed by de Wette into (1) *Begeisterung*, 'enthusiasm', (2) *Demuth*, 'humility', or *Ergebung*, '(trusting) surrender' and (3) *Andacht*, 'contemplatively rapt interest', or *Anbetung*, 'adoration' (de Wette 1831: 18-19; 1821: 63-67).

I am further supposing that Mark conquers his passions by expressing them, by telling the story he has to tell. Thus he converts his passions to actions, his passion to action, his action, in this case, in the case of writing a Gospel (Oakeshott would call it his 'exploit' [1983: 47]), amounting to telling words, telling words on papyrus or parchment, putting them into paperback or hardback, on to a roll or into a codex (Powell 1977: 113; Roberts and Skeat 1983: 61). Taking his actions together as one action, taking all his individual acts of expression as comprising one unitary act, it may be said that Mark's work is his act. The action, into which he converts his passion, is his Gospel.

It is the strength of his feeling that gives Mark his force. It is because the edifice of language that he has constructed has been well built that the resultant is as durable as history, more perennial than bronze. It is because he has succeeded in imagining well that we read him. Mark's imagining is not fundamentalist (he gets far too many things wrong), but it is fundamental. Could we not even

---

4.   Lumpp 1970: 215 (= Hamann 1762: 183), Nisbet 1985: 144.

5.   Lumpp 1970: 205 (= Hamann 1762: 163).

6.   And 1821: 20-72, cf. Fries 1905, cit. Hartlich and Sachs 1952: 103 n. 1.

say that just as 'love is strong as death' (Song 8.6), so art is strong as history? So why should we irritably reach for the latter? Might art even be in some sense more historical than history?

To say this and to say it this way is only to apply to Mark what Spinoza and Collingwood say of imagination and expression. Let Collingwood himself make the point, first in *The Principles of Art* (1938: 219):

> The problem of ethics, for him [sc. Spinoza], is the question how man, being ridden by feelings, can so master them that his life, from being a continuous *passio*, an undergoing of things, can become a continuous *actio*, or doing of things. The answer he gives is a curiously simple one. 'Affectus qui passio est, desinit esse passio, simulatque eius claram et distinctam formamus ideam' (*Ethics*, part v, prop. 3). As soon as we form a clear and distinct idea of a passion, it ceases to be a passion.

But the point was sufficiently important for Collingwood to return to it, in his last book, *The New Leviathan* (1942). Artists, or members of the human race (the distinction is without a difference—all men can be taught to speak well and women do not need to be), are agents of liberation, their own and ours, when they enable us to speak; enable us 'to make the strange discovery of freedom' (1942: 93). And 'the doctrine that a man acquires free will by conquering his passions is fundamental to at least three, if not four, major religions: Confucianism, Buddhism, and Christianity, with its offshoot Mohammedanism' (1942: 94). But

> 13.4. There is no sense in asking, when a man is found behaving in this way, 'why' he does it. The word 'why' has many well-established senses; none is appropriate here.
> 13.41. But there is much sense in asking 'how' he does it; and the answer is: '*By the use of speech*'.
> 13.42. A man liberates himself from a particular desire by naming it; not giving it any name that comes at haphazard into his head, but giving it its right name, the name it really has in the language he really talks.
> 13.43. Once he has done this he can do it again; most easily for another desire of the same kind; but in principle, with more or less difficulty, for any desire whatever.
> 13.44. Such at least is the doctrine common to Spinoza, the authors and divulgators of fairy-tales, and psycho-analysts (1942: 93).

Those who desire to find life can at least, from Mark, find out how

Mark found it. And finding out how he found it can perhaps better find it for themselves, giving it 'the name it really has in the language [they] really [talk]'. It is by *fingere*, 'making fictions', that we find speech. It is by reflecting on speech that we find philosophy.

For, to all this, there is an important *proviso*: art is only one moment in the movement of mind. The evolution of mind is not completed by the work of the imagination. The activity of *homo artifex* does not give an exhaustive account of human action. If art is properly (by Plato) defined as *cognitio confusa*, 'confused cognition', cognition certainly, but not cognition completely, then the work of the imagination has to be completed by the work of thought, of thinking. The work of art has to be completed by the work of interpretation, of explanation, of criticism. The imagining reed must think. Poetry, in Stevens's fine phrase (1960: 49), is (though, modestly, he says, 'possibly') 'a phase of metaphysics'. Without a firm foundation the house of mind cannot be built. With only the foundation there is no house. But when the poet founds and founds well, the house is implicit, as the oak *in nuce*, in the nutshell. An aesthetic philosophy must, in the end, complete the work of the poet, if 'the series of mental functions' (Collingwood 1942: 63) is to be complete. And this is why, in the *ecclesia semper reformanda*, Readings are complemented by Sermons, by the Children's Address, or by the coincidence of the latter with the former.

Thus Mark hits the nail on the head He is acting under the impress of agency, under the pressure of his sense of what is going on. He is under pressure to find words for what he feels. He is under impulsion to find a text. It is not just that his publisher is asking for copy, or his editor for *corrigenda*; he is labouring under the imperious demands of a topic, a topic as imperious as sex or love.

In speaking of God Mark is making, implicitly, a metaphysical claim and thus is on the way to meeting the needs of philosophers. He is neither writing the *Metaphysics Lambda* of Aristotle, nor the *Ethics* of Spinoza. In speaking of Jesus of Nazareth he is making a historical claim and thus is on the way to meeting the needs of historians. He is not writing history *tout court*; he is doing something more philosophical. He is producing an amalgam, of which history is one component and fiction the other. The disambiguation of the one from the other is not impossible, but is difficult and can only produce an incomplete answer. At the same time, while he is producing something that is more philosophical than history, he is not producing philosophy, but what implies a philosophy. This *tertium*, this third thing that is neither history on its own, nor philosophy on its own, is art, is literary art, is literature; vernacular literature, it is true, but literature all the same.

This is the nail that he hits on the head. It is 'the poetry of St. Mark' (Gardner 1959: 101-26) we are after. Mark is producing neither history, nor philosophy, but something more philosophical than both. He is producing poetry. He is producing fiction—fashioned discourse, dense and condensed; connotative, ambiguous, suggestive; inescapably indeterminate (Black 1979: 25).

Mark is expressing a contemplative judgment, of the sort that is clarified by Kant in his third *Critique*, but is expressing it in narrative form, in the form of folk-narrative, in the form of a folk-novel. Mark is writing this in the terms that are accessible to him, in the terms, namely, of a story of the end of the world. His *Gospel* begins with the beginning of that end, of which his every line 'bewrays' the sense.

It is possible that the beginning of John's Gospel is the response of a reader who is not responding to what is not there in the beginning of Mark. But it is possible that Mark, too, has Genesis in mind and that, with that 'beginning' in mind, is now setting out to talk of a greater beginning, the beginning of the end, and not merely the beginning of the beginning. In the jargon of the schools, he is engaged, not with 'creation', but with 'redemption', except that, with the creation of Genesis in mind, 'redemption', too, acquires creative colouring. In *that* sense, Mark's beginning is (to use Stanford's word [1936: 105]) 'stereoscopic'. Mark's double sense is (in Black's terms [1979: 26]), neither 'extinct', nor 'dormant', but 'active'. Only volcanic terms will do, only volcanic terms will answer. Mark's language is molten.

Mark is writing a novel about the novel, about a *novum*. And how does the novel, the *novum*, the new, arrive in history? And what sort of receptivity (German *Empfänglichkeit*) can pick up the signal? How is it possible to correlate the sign-event with ecstasy (Tillich 1953: I, 128-31)?

A Little Beginning

Mark's beginning is the beginning of a new book about the transition from nothing to something; or a new chapter in the transition from something less to something more. Cosmogenesis, anthropogenesis, birth, all spring readily to mind.

And Mark's beginning is the beginning of a story. For, as Aristotle did not tell Mark, 'A whole is that which has a beginning, a middle and an end' (*Po.* 1450b27-28). Peter (by one tradition, anyway), one of the triple pillars of the church transformed, in Galatians 2, into a hypocrite, forced by false forces into a false profession, dug into Mark's ear, and bred a booklet—the Healing of Peter's Mother-in-law may be said (Käsemann) to validate this tradition. The booklet begins at the beginning.

In Chapter 2 of the present book, it was claimed that Mark and John were historical novels with a science fiction component. The thesis was clear. Its demonstration less so; more a promise made than kept. *If* the thesis was clear. For in its inception it was unscientific and:

> [i]n unscientific thinking our thoughts are coagulated into knots and tangles; we fish up a thought out of our minds like an anchor foul of its own cable, hanging upside-down and draped in seaweed with shell-fish sticking to it, and dump the whole thing on deck quite pleased with ourselves for having got it up at all (Collingwood 1940a: 22).

But Mark is not philosophy, is not history; is art. The assertion so far was clear.

Beginning II

The Beginning of the Story of the End of the World

To judge by the interest his work has awakened, Mark has made a substantial contribution to world history. He is, in this sense, a man of substance. This is due not only to the fact that he has written well, but also to the content of his work. For the hero of his folk-novel (Jesus) was someone who had made, in Mark's view and the view of many of his readers, his own substantial contribution to what had gone on and to what was going on.

Although it is a novel Mark is writing and not a history, never-theless, because the hero is, by the best accounts (for there are worst), a historical figure, the novel is not a novel *tout court*, but a historical novel and, thus, a mixture of fact and fiction. Nor is there, at the present time of writing, universal agreement, either about the proportions in which the former is mixed with the latter, or the latter with the former, it being only agreed that there is disagreement. It is assumed here only that those who think either that Mark is 100 per cent historical, or that he is 100 per cent fictional are anything from 1 per cent to 99 per cent wrong. This will leave sufficient room for debate, a well from which Research Seminars (to call them that) may drink (Rehoboth [Gen. 26.22]).

My aim in the following pages is further to pursue the hypothesis that Mark, in particular his prologue (1.1-15), is a work of art, specifically a work of religious art. And my appeal to the reader takes the form, 'This is so, isn't it?' (Leavis 1969: 47) and invites dissent in the form, 'Yes, but...' (139). Farrer (1951: 30), despite his idiot vortices and epicycles, is on the right lines: 'St Mark's book is neither a treatise nor a poem, but it is more like a poem than a treatise.' The aim, here, is less to prove a negative, that Mark is neither history, nor philosophy, even if, in some way and in some measure, connected with both, than to 'place' a positive (literature) 'before the eyes' (ὅτι μάλιστα πρὸ ὀμμάτων τιθέμενον, *hoti malista pro ommaton tithemenon* [Aristotle, *Po.* 1455a23]). My aim is to enjoy Mark as a literary critic and to think about literary criticism. For while scholarship is mainly in the business of producing what is someone else's, it is not, in Britain at least and in Scotland certainly, in duty bound to produce everything else.

This means that we have to hold our course between the Scylla of history and the Charybdis of philosophy, deflected by no Celedones ('charmers'), or Sirens, or 'ostriches' (Isa. 13.21 [LXX], or owls).

It is not that history holds no charms, nor that Mark allows no access at all to the facts of the matter. But Renan (n.d.: xxxvi) is right to say that Strauss (1970) has done such a work as requires no re-working *(Je n'ai pas l'habitude de refaire ce qui est fait et bien fait,* 'I do not have the habit of re-doing what has been done and done well'), so that we may rest content with Conzelmann's round and typically laconic remark (1973: 31), that '[t]he account [of the

Baptism] is, of course, in its present form, legend'.

Nor is it that philosophy has no requirements. For what is to be made of our dumb friend, Jehovah, here? Criticism *s'impose*.

In what follows, both Scylla and Charybdis will need, no doubt, to find their physical and metaphysical location on the chart. But, nonetheless, the traveller must fare forward between them, smiting the sounding furrow, in a vehicle and on a course, that are themselves distinct. Literary criticism has the first call on our attention.

The word 'God' (we are not altogether surprised to find) presides over Mark's religious discourse. God, like any other agent in this text, gets things done—by moving mountains, by giving voice, by giving the bird. The 'unmoved mover' (Aristotle) moves other substances. 'Substance, cause of itself' (Spinoza) causes other modes of substance, but, in Mark, in a mode, or manner, that is neither Spinozist, nor Aristotelian. But the question remains whether it is not nonetheless true that Mark's mode and manner is in some way connected with the Substance and substances, the modes and manners of both. There is a way, hard though it be to find it, that leads from the 'logic of poetry' (Waismann 1977: 120) to the logic of philosophy. If God is one, if there is one world, a world that is both one and many, the modes and manners of the poet and of the philosopher are distinguishable, but not separable. There are many things to approach and many ways of approaching them, but none of these things nor any of these ways is absolutely unrelated to the others.

Mark is sufficiently laconic to mortify a Spartan, is less discursive than Proust. His style is a breathless parataxis: 'And immediately... And immediately...And immediately...' (Or has his language, like a weathered statue, lost its profile?) While he includes agents, with whom the historian is familiar, he includes others, God and Satan, who fill the conscientious historian with dismay, the thoughtful philosopher with alarm.

But Mark is writing neither history nor philosophy. He is producing something that is analytically distinct from both. He is producing some sort of a logaoedic thing, a 'discourse-song'.

Like *Macbeth* (Adam 1957: 381-87), of course, he successfully overlaps with history. And, like all works of art, he implies a philosophy. But to overlap with is not to coincide with. And to imply is not to be explicit. But if Mark is a work of art, it is a *religious* work of art. And this is why an assertoric, or propagandist, tone can be caught. But this tone might be better expressed by saying that he is an impassioned writer, writing under the impress here of God knows what, or of a kind of totality, of which one part is the poetry and song of his forebears and another the indefeasible garrulity (Peter's mother-in-law) of his contemporaries. He is stuck in a linguistic world, by which he is compelled, impelled. He is under impulse.

As Aristotle says he should, he begins at the beginning. As Horace says he should, he hastens to the middle: (the writer, the speaker) 'always hastens to the event and enraptures the auditory into the midst of the action as if the action were already well known to his hearers...' (Horace, *Ars Poetica* 148-49).[7]
Mark over-leaps the birth and the pre-natal period. Genesis (birth) and Genesis (creation) are neglected, at least explicitly. They are penumbral. Mark's notation is connotative. Pausing only long enough to say that the road builder can move mountains, he plunges into the bath, bath-bath almost, as the Germans say (Baden-Baden), hastens past sky, voice and bird (how differently Piero!), spends four lines on 40 days, till he lights on: 'the Kíngdom o God is naurhaund' (Lorimer 1983: 61 Mk 1.15 *ad loc.*), thus expressing the view, not that the old wine is best, but that this is a good year.

None of this is to hurry slowly. Screwing his courage to the sticking place, he hits the nail on the head.

Mark's art dislocates history. Mark's characterization re-delineates historical agents. His drama is less a conflict with the Pharisees than with Satan. The historian's picture, says Collingwood (1946: 246),

> must be localised in space and time. The artist's need not; essentially, the things that he imagines are imagined as happening at no place and at no date. Of *Wuthering Heights* it has been well said that the scene is laid in Hell, though the place-names are English; and it was a sure instinct that led another great novelist to replace Oxford by Christminster, Wantage by Alfredston, and Fawley by Marychurch, recoiling against the discord of topographical fact in what should be a purely imaginary world.

'History', says Eliot ethnically ('Little Gidding' V [= 1944: 43]), 'is

7.   'semper ad eventum festinat et in medias res
       non secus ac notas auditorem rapit...'

now and England'. Had Mark, the poet, been Eliot, the historian, he might have said, 'History is now and Palestine'. But had he been, he would have had as little right. For Eliot's place-names are English, but the scene is laid in Hell *and Purgatory and Paradise*. Mark's place-names are Palestinian, but his scene, too, is Eliot's. Like Eliot, he is not in Hell only. For Mark's scene is in No-place, Utopia, where the Second Adam is in conflict with a real snake. His scene is in the Nether Place, where the partly living are sufficiently alive to know that they are wholly dead. His scene is a place of purgation, where the leprosy of sin is prevented from giving birth to death.

Put it this way: like *Wuthering Heights*, Mark's scene is laid in Hell. But, like 'Little Gidding', not in Hell only, but in Purgatory and Paradise also, though if and only if, in a book that may, with qualification, be called good, the former two are recessive and priority given to the last. '[T]he saving action of Jesus over Satan is divided into a series of stories' (Robinson 1957: 30), while the whole is a cosmic struggle, in a 'three-storied' cosmos (Bultmann 1953: 1 [*drei Stockwerke*: 1988: 12]). The Palestinian place-names give place to Heaven, Purgatory and Hell and Hell and Purgatory in turn to Heaven. The katachthonic prison, the charnel-house, the 'graff chaumers' ('grave chambers': Lorimer 1983: 69, at the loch-side [Mk 5.2-3 *ad loc.*]) are, or are being transposed into the original garden, without original sin, into a garden city. For the macro-text, the book as a whole, transmutes the historical geography of the Holy Land into a fictive place. Mark makes place plastic to his purposes, into a setting for a 'myth of innocence' (Mack 1988).

Take Collingwood, again:

> Thus Shakespeare embodies history and fiction side by side in certain of his plays, but the plays are not mixtures of history and art, truth and beauty: they are art through and through, because the history and the art meet on equal terms; for the purposes of the play the distinction between them is non-existent (1925a: 13).

Mark is reality; history it is not—you can do history, of course, but would you not be missing the point?

But history it may become (some of it), when the historian (Conzelmann [1973], say, or say Morgan [1997]) gets round to it, reflects on the matter, for '(i)t remains as a historical fact...that Jesus emerged out of the Baptist's movement' (1973: 31). Hurrah!

But Conzelmann has just said, 'The account is, of course, in its present form, legend'.

But the word 'legend', before it came, in the Age of Iron (Hesiod, *Works and Days* 109-79), to mean 'what ought *not* to be read', meant once, in the Age of Gold, 'what *ought* (gerundively) to be read'. And the question pursued here is *not* what historical facts remain once the salmon of history have been purged of the sea-lice of poetry, but why the gerundive reading of 'legend' is not only an etymological, but a categorical imperative. What is wrong with 'what ought to be read'? Why not write to defend historical falsity, to defend true fiction? Do stories have a point?

Mark's legends are to be marked, learned and, like bread for 4000, for 5000, inwardly digested. His *fabula* (fable), his *fama* (report), his πλάσμα (*plasma*: 'fiction'—reality is *plastic* to his pen), his μῦθος (*muthos*: 'myth'), Aristotle's φασίν, *phasin* (again), 'they say' (*Po.* 1460b36, 1461a1), 'This is how [women] say the thing is', 'this is what is said'—all these terms require examination, not from the standpoint of the art historian, who is under an obligation to speak of legends pejoratively, but from the standpoint of the art historian, whose freedom and responsibility for what ought to be read precludes dispraise of what is worth reading. Mark has been taught by the tradition within which he is working to 'make false statements in the right way' (Aristotle *Po.* 1460a18-19, cit. Brink 1971: 223).

But what is worth reading? Worth, importance, import has to be *shown*. It has to be allowed to 'show itself' (Wittgenstein 1960: 82 [= *Tractatus* 6.522]).

Philosophy is no Charybdis to the philosopher. But there is no good reason for supposing that one man, or two women, cannot turn their minds both to philosophy and to art. And there is no adamantine law that can, or should, prevent the reader of 'the poetry of St. Mark' (Gardner 1959: 101-26) from turning either to Heidegger, or to Hegel, or to Collingwood, particularly if Aristotle is right to say that 'necessary or probable truths' (Aristotle *Po.* 1451b9; Heath 1991: 389-402) are somehow (but how?) embedded, or embodied, even in wonderful fables. But wonderful fables are first worth looking at in their own right and require their own methods of analysis, of synthesis, of heuristic illumination. There is a sense, surely, in which the literary criticism (and what is *that*?) of literature *ought* to precede the move from literature to philosophy. For, if to think is to climb, one cannot miss out a pitch: between literature and philosophy, cragged and steep, stands non-man-and-woman-fathomed literary criticism. *Pede temptim*, 'one step at a time', is the method.

Mark is acting under impress. One might as well have said that he was subject to inflation, or, with Longinus, to 'genuine passion' (γενναῖον πάθος, *gennaion pathos*) that 'as it were fills his words with frenzy' (οἰονεὶ φοιβάζον τοὺς λόγους, *hoionei phoibazon tous logous*: Longinus 1899: 8.4). Mark is phased by Phoebus. He is *there*, inside his story, as Homer inside his war 'shares the full inspiration of the combat' (οὔριος συνεμπνεῖ τοῖς ἀγῶσιν, *ourios sunempnei tois agosin* (lit. 'as a following wind, breathes together with the combats' [Longinus 1899: 9.11]). And when 'Longinus' goes on to say of Homer that, like Hector:

> Mad rageth he as Ares the shaker of spear, or as mad flames leap
> Wild-wasting from hill unto hill in folds of a forest deep,
> And the foam-froth fringeth his lips...[8]

(Iliad 15.605-607)

the reader will properly protest that Mark is not the *poeta vesanus*, the 'mad poet' of Athens (Horace, *Ars Poetica* 455; Brink 1971: 421-31), but is speaking the more Presbyterian tones of Jerusalem, under the more lapidary control of the pericope of Kings (2 Kgs 1.8), where God and a 'man of God' between them successfully 'consume' (κατέφαγεν, *katephagen*: 4 Kgs 1.10, 14 [LXX]) two commanders, two contingents of 50 men and a king (θανάτῳ ἀποθ-ανῇ, *thanato(i) apothane(i)*: 'by death you will die' (1.16). *Vesani poetae*—the Hebrews, too, had their frenzies.

But if Mark's lips are less foam-flecked than Homer's, is he not, nonetheless, being carried away? If he is not, why does he tell us that 'all' Jerusalem had gone down to the Jordan, leaving behind not a domestic pet? Or is it that are we dealing with something more banal, with the quotidian enthusiasms of the man on the Jericho omnibus, with the naïve hyperboles of the common man? But:

8.   μαίνεται, ὡς ὅτ᾿ Ἄρης ἐγχέσπαλος ἢ ὀλοὸν πῦρ
      οὔρεσι μαίνηται, βαθέης ἐνὶ τάρφεσιν ὕλης
      ἀφλοισμὸς δὲ περὶ στόμα γίγνεται...

> Must not the artist be stimulated or inspired by his subject? Is it not
> right and proper, and in the very nature of art, that the artist should
> enjoy the full use of his powers only when they are excited to
> activity by an exciting theme? (Collingwood 1929: 333).

And how, without inspiration, are we to explain his 'many
miracle stories' (Käsemann 1960: 215 [= 1964: 96]), to explain the
bird, that is waiting in the wings? This miraculous, marvellous,
remarkable element aligns Mark less with the *Iliad* and more with
the *Odyssey*, for '[t]he fabulous element prevails throughout this
poem over the real' (ἐν ἅπασι τούτοις ἑξῆς τοῦ πρακτικοῦ κρατεῖ τὸ
μυθικόν, *en hapasi toutois hexes tou praktikou kratei to muth-
ikon*). '[W]hat else can we term these things than veritable dreams
of Zeus?' (Longinus 1899: 9.14: τί γὰρ ἂν ἄλλο φήσαιμεν ταῦτα ἢ τῷ
ὄντι τοῦ Διὸς ἐνύπνια; *ti gar an allo phesaimen tauta e to(i) onti
tou Dios enupnia?*). The 'oneiric' (Wilder 1982: 166), intrudes,
'the element of the veritable dream'. Miracle, give or take the
tactile values of Jesus' hand (our medical warrants must be loose-
textured, 'no tight warrants are forthcoming' [Harvey 1967: 116]),
is, if ontological, a literary rather than a historical category: dis-
belief should be suspended, while reading, and belief suspended,
while not.

But to say, 'belief suspended', is again to leave the Aonach
Eagach Ridge of literature and abseil from Mark's text onto history.
No doubt, a historical formulation of belief might be thought possible, by speaking, for example, of 'God's history with man'. But
what, in that phrase (Gregor Smith 1966: 21), does 'history' mean?
But that question will be left to Chapter 12. And, no doubt, a metaphysical formulation is possible, by speaking, for example, of the
conviction that there is that than which nothing greater can be
thought.

But there are two other possibilities: first, the 'belching forth'
(*ructatur*: Horace, *Ars Poetica* 457), the 'vomiting forth' (ἐρεύγο-
μαι, *ereugomai*), that is spoken of in Ps. 44.2 (LXX): 'My heart is
inditing of a good matter' (Ps. 45.1 [KJV]). It is the 'uttering freely',
the 'vomiting out', that is spoken of by Ennius (*Ann.* 241: *evomere*,
cit. Brink 1971: 424). But of what? I mean the uttering freely of
poems and stories, of literature, of fiction in response to the poems
and stories, the literature, the fiction, the poetry of St Mark. Mark's

writing is an invitation to write, is an invitation to write something else.

And, secondly, the poetry of St Mark is an invitation to engage in literary criticism, to examine the form and comment on the content, but to withhold for a moment a more philosophical inquiry into the question how each poem and each story embodies, as poets do, probable and necessary general statements, not only Aristotle's τὰ καθόλου, *ta katholou*, but also the *communia* of Horace, sc. the 'generalities' of philosophy (*Ars Poetica* 128) and of Plutarch's adolescent poet (*Quom. adul. poet.* 34b, cit. Brink 1971: 206). The reader of Mark's literature can criticize it, or write his own.

It is these latter two, literature and literary criticism, that are being entertained, are entertaining here (*dulcia sunto*, 'let them be sweet': Horace, *Ars Poetica* 99), even if all climbers, especially when confronted by the Inaccessible Pinnacle, must sometimes deviate from the ridge, to the left or to the right. The *status quaestionis*, that is, the point that the current debate has reached, may not entirely permit the exclusion either of history or philosophy. But the poem, the poet, the poetics are the thing here, and 'as a thing, it is something of a thing' (Griffith *obiter dictum*). To put it with Wittgenstein (*attrib.* [so Brink 1971: 73]): 'How on earth does A [name deleted] think he can understand Blake? Why, he doesn't even understand philosophy!'

If, as Horace says, 'it is difficult to move from the generalities of philosophy to the particularities of poetry' (*Ars Poetica* 128: *difficile est proprie communia dicere*; see Brink 1971: 204-207), if it is difficult, that is, to turn philosophical statements into poetry, it is no less difficult to move from the particularities of poetry to philosophy, or from the pages of the New Testament to dogma. But it can be said, with some show of verisimilitude, that one of the generalities of philosophy to which reading of the New Testament can lead is the incarnational idea (so Trocmé 1992), namely, that the idea of the good must necessarily be instantiated, if 'in divers modes and manners' (Heb. 1.1), in the particularities of the sensible world (what Plato should have said!), or that all *modes* of substance are *in* substance and that 'whatever is is in God' (Spinoza 1843: 197 [= *Ethica* I, *prop.* xv]).

Of course, the idea of incarnation does not occur in the New

Testament (or, for that matter, any other idea, unless by an idea you mean what is not an idea at all). And, to be precise, it finds instantiation only once, as a metaphor: 'a word is a flesh' (Jn 1.14), a word is a man, a man is a word. But, though the idea does not itself occur *expressis verbis*, but only as the propositional tenor, or purport, of a metaphorical vehicle, there are nevertheless Markan analogues of what John says: 'a man is a son' (Mk 1.11) and 'a man's lungs breathe breath' (Mk 1.10). Mark does not, of course, say it quite like that, for what he says is that *this* man Jesus was a son, *this* man Jesus was in receipt of breath. And he says this, because what he finds *there* instantiated, he finds to be paradigmatically instantiated. Jesus is a paradigm case.

But there are paradigms and paradigms, examples and examples, including some that seem to be no examples at all. But he might have said, as Paul *did* say, that 'all men are sons' ('And because you are sons...'[Gal. 4.6]). Of course, Paul qualifies: the sons are 'adopted'. But, after all, a son is a son is a son. And had Mark only connected what he says in ch. 3 ('Whoever does the will of God is...my sister [v. 35]), he could have drawn the same conclusion as Paul.

For, if it is true that sacraments only make sense in a sacramental universe (Baillie 1957: 47), the same must be true of incarnation. But these two words, 'incarnation' and 'sacrament', belonging, as they do, to the staples of the theologian's trade, are introduced here, not as explanations (*explanantia*), but as those terms that have to be explained (*explananda*). For we are arguing here in terms of what is valid *etsi deus non daretur*, 'even if there were no God' (Bonhoeffer 1971: 359),[9] in terms of 'the non-religious interpretation of religious concepts' (Bonhoeffer 1971: 344). Man come of age, mature Woman, is looking back to the childhood of the human race, to a text '[w]oven with anticks, and wild imagery' (Spenser, cit. Johnson [1805], s.v. 'antick'), but without many epithets (cf. Auerbach 1953: 9). The metaphor, 'incarnation', is either universal (universally applicable), or useless.

But the ringing tones of the τηλεφωνή (*telephone*, the 'voice-from-a-distance') of the 'more or less elderly person in a tweed suit

9. Or, more exactly: *etiamsi daremus, quod sine summo scelere dari nequit, non esse deum*, 'even if we were to grant, what we cannot grant without the greatest wickedness, that there is no God' (Grotius 1853: I, xlvi).

living somewhere out of sight overhead' (Collingwood 1924: 124) must dissuade us from our abseil on to the far side of the ridge, from this lapse into philosophy. Mark's literature awaits our literary treatment.

The Beginning

Mark, Rhapsode and Liar

But '[w]e have to understand from where we are: we cannot do anything else' (Gregor Smith 1970: 31). And where are we? In a place, where we may not only have to argue *etsi deus non daretur*, but to imagine without the givenness of God. If modern thinking, if pre-modern, modern and postmodern (and post-ancient) thinking has to be done in a secular context, then modern, pre-modern and postmodern imagination are in the same plight, or the same opportune place. (Disasters are opportunities.)

For the attempt to do theology on the basis of Holy Scripture is like the attempt to do atomic physics on the basis of Lucretius's *De rerum natura*, in whom Higgs of Edinburgh expresses (1964a, 1964b, 1966) not a particle of interest. And yet the *De rerum natura* is a great poem. *Why* is it, one asks, that Lucretius's poem is likely to survive the demise of many (but not all) scientific papers? And *why, mutatis mutandis*, is the poetry of St Mark likely to survive the demise of many (but not all) theological books? But if Lucretius does not survive as science, neither does Mark as theology, as philosophical theology, as metaphysics. Mark's survival does not make him a thinker. It is to the 'feelies', and not the 'thinkies', that Mark belongs; to *Kunst* (art), not *Wissenschaft* (science).

We moderns, then, have to imagine, to feel, to express; and have to do so 'from where we are'; and, 'from where we are', we have to re-imagine where Mark was, to re-imagine his productive imagination. And we have to do this in a place where, and at a time when the idioms of the imagination have altered and the idioms of criticism have deviated from Aristotle, 'Longinus' and Horace. There are, now, different poet-practitioners, different poets. And we find ourselves, now, where those who answer to poetry, the literary critics, are asking and answering different questions (but which ones?). The laws of the Medes and Persians do not now run. Ciceronian Jerome found the prophets 'uncultivated' (*sermo horrebat incultus*: 'their uncultivated discourse filled me with horror' (Jerome, in Migne, *Patrologia Latina*, XXII 416 [= *Epistola* XXII. 115]). And we, after Jerome, find Mark quaint, bucolic, a people's poet with his 'blue guitar'

> bent
> Over words that are life's voluble utterance
> (Stevens 1955: 188)

Mark's is not 'the layered consciousness of a consciousness engaged in recollection' (Auerbach 1953: 542, on Proust), but 'sensory appearance' (Auerbach 1953: 49). His stories are stories that 'cling to the concrete' (Auerbach 1953: 44).

And his stories come, not 'in the form of historical events' (as Gregor Smith 1970: 40); and not 'clearly not a fiction' (as Gregor Smith 1970: 40). For we are plainly not plainly dealing with a 'historical, plain' narrative (Locke 1894: I, 27), if the narrative in question is a narrative, by which 'we cannot penetrate to the historical events themselves' (so Gregor Smith 1970: 40). It is the end of the fringe of the hem of a garment that we touch, not the one garbed (Lightfoot 1935: 225; 1962: 103).

This point is important and deserves brief expansion here, while more will follow in the final chapter (Chapter 12). However, as this whole book is about this small point, this brief expansion must be seen in the context of the whole of which it is a part.

I am dissenting from Gregor Smith here, but not just dissenting from him. For I am also agreeing with him, agreeing with some of the insights that he himself has. My relation with Gregor Smith is not Antiochian (Gal. 2) and antithetical, but dialectical. It is not that he is saying that we are dealing with history and that I am saying that we are dealing with fiction; but that I am saying that we are dealing with both, as Gregor Smith himself, at times, seems to say, and, at other times, to imply.

In his essay on 'The Resurrection of Christ', Gregor Smith speaks of 'the legends and embellishments of which even the canonical Gospels are full' (1969: 133). And he goes on: 'It needs a decided effort of the historical and literary imagination to think oneself into the world-view of the original shapers of these beautiful stories' (1969: 133-34). And, then, as we shall see below, he takes up (1970: 121) 'the dominant tendency in our society...the readiness of man to live out of the future'; and goes on, there, to say: 'The new, as such, has an almost magical attraction for man.' And (was this from the 'rough drafts' [1970: 18], from which Galloway and K. Gregor Smith had to work for the production of this posthumous volume?) he then goes on to speak of 'the place of so-called science fiction' (1970: 121).

Of 'the *classical physics*', of Galileo and Newton, Collingwood declares (1942: 246): 'This theory held the field until the late nineteenth century, when small, but to a scrupulous thinker fatal, defects in it began to be recognized by every serious student.' Similar defects, in the view of increasing numbers of critics, have begun to appear in the approach to the New Testament as history. The legends of the New Testament are not minor components, which can first be separated, as oil from water, and then excised. They are rather the major part, in so far as they constitute the major Christian doctrines. Moreover, they cannot simply be treated as isolated stories, or pericopes, for they themselves belong to and derive their meaning from a larger whole, a macro-legend, a macro-story, which, by scholarly nomenclature, lives under the name of 'apocalyptic eschatology'. And this 'study of the last things' draws 'protology', 'the study of the first', also into the equation, interfusing *Endzeit*, 'end-time', with *Urzeit*, 'primal time' (Eliade 1954). In the systematic account of 'Messianism' (Schürer 1979: 514-47), the resurrection is only one component of 11 items of an endless list. And no one of these 11 can safely be treated in separation from the other 10.

But if one asks, 'But what is named by the name and what *is* "apocalyptic eschatology"?' I would myself suppose it not altogether unfair to regard it as at least an analogue of what nowadays we call 'science fiction', granted that the science of the one is Einsteinian, or post-Fermatian (Wiles 1995), and the science of the other Aristarchic, Ptolemaic or Galenian.

That all this comes with history, of course, hardly anyone would deny. Nor would hardly anyone deny that the life and death of Jesus is somehow central to the picture. But the question surely is, Yes, but how do they talk about him? And how much more do they say than that his pastness has a place? And is history best dealt with by the historian? What place does the fiction-writer have? And which of these, the historian or the poet, is stating best the matters of most moment? And if it is to be said, as it surely must be said, that reality is correlative with imagination, and fact with fiction, then it cannot be said that any one of these categories can dispense with any of these others.

But the myth, the fiction, the poetry are, to my mind, the super-ordinate constituent of the texts. Fiction is mainly how they are about that about which they are. And that about which they are is more than only history, especially if one cannot, even 'doggedly' (Johnson's word), set oneself to write a history of the future: there is no place for such a time in the historian's chronography.

Not just one mode of inquiry is in order here. But there are two further questions: first, whether one might equally speak of fictional history as historical fiction, for the former gives more weight to the history that can actually be inferred; and, second, whether any history at all can be written without fictional tools, for how historical can a historian actually succeed in being? If Mark is offering us 'not just an artist's story' (Collingwood 1925a: 13), he is not just offering us a historical narrative either. Nor is he, on the other hand, offering us both, but he is offering us *some third thing*, a τρίτον γένος (*triton genos*, a 'third kind'), that allows both literary and historical analysis. He is offering us a unity, which we must only subsequently analyse, an undifferentiated matrix, out of which both history must be carefully extracted and literature carefully criticized.

But what is this 'something'? Have we a name for such a thing? It is 'art through and through' (Collingwood 1925a: 13), an 'artist's story', if not 'just an artist's story', and is, as an artist's story, no less than history, about reality. He is offering us *ein bestimmtes Woraufhin*, an 'about what' (Bultmann 1952: 218, cit. Malevez 1958: 169). If this is true, then we need, for the interpretation of what Mark is (not historiography), not the historical-critical, but an *artistic*-critical method for the criticism of a work of art; we need a method such as the young de Wette devised. The old de Wette was 'more cautious, more academic[!], more un-revolutionary' (*vorsichtiger, akademischer, unrevolutionärer* [Smend 1958: 136]). The young de Wette might have carried through his critical project on the New Testament, though even here, at least in *Ueber Religion und Theologie* (On religion and theology' [1821: 188-90]), where he deals with the resurrection as 'fact' (*Factum*), 'occurrence' (*Begebenheit*) and 'miracle' (*Wunder*), he walks too delicately and with feline feet. But even '[o]ld men', too, 'ought to be explorers' (Eliot, 'East Coker' V [= 1944: 22]). Why run rings round Moses and leave the resurrection of Jesus more or less untouched? Why eruct more roundly on the Ascension than on the resurrection, for, as de Wette himself admits, 'actually, this miracle can nowadays hardly say anything even to the crudest mind' (*eigentlich genommen, kann dieses Wunder heut zu Tage kaum noch dem Rohesten zusagen* (de Wette 1821: 190). In his introduction to the second edition (1821: xi), de Wette speaks of 'the incisive sharpness of critical examination' (*die schneidende Schärfe der kritischen Untersuchung*). But was the first edition (1815) more Bultmannian in its candour? 'Intellectual honesty in all things...' (*Intellektuelle Redlichkeit in allen Dingen...* [Bonhoeffer 1992: 106 (= 1955: 34)])!

Mark is in the trade of 'telling lies'. But he is 'telling lies as he ought'. He is telling lies 'skilfully': 'It is Homer who has chiefly taught other poets the art of telling lies skilfully' (δεδίδαχεν δὲ μάλιστα Ὅμηρος καὶ τοὺς ἄλλους ψευδῆ λέγειν ὡς δεῖ, *dedidachen de malista Homeros kai tous allous pseude legein hos dei* [Aristotle *Po.* 1460a18-19]). Here Aristotle, Lucas tells us (Aristotle 1968: 228 [= *Po.* 1460a18-19 *ad loc.*]), 'is in direct conflict with [Plato] *Rep.* 377D where Homer is condemned because μὴ καλῶς ψεύδηται [*me kalos pseudetai*]' ('because he does not tell lies well'). The debate is a very old one. And we do not seem to be much further on. But if the Greeks, if Homer in his agora could do it and find Aristotle's approbation, why not the Semites in their souk? The Bible, surely, will do, provided we do not think about it. Where would we be without the possibility of the paralogism?

If, as Bywater tells us (Aristotle 1909: 318 [*Po.* 1460a18-19 *ad loc.*]): τὸ θαυμαστόν [*to thaumaston*, 'the marvellous', 'the miraculous'] is a truth with a πρόσθεσις ['addition'] of falsehood, and the lie artistic (ψευδῆ λέγειν ὡς δεῖ ['telling lies skilfully', 'the art of framing lies in the right way']) a falsehood with a πρόσθεσις of truth', we have two options: subtract the lie and arrive at history, or enjoy the lie and arrive at theology.

Does it not all come down to plausibility? Take the sentence of Aristotle that immediately follows: 'the poet should prefer probable impossibilities to improbable possibilities' (προαιρεῖσθαι τε δεῖ ἀδύνατα εἰκότα μᾶλλον ἢ δυνατὰ ἀπίθανα, *prohaireisthai de dei adunata eikota mallon e dunata apithana* [1460a26-27]).

What does monotheism do to the notion of plausibility? Why should it, why does it (for it can, can it not?) become plausible to 'meet the Lord in the air' (1 Thess. 4.17), so long as θεός (*theos*: God [1 Thess. 4.14]) is a co-component of the pericope? What else than monotheism makes it plausible that a man should emerge from a handful of dust? It is, after all, as the rabbis, or the daughter of one of them (Gamaliel II [*b. Sanh.* 90; cit. Bultmann 1960: 28]) held, *prima facie* implausible that a man, or a woman, should emerge from 'a drop of water' (i.e. semen). Is there any reason why a man, or a woman, should not be, or come to be, above it all, even after he, or she, has been reduced, or re-reduced, to a handful of dust? Is there any reason why something should not come of nothing, if we grant that the something we are once was not, and the all things once were not, that all things are?

Mark, then, is telling lies as an artist ought to tell them and as Mark the artist has learned to tell them, standing in the tradition in which he does, the tradition of 'the Hebrew epic' (de Wette 1807: 31), the tradition of poets and prophets, or poets and poets. His 'absurdities' (ἄλογα: *aloga* [Aristotle, *Po.* 1460a36]) are veiled by the poetic charm with which he invests them (τὸ δὲ θαυμαστὸν ἡδύ, *to de thaumaston hedu*: 'the wonderful is pleasing' [Aristotle, *Po.* 1460a17]). And he passes from the sublunary to the transmundane, from 'this side' to 'the other side' (Bultmann 1953: 10 n. 2 [= 1960: 22 n. 2) with the same 'equal foot' (*aequo pede*: Horace, *Odes* 1.4.13) with which pallid Death strikes the hovels of the poor and the palaces of kings.

Eliot's *Quartets* speak with many voices—philosophic meditation, lyric, desiccated prose. Mark neither interrupts his narrative, nor alters his style, when he indifferently passes from the bath of the Baptist on the ground to the love of God in the sky: *Yu Pikinini bilong mi. Mi laikim yu tumas. Bel bilong mi em i gutpela long yu* ('You piccanini belong me. Me liking you too much. Belly belong me him he good-fellow belong you': *Nupela* [New-fellow] *Testamen bilong Bikpela* [Big-fellow] *Jisas Kraist* [Mk 1.11]). His moves from the rational to the absurd are effortless, his transitions 'kwiktaim' (*Nupela Testamen* [Gk εὐθύς, *euthus*]).

These are 'useful' lies (*utile*: Horace, *Ars Poetica* 343).[10] The

10. Cf. Neoptolemus of Parium, *apud* Philodemus, *Poemata* v. 13.8-10,

phrase (Horace, *Ars Poetica* 334), *volunt...poetae...idonea dicere vitae*, 'the poets want to speak of matters that are apt for one's life', is instructive. Mark functions to offer the human animal an alternative government, an alternative election, another alliance. And these useful lies are 'pleasant' (*dulce*: Horace, *Ars Poetica* 343, cf. *delectare*, 'delight' [333] and *iucunda*, 'jocund' [334]). And his proper commentator is Piero in his painting of the Baptism (Lightbrown 1992: 103-17; Lavin 1981). *Ut poesis pictura*, 'painting is like poetry', one might say, reversing Horace's dictum (*Ars Poetica* 361; Brink 1971: 368-72).

There is a dialectic in all these things: the interpreter has to stand near and far, *in* the work and outside it. In a tank battle in the Ardennes an Englishman would do no less (Mackenzie *obiter dictum*). It is a dialectic of engagement and disengagement. In the silence of the university, that 'interval' between adolescence and working life (Oakeshott 1989: 101), broken now, not by 'the sound of splitting hairs', but of landing circulars, not by the sound the universe makes when being destroyed by God (ῥοιζηδόν, *rhoizedon* [2 Pet. 3.10]), but by the sound the university makes when being destroyed by Government, there should be, or there should have been, time to 'play the texts'.

Horace knew this humour, this self-deprecating distancing. And knew the necessity for the industrious application of *ars* ('art', 'technique'). But he knew also about the involvement of *ingenium*, 'genius', the ability, under the impress of the Muse, to be inside something, to be inside a work, when the work is all (Brink 1971: *passim*).

When the contemplative judgment of the reader of Mark's text, as of Piero's *Baptism*, is engaged, as Mark and Piero were engaged, anxious reaching after fact is stilled. This is what Eliot means when he says that 'you are the music / While the music lasts' ('The Dry Salvages' V [= 1944: 33]). If the reader, after the contemplative, unitive moment, is then to interpret, to move on to questions of meaning, truth and fact, he, she, must first read the work *as artist*, must first read as if the reader had been the writer, as if the admirer of the thing made had been the maker. The distinction between

cit. Brink 1971: 352; esp. ψυχαγωγία, *psuchagogia*, 'the leading of the soul'; ὠφελεῖν, *ophelein*, 'benefit'; and χρησιμολογεῖν, *chresimologein*, 'say something useful to'.

artist and audience must first be broken down. How else is one to know what it is that is being interpreted? The illusion must first be complete, before it is broken.

But sleepers wake and the illusion can, and should, be broken. For the 'oneiric' moment is only a component of a life. And we are urged by the importance of our non-reading lives to find a metaphysic, a system of thoughts to live by, to find what is 'absolutely presupposed' (Collingwood 1940), what is fundamental, to find how *this* text bears on *that* and how both bear on the world.

And *if* this text of Mark can be distinguished from, while 'overlapping' with (Collingwood 1933), historiography, *if* Mark's text really is the imaginative expression of an artist and not the critical history of a thinker, what does 'bear on' mean, when the artist is religious and the thinker is secular? What kind of move leads from the text to what the text is about? What is the relation between Mark's fiction on the one hand and fact and truth and reality on the other? Is fiction a loss? Is to call Mark fiction to bar access to reality? Or is to call it fiction no more, if no less, than to make precise the mode in which access is gained?

And how in any case do words bear on these? How do words bear on reality? What is the place of language in the economy of an animal? How does oral gesture and gesticulation relate to touch? *Tango, ergo sum*, 'I touch, therefore I am', says Macmurray (1957: 104-26 [very nearly]). Should we be touching, not speaking, nor writing, nor reading?

But the trade of the academy is words. And Mark's trade, as we know it, was words. And yet, while there are mere words, there are also words with 'tactile values' (Berenson 1952: 40-46), there are words with five-sense values. There are classical words. There are classical words, from which we can get more. There are classical words from which thought can get more, but not thought only, but imagination, too, and sense.

But there exist those to whom fiction is a loss. Is it possible to offer them something more than cold comfort? What is to be offered to the fundamentalist on the one hand and the 'cultural fundamentalist' on the other, to the devotees of fact and history, is this, that Mark has rhymed, but has rhymed with reason. And he reasons about the real. He is acting under the urgent impress of that to which he is receptive. Thus '(t)he work which is authentic and true corresponds to a necessity in the one who has created it' (Dufrenne 1973: 504). Mark has 'opened for us a unique and irreplaceable world' (Dufrenne 1973: 507). But 'It is against the real that we must finally measure the truth of the aesthetic object. In this regard, it is the content of the work that must be considered and no longer its relationship to the subject, its existential truth' (Dufrenne 1973: 507).

A Short End of the Beginning

It is likely that J. Enoch Powell will be disbelieved by half of my reader for his political and by the other half for his theological views. Nevertheless, on Gethsemane, Powell has a point. Powell is dealing with the 'central passage' of the story (Mk 14.32-42), which Mark has in common with Matthew and Luke, or they have in common with him. This 'central passage' is 'roughly as follows':

> With the injunction to watch and pray, Jesus leaves Peter and two other disciples at a certain spot and goes some distance away from them. When he returns he finds them asleep; but the narrative tells us not only what he did but what he said in the meantime. He prostrated himself in prayer, and he said, 'Father, if it is possible, let this cup pass me by; nevertheless, not what I will but what thou wilt.'
>
> Whoever first composed that central passage took great pains to make plain what sort of narrative he meant it to be. The words were uttered out of earshot of the closest disciples and in any case those disciples were by then asleep. Either trait by itself would have been sufficient to mark the intention, but both together are irresistible. Understood as history, there is no possible evidence for the crucial words of Jesus: the narrator has deliberately, and even superfluously, by the narrative itself removed the possibility of evidence. Short of the grotesque and almost blasphemous notion that on awaking the sleeping disciples, the Master said to them: 'By the way, I think I ought, for the record, to tell you what I have just said to my Father', there is no possibility of source. The narrative and its truth is not that of history; it is that of poetry, of imagination (1977: 87-88).

But what if what is true for a part is true for the parts, and if what is true for the parts is true for the whole, give or take the admixture anywhere of more history, or less history, or no history at all? If Piero's pigeon (*The Baptism*) embodies wind, and blows 'a wind of change' (πνέων τροπαίαν, *pneon tropaian* [Aeschylus, *Agamemnon* 219]), how does one best reason about the products of the imagination? How does one reach reason about the real?

Endless

But by what hook, or crook, the literary critic might here go further, it would, at the present juncture, be senseless to attempt to say. For I fear

(To a chapter without closure the
following chapters are supplements.)

A Metaphysical Poem in a Space-Fiction Setting: The Name and Nature of the Prologue of John (John 1.1-18)

'Being' and 'becoming' (Kermode 1986) are terms that appear in John's prologue. And 'sending' (Bultmann 1967: 57, cit. Ashton 1986: 7; Meeks 1972) is a term that appears there and throughout the Gospel. Then why should we not say that the term, 'metaphysical', applies equally to John as to Donne?

Kiss Jesus, the frog, and he will turn into a prince. Throw Jesus against the wall (as the Grimms's princess [1954]), and he will turn into a pauper.

In *Understanding the Fourth Gospel*, Ashton, for garrulity is the normal attitude adopted by the theologian when confronted by the ineffable, speaks of 'the fairy-tale atmosphere of the resurrection stories' (1991: 511).

All John's stories are fairy-tales?

All John is a historical novel?

The historian's 'picture must be localised in space and time. The artist's need not' (Collingwood 1946: 246). But John's 'Jerusalem' is almost a fiction. Where the reader reads 'Jerusalem', he might almost as well read 'Ephesus'. Almost, but not quite, for John's 'Jerusalem' does a double job: it plays the rôle, not only of the town, where John put pen to paper (and Ephesus, of course, is only one guess among more), but also of the place where Jesus, in point of historical fact, had something to do and something to be done to him, much as, in Scott's *Waverley* (to compare like with unlike), the Young Pretender in Edinburgh.

'Secondly', Collingwood goes on (1946: 246), 'all history must be consistent with itself'. By no stretch of the imagination (but only by a stretch of the artistic imagination—John's Palestine is plastic to John's touch) can Jesus' visits to that city in the Fourth Gospel be made consistent with his visit in Mark. Had the liturgy demanded it (as some think it did), John would have been perfectly happy to have had Jesus visit the city on all feast-days of obligation, to have him commute there weekly, daily. The consistency of Jesus' visits with anything other than the necessities of his aesthetic-religious imagination was as little troubling to him as Farewell Discourses twice: 'Arise, let us go hence, after two more chapters' (15.31).

'[P]urely imaginary worlds' (Mark's and John's!) 'cannot clash and need not agree' (Collingwood 1946: 246). John is not always even consistent with himself and has no earthly reason for being consistent with anyone else. We must allow, says Gregor Smith somewhere (but he says it differently), the Holy Spirit to get up to its tricks, to produce assertion A in one mouth and not-A in another: if discourse on infinite topics by finite subjects can never differ from nonsense but only by a little, then there may be very little to choose between saying that something is so and that it is not. Does Cusanus's *coincidentia oppositorum*, 'co-incidence of opposites', help us here?

Collingwood's final point of difference (1946: 246) is 'evidence'. But what is evident to the artist, be he religious artist, or no, may not be evidence for the historian. What kind of *historical* evidence is the journey past the aeons, those abstract nouns of Gnosticism that clamour, like stupid sentries, for the password, or the journey, by whatever route, of the *logos*? If, by saying that 'the word became flesh' (1.14), John is trying to tell us that Jesus of Nazareth was born, he is going an odd way about it.

> As works of imagination, the historian's work and the novelist's do not differ. Where they do differ is that the historian's picture is meant to be true. The novelist has a single task only: to construct a coherent picture, one that makes sense. The historian has a double task: he has both to do this, and to construct a picture of things as they really were and of events as they really happened (Collingwood 1946: 246).

Collingwood, here, is concerned with *historical* truth. Collingwood might also have said, as he does say elsewhere (1938: 286-87), that the novelist's picture is meant to be true—and that, not only in his (sc. Collingwood's) sense of the true expression of emotions that have been truly felt, but in Aristotle's sense (λέγει τὰ καθόλου, *legei ta katholou*: '[poetry tends] to express the universal' [*Po.* 1451b6-7]) of that *about which* the expression is true. But

Collingwood, here, is concerned with *historical* truth. And John, the artist, is concerned rather with the truth of the *secreta cordis*, 'the secrets of the heart', the secrets of the imagination of the heart, and goes to the heart of the matter in a different way. The heart shapes its deliverances differently. The two callings differ, not *toto caelo* and *tota terra*, but in that, in what is a mixed form, a form that is both 'historical' *and* a 'novel', the historian differs from the historical novelist, in that the freedom from what actually happened is greater in the case of the second than in the first.

The difficulty of supposing that Mark is a historical novel lies partly in the fact that the part played by Jesus of Nazareth in Mark's work is less minor than the part played by the Young Pretender in *Waverley*. The objection to a comparison of the Gospel of John with the Good News, or the Good News In Parts, of a character who wavers between Highlands and Lowlands, Scotland and England, is in some measure countered by the fact that, while the hero of John plays a major part, not even a minor part, if the critics are right, is played by *what Jesus actually said in history, said as a matter of historical fact*. And how many of the minor parts, Nicodemus, say, are fictional constructs, mere opportunities for Jesus to say what he did not?

John plagiarizes, of course, from earlier writers, or tellers of tales, and replicates many of the *thaumasta* (θαυμαστά, *thaumasta*: 'elements of surprise' [Aristotle, *Po.* 1452a4, etc.]), that are found there, though it seems that his interest does not lie there ('blessed are they who have not seen...' [Jn 20.29]). His heart is not in them. For he hurries over them with almost Markan terseness just as he hurries over others of his own that other writers did not have (e.g. the Marriage of Cana!). But something else is shining through the *haar*, which does not perhaps deserve the name of *dianoia* (διάνοια, *dianoia*: 'thought' [Aristotle, *Po.* 1450a10; Ashton 1994: 168]), which should perhaps be reserved for the rather more intellectual, almost intellectualist, exchanges in Greek tragedy, between, say, the 'ninefold parechesis', or 'succession of similar sounds' (see Sophocles, *Oedipus Tyrannus* 371, Jebb *ad loc.*) of seeing Oedipus, who does not see, and the blinded ears of unseeing Teiresias, 'old man with wrinkled dugs' (Eliot, 'The Waste Land' III [= 1936: 69]), who does: τυφλὸς τά τ᾽ ὦτα τόν τε νοῦν τά τ᾽ ὄμματ᾽ εἶ, *tuphlos ta t'ota ton te noun ta t'ommat' ei*. It is rather φαντασία (*phantasia*:

'imagination') we have to do with here.
The religious community is

> founded and confirmed by the symbolic structure of sacred
> memorial and usage (*gestiftet und festgehalten durch die Symbolik
> heiliger Denkmäler und Gebräuche)*... About this sacred centre
> there is then, too, described a circle of free poesy (*Dichtung*), in
> that the imagination (*Phantasie*), supported by sacred teaching and
> a system of symbols (*Symbolik*), in the service partly of dreaming
> [oneiric?] curiosity (*im Dienste träumender Wissbegierde*), and
> partly of the sense of beauty (*Schönheitssinnes*), sets forth pictures
> of eternity it has itself constructed (selbstgeschaffene [*sic*] *Bilder
> des Ewigen... aufstellt*) and gladly goes on to transform original
> symbols into historical sagas (*und daher gern ursprüngliche Sym-
> bole in Geschichtssagen verwandelt*). We call this *Mythology*, and
> distinguish it as the free play of poetic creativity (*freies Spiel der
> Dichtung*) from the symbolism which is the object of worship' (de
> Wette 1830: 24).

By happy coincidence for an 'intelligible' circle, of which 'the circumference is nowhere and the centre everywhere' (*sphaera intel-
ligibilis, cujus centrum est ubique, & circumferentia nusquam*
[Bonaventura CIƆIƆ·CC·LIV: 354]), the word for 'point' in Euclid
(1955 *ad init.*, cf. M.CCCC.LXXX.II *ad init.*) and so for centre and
centre point (σημεῖον, *semeion*)[1] coincides with the word for
'sign' in John [*passim*]).

If John's work is thought, what is John thinking, when he thinks
it? Is he not just being open to what was once called 'openings'?

And yet John is sufficiently distinct from the Synoptists to
prompt Renan to speak, fastidiously, of *ces leçons de méta-
physique abstraite* (these lessons of abstract metaphysics [n.d.:
LXII]). But one has to rejoin, that, whatever his differences from
the Synoptists, John is different again from the metaphysics of Aristotle, and Plato in his less, and even in his more, mythological
moments, for Plato's stories, his myths, are more transparent to the
philosophy that underlies them than the Johannine.

The prologue, capitalized or not, is best, I think, taken as a
Hebrew poem, the parallel clauses sometimes, moreover, being
marked by the rudimentary device, whereby the last noun of one

---

1.   σημεῖόν ἐστιν, οὗ μέρος οὐθέν, *semeion estin, hou meros outhen*
(Euclid 1955); cf.: *Punctus est cuius p̄s n̄o est* (Euclid M.CCCC.LXXX.II), 'a
point is that of which there is no part/that which is indivisible'.

clausula becomes the first in the next, and so on. 'Step-parallelism' is a term used of the phenomenon. And the central image, *logos*, is the image of dialogue (Woods 1958: 173-84): A says B to C about D. It is the image of dialogue, or speech, or expression in language. The whole might be mistaken for a philosophic meditation, as a poet might bring it off, but should nevertheless be distinguished from what Eliot undertakes, at the beginning of 'Burnt Norton', say, for Eliot had done his apprenticeship on Bradley (Eliot: 1964) and had had, prior to Burnt Norton, some acquaintance (I put it no higher) with the *Posterior Analytics* of Aristotle (Eliot 1960: 10; 1964: 9).

What is it, one might ask, for a poet to write poetry who has read some philosophy? And what, speaking generally, is the relation between emotion and thought in such poetry? Dante, says Colling-wood (1938: 295), is writing poetry, not philosophy, but is expressing the *emotional* 'charge' of *thinking* in a certain way; is finding language to *express the emotions* of a poet who is living within the system of Aquinas.

But the Hebrews, before Spinoza (Maimonides?), *had* no philosophy. Just sophy, 'wisdom'. What Hebrew scientists call *hokh-mah*. And there is a great deal of difference between saying,

> A continual dropping in a very rainy day
>   and a contentious man are alike (Prov. 27.15).

or

> Better is a dish of herbs, where love is,
>   than a stalled ox and hatred therewith (Prov. 15.17).

and saying,

> without sense-impressions no one could learn or understand any-thing, and in scientific thinking one must with one's thoughts contemplete [*sic*] images (phantasmata).
>   (Aristotle, *de Anima* 432a8-9, cit. Guthrie 1981: 312)[2]

It is Philo, who, among the Hebrews, perhaps approximates to the disinterested spectator of time and eternity, but still has his

2.   Or (more exactly), with Hicks 1907: 144-45 (?): ἀνάγκη ἅμα φαντάσματι θεωρεῖν· τὰ γὰρ φαντάσματα ὥσπερ αἰσθήματα ἐστι..., *anangke hama phan-tasmati theorein; ta gar phantasmata hosper aisthemata esti...*: 'when he is actually thinking he must have an image before him. For [Aristotle goes on] mental images are like present sensations...'

plaid very much twisted in 'what people say'. For his is a mixed *oeuvre*, an uneasy conflation of Greek philosophy and Hebrew poetry (much as Bultmann mixes mythology and existentialism). John's natural symbols of 'light' and 'darkness' remain implicated in the natural phenomena from which they arise; 'truth' and the 'lie' anchored in the fidelity and betrayal of persons.

But the Prologue *is* a theistic poem. The image of dialogue is intended to say something about how a single, infinite object is related to, at least temporarily, finite persons. And post-Machiavellian exegesis (Bonhoeffer 1971: 359) must do something here, at the very least by drawing out some of the anthropological implications of theistic utterance, such as, for example, that people are 'not fated, but destined' (Gregor Smith *obiter dictum*), however much appearances may counter this reading. But philosophy is as little John's *forte*, as mathematics, or the organization of the animal kingdom into phylums, orders, classes and families.

Nor is it history. Gone for a Burton is Bethlehem—except on the lips of the ubiquitous ὄχλος (7.42 [*ochlos*: 'crowd']). And the whole terminates in 'the fairy-tale atmosphere' of the resurrection. Thucydides, Conzelmann and Morgan are to seek; von Ranke quite out of sight.

By the whole, however, is implied a neat metaphysic, pure and undiluted by all but the 'water of life'. But *what* is it that implies it? In what *form* is truth or supposition being conveyed? A poem? A historical novel? A historical novel with 'sci-fi' components? A phantasy, even (Aichele 1992)? What is quite clear is the unitary nature of the direction, in which the author steers between the rocks of history and philosophy, *measuring* by the stars, like Oedipus, his distance from home (*Oedipus Tyrannus* 795: ἐκμετρού- μενος *ekmetroumenos*)—it was, for Oedipus, for Swellfoot the Tyrant, the wrong home. John goes about and about, of course, 'in a style that is distinctive to the point of monotony' (Ashton 1986a: 16), but makes, in Yeats's phrase (1950: 210), no 'widening gyre'. For he is going about a point. This falcon hears the falconer. All the time, with all the resources at his command—'light', 'truth', 'life', he is homing in on the nature of 'the man' (19.5). He cannot do this without metaphysics, the metaphysics, not of the philosopher, but of the artist. He cannot do this without implicit metaphysics. John has central concerns. His movement is centripetal.

Supposing then that the object by which we are confronted, the prologue, is neither a historical, nor a philosophical one, what are we to do with it? If historical criticism is instructive chiefly for its irrelevance, except in so far as it highlights the local idioms of the artist, his parochial place, what are the right questions to ask? If philosophy is present in the text only as embedded and embodied, is the proper task to disengage it? And if philosophy, why not history also? Is history, too, not embodied, in the enfleshed 'word' of 1.14: the word became a man, so was one? Why not disengage history also, use *Macbeth*, so to speak, as a historical source (Adam 1957)?

Jesus of Nazareth was articulate and John is articulate about him, but not sufficiently interested in what Jesus articulated to tell us what this was. John had other interests than *ipsissima verba*. For John has given us his estimate, an estimate that takes the shape of what is being estimated. The Johannine estimate takes the form of a story about Jesus. Jesus lives, yet not Jesus, but John lives in him. The mouth of Jesus is inhabited by the words of John. The hero is evaluated and the hero evaluates—himself. The mouth is the mouth of Jesus, but the words are the words of John. Or, in the prologue, it is 'we' that evaluate. It is not John only, but John and his conventicle that evaluate: 'We have seen..., *we* can give a reading of the given—of the *data*, of the *danda*, of what ought to be given and is being given, because it ought to be. ' "History" (or History) is now and Ephesus.' And it is an estimate that the reader is invited to share.

John, as a poet (Kermode 1986), is exploring history (just) and metaphysics (more than just a little). He is less exploring history than the conditions that make history possible. And it is that the world is that makes history possible. All the world's a stage and you cannot act if you do not have a stage to act on (von Balthasar 1988). But John is doing this 'as a poet'. He is offering secondary reflections on a story (Genesis). But it is not so much reflection as allusion. He makes explicit what is implicit, or what can be taken to be implicit, in Mark's 'beginning' (Mk 1.1). And the history that is made possible, by the fact (asserted by a fiction [Gen. 1]) that the world is, is a poet's history: 'A man is a word', is as good as his word, no, he is one.

'A man is a word'? He is nothing of the kind. Only provided that he is not a Scotsman, and so not taciturn, but tacit, a man is a speaker, rather. But this speaker (Jesus) is seen as a word spoken. But by whom? For this man is someone else's word, is *God's word*?

But is God a speaker, if and only if he is not, as for Xenophanes, a Scots god (Clement, *Strom.* 7.22.1)?[3] God is nothing of the kind—as little, one might point out to Mark, as a pigeon fancier, sending an aleatory bird (Mk 1.10), but God does not throw dice. But what of a *poet's* God? What are the proper parameters of a poet's God? What are the restrictions, the liberties here? If Aphrodite allows Euripides in the *Hippolytus* to write an essay on sexuality (Collingwood 1940: 207-10), the lips, teeth and tongue of Jehovah can do the same, if one is setting out to write variations on a Hebrew theme, the theme of God as speaker. And this theme allows John to write an essay that sheds light on life and liberty. But how does poetry arise? And what is the origin of language? And what is the origin of language about life and liberty? If, that is to say, what Euripides says about Aphrodite in the *Hippolytus* is non-vacuous, if it is sense and not nonsense, there is equally no reason for holding the view, that the *sense* of the word 'word' in John and the *sense* of the words, 'lips, teeth and tongue', there implied, are senses that have no *reference*. Poetry, in a word, is rooted in ontology. And is here rooted in a history that the author is not much inclined to narrate.

The frequency of the word 'word' in Lutheran Protestantism is no less mysterious than its frequency in the prologue of the Fourth Gospel. The mystery is caused, in part, by the fact that the 'word' comes there *without* lips, teeth and tongue. But a word can be spoken without lips, teeth and tongue as little as a walk can be taken in a garden without thighs, calves and feet (Gen. 3.8). Further, ἐσκήνωσεν, *eskenosen*, 'made his wonnin amang' (Lorimer 1983: 159 Jn 1.14 *ad loc.*), 'pitched his tent', comes as much

---

3.   Diels (1906: 168) *Fragment* 168 ('Scots' is curiously missing from this text):

Αἰθίοπές τε <θεοὺς σφετέρους> σιμοὺς μέλανας τε
Θρῆκές τε γλαυκοὺς καὶ πυρροὺς <φασι πέλεσθαι>.

['The Ethiopians say that their gods are snub-nosed and black, the Thracians that theirs have light blue eyes and red hair'] (trans. Kirk, Raven and Schofeld 1983: 169).

without the tent pegs as the 'alien' (Meeks 1972), despatched by the Despatcher on his *good* errand (unlike Milton's Satan on his 'bad' one), arrives from outer space without any indication of the route by which the arrival comes about. The reader just has to make something of these. If John is 'fraught with background' (Auerbach 1953: 12), the freight has to be unloaded. And if it cannot, its absence has to be explained.

Some people some of the time become sufficiently impressed by something to say it. If what John means by *theos* is 'incomprehensible', but is what must be supposed, if anything is going to be comprehended by anyone; and if what John means by *theos* is supposed by John to be 'apprehensible' (von Hügel), by his following out the hints and guesses, the implications of what he is supposing, then it should not be cause of wonder that he should have recourse to models and metaphors for the expression of the complexity, and simplicity, of what is so apprehended, though not comprehended. But these implications are not the logical implications of a supposal, but its poetic expression. What, I think, remains, perhaps *must* remain, unclear is whether, if anything is being apprehended at all, what is being poetically expressed is the supposal itself, or its implications.

John is expressing the feeling of having something to say and Jesus of Nazareth is the one about whom he is saying it. And he is saying here, not that Jesus was a speaker (though he was), but that he was spoken, like a text to be read, a situation to be 'read', or a statement to be interpreted. This may be an odd thing to say, and '[s]imple-minded modern readers can hardly restrain their indignation' (Collingwood 1940: 209), but is no odder, if no less odd, than a metaphor, which it is, if humans, literally, are not spoken, but speak, if they are spoken to and, if not, remain silent. It should be remarked that there may be an admonition here to those whose books should never have had a beginning.

But for John the case is this, that his 'belly is as wine which hath no vent; it is ready to burst like new bottles' (Job 32.19, cit. Hamann 1950: 196). What form, for John, does that, which is exploded, take? Hamann (in Gregor Smith 1960: 196) goes on:

> Poetry is the mother-tongue of the human race, as the garden is older than the field, painting than writing, song than declamation, parables than inferences, [*] barter than commerce. The rest of our

forebears was a deeper sleep; and their movement was a tumultuous dance. Seven days they sat in the silence of reflection or astonishment; and opened their mouths to utter winged words. Senses and passions speak and understand nothing but images. The whole treasure of human knowledge and happiness consists of nothing but images. The first outburst of creation, and the first impression of its historian, the first appearance and the first enjoyment of nature, are united in the words, Let there be light. Herewith begins the experience of the presence of things. [**]

[*] 'As hieroglyphics are older than letters, so parables are older than arguments,' says Bacon, my Euthyphro.

[**] 'Anything that becomes visible is light,' Eph. 5.13.

When John's belly bursts, what bursts from it takes the form of poetry. Like Socrates, prompted by 'the horses of Euthyphro' (sc. Euthyphro's inspiration: Plato, *Cratylus* 396d, 407d, cit. Hamann 1950: 197), and like Hamann prompted by Bacon, John seizes

a prey of divers colours,
   a prey of divers colours of needlework,
      of divers colours of needlework on both sides,
         meet for the necks of them that take the spoil (Judg. 5.30).

and seems to be 'quite like a prophet newly inspired, and to be uttering oracles' (χρησμῳδεῖ, *chresmo(i)dei*: Plato, *Cratylus* 396d, 407d, cit. Hamann 1950: 197). But if Mark's 'horses', his inspiration, make Mark breathless, John's amble at leisure. Their pace is not *kwiktaim* and *ventre-à-terre*, but measured. The 'becoming', the genesis, of the Baptist and Jesus are contrasted with and counterposed, not to ontology, the '*study of* being' (and so philosophy), but to 'being', for example, the being of the word (cf. Kermode 1986: 3-16): the 'word was', while John and Jesus 'came to be' ('became').

The origin of language is to be sought in the poesy of God, as 'makar' ('poet' [Scots]) and maker (creator). Creation and creativity are cognate terms. You can make a universe, or a poem and both may be described as creative acts. And John's language of being, or at least his use of the verb 'to be', introduces an atmosphere of timelessness as a pendant to his temporal narrative, his fragments, here in the prologue, of narrative. It is not that nothing happens, but that there are timeless conditions for the happening of anything.

And the condition of becoming conscious of anything happening is itself timeless, if '[t]o be conscious is not to be in time' (Eliot 1944: 10), even if the language, in which timelessness finds expression, is conditioned by time, so as to be changing over time: John's and Eliot's idioms differ. It is all language as gesture, perhaps, in this case, the language of *ritual* gesture, regular gesture, gesture frozen into fixed form, with all the mobile immobility of the sculpted figures of the Phigaleian Frieze: the still, by *Gestalt*, becomes the moving picture.

The author is not undertaking a conceptual analysis. He is offering prosopopoeia (Lowth 1821: 120-28 [= 1847: 143-52]), 'personification', the *curriculum vitae* of an abstract noun, a *curriculum vitae* that is replicated by the life of the hero. And this hero is the protagonist, who does not come into his own with his own (Jn 1.11). But this is not the end of the story.

One of the recurring questions here in this essay is how a historical-critical should differ from a literary-critical method. Hamann's *Aesthetica in nuce* has as subtitle, '*A Rhapsody in Cabbalistic Prose*'. And the occasion and the butt of this particular crusade of Hamann were the Enlightenment methods of Johann David Michaelis (1717-91). For Michaelis, in his *Beurtheilung der Mittel, welche man anwendet, die ausgestorbene Hebräische Sprache zu verstehen* (Evaluation of the means, which are applied in the understanding of the extinct Hebrew language [1757: 88]):

> The Jews attribute to the Hebrew language a special sanctity and an entirely divine origin, that extends as far as all the minuscule characteristics of the letters, in which the Kabbalist even searches for a multitude of vain secrets. They reckon among the divine prerogatives of these, that they express the essence of things: these propositions being repeated by a whole troop of credulous Christians.

But is it altogether so easy to discriminate sense from nonsense in texts of this kind? And is it easy to do so in *this* text (John), of whatever kind soever it is, particularly when the text is dealing with the sort of fundamental matters that are metaphysics, but are here metaphysics in the form of poetry? If the text itself, being a poetic text, is already an *umbra*, what kind of clarity and distinctness can be expected, where the *pen*umbra is in question? If sense has to be discriminated from nonsense, nonsense has, in its turn, to be discriminated from the kind of 'super-sense', in which the supersensible must find expression.

If the mythology is the thing itself, if 'this mythology...is the thing itself' (Bonhoeffer 1971: 329), if fiction, poetry, story is 'the thing itself', what kind of study is appropriate to the thing itself and in what terms are the results of that study, post-Machiavellian, post-Spinozist, to be expressed? Are there terms for the expression of a sense of *scripta*, or *scriptura*, that is at the same time mystical and modern? How did John get away with it and what was it, with which he got away?

The Johannine philologist, John, the lover of the word, is the author of a would-be metaphysical poem, makes use of would-be *concetti metafisici ed ideali*, 'metaphysical and ideal conceits' (Testi [no ref.], cit. Grierson 1921: xv), makes use of *theos* and *aletheia*, of 'God' and 'truth'. Would-be and will-be, for Aristotle, refracted by Aquinas, has entered into Donne, but has not yet entered, but will enter, *via* criticism and the critic, into John. Jesus is just John's 'necessary angel' (Ashton 1994: 71-89; Stevens 1960), not necessary in Stevens's sense, as 'the imagination that redeems the earth' (Kermode 1960: 85), 'the necessary angel of earth' (Stevens 1955: 496), but in Ashton's sense, as necessary to explain the inability of the fourth Evangelist to make up his mind on what rung of the ladder to suspend his hero: the trouble with John is that he thought Jesus was an angel and about angels it is easy to hum and haw, as being not easily to be disambiguated entities.

John, then, is the author of a metaphysical poem, unlike Donne, in that he did not have the benefit of access to 'the things after the physics', but like Donne, in that he was a poet; and no less sophisticated, if sophisticated in a different way. And, if Stevens is right in *The Necessary Angel*, that '[t]he major poetic idea in the world is and always has been the idea of God' (Stevens 1959: xv, cit. Morse 1958) then, as things now stand, cruciform, acantho-cephalous, in a time in which the charioteer of Plato's *Phaedrus* remains only as 'the emblem of a mythology, the rustic memorial of a belief in the soul' (Stevens 1960: 4, cit. Kermode 1960: 86), the angel of the imagination is necessary, if the poet is to fulfil his function 'to make his imagination become the light in the minds of others. His role, in short, is to help people to live their lives'

(Stevens 1960: 29, cit. Kermode 1960: 87). 'He…gives to life the supreme fictions without which we should be unable to conceive it' (Stevens 1960: vii, cit. Kermode 1960: 87). The cruciformity of John's imagination is implied in 1.10-11 ('knew him not…received him not') and will be explicated later in the body of the book.

Thus a metaphysical poem, the prologue, precedes a historical novel. A supreme fiction of one kind precedes another of another.

But someone will say that John is not forming fictions, but stating facts, that the universe had a beginning in time and the Christian movement a beginning in history; that the movement had its antecedents and its *diadochi*, its torch-bearers, that set alight more heather. Thus we have natural science (astronomy) and history, the facts about Jesus of Nazareth. And we have a statement of the causes, or the Cause, of both, reached by a process of inference from observation and evidence, inferred from Betelgeuse and corroborated by Josephus. Moses was an eminent man, Jesus more eminent still. And operating in a field, that, while cognate with law, is not identical with it, for 'grace' (the term used) is what comes into play, when law is to be obeyed, or when law has broken down. Give or take undoubted poetic form, the content is fact. The objection, that a cause does not have a 'bosom', where the cause is God, may be answered by saying that metaphor is a familiar device and that this metaphor is asserting that the cause of nature and history, the cause of movement in both spheres, was in this case, an uncommon one, not resisted. Jesus of Nazareth was obedient to the voice of his calling. If Aristotle was right to say (but is he?), that '[e]verything said metaphorically is unclear' (Aristotle, *Topics* 139b34, cit. Guthrie 1981: xvi), it still remains true that something, even some things, can be clarified by analysis. And Collingwood's *Religion and Philosophy* (1916) is one such attempt.

The content is fact, the facts of cosmogony and history. But no attempt is being made here to deny that these are facts. All that is being claimed is that these are facts that are not being stated. If these facts come, as come they do, they come in the form of fictions: 'The whole treasure of human knowledge and happiness consists of nothing but images' (Hamann, trans. Gregor Smith, 1960: 196). Jesus has only one father in the prologue, a father not historical (Joseph), but metaphorical (God). The word 'bosom' is non-isolable, is not the only metaphor, is not unaccompanied. It comes with the person, whose bosom it is, in a textual sequence 'saprophytic' (Collingwood's word [1927b: 6]) with anthropomorphism.

It is true that the text does not say either that the world was made, or that a garden was made in it, or that fig-trees were made in the garden. It speaks more baldly of genesis, of 'what came to be' (Jn 1.3). But speech is implied by the word 'word', which in turn implies 'tongue', which in turn implies 'hand', the hand of the maker of 'what came to be'. But the deforestation of a luxuriant undergrowth of metaphor, if John and *tanak* are compared, may be significant. 'The mother-tongue of the human race', it seems, is on the move from lisping infancy, to P from J, to Jn from P, and from Jn... The smile has lost the cat, but the smile is the smile of a cat.

The question remains, that is, whether poetic form does not betray the presence of poetry, the poetry, certainly, of embodied philosophy and metaphysics, for the philosophical reader at any rate, and of embodied history for the historical reader at any rate. But the poetry is the poetry of a writer, who was neither, nor trying to be. John was neither philosopher, nor historian. 'The symbol gives rise to thought' (Ricoeur 1969: 347), but is not thought. The symbol is thought inchoate in feeling. For 'man is defined by his senses and passions, not by his thought. Accordingly his whole mental and spiritual possession is constituted by pictures...' (Lumpp 1970: 51).

To Bacon's partition of the human sciences into '*Historiam, Poesim, Philosophiam*' there correspond three faculties of the intellect, '*Memoriam, Phantasiam, Rationem*' (Bacon 1858: I, 423-837, cit. Lumpp 1970: 58 n. 43). It is *Phantasia*, 'imagination', that is relevant to the argument here, and the feeling of which imagination is the expression (Benedetto Croce [1922, 1927] lies behind Collingwood [1938]). John, Michaelis might have said, as he did of Jotham in Judg. 9.7-15, is *prisci et horridi dicendi moris tenax* ('tenacious of a mode of speaking that is ancient and uncouth' [Michaelis, in Lowth 1758: XXXII, cit. Lumpp 1970: 53]). But we cannot get by without either stories, or poems. Why should we try to? We must tease them into thought, but why should we tease them away? No doubt, we should treat them with caution, but why should we expel them from the city? But even John's prologue, as among 'hymns to the gods and praises of famous men' (Plato, *Republic* 607a), would have got by with Plato. And if Plato could be satisfied here, then why not us? 'I am a worm and no man', says the Psalmist (22.7, cit. Hamann 1952: 38, cit. Lumpp 1970: 55),[4] which is no less true, because he is not.

High-nosed contempt for art is a legacy of the Enlightenment, that we need not share. Why be ashamed of a narrative sky (*caeli enarrant...*: 'The heavens are telling...': Ps. 19.1)? Why be ashamed of an enarrative sky (Murray 1888–1933, s.v.), a sky that is capable, not of telling only, but of 'showing' (Funk 1988: 134-61)? Of the unenlightened attitude to the documents, of whatsoever sort they are, of the Enlightenment historians and their modern (postmodern?) successors, the best that may be said (as Ducasse of his theory of art [cit. Collingwood 1931: 386]: *citius emergit veritas ex errore quam ex confusione*: 'truth emerges more speedily from error than from confusion'). To ask the wrong question and to show that it is the wrong question is to progress, if to progress slowly.

The New Testament, it was said above, is reticent about incarnation. Indeed, the word itself, or what the word itself is after, appears only once, if the thing itself more often. And it appears here in the prologue. And we have it *in nuce*, 'in a nutshell'. And what appears is something better than 'incarnation'; something less abstract, more concrete; more Hebrew, less—no, more Greek: 'became flesh'.

Language is what people get up to, but they get up to other things as well. If Spinoza is right, reality has (at least) two aspects: the mental and the bodily. We are dealing not with '*psycho-physical parallelism*' (Collingwood 1942: 8 [*sic*]), but with one thing, which has two aspects. What John is saying and, with John, Manilius (*Astronomicon* 4.895, cit. Hamann 1950: 198)[5] is this:

Each man is an example of God in a small image.

The prologue of John is a poem, that embodies, incarnates, sc.

4.   The Psalm is cited in connection with Hamann's debate with Lessing: at what point, or points, is Enlightenment rationality open to criticism?

5.   *Exemplum*que D E I quisque est in *imagine parva*.
This line of Manilius appears in Hamann's, not Housman's (1920: 121) heterography—the spacing, the capitals, the italics.

gives form and content to, the assertion that there was a man, once, who not only came both before and after the man, who came before him, but also incarnated, sc. gave form (one-liners and short stories, or [so John] many lines) and content (his actions and his thoughts were of a piece) to the assertion that there is that, than which nothing greater can be thought. John, that is, is writing a poem about a poet, who was also a man of action. He was as good as his word. He embodied his images. He expressed in action what he expressed in language. Or, insofar as language is itself already a form of action, he expressed himself also non-linguistically, by touch, for instance, and by gesture.

'Incarnation', in a word, can be understood as an aesthetic concept, but that in a context where aesthetics are related to ethics and both to ontology, with logic thrown in for full measure. John's assertion is aesthetic, for to assert, that 'a man is a word', is not more prosaic than the assertion, that it is raining cats and dogs, thus inviting quodlibetal questions into *genera* and *species*.

'Speak', says Hamann (trans. Gregor Smith 1960: 197; Lumpp 1970: 55 n. 30), 'that I may see thee'. But what if the speech is the speech of God? If the world, if narrative sky, narrative earth, narrating humans—if all these, if the universe is the poetic speech of its poet, its maker, so too, as man in the world, this poet, or *makar*: Jesus.

But if the name of John, too, is 'poet', if 'poet' is properly what he should be called, and if the nature of what he is writing is a poem, then it cannot be interpreted as prose, nor he prosaically. Would the difference between John's prologue and prose be better prehended and appreciated by reversing the initial proposition and saying,

> In the beginning was the body...

and by continuing,

> And the body became word
> and pitched its tent...?

Tents, after all, are pitched more easily by bodies than by words (though I have known sergeant-majors in my time, who would have disagreed). The subtitle of Hamann's *Aesthetica in nuce* is *A Rhapsody in Cabbalistic Prose*. Thus thing, on the one hand, and adequation of the intellect to the thing, on the other, would be better matched by a rhapsody than by a commentary.

But if a poem is not thought, but feeling, if a poem is not thought, but that which 'gives rise to thought' (Ricoeur 1969: 347-57), is the commmentator not bound to give an account of that thought to which the poem gives rise? No doubt, a poem can give rise to poems. The hymn books, the song books, the bad poem books, 'the traditional low-brow arts of the upper classes' (Collingwood 1938: 72), are full of them. But the task of the critic is different.

But what is the name and nature of the critic? 'A bee who buzzes in a corner' (γωνιοβόμβυξ, *goniobombux* [Capper's word])? The Greeks have words for many things. But what is named by *goniobombux* is not 'critic', but 'grammarian'. Crates of Mallus, however, has *kritikos* and the 'distinguished but over-heated mind' of Longinus (Brink 1971: 76) comes up with *logon krisis*, when in *On the Sublime* (6.1) he says that 'literary judgement [λόγων κρίσις] comes only as the final product of long experience'. Only grey hair is consonant with wisdom.

The literary critic is one, who responds with words to words, responds with words to a poetic *corpus*, to the *corpus* of the poet. But the words of poets are the words of speakers, or writers. And speakers and writers are persons. And persons speak and write, some of them, about other persons. And persons, some of them, are embodied. And even critics, a few of them, are embodied, too. If language is 'gesture' (Blackmur 1954: 3-24), the gestures are the gestures of bodies. The gestures are the gestures of actors. *Am Anfang war die Tat* ('In the beginning was the act': Goethe, *Faust* 1: 883, cit. Dodd 1953 *ad init.*).

But what if persons are disturbed in a disturbed world and can produce only what Hamann called *Turbatverse*, 'a confusion of verses' (trans. Gregor Smith 1960: 197). But just suppose that there came to be an *undisturbed* person in a disturbed world. With that person in mind, what could not a body do then? What could not the body of a poet do then? And would not an undisturbed person go on to create a nuisance and disturb the peace, the peace of those who are at war with themselves and with everyone and everything else—*homo homini lupus* (man is a wolf to man)?

Is not Mark's 'myth of innocence' (Mack 1988) mythically true? Is not John's fiction fictionally true? Is it not metaphorically and fictionally true that 'the word become flesh' (God n.d., cit. Jn 1.14). And with this word the Great Authour laid down his pen, not made with reed, *and has done nothing since. Floruit et tacuit* ('he flourished and became silent' [Eliot 1960 *ad init.*]).

John's pictures, like Hamann's, 'themselves contain the hidden truth, which he declares not otherwise than in them' (Lumpp 1970: 58). To do otherwise is to be other than wise. For what is to be said of the attempt to translate poetry into prose? 'This kind of translation [Hamann 1960: 198] is, more than any other, like the underside of a carpet,

And shews the stuff, but not the workman's skill

or like an eclipse of the sun, which can be seen in a bowl of water.[*]'

And Hamann adds, in a footnote:

[*] The one metaphor is borrowed from the Earl of Roscommon's *Essay on translated verse*; the other from one of the leading weeklies (*The Adventurer*): there, however, they are used *ad illustrationem* (as ornaments of the dress); here *ad involucrum* ['as a covering'] (as a shirt on the naked body), a distinction taught by Euthyphro's Muse.

For something to appear *in* a picture is, no doubt, what Bonhoeffer meant by 'the mythology...is the thing itself' (1971: 329). But the *critic's* job, presumably, is to say, or to attempt to say, what it is that appears there. But can the critic succeed in what the critic attempts? Or can criticism be no better than the inversion of a carpet, or the substitution of a reflection for the sun in glory, passing through shadow from glory to glory, or the preferring of drapery to the nudity it clothes. Criticism can only be a very modest trade.

Many of the above reflections in this chapter have been concerned with the distinction between literary criticism and historical criticism, with the interpretation of poetry as distinct from the interpretation of prose, with the language of emotion as distinct from the language of thought, with cognitive emotion as distinction from cognition *tout court*.

It is suggested that there is an alternative to historiography and that that alternative is the alternative that John has chosen, an alternative, 'not between, but of':

He had to choose. But it was not a choice
Between excluding things. It was not a choice
Between but of

(Stevens 1955: 403)

And these reflections have been undertaken in a secular age, an age of 'secularity', or 'radical secularism' (Gregor Smith 1966: 172). But what is to be interpreted, the prologue of John and the whole of what that prologue introduces, was done, was *made* (*poiesis!*), was formed and fashioned in a sacred age, when 'all things' had been, not as for Thales 'full of gods' (Aristotle, *de Anima* 411a7 [= Diels 1906: 91]), but full of God. It was an age, not of polytheistic (and so pluralistic), but of monotheistic science, sc. *scientia*, sc. systematic knowledge of whatever kind (Collingwood 1940: 201-27). What, in particular, is to be interpreted is the prologue of John, in the conviction that what holds for part of John's text will be found for the most part to hold for the whole.

It has been supposed, above, that Hamann's *Aesthetica in nuce* is attuned to these questions, but that his dark sayings may become brighter with the assistance of ancient literary criticism on the one hand (Aristotle, Horace, 'Longinus') and modern literary criticism on the other (Kermode, Blackmur, Crane, Gardner), the great gulf fixed between poetry and prose, and poetry and criticism, being paradigmatically bridged by such poet-practitioners of criticism as Eliot and Horace and, in a measure, Stevens, whose poetry, prose and aphorisms alike have the supposititious correlation of imagination with reality as an explicit theme.

And the key of the door, in this chapter and elsewhere throughout, is not 'myth', but 'fiction'. And the question being considered is, not how fiction functions, but *what it is* that has this function, if, and only if, fiction has a meaning that is wider than Heliodorus (1935-60) and Barbara Cartland (1982 and *passim*) and is the synonym of poetics, or poetry.

And the questions and queries of this particular chapter are only as eccentric as Ashton (1986a, 1986b, 1991, 1994) and Meeks (1972) and, of course, the darkened and darkening abstrusities of Bultmann (1950 [= c. 1971]), author of the only worthwhile commentary for the thinking man, or pensive woman, of the present era. But Bultmann is difficult, because he makes himself doubly obscure by the opaque qualities of Martin Heidegger. For what are the rules by which Bultmann translates the landing and levitation of the alien from elsewhere into the non-German (1927), or non-English (1962) of Heidegger's *Being and Time* on the one side and Martin Luther and others of that clan on the other.

It is *not* claimed here either that the question is barred, that leads towards history, towards 'what really happened', or the question ruled out of court, that leads towards philosophy, be he, or she, Heidegger, or any other; but only that the treatment of poetry and fiction by such aesthetic philosophers as Aristotle (1907b), Collingwood (1938), Croce (1922), Dufrenne (1973) and von Balthasar (1961-69, 1988) is to be taken into account as relevant.

These questions are shown to be eccentric neither by considering what is being done, nor what has been done, for there is a golden thread that leads through the labyrinth from Lowth through de Wette, with Kant (1915) and Fries (1805), with Rogerson (1992) and Davidovich 1993) and the work of that great pioneer, David Friedrich Strauss and his intelligent translator, George Eliot (Marion Ann Evans).

And all these things allow an approach, not only to God's 'turn towards language', the *logos*, but to God's *kolpos*, or 'bosom', an expanse to be known by Hebrew knowledge (the word 'empirical' springs to mind!). For 'natural piety should be the clue to metaphysical thinking' (Collingwood 1940: 172), of which Samuel Alexander is Collingwood's paradigm. And that natural piety is the clue here to this metaphysical poem, John's prologue, that constitutes the prelude to his historical fiction.

It was no great matter that Lowth in 1753 was collated (Hunt 1893: 214), but great matter for him, no doubt, that he was married the previous year. And great matter for him, too, that his lectures on *The Sacred Poetry of the Hebrews* saw in the same year (sc. 1753) the light of day. But what was great matter for Lowth was great matter for Hamann. And not only for Hamann, but for the *merus grammaticus*, 'the mere and unadulterated grammarian', Johannes David Michaelis (Lowth 1821: 389). For here for the mere grammarian was a book by a 'bard': *aliter enim poetas vates tractabit, aliter merus grammaticus*, 'for the bard (Lowth) was treating poets otherwise, otherwise the mere grammarian' (Michaelis, in Lowth 1821: 389). Here was a critic with a poet's sensibility.

The question has already been raised above, what de Wette might not have done to the New Testament, had he held and hit it with the same hammer, with which he had earlier hit the Old. Had Lowth, one might ask, turned his hand to the *Sacred Poesy of the Early Christians*, what might he not have been able to say?

What we have to do with here is the castrametation of the logos. Reference has already been made above to Lowth's 'Praelectio XIII' (1821: 120-28 (= 1839: 136-46), to the first kind of *prosopopoeia*, or personification, 'when action and character are attributed to fictitious, irrational, or even to inanimate objects' (1839: 136), *cum rebus vel fictis, vel ratione ac sensu carentibus, actio ac Persona datur* (1821: 120). Here in John's prologue, the word 'word', goes, to speak in a pre-Grotian fashion, on a camping holyday, or in a post-Grotian fashion, holiday—the move from holy day to holiday is a secularist move to an age, in which the force of theopoetic abates.

But the protracted prosopopoeia of the *logos*, whereby an abstract noun describes a parabolic curve that touches the earth at a particular point, or *semeion*, is the mere and unadulterated prefix only to the second kind of personification, 'when [or 'whereby'] a probable but fictitious speech is assigned to a real character' (1839: 136), *cum verae personae probabilis Oratio tribuitur* (1821: 120). Jesus' discourses are John's fictions. Everyone, my wife and I, agrees on this.

Now the resort to historical fiction is something that aligns the Fourth Evangelist, not only with Cartland, but with Scott. Sir Walter and St John form a syzygy. We may compare them and contrast them. And in comparing and contrasting we are only following St Paul. For even Paul, when comparing, contrasts: 'That which has been glorified has not been glorified...' (2 Cor. 3.10). Paul is comparing and contrasting two dispensations. I am comparing and contrasting two writers. Totally different, they are totally the same.

John's prologue is a metaphysical poem, that is concerned less with history, less with the historical explication of the entrance onto the stage of history by the Baptist and by Jesus, than with the conditions, the existence of a fashioning and fabricating God, without which history would not be possible. But few would deny, though few do deny, that he has no concern with history at all. But what benefit accrues to the writer of fiction, that is unavailable, or less available, to the historian?

Scott (Anderson 1981: 8)

> was emphatic about the value of old poetry, plays and romances, commonly ignored by the general historian. Poets were the first historians of all nations, and the traditions they hand down, however corrupted, are not to be hastily rejected. They can supply solid information—a mediaeval romance may elucidate the laws of knighthood—but the chief value of the older literature is that while annals tell us what people did, poetry tells us what they were; in this respect a mediaeval romance is preferable to 'dull and dreary monastic annals' [Scott 1877-82: *Prose Works* XVII, 17]. He went so far as to say that a history of Scotland could be compiled from ballads and similar material, though he did admit that the result would be 'very curious' [Scott 1877-1882: *Poetical Works* I, 14, 40, 213].

John is 'very curious', indeed. He is, indeed, curiouser, more than very curious.

If 'Scott's memory resembled less a set of pigeon-holes than a melting-pot' (Anderson 1981: 18), did John melt less? You can, of course, melt more, like Carlyle on the battle of Dunbar: 'The moon gleams out, hard and blue, riding among hail-clouds; and over St. Abb's Head, a streak of dawn is rising' (1904: II, 99, cit. Anderson 1981: 20). This is more than 'it was night' (Jn 13.30).

With Scott 'nearly all the novels employ a historical background, whereas the foreground is occupied either by fictitious characters, or by fictitious incidents involving historical characters' (Anderson 1981: 37). Here John's foreground is occupied by a historical character, the incidents fictitious (the Feeding), or melted history (the Arrest), and the background partly the ups and downs of life, not in Jerusalem, *about which* he was writing, but in Ephesus, *where* he was writing. And what he was writing is (I think) partly an analogue of sci-fi, 'the folk literature of [the twentieth] century' (Mackenzie 1966: 402), the arrival, with abbreviated itinerary, of Meeks's alien (1972). He is writing the sci-fi of the first.

'While the *Waverley* novels are an epitome, not merely of one man's personal experience, but of the records of several nations over many centuries' (Anderson 1981: 38), for the novelist not only has the freedom (Collingwood 1946: 242-46) to be more philosophical, but, 'if annals tell us what people did, poetry tells us what they were', to be more historical than history, John's period runs not from Abraham to Wittgenstein, but from 4004 BC to 100 AD, with special reference to the period 30–100 AD.

Moreover, in *Waverley*,

> a certain amount of matter is transferred straight into the story from the historians of the '45—that is, from the actual historical context of real life into the identical historical context in fiction. This matter, drawn chiefly from writers like John Home, relates mainly to the military operations, and in particular to Prestonpans and Clifton... The interesting point is that this policy of direct incorporation accounts for so small a proportion of the complete work (Anderson 1981: 39).

But even if John had eyewitnesses to rely on, or was even an eyewitness himself, the question is first *what kind of eyes he and they had*. Was there anyone there in that part of the world and in that social grouping who had Thucydidean eyes to see with? Any Ephesian John would be treated with proper suspicion by any Ephesian David Hume. And even where John, the Fourth Evangelist, is patently relying on what earlier people had said, and even if it must be conceded that earlier *logia* of Jesus shine, more or less fitfully, through what John's Jesus says (e.g. Ashton 1991: 184), '[t]he interesting point is that this policy of direct incorporation accounts for so small a proportion of the complete work'.

There is no 'evidence at our disposal (that) obliges us to conclude' (Collingwood 1940: 56) that John had, in Ephesus, 'an office at the Register House', like Scott in Edinburgh (Anderson 1981: 2). And even Scott's having one did not do much to curtail his sovereign freedom to introduce, for example, into the '45, material that belonged to 1742, 1715, 1702, 1689 and 1563! And the character of Bradwardine derives from John Sinclair, author of memoirs of the Fifteen (Anderson 1981: 39-43). Even where Scott has access to history, or to what we should call history, he is doing something other than, and more than history. He is doing history '*and more*' (Ramsey 1967: 50 and *passim*).

And even where he has access to literature, he is doing something other than, and more than, repeating, transcribing it. For he is drawing 'on an equally rich literary background' (Anderson 1981: 44), 'not to mention the background of personal experience which every artist must have, to produce a most extraordinary amalgam of the life, experience and feelings of Western man through many generations, set out in the long series of the Waverley novels'.

A final catena of transcriptions should make as plain as an Abbotsford pikestaff the parallels between the authorial methods of these two creative writers:

'There seems to be only one character in the novels who clearly represents Scott himself, and that is the Edward Waverley of the early chapters [of the eponymous novel], whose education and reading are Scott's own...' (Anderson 1981: 86). Scott himself was, 'in one aspect of his personality, a dreamer, living in an ideal world...' (v. *Journal*, 27 December 1825 [pp. 87-88]). 'Every novel of Scott's has a strong infusion of Regency life and thought which renders period authenticity impossible...' (87-88). Scott's romances 'contain pictures of manners that never were, are, or will be, besides ten thousand blunders as to chronology, costumes, etc.' (Sharpe 1888: II, 517, cit. Anderson 1981: 92). And Scott,

> like Robert Henry, presented 'the history of Scotland and its neighbours on a New Plan'—a much more original plan than Henry's, involving the free handling and presentation of the material on aesthetic, not scientific, principles, and aiming at general fidelity to human nature rather than at close adherence to the historical structure of a given period. History, in fact, is given no special status; it is an extension of the artist's personal experience, and Scott's commonsense rules for its treatment are the commonsense rules which govern the treatment of any material whatever (Anderson 1981: 92).

The case rests.

Biblical writers in general and John, and John's prologue in particular, are consumed with 'this strange human passion for never saying what one means but always something else' (Farrer 1972: 24), for

> when we are not being scientists, we do not use language to break things up into factors, we use it to describe the quality they have. I do not now want to know how a thing can be analysed, I want to know *what it is like*: I am interested in its individual character (p. 30). And '[t]his gift can only work by inspiration' (p. 32).

And with what is inspiration clothed? Thus de Wette (1831: 33):

> The appearance of symbols and myths, as such, can be denied by no-one who knows the ancient world. They are the necessary

integuments of super-sensible truths for a people operating within the bounds of sense and incapable of untrammelled thought.[6]

If Scott can do it, John can do it. If John can do it, Scott can do it. If there is 'poetic truth' (Farrer 1972), then fairy-tales (the resurrection) are true; 'fairy tales and newspapers make up the lack of our historians'[7] (Hamann 1950: 205). If there is poetic truth, then metaphysical poems are true. Then John's prologue is true. Thus Hamann's *philologia* crucis, 'philology of the cross', has an apt Johannine complement. It is complemented by John's *philologia incarnationis mortuorumque resurrectionis*.

There are *Tunes of Glory* (Mackenzie 1993). John, too, as we have seen (1.14), 'sings glorious numbers', *numeros canit gloriae*. He is telling a fairy tale. 'A circle of which the circumference is nowhere and the centre everywhere' (Bonaventura 1754: 354)? He is describing the progress of an itinerant noun for the eccentric, or concentric, mind of the literary critic, that is itself prepared to be itinerant. If it is fictionally true, that 'he that has heard my words has already passed from death to life' (Jn 5.24), then John is not 'undoing the past' (Templeton 1993: 43-60), but the future. And undoing it now (Bultmann 1957: 155).

6.   'Das Vorkommen der Symbole und Mythen, als solcher, kann kein Kenner des Alterthums leugnen. Sie sind zur Einkleidung übersinnlicher Wahrheiten bey einem sinnlichen, des freien Denkens unfähigen Volke nothwendig.'
7.   'Feenmährchen und Hofzeitungen ersetzen den Mangel unserer Geschichtschreiber.'

8

Through a Glass Brightly: The Magic of Metaphor (Paul Apostle and Genius: 2 Corinthians 3.18)

> [T]he reader, wandering about as though in some kind of confusing labyrinth or winding maze, does not see very well whence he has entered or how he may leave (Erasmus 1984: 13).

> It might just as well occur to such thoughtless eloquence to laud Paul as a stylist and for his artistic use of language, or still better, since it is well known that Paul practiced a manual trade, to maintain that his work as an upholsterer must have been so perfect that no upholsterer either before or since has been able to equal it (Kierkegaard 1955: 105).

The attempt to follow the mind, or imagination, of the apostle Paul is a demanding task. He twists like a serpent and says (like most theologians) least, when he should be saying most. But why has he won a fixed place in the Western canon? One answer is that he could write and another answer is that he had something to say. But if he could write and turn a trope with the best, why should we be prohibited from saying that his religious is paired with an artistic genius? But how easy is his art to understand and what does understanding mean when it is religion that is to be understood, in whole or in part?

But he (or she) that will endure to the end of this chapter may not be able to endure to the end of this book.

What shape does God's breath take, when it passes through Paul's lips? With what tones and 'voices' does he makes his 'senses and passions' (Hamann 1950: 197 [= Lumpp 1970: 205]) articulate? How is the angularity to be specified and explained, with which Paul attempts 'to purify the dialect of his tribe' (Eliot, 'Little Gidding' II [= 1944: 39])?

It is difficult to be determinate about an infinite text. This text is infinite, partly because texts are infinite, because 'inexhaustibility is one of the marks of a work of art' (Gardner 1963: 14), and partly because the *Woraufhin* of *this* text, sc. 'the whereonto-from-here', what it is *about*, is God.

But even if God were not being given, a great many fields, and fields that encompass fields, are covered by Paul in what is a coruscating display of verbal pyrotechnics. If John is no slouch, nor is Paul neither. Both can write.

Truth is related to Paul's text, much as aesthetics is related to literary criticism, when '[e]sthetics sometimes seems only as implicit in the practice of criticism as the atomic physics is present in sunlight when you feel it' (Blackmur 1954: 387). What does Paul say here? What does he not? What does he not!

God is my general, 'who...always leads us in triumph' (τῷ πάντοτε θριαμβεύοντι, *to(i) pantote thriambeuonti* [2 Cor. 2.14]). God is my ally and Paul an ally among allies (διακόνους καινῆς διαθήκης, *diakonous kaines diathekes*: 'ministers of a new covenant' [2 Cor. 3.6]). Jesus of Nazareth is the 'insinuation' (Craig's word (*obiter dictum*, not in Templeton 1991) of creativity, of destiny, into the stony heart of adamantine fate and unalterable law (ἐκ σκότους φῶς λάμψει, *ek skotous phos lampsei*: 'Let light shine out of darkness' [2 Cor. 4.6]).

There is 'the agony of death and birth' (Eliot 'East Coker' III [= 1944: 20]) and agonies, that occur, or may occur, between these. Paul of Tarsus was one of those good men, whom no one could nail down, though many tried. Like Longinus, he was 'a distinguished, but over-heated mind' (Brink 1971: 76), though his surplus heat was dialectically controlled by 'freedom' and 'responsibility' (Gregor Smith 1969: 15 and *passim*). Mackinnon's word, 'receptivity' (1957: 255), a receptivity to that which, in Eliot's words ('Little Gidding' II [= 1944: 38]), 'compels the recognition it precedes', fastidiously names the attitude to the source and origin of Paul's pedestrian balance, the balance of the walker, that is the resultant of a sequence of imbalances, the walker shifting antithetically from one leg to the other and *getting on*, as soldiers do ('Our mission is to get on', says the Company Commander). Thus, if you like, Paul is attributing the authorship of his insights to an agency that is other than his own, for, if something comes to him, it comes from somewhere and from someone, or from some thing. As Gregor Smith was the most unbalanced theologian of his day and places (Siena), so Paul, of his day and places. 'Damn braces', said Blake. 'Damn balances', says Paul.

> And [Onesiphorus] went by the king's highway that leadeth unto Lystra and stood expecting him, and looked upon them that came, according to the description of Titus. And he saw Paul coming, a man little of stature, thin-haired upon the head, crooked in the legs, of good state of body, with eyebrows joining, and nose somewhat hooked, full of grace: for sometimes he appeared like a man, and sometimes he had the face of an angel (James 1924: 273).

Paul's body, singular, is a member of a body, corporate. Both bodies are subject to disintegration. What disintegration? What was *going on* in Corinth? What natural and unnatural shocks?

Even if literary criticism is to be distinguished from scholarship (Blackmur 1954: 394-96), neither can safely be separated from the other. The scholar, in particular the scholar in the business of reading letters not written to scholars, is forced to guess—without guesswork, in this business, one does not get on. And Murphy-O'Connor's guess is as good as any (Murphy-O'Connor 1991: 14): Apollos was an intellectual, deracinated, an intellectual *in sensu malo*, overheated by a religion non-somatically conceived, and Peter, sold on 'Right Conduct, or action according to the recognized rules...the low-grade morality of custom and precept...was shutting his eyes to anything that might convince him that his ready-made rules were not an adequate guide to the conduct of life' (Collingwood 1939: 105-106). Both had the stick, but each by the wrong end (Tabraham 1996: *passim*) and by a different end: the stick should be held in the middle and twirled and tossed in the air. No pipe-major can do less (he that has seen can testify).

But Paul was a *via media* man, of a very extreme kind, of the kind that goes, that is prepared to go for the fundamentals, the fundamental agonies of birth and death, of affirmation, negation and reaffirmation. There is a triple movement: life, death and the creativity of God, the poet (*der Poet am Anfange der Tage*, '[t]he poet at the beginning of days' (Hamann, on 2 Cor. 4.6, 1950: 206).[1] Death is the birth of 'orient' wheat (Traherne 1908: 157, cit. Martin 1990: 210).

But on what facts are Paul's fictions parasitic? What do they feed on?

---

1.   Lumpp 1970: 219; Crick in Nisbet 1985: 145.

There are, first of all, the historical, plain facts that feed on Paul; historical, plain people, like Apollos and Peter and those who meta-schematize themselves as apostles, but are none (μετασχηματίζε-ται, *metaschematizetai* [2 Cor. 11.14]). And the Corinthians, like sheep without a shepherd—and, like sheep without a shepherd, not at all incapable of getting in among the bluebells and so abhor-ring the plain fare of dour grass. All they, like sheep, have gone astray (incest and vegetarian idol-meats, a pusillanimous diet).

And there are, secondly, the metaphysical facts, that reside within Paul's language, as atomic physics in sunbeams (as Blackmur above); such facts as the existence of God, the existence of a world, the existence of Jesus now, who existed then. Such are the metaphysical facts, that confront Paul and his brothers (not count-ing the women [or counting them only?] and children).

Without the second, the metaphysical facts, there would be none of the first, the historical, plain facts; without the metaphysics, no history. And without the history, one might add, no language for the metaphysics, for you cannot have God for an 'ally' without the whole apparatus of Near Eastern politics, nor God for a 'general' without the pomp of Rome, nor God for 'creator' without the craftsmen and scribes, the arrow-makers and the pushers of the *calamus*, or pen (see [again], and again) the Arabic analogue of the Hebrew *bārā*, 'create'). We think about metaphors, we think about images, and we find the analogies, for 'what are analogies but sober and criticised images?' (Farrer 1948: 62) As an Orcadian, or any 'Albanian' lochan (Lynch 1992: xiii) is a reflex of heaven, the sky (Oman 1960: 43), so history mirrors metaphysics, the world mirrors God (τὴν δόξαν κυρίου κατοπτριζόμενοι, *ten doxan kuriou katoptrizomenoi*: 'beholding [in a mirror] the glory of the Lord' [2 Cor. 3.18]).

So if it be asked whether Paul's use of language is a *poetic* use at all, the answer is, I submit, that it is poetic through and through—give or take, for example, what seems to be an excessive preoccu-pation of the Apostle with finance, though even here, in this exam-ple from the charitable lottery of financial giving, Paul's macro-text, his constructed pattern, his fictive coordinates shine through: 'for your sake he became poor' (2 Cor. 8.9). The empirical detail (finance) is transparent to its fundamental ground (God's agent).

And if it be objected that the language of Paul is not poetic, but the language of dogma, then it should be answered *either* that this is not to construe, but to *mis*construe what he said, to read as dogma what is not dogmatic. For the words of dogma (just as the word 'dogma' itself) are words, from which the meaning, the unmanageability, has evaporated; are words petrified. But was Paul operating within the limits of the manageable, when the words came into his head, came on to his pen? Or it should be answered that dogma is to be defined, or *re*-defined (Walls *obiter dictum*) as 'that which cannot be said, but can only be sung'. If dogma is song, Paul is writing it; if dogma is said, he is not.

Like a lochan, Paul's text, rightly read, is an enarrative text, in the especial sense of stripping the veil. The word 'stripping' is not too strong for Paul's acerbic intelligence. For it is a stripping of the veil from all that conceals a 'fundamental view of life' (Blackmur 1954: 397), stripping away the 'fig-leaves' (Hamann 1950: 198),[2] the 'disgraceful, underhanded ways', τὰ κρυπτὰ τῆς αἰσχύνης, *ta krupta tes aischunes* (2 Cor. 4.2).

And, if so, it is a text that must be read by those who are 'drunk with sober drunkenness' (μεθύοντες... τὴν... μέθην... τὴν νηφάλιον, *methuontes...ten...methen...ten nephalion* (Philo, *Vit. Mos.* 1.187.5), or with drunken drunkenness (as Longinus reads Sappho: 'Are you not amazed how at one instant she summons...'[Longinus 1899: 10.3]). The body of Paul's *oeuvre* is not a corpse.

So some sort of 'technique' must be found, which 'resembles scholarship', but passes beyond it 'in that its facts are usually further into the heart of the literature than the facts of most scholarship', so as to manifest 'the thing itself from its own point of view' (Blackmur 1954: 397).

'The thing itself'! If *diese Mythologie...ist die Sache selbst*, if 'this mythology...is the thing itself' (Bonhoeffer 1971: 329 [letter of 8 June 1944]), what is that which can throw light upon it 'from its own point of view', which is not scholarship, but is literary criticism?

Where 'the thing itself' is known, is known to Hamann, the language-game is of 'blood and fire and vapour of smoke', or:

2.   Gregor Smith 1960: 197; Crick, in Nisbet 1985: 141.

Blut und Feuer und Rauchdampf

(Hamann [*sic*], in Lumpp 1970: 215 [= Acts 2.19])[3]

For Paul this is a linguistic and experiential realm, where there are no rules, but freedom. It is a realm where 'law' is transcended by 'love'. Paul, that is to say, is concerned with a category, 'love', that comes higher in 'the scale of forms' than 'law' (Collingwood 1933: 54-91). Is Collingwood, here, with his theorem of the 'overlap', the key to making single Paul's double tongue, his perplexing tendency both to attack the law and defend it? But the exegete, too, must try to probe the imaginative expression of Paul's passion. The literary critic, too, has something to do, which is not the application to literature of a philosophical theorem.

But is Paul concerned with something higher than aesthetics? Did he think of himself as an artist, and not rather as an apostle? Then what is the relation between these, between artist and apostle? Is there a difference, an opposition, between the 'receptivity' (Mackinnon 1957: 255) of the artist and the apostle? But even if there is a difference, does Paul nevertheless exhibit the *notae poetae*, the 'marks of a poet'? Does his speech not exhibit condensation, thickness of speech, idiocy, even? Is there not a remarkable unity in what he says?

These questions feel their way. Artist? Apostle? If Kierkegaard denied the equation, can Kierkegaard's denial be denied? Why not look closely at what Paul said?

Is it not the business of the poet to strip off the veil of linguistic habit? Surely Paul reveals *ingenium*, or genius, or something very like it, and has picked up sufficient *ars*, poetic technique, to express himself, at least on paper (2 Cor. 10.10)? Is de Wette's compound epithet, 'aesthetic-religious', not valid for Paul, doubly valid in *both* its halves? And if so, why should both halves not be combined into one whole? And this would make him neither: apostle, but not a genius, nor: genius, but not apostle, but both together in one.

As noted just above, Hamann speaks of God as poet, 'The poet at the beginning of days' (1950: 206).[4] Moreover, Hamann refers there to a later verse in this very same segment of this very same

3. Crick, in Nisbet 1985: 144.
4. Crick, in Nisbet 1985: 145.

letter, 'Let light shine out of darkness', or (more or less) as it originally appeared (1762: 190 [= Lumpp 1970: 219]):

Der Poet [* * *] *am Anfange der Tage*

[* * *] *2 Kor. IV, 6.*

When this poet speaks, he makes male and female. When this poet makes, he makes man out of dust, the dust of the earth, the dust of the grave, the grave of Pharisaism and the law.

If the Great Dictator, dictating to Paul, not only produces physical facts from verbal feats (viz. creates a world), but is producing the kind of verbal feats that poets do, how much more does that not make Paul a poet, though a lesser poet than God, the greater? Is God, too, a genius? And can, then, a genius who sends an apostle make of an apostle a genius? 'We are ambassadors for Christ' (2 Cor. 5.20). But are we not geniuses for him and by him, too? If de Wette is right, at least on the Old Testament, that, taking into account the modes of Hebrew expression, the epithet should be double, not single ('aesthetic-religious'), is there not a chance that that compound epithet should also apply to the New and, moreover, that what is double in the former should be trebly retripled in the latter?

Is not Paul, too, among the poets?

If we are after, not the assertion, but what is asserted in the assertion, if language has to be subtle, if it is to investigate the traces of God, can we not say that Paul, in converting his theological passion into action by finding speech (to allude [again] to Spinoza, *Ethica* V, prop. III, cit. Collingwood 1938: 219), is finding *poetic* speech? The requisite intensity, at any rate, is there.

And if Gregor Smith (*obiter dictatum*, to a Scottish audience) was right to say, that Kierkegaard was wrong to reject Regina, was Kierkegaard not also wrong to drive a wedge between the apostle and the genius?

For how are metaphors found? Is Aristotle not right, over against Kierkegaard, to say of the command of metaphor, that:

> This alone cannot be imparted by another; it is the mark of genius,
> for to make good metaphors implies an eye for resemblances
> (Aristotle, *Po.* 1459a6-8, trans. Butcher 1925a: 87).

And Paul makes good metaphors.

If it is right, in what after all is conatively a theological work, to fall 'amang thrissles' (Mk 4.7 [Lorimer 1983: 67]), is it not also right, not that 'the eternal once appeared in time' (Kierkegaard 1955: 76, cit. [*sic*] Pattison 1992: 82), but that the eternal, that appeared once in time, appears always and everywhere in time? Does one need to make oneself contemporary with the eternal, that appeared once and not rather with one's own time, where the eternal appears always? One does not need to be transposed, but only to be located, where one happens to be.

This appearance, certainly, is in the mode of non-appearance (*absconditus*, 'hidden'), the mode of one who plays possum, such that *non possumus* (we are unable), and, according to some reports (Altizer 1967), has been run over and lies flat on the highway (the sight is not uncommon in Ohio). If that is so, if absconditus, if *abscondence* is a *mot juste*, though not justly the only one, then new words have always and everywhere to be found.

Thus there is a need for invention, for invention and invention; for invention in the double sense of 'revelation' and 'discovery'. Both. And both together. Granted that the noun, 'apostle', what-ever may be true of the adjective, 'apostolic', should have a use that should be restricted to the period that runs from Q to 2 Peter, from c. 40–c. 31 December 150, why should we not say that, though all apostles may not have been geniuses, some were; and among these John and Paul. God, if there is a god, is not, like a lecturer to Scottish students. We must speak, not of dictation, but of co-authorship.

But, to return, in this complex and plural text, the third chapter, in its context, of Paul's Second Dictation to Corinth, there is also unity and simplicity. Moses and Jesus are comparable. And they may be contrasted. And with the comparison and contrast of two persons, Moses and Jesus, one may compare and contrast, equally, two things, with which these two persons were engaged. I mean 'letter' and 'spirit'.

'Death' is connected importantly with the former, 'freedom' importantly with the latter, though this may *not* be to say that 'death', in a somewhat different sense, may not be importantly con-nected also with the latter. For there is a freedom to 'die' to self, and to die *simpliciter*, as a free man under tyranny, for example. Similarly, for words are chameleons, freedom can be connected, if

in a less perfect sense, with the former, too. I mean the freedom to
choose, the 'choice not between, but of', the freedom to respond
to ethical imperatives (the aesthetic realm is not divorced from
others). It should not be cause of wonder, if in a complex text the
relation between terms should be complicated.

What perplexes about this text, and Paul's *oeuvre* as a whole,
what perplexes here about the relation between letter and spirit,
law and grace, is the shuttling to and fro of affirmation and negation, where what is affirmed seems now to be denied and what is
denied seems again to be affirmed.

The formal key, I guess, the right analytical tool, the appropriate
philosophical theorem is *sublation*. For 'the purpose...is altered in
fulfilment' (Eliot, 'Little Gidding' I [= 1944: 36]).

Spirit stands highter than letter in a scale of forms: 'The higher...
negates the lower, and at the same time reaffirms it: negates it as a
false embodiment of the generic essence, and reaffirms its content,
that specific form of the essence, as part and parcel of itself'
(Collingwood 1933: 88). Letter differs from spirit at once in kind
and degree, is related to spirit at once by distinction and opposition.

> If, as St. Paul believed, law is given for the better ordering of life,
> and grace is something of the same general kind but a higher term in
> the same scale, it is no paradox that grace should perform exactly
> what law promised to perform but did not (Collingwood 1933: 89).

But to say so much is to shed some light, or glory, on the
structure of what Paul is doing, though yet very little on what is
structured *by* his structure.

Would an Erasmian paraphrase take us further?

'We for our part', says Erasmus (1984: 14), in the proem to his
first published paraphrase (1518), *The Argument of the Epistle of
Paul to the Romans*,

> have attempted to remove (*amoliri*) the difficulties to the best of
> our ability, except for certain words which are so peculiar to the
> language of Paul (*adeo peculiaria sunt*) that they cannot be
> expressed in more than one way [or 'that sometimes/on some occa-
> sions/quite often/they cannot be paraphrased' (*ut aliquoties mutari
> non queant* (trans. in a kind communication, Wright)]; these for
> example: faith, grace, body, flesh, member, spirit, mind, feeling, to

build, and others of this kind which, although it was not possible to change outright, we have striven to soften (*emollire*) as much as possible.

But what δῆθεν, *dethen* ('pray!', 'forsooth!!', *'Du liebe Zeit!!!' 'O tempora...'*, 'What are things coming to?') is to be said for a paraphrase that, when it comes to the central terms of the text to be paraphrased, can do no more than 'soften as much as possible'? Is not this to produce *Hamlet*, if not without the Prince, yet with the Prince mollified: 'Almost to be, or more or less not to be'?

Would not even ten minutes *Nachschlagen*, 'looking up', of *ruach*, 'spirit', in the magisterial *opus* of Brown, Driver and Briggs, s.v. *ruach* (also Briggs 1900) have given Erasmus pause for thought? Can a 'philosophy of Christ' (Erasmus 1984: xxxviii) be written by a 'softening' of its central terms? This is a Grand National, in which the horse is almost taking the jumps. It is not a winner.

'Texts', says Paul boldly, 'are not worth the paper they are written on'. Persons take priority over texts. And they take priority, much as warm hearts take priority over cold stones, as soft wind ('Favonian' [Horace, *Od.* 1.4.1]), as *egelidi tepores*, 'very cool warmths' (Catullus, *Carmina* 46.1.), as gentle breath overrides hard laws, that, like the laws of the Medes and Persians, alter not.

'A text', says Paul boldly, writing one, 'a text is only a text'. For texts *are* about something. And what *this* text is about is warmth. Breathing, vulnerable warmth.

This text about the priority of persons (more than three of them!) expresses Paul's δός μοι ποῦ στῶ καὶ κινήσω τὴν γῆν, his *dos moi pou sto kai kineso ten gen* ('Give me somewhere to stand, and I will move the earth' [Archimedes, cit. (*sic*) Bonhoeffer 1971: 240).[5] It expresses something central in Paul's standpoint, his *Fragestellung*, 'the position from which he asks questions and answers them'.

But this standpoint is non-philosophical. Or pre-philosophical, implicitly philosophical. The mode of Paul's expression here is the mode of 'symbolical hypotyposes': 'If we are to give the name of cognition to a mere mode of representation...then all our

5. But: ...*pou stân* (*sic*) (von Balthasar 1965: 16); πᾷ βῶ καὶ κινῶ τὰν γᾶν, *pa(i) bo kai kino tan gan* (Simplicius, *Commentaries on Aristotle's Physics* 1110.5d).

knowledge of God is merely symbolical' (Kant 1914: 250).[6] Such expression, if taken as literal, not metaphorical, as factual, not fictional, 'falls into Anthropomorphism' (Kant 1914: 250) (*gerät in den Anthropomorphism* [Kant 1915: 213]). It is the mode of symbolical supposal.

Paul is in too much of a hurry to trouble his head about what he is saying to have time to stop to consider what it is that he is saying, when he says it. His warm, his hot, his 'overheated' stand-point allows him, in freedom, to spring from the undoubted historical fact that, far from coming up with a reference, Jerusalem, like the deaf adder, has remained obdurately dumb, to the undoubted fiction, that God, by 'inking' the Corinthians, has himself come up with a fiction. 'You are my letter' says Paul (2 Cor. 3.2; Kromer 1989 [unpublished]). And God has 'spirited' it. It is 'written not with ink but with the Spirit' (2 Cor. 3.3).

It is not that Paul's *intellection* is firing on all cylinders, but that his intelligent *imagination*, at maximum revolution, is going through a series of Protean transformations (some engine!). And these transformations force him to, or there is a transforming force that forces him, wins him to move (he is 'receptive') from the realm of ecclesiastical history (church-life in Corinth in the early years of our era) to the co-implication and inter-implication of history with metaphysics.

But these are metaphysics in the mode of imagination. These are implied metaphysics. His subject is less the ink, of which Jerusalem is resolutely supplying none, and more the warm-hearted enthusiasm, by which all real persons may, if they are lucky, become animated, even when they are writing, but especially when they are not (Sayers, in Dante 1950: 32).

When Paul's cachinnation somersaults down the long strath and

Halloos your name to the reverberate hills
(Shakespeare, *Twelfth Night*, I.v.256)

the hills break in fragments. Whose name? 'The name that is above every name'? Such is the force of his poetry, such is the central force, the central force of a 'major man', of Paul, the 'major man'

6.   'Wenn man eine blosse Vorstellungsart schon Erkenntnis nennen darf...so ist alle unsere Erkenntnis von Gott bloss symbolisch' (Kant 1915: 213).

(Stevens *passim*). It is hard to unravel the complications of his echoes.

But these are *localized* fictions, they have a local habitation and a place. *Darstellung* (placing there), *Vorstellung* (placing before) has a history. There is a stylistic shift from the figures on an Egyptian frieze, *via* Watteau to the late Picasso, tormented by age and the Church. But this is not to say that there is not a line that leads from what the French call *alliance* ('alliance' [Eng.]) to the Auld Alliance (Scot.) between Scotland and France, and from there to NATO, SATO, WATO and EATO. For (again), just as 'there is no specifically religious language' (Davis 1994: 115), so there is no peculiar alliance for a peculiar people (Tabraham n.d.), though parliamentary Scots may be a peculiar exception to the general rule. And the term 'alliance' is also to be linked backwards also, to the older 'covenants' with Hiram of Tyre. But this is not to say that the continuities of these historical connections are not dirempted by caesuras, *Umbrüche* and *Diskontinuitäten*, to use some favoured terms of Käsemann (*passim*). And he should know, for he did guard duty in Corinth in the Second World War.

In his *Autobiography* (1939), Collingwood puts the point of Newman's *Essay*, but more briefly: questions and answers change over time (1939: 29-43, 53-76). A line of questions and answers, that give rise to new questions and answers, leads from the Corinthian mirror of 2 Cor. 3.18 (*speculantes*: 'beholding in a mirror') to the Hubble telescope. But the mirrors, the Corinthian (Murphy-O'Connor 1983b) and the Hubble (Tanvir, Aragon-Salamanca and Wall 1997) are not the same. If a trireme is a sort of steamer, adds Collingwood (1939: 64), if Hobbes's state is Plato's, it 'has got *diablement changé en route*' (61).

The questions Paul asks and the answers to these questions, that he imagines in an imaginative tradition, are particular and local. Not only does each image, each metaphor, have its history, but so too the mode in which the images are collocated, organized. Here, in Paul, and everywhere in Paul, they are organized messianically in terms of the emergence, or 'having-emerged', of a great leader, who leads from below. But (again) there is a line that leads through More's *Utopia* through Orwell's *1984* to Adams's 'trilogy in five parts' (1995), the denomination of this latter book, sc. 'science fiction' (μυθιστορήματα ἐπιστημονικῆς φαντασίας, *muth-historemata epistemonikes phantasias*), retroactively lending heuristic validity to the denomination of the *Ko-ordinatensystem* of the Apostle. Science fiction and thinking about a messiah are not without analogy.

In sum, then, Paul's 'covenant', his 'alliance' is a political metaphor and, *qua* metaphor, a fiction, is Isenberg's 'stroke of art' (1973: 115), Ricoeur's node, where 'is' contends with 'is not' (1978: 248). In comparison with the 'old', Paul's 'new covenant' is *divinement changé en route*. It is a covenant for a community, of which God, too, is a member, and is unrestricted in its membership. This little fiction has its *locus* in the messianic sci-fi. The Lord is my shepherd (Black 1979: 22) and takes his seat, when the Treaty Organization sits.

But the question of the historicity of images and their organization is a question about a text, which is not itself historical, in the sense in which Luke, to judge by the *appearance* of his Prologue, *appears* to be historical, *appears* to be *about* history. But, by our hypothesis, Paul's text is an artistic text, in which history is included (Peter has refused a reference, Corinth is a town, where Paul has been active). But not history only, for philosophy is implied (this 'alliance' implies that among the allies there is that ally, than which a no more allied ally can be conceived, or that all other allies are such that they could be otherwise). Paul's text is a text, in which a constellation of discrete metaphors is thematically unified by irradiating light. 'Glory' is a pervasive theme.

But some localized fictions, the parts of them and the whole of them, have the ability to transcend the time and the place in which they were written. And this is so, when the particular fictions in question are the fictions of an apostolic genius, when they are the fictions of a genius, who not only *felt* he had something to say, but *had* something to say. A localized fiction, a fiction limited to a locality, has become unlimited. A limited story has become a story without limits. We have a name for this and we call it a classic.

Two questions then arise: (1) Why does this writer deserve this evaluation? and: (2) To what kind of further classics has this writer given rise and to what is he giving rise? The critic is invited to expatiate on the first, the writer, with the critic, on the second. Or the two tasks can become conflated; and then we have the critic-writer. Immanuel Kant would add the purveyor of bombast, the buffoon[7] 'of whom we say, that he hears himself talk, or who stands and moves about as if he were on a stage in order to be stared at; this always betrays a bungler' (1915: 174 [= 1914: 205]). While Kant here is speaking of mannerism in art, his words may be taken to apply to criticism of the baser sort.

But by what is Paul prompted to produce his fictions? Because, on the one hand, he has legal problems on his hands and lawyers on his toes and because, on the other, he has the freedom, because the standpoint he occupies permits him to pick and choose: *this* is to be obeyed, *that* not. Paul's meals had no prescribed menu. Paul's meals are either *à la carte*, or duck's feet from the kitchen.

But any observation about the localization of Pauline doctrines is no more than a banality, no more astounding in itself than the taking note of the peculiarities of the Pauline idiolect. And while there is as much chance of our ever understanding Paul as Paul understood himself, as there is of knowing 'how Nietzsche felt the wind in his hair as he walked upon the mountains' (Collingwood 1948: 296), it is hardly credible that the task should be thought a hopeless one. But it is the the task of following Paul's mind through the labyrinth (Erasmus 1984: 13), of replicating in the critic's own mind the motions of the Pauline Meander. But the localizations and peculiarities of Paul's mind and imagination have their analogues and are related to the general condition of things, as this general condition is specifically understood at any particular time by specific individuals and groups. If justice, verdict, guilt, life and death, are not eternal verities, they are sufficiently like them to give us some purchase on them. And while 'some' may not be 'all', 'some' may be enough.

It is Paul's contention, that on this general condition as particularly appropriated, Jesus of Nazareth sheds light, with which the light shed by Jewish principles and procedures may be compared and contrasted. Sunlight and candlelight and Broneer's oil lamps (1977) are analogues. How much brighter is the sun! But the sun is the son. And the son is mirror to the sun and mirror image to the observer and sculpture to the sculptor. God, as the craftsman who made the mirror, is father, sculptor, the one reflected in the

---

7. '...von dem man sagt, dass er sich sprechen höre, oder welcher steht und geht, als ob er auf einer Bühne wäre, um angegafft zu werden, welches jederzeit einen Stümper verrät.'

mirror of the world. And his son is the spitting image (semen [Cupitt 1990: 1]) of his father, the clay image of the worker in clay, the mirror image in the looking glass of the world.

Mirror image and sculptured image are parables. Of what are they parabolic? What etching, what outline, what stroke, what writing of what pen? And who is Hamann's 'poet', who makes, not *works of art*, but *things*? Who makes, not works of art, but *all* things?

Paul of Tarsus is much too cunning a writer to leave himself with nothing to say. Just as 'kingdom' is a parable in brief, just as a parable of the kingdom is a parable less brief than the metaphor, 'kingdom', of which the parable is an explication, just as Jesus can turn from a parable to a parable, Paul vaults (he is free to) from mirror to model, from the visual to the tactile. Paul's mind is 'wind-swift' (ἀνεμόεν φρόνημα, *anemoen phronema* [Sophocles, *Antigone* 354]). Sitting light, Paul never sits for long. From mirror to sculpture, from the creation of the artist to the procreation of the parent (Christology as a play of images), Paul turns to 'spirit'.

The mind has 'cliffs of fall' (Hopkins 1970: 100), and heights (else where could you fall from?). And the wind, that beats against the heights (Darling 1937: 123), makes itself visible in snowflakes and leaves; tactile in its contention against the face.

In this sense, 'spirit' is a concrete phenomenon, if, as zephyr on 'The Ripening Seed' (Kerr 1993: 31), falling short of abstraction by the merest susurration:

> To have let go
> would have been
> to go with the wind
>
> back to summer...

And add the 'flying eddy' of Caiseamheall, 'the Rounded Hill of Cheese' (Darling 1937: 123). As the wind is malleable, 'spirit' is Protean, both in its form and in what it forms.

There is that by which things hang together, that may be invoked, when they fall apart. What Paul wrote was written in some such conviction as this. But by the law of the historicity of *rerum mortalia*, the mortality of things, and by the law of the historicity of the language, by which we speak about them, Paul's language is local and one would need the whole of the Apostle's work for the examination of how his experience is mapped by his words (Bultmann provides a classical example, gives a systematic account of Paul's 'thought' [1961: 187-353 (= 1952: 187-352)]. What cannot be denied (for it obtrudes) is that the present section of the Second Letter to the Corinthians is the preternaturally rich production of a rich writer, who can deal as eloquently with poverty as with wealth. And 'Spirit' is one of the ways, by which he does it. 'Spirit' (*pneuma*) is one of the central terms by which the burden of the glory of Paul's experience is carried, the lightness of its being and tautologously the 'weight' of its 'glory' (2 Cor. 4.17 [*kabod* (Heb. means indifferently 'glory'/'weight')]).

But, from one point of view, 'spirit' is the least successful locution, the least successful *parole* of the Pauline *langue* (de Saussure 1960: 7-15), the mere hypostatization of a natural phenomenon, a phenomenon that ranges from that, by which Torridonian flanks and Lewisian gneiss are beaten, to the thinnest susurration, that cannot be distinguished from stillness.

But, from the opposite point of view, the very plurality of the *Umwandlungen*, 'transformations', through which this natural phenomenon passes, is the very ground that 'licenses' (Ramsey: *omnia opera passim*) an almost infinite variety of *Rede*, not *Gerede*, not 'chatter', or 'idle talk', but 'speech' (Heidegger 1927: 160-70 [= 1962: 211-14]). Whether, when 'spirit' appears in Paul, we have to deal with a *symbol*, embedded in the natural world (wind), as Ricoeur might say (1976: 61) and *Ricoeur a ses raisons que la raison ne connait point*, 'has his reasons of which the reason knows nothing', or with a *metaphor*, is not much here to my purpose to discuss, though in either case I should wish to insist that a metaphorical, or symbolical, 'proposition' is a fiction, in that that is not, or not only, literally that which it is said to be. Despite, however, this limit to the story fiction can tell (it is not literal), nevertheless, fiction, because of the gap between itself and fact, has the advantage over fact of being more open-textured in its approach to, and its construction of, reality (Hepburn 1990). And 'open-textured' links with Richardson's 'adaptability' (1995: 121). 'Fiction' allows fluidity in the fluid world of Heraclitus (and foments it in the world of Bacchus!).

For where a writer is intending to say two things, it is a fallacy that the critic should choose between them. No doubt the word

'spirit' (*ruach*, *pneuma*, 'wind', 'breath'), by the time it reaches
Paul, has travelled a long way from Gen. 1.1, where the translators
have to halt between two opinions: 'the wind moved'/'the spirit
moved over the face of the waters'. But the fact that the novelist's
Jesus of Jn 3.8 ('the wind'/'spirit' 'breathes'/'blows', 'where it
wills'/'the molecules permit') and the teller of tales, in the *emphy-
sema* of Jn 20.22 ('he breathed on them...', ἐνεφύσησεν, *enephus-
esen* [Gen 2.7]), does not halt between, but straddles both opinions
(the poetic mind is an acrobat), at least demonstrates that even the
creative impulsions of a later writer than Paul could be aware of
this history made in the making of it, aware of what had been
written, as he came to the point of writing: it is important that the
primal sense (to call it that) of 'wind' and 'breath' still shines
through for John despite that usage, contemporary with himself, by
which the word applies to the higher ranges of the mind and what
lies beyond.

Diachronically and synchronically, 'spirit' has many meanings.
'Spirit' is a mustard tree, in which many birds can nest. 'Spirit' is a
bird, under the brooding of which all the fowls of the air can
breed. Its semantic range is astonishing.

What does not breathe is not alive, even if one may be forgiven
for supposing that there are times when what *does* breathe is very
nearly dead. While life under law is end, or goal, life under law is
end, or gaol. Law by spirit is 'reaffirmed' (Collingwood 1933: 88).
Law by spirit is 'opposed' (88). For what are the rules that apply to
the heart?

By Piero's foreshortened perspective (*de prospectiva pingendi*
[1984])in his painting of the 'aetiological cult-legend' (Dibelius
1929: 203), the baptism narrative at the beginning of Mark's novel
(Mk 1.9-11),[8] the 'spirit' as dove, white enough to indicate that
Jesus is candid, shows sufficient courtesy to the styles and conventions of *The Observer's Book of the Holy Spirit* to allow its identi-
fication with Canon Tristram's *Turtur garrulus risibilis* (1885:
121). But Paul precedes Piero, as he precedes the Conrad of
Typhoon (cit. Ramsey 1973: 3-4) and 'the west and southwest
winds' of George Adam Smith's *Historical Geography* (cit. Ramsey
1973: 5). And, preceding all these, Paul precedes Mark also.

---

8. Cf. *Glaubenslegende*, 'faith-legend' (Bultmann 1958: 264 [= 1963:
248]).

There are, in Paul, a number of leading categories, 'death' for one and 'spirit' for another. What is the *Pauline* profile of 'spirit'? What is its *Corinthian* distribution, habitat, display, reproductive behaviour?

On 'spirit', that is, Piero, in *The Baptism*, produces a bird-shaped cloud, or cloud-shaped bird and refuses to disambiguate. In *Models for Divine Activity*, Ramsey, via Conrad and George Adam Smith, has recourse to wind.

In order to probe Paul further, are we to turn to Cowley for an 'imitation' (of a Horatian ode), to Erasmus for a 'paraphrase', or to Hobbes (1844: Alala!)[9] for a 'metaphrase' (Dryden 1962: 268-69, cit. Prickett 1986: 29)?

It might, indeed, have been possible here to have made an attempt at a sub-Erasmian paraphrase, or imitation, of at least a vestigial part of what Paul is saying from: 'God…leads us in triumph' (2 Cor. 2.14) to 'We ar but bruckle piggs for sic a treisur tae be pitten in' (Lorimer 1983: 309, 2 Cor. 4.7). It is Paul's essay on development, the development of ethics (Walls *obiter dictum*), the development of ethics, logic and ontology.

In a plural world, with a Roman transport system, in which boats ply and, for Paul, sometimes tunnel (2 Cor. 11.25), there is neither Achaean, nor Judaean, neither feminist nor virist. All are united in a bond. Paul is living in a world in which ethnic ethics cannot survive, in which carnivores and vegetarians, the mutilated (sc. circumcised) and unmutilated must learn to tolerate one another and (*per impossibile*) women men. More than one tribe and trend comprise the community that houses within Paul's symbolic construct. History is a process of permanent sublation. Things, to speak ontologically, will be what they will be. While people must remember from where they have come, resistance to change is criminal folly; is not life, but death. History is a process that moves faster than texts.

And it should then have been sub-Erasmian, a meta-sub-Erasmian paraphrase, in the sense of something undertaken in what Bonhoeffer calls a post-Grotian, or post-Machiavellian world, in which we may speak in a way that would remain valid, *etsi deus non daretur*, 'even if God were not being given' (1971: 359). But, for Paul: *dandus est et datur deus datus*, 'God, who has been

9. = 1675 *Odyssey* 299, *Iliad* 214.

given, is being and is to be given'. And (this is the contention here) is given in the language of story and song. Paul was a great singer and is writing within a tradition of song. This singing tradition, this *cantabile*, is the rock from which his language is hewn: Moses sweating under un-sublated *lex* and the starting of light by a genetic locution.

But Paul hones what he hews in his own peculiar way. Gone are the winds of Elijah's Carmel (1 Kgs 19.8-12; cf. Prickett 1986: 6-18), like *An Teallach*:

> When the snow is down, an east wind blowing hard, the sky leaden, and the tops partly hidden, Beinn Dearg and An Teallach roar to one another from the unapproachable country of their summits. I do not know what causes this deep song in the high hills during the weather I have outlined. It cannot be explained away purely on the basis of wind and rock surfaces, for the roaring should be heard then under other sets of conditions which included high wind (Darling 1937: 11).

Figure 5. *Loch Toll an Lochain with An Teallach hills* (March 1925) by R.M. Adam (1885-1967) (reproduced by courtesy of the University of St Andrews Library)

But abbreviation is Paul's eloquence. Taciturnity, almost. Elijah comes without the pyrotechnics. In contrast with the Old Testament Paul's language is reduced. He does not narrate; he alludes. We do not have 'spirit' clothed in a story. We have 'spirit' unclothed (nearly). A mere word (nearly).

But what is this 'mere word'? What is 'spirit'?

With the exception of the noun 'God', and a handful of adjectives, by which the writer directs the reader to the noun, adjectives such as 'whole', 'hale' or 'holy', 'there is no specifically religious language' (Davis [again] 1994: 115). With these exceptions we have only qualifiers to indicate how the non-religious is being used. We have only secular models and metaphors and the implied assertion that there is that which is modelled by them, that there is non-literally that, which is literally so. Every time Paul passed a mirror, he took out his notebook and noted it for non-literal use. And the assertion is grounded rather in what follows from it than in what leads to it. The models are empirically fitting. They give us something to live by.

It is not that Paul does not belong in our world; it is that he does not seem to. 'Spirit' is what inspires and is expired. There is something to breathe. What happens in 2 Corinthians 3 is that this terminology, rooted in physiology (the lungs) and the physical (air, breath, wind) is transplanted into the metaphysical sphere with cultural effect. For in 2 Corinthians 3, 'spirit' is what inspires the human animal to take up critical distance from law. And both affirmation and negation are involved.

But 'spirit' and words like it (such as 'grace'), these images, these metaphors, these symbols, are not just suspended in the air, like grouse on the twelfth in a 35-knot wind, with Strauss and Bultmann among the beaters, Freud and Feuerbach among the guns. For these images, metaphors, symbols, whatever they should rightly be called, 'press beyond poetry into ontology' (Mackinnon 1986: 168). Or, if '[t]o write in these terms is not to belittle the work of the poets' (1986: 168), but, nevertheless, to run the risk of doing so, it may be said rather, that poetry instantiates the ontology, embodies it, the ontology being in, rather than beyond the poetry. For (so Bonhoeffer [again] *die Mythologie ist die Sache selbst*, 'the mythology is the thing itself' (1951: 162).[10] As Aristotle lapidarily

10. = 1971: 329 (letter of 8 June 1944).

and punctually puts it, the poetry 'says' it (λέγει, *legei*: *Po*. 1451b7).

'Not all the objects', writes Oakeshott (1983: 31),

> which compose the present of historical concern are mere survivals from bygone worlds of practical engagement. It contains also mathematical and scientific theorems, philosophical investigations, musical compositions, poems, works of art and so on. These also are *res gestae*, performances which have survived. But if there are to be genuine histories of science (as distinct from historical accounts of the place occupied by scientific engagement in a *Lebenswelt*), or of philosophical reflection (as distinct from 'the lives of the philosophers'), of music, art or literature, then these surviving objects must be distinguished in terms of the universes of discourse to which they belong and understood in terms of their appropriate modal provenances.

Paul's 'performance' here belongs to 'works of art', to 'art or literature'. Paul is no historiographer, though history may be by implication included: 'Peter refused me a reference.' In so far as Paul writes about the past, he writes about it only as it has passed through the crucible of his imagining mind. The past is plastic to his touch: the Exodus pericope about Moses and the veil implies that Moses put it on out of consideration for his interlocutors, while Paul implies something more sinister, that there was a failure in communication, a withholding of the damaging information, that the rule of law, the rule of *this* law, had its limits. And the future is his primary aim, not the past.

But Paul has, like the sea, texts have, like the sea, 'many voices' (Eliot, 'The Dry Salvages' I [= 1944: 26]). And if 'the pre-eminent voice' (Oakeshott 1983: 48) of Paul's text is the future, is (what is called) 'eschatology', is every new moment, is the attempt to per-suade the addressees to go for a higher option than law, there are simultaneously other eminent voices, such as (the reader may infer) a concern with the historical event (whatever this was) of the emer-gence and continuance of Hebrew law, with all its defects, and the sublated significance of this historical event for the development of a community that will be truly international. There is a concern with the historical event of the emergence (whatever this was) of the Christian movement and its contemporary relationship with the synagogue in general and in particular in Corinth, the...ΑΓΩΓΗ ΕΒΡ..., ...AGOGE HEBR... (Merritt 1931: 78-79), a body, that Paul

finds to be obtuse, a dead body, a corpse. For God can make a
human being out of a handful of dust (*b. Sanh.* 90b).[11] 'Spirit' is an
unspecifiable vantage point from which the Mosaic past can be
surveyed. It is a place where a purer air can be breathed, the locus
of the free man, the *loca* of free women.

Of any text it may be asked, What is the pre-eminent voice of the
text? And the question has been asked here, What is the pre-
eminent voice of *this* text? And, to what was said above, it may be
added that 'it contains Paul's *apologia pro vita sua* and some of
his most profound reflections on the theme of grace and nature'
(Mackinnon 1957: 257). And it may be added also that Paul is as little *pre-eminently* concerned merely to *impart information*, as

> the Gospel according to St Mark, a Persian carpet, Hobbes's
> *Leviathan*, the Anglo-Saxon Chronicle, the score of *Figaro*, a parish
> register of marriages, Fountains Abbey, a field path or a song. Each is
> a *res gesta*, an exploit which was performed in bygone times and
> has survived exactly as it was performed except for the damage it
> may have suffered on the way. And each is an oblique source of
> information which may be used in seeking answers to a variety of
> historical question about the past, but was certainly not designed to
> supply any such information (Oakeshott 1983: 48).

Amid such a euphony, or cacophony, of voices there is a danger
of being too tidy.

Paul's pre-eminent voice is literary, is the 'excited' construction
of fiction (Alexander 1933: 50). Paul is writing literature, though
literature with the quite practical, rhetorical purpose of persuading
the Corinthians to adopt a Pauline position. Paul has learned a
language and, in order to understand him, we need a 'dictionary or
a grammar of the language of Christian symbolism' (Oakeshott
1983: 50). And we need here a dictionary of *Pauline* symbolism,
which Paul was much too busy writing to write. The *mentalité* of
the futurologist of Paul's kind is under pressure. When Paul says
something, he knows what he is saying and what he means by
saying it, but is much too busy to reflect on either.

But if it is the scholar's task to write the dictionary and the grammar that Paul did not write, Blackmur's question (1954: 394-96)
still arises, whether scholarship and literary criticism do not necessarily *not* coincide, whether they are distinct and distinguishable

11. Cit. Strack and Billerbeck 1956: I, 895, cit. Bultmann 1960b: 28.

things, whether there are techniques, not of scholarship, but of
literary criticism to be pursued, that can examine, but press beyond
style to reach content and ontology, divinatory techniques, that,
while failing to say what the text has said, when the text is such
that what it has said cannot be said otherwise, nevertheless confront the reader, in some kind of appropriate way, not with the
critic and the critic's views, but with the text the critic is criticizing. How is a cool head to confront a hot text, when literary
criticism is a mere pink postulant among senior monks, seeing that
its history as a university discipline has been so brief, in Cambridge
only 'towards the close of the first world war' (Leavis 1969: 11)?
One thinks here of Yeats's scholars (1950: 158):

> Bald heads forgetful of their sins,
> Old, learned, respectable bald heads
> Edit and annotate the lines
> That young men, tossing on their beds,
> Rhymed out in love's despair...

What kind of twentieth-century analogue to Paul's first-century
performance would be the right one to identify for the reader what
Paul is performing? How is one to see (and, seeing, to *see*) the
colori cangianti, the 'changing colours' (Lightbrown 1992: 107) of
Paul's painting, Paul's 'contrasted studies' (1992: 107) of the faces
of Moses and Jesus?

This Corinthian Letter is an early work in Paul's more mature
style. The Epistle to the Romans is to seek. How is the scholar to be
directed by the critic to the 'magical reflections' (Lightbrown 1992:
107) in Paul's text ? 'How do words', so Alexander (1933: 23), 'get
diverted from their practical use, and become enchanted? How
does the magic get in?' (23). Are the subordinate figures in 2 Cor.
2.14–4.7, like the disrobing catechumen and the Jews in Piero's
Baptism, 'scaled not in rigorous perspective according to their real
distance from the principal figures but in a diminution proportional
to their importance in the story... [a] scaling for purposes of
narrative subordination' (Lightbrown 1992: 107-108)?

What magic, what miracle allows Paul's words to leave the river-
bed, in which they flow (as the Jordan in Piero's *Baptism*), so that
the redeemer and the reader can stand dry shod to contemplate?
Ornithology, a bird, is Piero's answer. The 'spirit' Paul's.

If one supposes, on a hypothesis shared by de Wette and von

Balthasar, that Paul, like Piero is an artist, using *Pictures as Arguments* (Hess 1975), that Paul is arguing more like an artist than a philosopher, then there will be a relation of peculiar intimacy between what he is saying and what he means by saying it, between his poetry and his ontology.

An extended quotation from Alexander (1933: 37-38), speaking 'like the good and wise man he was' (Collingwood 1940a: 174), makes the point:

> The meaning which in customary speech is attached to the sound of the word is in art blended or fused with the sounds. The sounds not only have meanings, that is they refer to things, but they are charged with their meanings and indissolubly one with them. For words or other expressive products become the material of art when they are used not for the sake of the things which they mean but in themselves and for their own sake. It is therefore mistaken to hold all spoken words to be aesthetic; they are in general purely semantic. Language becomes aesthetic only when it in turn becomes an object, and as such is revealed to the speaker charged with its meaning. It now not merely means its meaning and serves as a guide to the thing it means, and as in general happens, passes out of the mind when the mind is directed upon the thing through it; but is held there and becomes itself the thing which occupies the mind, and no longer has a meaning but is charged with meaning or fused with it.

What Paul writes is not only *about* ontology, it *is* itself ontological, *is* a poem, a thing made. Paul is writing *about* something and Paul's writing *is* something.

This section of 2 Corinthians is a high octane mixture, the antithesis to pedestrian prose. It is not the castration of his opponents that 'excites' him here ('Sall, but I wiss thae din-breeders amang ye may gang on an libb themsels!' [Lorimer 1983: 326] [Gal. 5.12]); he is 'excited' by the fight for his life, his *apologia*. He here performs the 'exploit' (Oakeshott 1983: 48), that imaginatively expresses his excitement. And thus, like Coleridge's iridescent geography in 'Kubla Khan' (Shaffer 1975: 119), or Luke's in the Pentecost pericope (Acts 2.2 and Loisy 1920: 186), Paul subtly elides a saga and a myth, the story of the birth of the law and the creation of the sun (2 Cor. 4.6).

We may forgive Erasmus for being so baffled by Paul's brevity, that he is prepared, on some occasions (*aliquoties*), to do no more for Paul than to repeat him. Thus on 'spirit', Erasmus repeats Paul. But why repeat, when you are meant to be paraphrasing? And what are you repeating? 'Spirit' is less a *Grundbegriff* (Wölfflin's word [1917]: 'principle', 'foundational concept') than a *Grundbild* (foundational picture). 'Spirit' is a 'root metaphor' (Tracy 1979), a 'model for divine activity' (Ramsey 1973). Paul resolutely tells no tale, for you cannot draw the *desegno* (Piero della Francesca 1984: 63), the 'outline', of the wind, or delineate a susurration. In the historical, or the theological sense of the word 'cause', one is sometimes persuaded by persons, or supersensibles, to take some kind of account of either, or both. Does scholarship come to the aid of criticism here? Are we to summon up Briggs's classical article (1900)? Or resign ourselves to Erasmian exhaustion?

But even single words can bear a weight of meaning. Take 'take', for instance:

> Daffodils,
> That come before the swallow dares, and take
> The winds of March with beauty.
> (Shakespeare, *Winter's Tale* IV.iv.118, cit. Alexander 1933: 39)

And take: 'beholding in a mirror' (κατοπτριζόμενοι, *katoptrizomenoi*), '...beholding the glory of the Lord' (2 Cor. 3.18). 'Us believers...luiks on the glorie o the Lord as in a gless' (Lorimer 1983: 309). The word occurs within a passage, the whole of which (2.14–7.4) is printed by Loisy (1922) in verse form.

'The world', Hopkins tells us ('God's Grandeur' [1970: 66]) 'is charged with the grandeur of God'. Take, moreover, Philo (*Leg. All.* 3): 'nor would I find the reflection of Thy being in aught else than in Thee Who art God', μηδὲ κατοπτρισαίμην ἐν ἄλλῳ τινὶ τὴν σὴν ἰδέαν ἢ ἐν σοὶ τῷ θεῷ, *mede katoptrisaimen en allo(i) tini ten sen idean e en soi to(i) theo(i)* (cit. Thrall 1994: 291). From Philo it may be inferred, *perhaps*, that *both* objects in the world *and* the world itself as a whole may be a mirror that reflects God's grandeur. Does not then Paul's speech betray him as 'bewitching' (Alexander 1933: 39), as a writer of verses that sing. And if Paul took it from Philo, is it still not a tribute to him that *he* saw it, too, and a tribute to him that he saw how to alter it. Theft, too, is a 'mark of genius' (Aristotle, *Po.* 1459a7), the theft from one talent by another genius.

But the world reflects, only if it is seen to do so. And we have the privilege of remaining content with puzzling reflections in a mirror, of seeing *durch einen Spiegelglas in einem dunklen Worte* ('through a mirror-glass in a dark word' [1 Cor. 13.12]; so Brahms, *Vier ernste Gesänge*). The composers of the West have been right to set Paul, and Luther, to music.

When that than which no greater can be imagined (for the imagination needs space to move in and the fact that it needs it does not prove that it does not have it) looks into the mirror of the world, the mirror image of that which, being greater, must be the greatest, not *maius*, but *maximum* (Cusanus 1954: *passim*), is Jesus. Into this mirror the inhabitants of the world may gaze and be changed. The object of Paul's *Ahnung, Ahndung*, 'intimation', is here specified as a Corinthian mirror, the image in it and what is *imaged* by that image..

Exegi speculum hocce aere perennius, Paul might say, after Horace (*Odes* 3.30.1), Paul has here executed a mirror more perennial than bronze (cf. Murphy-O'Connor 1983b: 23-36, Davidson 1952: 182-83).

The illusion of truth and the truth of illusion can both be done with mirrors. We must learn to see, not only Paul himself, but the language of Paul, as 'false, yet true' (ὡς πλάνοι καὶ ἀληθεῖς, *hos planoi kai aletheis, ut seductores et veraces* [2 Cor. 6.8]). Can the poet understand his life, if he does not fictionalize it? Can the theologian theologize, if he cannot play truly, not only among the false, but *with* it?

9

The Intrusion of a Locution and an Assumption into the Autobiography of a Man in Difficulties: But You Can't Nail a Good Man Down (Paul and the Catalogue of *Peristases*: 2 Corinthians 11.22–12.10)

ἀλλὰ ὑπάρχων πανοῦργος
2 Corinthians 12.16
but, the loupie loun at I am
Lorimer, *The New Testament in Scots*

In a given circle to inscribe a fifteen-angled figure which shall be both equilateral and equiangular: let ABCD be the given circle; thus it is required to inscribe in circle ABCD a fifteen-angled figure which shall be both equilateral and equiangular

Euclid, book IV, prop. 16

This Pauline passage looks like straightforward autobiography, but the plain, autobiographical framework is broken at two points, though there are maybe more of these. What is to be made of these two points, Paul's voice from the sky: 'My grace is sufficient...' (2 Cor. 12.9) and Paul's travel to it (in whole or in part): 'caught up to the third heaven' (2 Cor. 12.1-5)? Doing a bit of Euclid helps the spectator to get inside Piero della Francesca's *Baptism*? Can anything as lucid, even to the geometer schoolboy, help us with Paul? Some language may legitimately be odd. But even the legitimately odd may have perspicuous, even Euclidean form.

And looking only at the straightforward autobiography, if all that happened to Paul, why did not he just roll over and float belly up, as the sea seems more than once to have given him some opportunity of doing? He seems to have had 'difficulties', *peristases*, with which to contend.

If Brahms could put 1 Corinthians 13 straight into music, to do something here would take, to catch it, the Stravinsky of *The Rite of Spring*. But the (w)rite Paul writes is antiphonal, contrapuntal, written, because written by Paul, not in Spring simply, but in Midwinter Spring, dialectically.

Or should it be the horn theme of Strauss in *Don Juan*, the musical analogue certainly of Rom. 8.38, of ὑπερνικῶμεν, *hupernikomen*: 'in all these things we are more than conquerors'. Jerome is weak here: *in his omnibus superamus*, 'we conquer in all these things'. But where is the 'hyper'? We had better, if I understand him, have Lorimer (1983: 268 *ad loc.*): 'But aa thir drees an ills, we ey waur an better nor waur them aa.'

Or should it just be sung through the nose, like any singer from the *souk*?

But (Mackenzie *apud* Thorpe Davie 1953, *obiter scriptum*) it is not *Don Juan* we want, as the musical analogue of Paul 'in it', of Paul in deepest trouble, of Paul in *tribulation* even (Macdonald's distinction [*obiter scriptum*]), of Paul 'in it' and at the same time above it all. What we want rather is the horn theme from the last movement of Brahms's First Symphony. 'That ass, Tovey' (Wittgenstein 1980: 81e, contra Mackenzie 1993: 85) writes:

> there is a moment's darkness and terror, and then day breaks. There is no more tragedy. The mode of the principal key changes to major for the last time in this symphony as the solemn trombones utter their first notes, and the horns give out a grand melody that peals through the tremolo of muted violins like deep bells among glowing clouds (1935: 92).

But the burden of Paul's deliverances here is clear: he is not one to crouch in the desert with his *burnous* over his head amid the graves of his hopes. An elision of collisions, this passage: Paul collides with almost everybody, but says almost nothing about anyone. He speaks of 'dangers of rivers' (2 Cor. 11.26), but if he stood on the banks of the Meander, and if, as he stood there, he asked himself whether the river was 'a strong brown god' (Eliot, 'The Dry Salvages' I [= 1944: 25]), or was merely a problem for the builder of boats, he does not tell us he did so. But if his narration is short, his list (and *List* [German: 'cunning']) is long: the list is long and cunningly crafted (Weiss 1897: 23-25, 29-30).

You can measure a man (*this* one), says Paul, by what he has been prepared to put up with. He is

> in this earthly world, where to do harm
> Is often laudable, to do good sometime
> Accounted dangerous folly...
>
> (Shakespeare, *Macbeth* IV.ii.75-77)

Oppugned, he defends and accordingly produces a selection from an abbreviated autobiography.

The selection is formally excellent: anaphora (e.g. 'dangers': eight times repeated [11.26]); anaphora, with climax ('I, too...I, too...I, too...I, *more* than all' [11.22-23]); dyads (three times, e.g. 'hunger and thirst' [11.27]), followed by monads (e.g. 'fastings'), in concatenation; adverbial numbers (four times [11.25]) arranged according to the idiosyncratic ordinal of a cardinal figure of the early community (e.g. 'five times...three times'); rhetorical questions, answered rhetorically by this rhetorician, questions that are rhythmical, of which the rhythm is varied ('Who is not weak and I am not weak...' [11.29]); the whole culminating in a near-perfect chiasmus: 'is sufficient [A] for you [B] my grace [C], for power [C'] in weakness/in you, weak [B'] is perfected [A']', the whole pervaded, interfused, by the characteristic writhings of the Pauline mind: 'I know...I do not know, God knows...'—and, perhaps, the desperate writhings of the glossators of the text, 'the damage it may have suffered on the way' (Oakeshott 1983: 48).

Was not M. Loisy right to print the New Testament (1922) as, in some considerable measure, poetry, a man (M. Loisy), whose *Duel with the Vatican* (1924) is here replicated by his duplicate (M. Paul)? For on Paul's 'thorn in the flesh' (2 Cor. 12.7) the exegete is faced with the choice of epilepsy, cerebral malaria, or St Peter. It is not unfair to say that not everything speaks against the view that under that phrase, 'thorn in the flesh', the last of these may, even if not alone, be subsumed.

For M. Loisy, who can speak intelligent French, says (1933: 49 n.; he has been saying, that[1] 'Their [sc. Nos Evangiles...] form, their oracular and liturgical style, of which the character is impersonal, answers to their object'):

> The question of the New Testament style is still under examination. It is certain that the discourses in the Gospels, even those in the fourth, were originally short writings composed in the rhythmic

1. Leur forme, leur style oraculaire et liturgique, de caractère impersonnel, répond à leur objet.

form peculiar to the poetic writings of the Old Testament, Psalms, Proverbs and the discourses in Job. It is equally certain that some parts at least of the Epistles and the entire Apocalypse were put out [?edited?] at first in rhythmic form. The same may well be true of the Gospel stories] (Loisy ET 1948: 43-44).[2]

M. Loisy's text (not in the English translation) continues:

A considerable sketch of this problem has been made by Fr. Jousse in a dissertation with the bizarre title: 'The oral-rhythmic and mnemo-technic Style among the Verbo-motors'[3] (1925). The response to this dissertation is eagerly awaited. Some pointers were offered in my article on 'The rhythmic Style of the New Testament' (*Journal de Psychologie*, 15 May, 1923). The earlier published studies of Fr. Schmidt ('The strophic construction of the complete text of the four Gospels', delivered to the Academy of Sciences of Vienna [20 April, 1921]) have found little response.[4]

Each time a book of M. Loisy appeared on the Presbyterian shelves of the Edinburgh Faculty of Divinity, it (and some readers) began to smoulder slightly, with (some detected) a slightly acrid odour. But Cambridge (of course) and the National Library of Scotland (the [next] Secretary of State for Scotland be praised!) permit the citation of some further sentences, a part selected only with

2.   'La question du style néotestamentaire est encore à l'examen. Il est certain que les discours évangéliques, même du quatrième Evangile, ont été libellés d'abord dans la forme rythmée qui a été celle des écrits poétiques de l'Ancien Testament (Psaumes, Proverbes, discours de Job). Il est certain également que telles parties au moins des Epîtres [Phil. 2!] ont été rédigées de la même façon, et aussi l'Apocalypse entière. Il pourrait bien en être de même pour les récits évangéliques ['The Samaritan' and 'The Prodigal'!].'

3.   Loisy has spoken of a *dissertation au titre bizarre*. The term, *Verbo-moteurs*, certainly qualifies as a component of such a title. Might it be, asks hesitantly, and speculatively, Laver J. (in a kind communication), that 'glosso-lalic speakers might be thought to speak with their 'speech motors' unable to be switched off for a while?' We are doing the best we can.

4.   'Ce problème a été largement ébauché par le P. Jousse dans une dissertation au titre bizarre: "Le Style oral rythmique et mnémotechnique chez les Verbo-moteurs" (1925). La suite de cette dissertation se fait beaucoup attendre. Quelques indications avaient été données dans mon article sur "Le Style rythmé du Nouveau Testament" (Journal de Psychologie, 15 mai 1923). Les études publiées auparavant par le P. Schmidt "Der strophische Aufbau des Gestamttextes der vier Evangelien, communication à l'Académie des Sciences de Vienne", 20 avril 1921) ont trouvé peu d'écho.'

difficulty from a longer whole of (the still untranslated) volume, *Les livres du Nouveau Testament* (1922).

There are first some introductory remarks on the religious writings of the most primitive peoples, with their 'incantations and rhythmic ballads (*cantilènes*), in which the choice of words contributes to the effectiveness of the formulae, and the parallelism, the rise and fall (*cadence*), the assonance assist the memory and pace(?) the ritual gestures'. These are then followed by some further remarks on the 'poetic rhythm and the oracular style' of the Old Testament, which has impressed itself on the New, on the rhythm of the sayings of Jesus, 'which recalls the parallelism of the Hebrew poems, which is furthermore not without analogy with the oracular style of pagan mysticism', and finally on the style of the Fourth Gospel, where 'the mysticism is coloured by lyricism' (*le mysticisme se teinte de lyrisme*). M. Loisy then goes on:

> Even the epistles hold more or less firmly to the mystical and liturgical style, with its cadences and rhythms. All of this, without being classical, is more or less studied, sometimes cunningly arranged and harmoniously turned (1922: 14).[5]

It is here inappropriate to labour the point, or to labour it further, but Loisy's book and his insights, registered by and embodied in the appearance of the translated text on the printed page, are (I think) of immense importance. *Loisy locutus, causa finita*, Loisy has spoken, the case is settled. But Loisy is not alone in so speaking. He is accompanied by Burney (1925) and Black (1954: 105-42) on the Hebrew verse form of the Jesus tradition and by Johannes Weiss (1897) on rhetorical form in Paul.

Loisy has spoken, indeed, and the question that arises is this:

What is to be made of a *content* which takes *poetic form*?

This, and what follows from this, when this is thought through, is the purport of the present book.

Loisy locutus, causa finita. But what is the case that has been settled? It is this, that, if the whole of the New Testament in considerable measure takes poetic form (which it does), then it is poetry and it is as poetry that it is to be interpreted.

---

5.   'Même les épîtres tiennent plus ou moin de ce style mystique et liturgique, cadencé et rythmé. Tout cela, sans être classique, est plus ou moins étudié, subtilement agencé parfois et harmonieusement tourné.'

The case rests.

And does not rest, for the debate continues.

It is not that Paul is taking time to write well; it is just that he can. It is not that he is a disengaged aesthete; it is that he feels his theology and, in feeling it, feels its shape.

And he glories in paradox: 'I am proud of what I should be ashamed of'; 'My achievements consist in my failures'; 'My actions are passions'; 'Only he is strong, who is without strength'.

The man is a fool, irritated by the hierarchy into blowing his own trumpet.

But what kind of a fool? The wisest in early Christendom? If irritated by his enemies, by what is he stimulated? By Jesus' last gasp? By the last *tuba* (trumpet), scattering a surprising sound (*mirum spargens sonum*)? By the nails that nailed a good man down?

Paul, like Jesus before him (Paul makes the point), has fallen foul of law and order. What could be more patent than that Paul is making use of the 'historical, plain Method' (Locke 1894: I, 27, cit. Collingwood 1946: 206) in narrating his decline and fall from Damascus in a way that would have taken Gibbon longer.

The supposal, that the New Testament is fiction, can hardly be sustained by a passage that looks more like plain history than almost any other passage in the whole collection. It is history in the form of autobiography. It is history well shaped. But history is what it is. It is history Paul is writing.

But is that *all* he is doing? Is it only the 'historical, plain Method' that Paul is using and not also the 'theological, obscure Method'?

For from where does his near-perfect chiasmus (2 Cor. 12.9) derive? From his English classes, as a schoolboy, in Tarsus? Quite apart from training under one schoolmaster from earliest infancy to throw a javelin at Jerusalem, as he wrestled on the banks of the river, Cydnus (Harris 1964: 133-35), was another of Paul's school-masters a schoolmaster unto the pre- *progumnasmata* of Hermo-genes of Tarsus (2nd century AD), the antecedents of his 'prepara-tory exercises in rhetoric' (Forbes 1986: 22-24)? Is Paul's use of chiasmus in 2 Cor. 12.9 sufficiently explained by his education?

For, by Lowth's prosopopoea (1839: 136-46), it is the poet, who puts words into the mouth of God.

Or is it that the *content* is discovered and the *form* invented? Is it that *what* is said is supplied (by another) and *how* it is said constructed (by Paul)?

Is Mackinnon's 'receptivity' (1957: 255) to be exhausted by what Paul learnt at his teachers' knees, or across them? Where do insights come from? And from where do *judgments* about insights derive?

Judgments are best left to the sovereign, Hobbes, in the *Leviathan*, supposes. We may agree with Hobbes that insights and judgements can have fissiparous results (*homo homini lupus*... etc.), but we need not agree with him that no one has the right to run foul of law and order. While there is nothing wrong with caution, there may, at any time, be nothing wrong with throwing caution to the winds. Was Socrates right? Was Paul?

Chiasmus features here.

But space travel also: 'I know a man in Christ... such a one caught up' (2 Cor. 12.2). Irruption and eruption: a locution irrupts into Paul's world and Paul from Paul's world erupts in rapt locomotion.

And this is so, this irruption is happening, in a passage where Paul is at his plainest, where Paul is going in for historiography, where he is writing about the past, a past that is his own past, even if he is not merely remembering what one would be forgiven for thinking unforgettable, but consulting his diary, an extract from which is given immediately below, some of it the merest jottings from a life cumbered about by much apostolicism:

Diary of an Idiot in Word

[This diary was recovered by divers from the black box of a sunken quinquereme, refitted and converted for use as a merchantman (or merchantwoman). The quinquereme was found at a depth of 39 fathoms, one night and one day's swimming distance NW of Troas. The box was concealed at the base of some 401 tons of (now calcified) lentils. It was, no doubt, these, which had caused the ship to founder.]

boat departure times [KS Enkephalides],
take tablets of stone (copies),
   for ballast and bottom
      (n.b. effect on Plimsoll lines),

as legend for on-board exegesis workshops (pack saws, cork):
    the Law and Sin/*Sinn*;
handle inquiries of stevedores, concerning
    item: trinkets (hierarchically priced) for Rome,
    item: Palestinian sherry for *Hispania Citerior*,
    item: withies (basket-making) [bound to come in handy:
        physiotherapy (senior legalists)? defenestration?]
    item: coracles assault (river crossing)
    item: Judaiser identikits (the Damascus & X-Files)
    item: one (1) one-woman tent for, tracts for distribution by Phoebe,
    item: addresses of police stations, Asiarchs, etc., in:
    Illyricum, Italia, Hispania, Lusitania—
        would I were in Alba
        able were I were I to see *Alba*
            εἴθε γενοίμην (?)
            μὴ γένοιτο (?)
        [memo: must investigate 'legal fictions']
memo: sheer pain—reflect on:
        pain within the brackets of beauty (?)
            (beauty as metaphor, not analogy)
        weakness within the brackets of strength
        disgrace bracketed by grace
        the beginning, middle & end of a story, bracketed by
            'to be begun', 'to be continued…'
        physics/metaphysics, implicit/explicit
            explicitated by Hebrew texts
            critical assessment of sagas
            exploitation of myths
            sensible phenomena capable of
                supersensible employment:
                item: mirrors
                item: inkpots
                item: *ostraka*
                item: snakes
                (anything in snake-handling, I wonder?)
                (snake-handling and the liturgy?)
                (memo: must try Malta)
                (with luck no snakes there)
                (memo: pack grass snake)
                (sure to come in handy)
                ('handy' *mot juste*!)
            (might ask Timothy if he can manage the hand-
            luggage)

```
[memo: disk-world & Euclid on
      centre & circumference—Aristarchus in ship's
      library?]
[memo: propheta—vates ('prophet—poet')
      teacher? 'those who can do'?
      'apostle' as pro-agent
            [Q: can pro-agents be pro-active?]
            vocation as topos
      [MEMO: must prioritize
            or did I do that already (1 Cor. 12.28-31)?
[memo: all this Greek nudity in
      bad taste—must get this into
      earlier bit that I shall write
      later—would go well in Chapter 5 ad init.
         (I think)
      memo: try tent again]
[memo: nocturnal invasions of Phoebe
[memo: more ditto.]
      it's a rum thing, but there doesn't
      seem to be any drink on this ship,
      better, for my stomach's sake, to
      try the hold, if the undergirdings
      can hold up in this weather
      (must remember to wrap Diary
      in protoplastic folder, if danger
      of being submerged for a night
      and a day)
```

[cetera desunt]

But Paul is sustained here by more than mere autobiography. Paul's thought is carried by something else, by the 'oneiric' (Wilder), or whatever one should call it—and I want to call it 'fiction', the shaping of one's experience by conversation, to include conversation with supersensibles, or one's travelling (or not travelling [Paul is either not clear on this, or is modest about this]) to meet supersensibles, much in the same way as Eliot is unable to return home, after an air raid, without entering Purgatory, or re-enter his home, without fusing his return with the *Purgatorio* of Dante ('Little Gidding' II [= 1944: 38-40]), the poet, thus, in Kantian terminology, fusing what he *understands* with what he *imagines*, or *re-imagines*.

Man cannot live with Paul alone, nor woman (far less) neither. And for this reason: in the rather unbalanced régime of Adolf

Hitler, Dietrich Bonhoeffer, in his *Ethics* (1955a: 16, 89 [= 1992: 78, 148]) shows his philosophical, or implicitly philosophical, balance by speaking there of Jesus of Nazareth 'incarnate, crucified and risen'. Not one of these three words is undeserving of critical inquiry, for we have (do we not?) two metaphorical fictions ('a word is flesh', 'a dead man is awake'), and a fact ('crucified') surrounded by fictions (e.g. 'sacrifice'). Jesus was not sacrificed. He was executed. But, even where such inquiry is not undertaken, the general purport is clear, a purport of affirmation, negation and reaffirmation. Or life, death and life after it.

What *carries* Paul's text, what *carries* his history, his personal history, his autobiography, in 'The Fool's Speech', appears, as it were, only at the edges of his discourse, winks round its corners: sc. the space travel and the chiasmus. But if this text is inserted into the context of Paul's *oeuvre* as a whole, then (I would argue) that the *carrying* text (Käsemann and Meeks), that carries the texts is Gal. 2.19, 'I have been crucified with Christ', Χριστῷ συνεσταύρωμαι, or as St Jerome (if the epithet, or title, can be unambiguously used (Henderson *obiter dictum*)[6] would put it: *Christo confixus sum cruci*. Many other analogous texts might be cited (2 Cor. 4.10 etc.).

The text is, of course, a fiction, which could not, had it been true, have been written. For crucifixion (literal) is not a possible posture for the writer. But, for all that, the thrust, the force, the transfixing power of the metaphor declares that Paul is palmarily dealing with, or is imagining he has to deal with, *der gekreuzigte Herr* (the crucified lord [Käsemann 1960: *passim*]) as his 'crucified' servant:

> Like any good Hellenistic moralist, Paul puts forth his own life as a model to be imitated, but by his 'biography of reversal' [Paul's former life goes into reverse at his conversion (Schütz 1975: 133)] and his application of the Cross as a metaphor to his own mishaps and sufferings, he transforms that commonplace into something new (Meeks 1983: 131).

The point is sufficiently central to the work of the cantankerous

---

6.   But cf. Henderson (1967: 5), where the epithet is withdrawn from Augustine 'with his preposterous depreciation of marriage as licensed fornication, a view not unconnected with his own abandonment of the woman who had been his mistress'.

Käsemann to require the citation of no part of his work except the whole of it.

But the centrality in Paul of this metaphorical predication, 'crucifixion', and the centrality of the peculiar fact, a fact both historical and, by implication, metaphysical, on which this predication is based, co-equally perhaps conjoined with 'resurrection' from that ἐγέρσιμος ὕπνος, *egersimos hupnos*, 'that sleep from which one wakes' (Theocritus 24.7; Nonnus, *Paraphrase of John* 20.42, 21.78),[7] threatens balance, which could be restored only by being better on 'incarnation'. It is the *triad* of terms that provides a solid structure. 'Crucifixion' and 'resurrection', on their own, are not enough.

Does John do better? Or would one be right to say (but two to differ) that Paul, with all his pain, would have benefited from Hopkins (for all his pain, also) on kingfishers and Bonhoeffer on 'the right to bodily life'? The question is worth raising and not beyond answering.

Sanday and Headlam are right to wax lyrical on the travailing and groaning of the cosmos (1902: on Rom. 8.22), but are they right to say that Paul waxed lyrical, that '[h]e is one of those (like St. Francis of Assisi) to whom it is given to read as it were the thoughts of plants and animals' (Sanday and Headlam, Excursus on Rom. 8.18-25: *The Renovation of Nature* [1902: 212]). If Paul, here, 'seems to lay his ear to the earth' (1902: 212), it seems to be over my dead body that he does so.

> θαμίζουσα μάλιστ᾽ ἀηδὼν
> [the nightingale, a constant guest]
> (Sophocles, *Oedipus at Colonus* 672 [trans. Jebb])

is after all not a line in Paul. For it is Sophocles' nightingale, that in the Academy (Jebb on 675-76), 'trills her clear note in the covert of green glades, dwelling amid the wine-dark ivy and the god's inviolate bowers, rich in berries and fruit, unvisited by sun, unvexed by wind of any storm' (671-78), that 'deafens daylight...in the gymnasts' garden' (metatrans. Yeats, 'Colonus' Praise' [1950: 245], contra Sophocles, *Oedipus at Colonus* 1239-48, Yeats, 'From Oedipus at Colonus' [1950: 255]).

But when that has been said, this foolish man, Paul, can be

---

7. Cit. Gow 1952: 416, with ref. to 360.

accused in this speech of writing an exegesis of Gal. 2.19. It is as if Paul were saying that by the Galatians metaphor, 'crucified with Christ', *what he literally means is what he recounts in the Fool's Speech* of 2 Corinthians. When Paul says metaphorically that 'he has been crucified', what he means, in point of literal fact, is that he has been beaten 'five times' by the Jews and 'three times' by the Romans (2 Cor. 11.24-25), and so on. In *this* sense the Corinthians Speech is parasitic on the Galatians metaphor.

Fiction, in other words, breaks through this 2 Corinthians text like Lewisian gneiss. History is *now* and Corinth and was *then* before it. But history is not all there is. What is happening here is that, by Vaihinger's 'fictionalism', 'an idea recognised to be untrue may nevertheless have practical value' (Macquarrie 1963: 81). It is *als ob*, *'as if* (Vaihinger 1920 (ET 1924), cit. Gallagher *obiter dictum*), the Great Authour of our Salvatioun and Damnatioun has made of Paul, not only an 'authorial self' (Cohen 1994: 77, *u.ö.*), but an authored self, whose writing (Paul's) has been written by writing (God's [2 Cor. 3.3]) and whose writing (Paul's) is metaphysics, but implicit metaphysics, in the form of space fiction etc. *That* is Paul's pre-eminent voice, while the eminent voice of the writing *here* (Paul's) appears as history (sc. autobiography). But it is a history, into the edges of which there has been 'insinuated' (Craig, see Templeton 1991) other writing (God's), which is more closely to be defined as 'fiction', for this is the writing of a writer (God), who is capable of performance in more than one *genre* (sc. history and metaphysics also, as well as poetry).

For if human beings cannot get by without art, the art of the imaginative expression of emotion; indeed, if no human being can get by without this (for art is co-extensive with language as such, and '[a]rt must be language' [Collingwood 1938: 273]), then how much more should this not be true of God? It is simply too narrow to suppose that history only is God's *forte* and a mistake, or a localized prejudice merely, to suppose it, since Reimarus, his *fortissimo*, or her *fortissimiore con crescendo* (*Madame Rossini*), *sfz*.

For God's voices are neither a solo instrument, nor yet a quartet, or a quintet, but an orchestra, of which the music

> is not heard at all, but you are the music
> While the music lasts.
>
> (Eliot, 'The Dry Salvages' V [= 1944: 33])

The auditory, the audience (*hupakoe*, 'hearing', 'response') is receiving an invitation to dance: 'you must move in measure, like a dancer' (Eliot, 'Little Gidding' II (= 1944: 40), or, in Sydney Carter's more vernacular idiom ('The Lord of the Dance') and Aaron Copeland's music, the *Appalachian Spring*, you must learn to 'dance with the devil on your back'.

But these things, Hamann (1950: 197) after Bacon (*de augmentis scientiarum* 2.13 [ET = 1870: IV, 317]), would say, are parables *argumentis antiquiores*, 'older than reasoning' (Crick, in Nisbet 1985: 141).

But I am not so much entertaining a hypothesis here as making an assertion; the assertion, namely, that there is that, than which nothing greater can be conceived; and not making merely, but following out the implications of an assertion, being committed to it and being committed to following it out, if not committed to not following out the objections to it. For it is, regrettably, true, fictionally true, that Job lost his children, if it is also true, fictionally true, that he found them again, Jemima, Kezia and Keren-happuch (Job 42.14), even if it might still be objected that neither a replacement, nor a clone, nor a series of clones should be regarded as adequate substitutes for the originals (Job 1.15). And anyway three daughters must have been a handful and especially at one's latter end. But objections, at one level, to deity are valid and are not unknown to the authors of Hebrew fictions. And objections to deity may be all the more valid, if (to speak in a Tillichian way [1957: 154]) 'we do not find symptoms of repression of doubt in the picture of Jesus as the Christ'.

But God, too, like the gods, and like the sea, 'has many voices' (Eliot, 'The Dry Salvages' I [= 1944: 26]). And 'like the gods' is no idle insertion, if '[t]he death of one god is the death of all' (Stevens 1955: 381 [= I: i]). If Christian polytheists, or trinitarians, can talk sense, there is no good reason for supposing that others cannot also, if (for example) Collingwood is right to speak of 'the college of medical men attached to the temple of Asklepios at Epidauros' (1940: 204), who were practising pluralistic science (in this case, medical) in a polytheistic context. For why should theology be Hebrew, or Christian, if it is to be right? For myth, any myth, or fiction, any fiction, implies an 'understanding of existence' or *Existenzverständnis* (Bultmann 1960a: 23 [= 1957: 11]). And if any understanding of existence is wrong, or is something less than another that is better, it may nevertheless not be *all* wrong, so that it may be said that the understanding, or the myth, or the fiction, is at least true in parts. Monotheistic may be an improvement on pluralistic science, but still that 'college of medical men' may have known a thing or two.

However true it may be, that there is between Athens and Jerusalem an overlap, a relation at once of distinction and opposition, of re-affirmation and discomfirmation, Paul's assertion here, that there is that which is other than history, is not an assertion *tout court*, but an 'assertion', that comes in the form of a venture into space. It is sci-fi for a purpose, but it is sci-fi nonetheless.

But what is the function of such an 'assertion'?

What is implied by such talk is that human beings can, and do sometimes have, and that Paul, in Paul's view, *did* have access, not to history, but to a perspective on history. How does the new occur in history? How does one gain access to neoterism, to novelty? Is religion, Paul asks, for the Jews? No, religion, Paul answers, is for Jews and Greeks. But because some Jews object to Paul's answer, conflict follows, they beat him 'five times'. But conflict can be withstood. How can it be withstood? Here Paul has the benefit of the audition of a locution: 'My grace is sufficient for you...' But what kind of a locution? *This* locution is different from Peter's locution, or the Jerusalem locution: 'I refuse to write you a reference' (2 Cor. 3.1). For *this* locution (2 Cor. 12.9) is a locution from the sky. The two locutions are not on all fours. For such a locution, as God's or Jesus' locution (and, if so, it is after all, a post-mortem one), is not on all fours even with the absence of one from an unwilling Peter, or an unwilling Jerusalem. The former is not on all fours with the latter, but on all *sevens*.

But this *sevens* needs an explanation:

In a 'Foreword' to one of his publications (1954: 163), e.e. cummings writes as follows:

> Ineluctable preoccupation with The Verb gives a poet one priceless advantage: whereas nonmakers must content themselves with the merely undeniable fact that two times two is four, he rejoices in a purely irresistible truth (to be found, in abbreviated costume, upon the title page of the present volume).

The 'present volume' was *Is 5* (1926, also in 1954: 161-219). But if, for the poet, 2 + 2 = 5, it may be said, at least of *some* poetry, *religious* poetry, that 2 + 2 = 7 and it may be claimed that Paul's poetry here is poetry of that kind, that the locution of Paul's audition here in 2 Cor. 12.9 is an *Is Seven* locution. This is a locution that is not a mere locution, for:

> ...the communication
> Of the dead is tongued with fire beyond the language of the living
>
> (Eliot, 'Little Gidding' I [= 1944: 36])

Or do poets lie? *Or* is that being said, which cannot be said otherwise? Truth and the lie are relative to the discourse, *in* which they occur and *about* which they are. By Collingwood's doctrine of 'absolute presuppositions' (1940), such assertions are not themselves grounded, but are themselves the grounds for others. Thought, at particular times and in peculiar places, has to stop somewhere. No supposal can be made without the presupposition of something.

But is all this to transgress the limits of what can be said? Paul himself seems very well aware that his travel has taken him to a place, where his language, for one reason or another, has reached its limits—like Nicholas, the Cusanian, that 'errotic black' (as von Balthasar calls him [1965 III.1: 556: *beinah ein erratischer Block*), Paul knew the importance of 'learned ignorance', of *docta igno-rantia*: '*now* I know *in part*; but *then* shall I know, even as also I am known' (1 Cor. 13.12). And he seems to be somewhat uncertainly straddling the border, rather like Jesus, circus-riding on two pack animals: 'upon an ass and upon a colt the foal of an ass' (Mt. 21.5). And what he has said about necessary ignorance in 1 Cor. 13.12 finds its analogue here: 'And I know that this man was caught up into Paradise—whether in the body or out of the body I do not know, God knows—and he heard things that cannot be told, which man may not utter' (2 Cor. 12.3-4).

At what point do we reach the edge of language and can the edge be easily discriminated from what lies on the edge's other side?

These edges are occupied also by the poet and the lover (Van Buren 1972). 'Now I, Joseph, was walking, and I walked not' (*Prot-evangelium of James* 18.2, cit. Walker 1942: 156). Come, come, Joseph, were you, or were you not? But people of this sort say this sort of thing. All one can say is that the authors of science fiction are transparently not easily deterred. Or poets. Or lovers. Or the painters, for of van de Velde (1932: 39)—or of Ruysdael (1917: 43) Wölfflin writes: 'The inexpressibility of an infinitude of form which seems to defy any attempt at fixation has here been mastered by painterly methods'.[8] The infinite here has been finitely mastered!

We are all, in a sense, in Tegel, in *Wehrmachtsuntersuchungs-gefängnis Tegel* ('Tegel: Prison for Military Investigation' [Bonhoeffer 1992: 7]), we are all mortal, though not, of course, in the sense that made of Dietrich Bonhoeffer a paradigm. For Bonhoeffer Berlin, for Paul Jerusalem, Jerusalem as Babylon. These, respectively, were their historical contexts, contexts in various ways extreme.

But whether or not he is telling history, or fiction, or a mixture of both, the question that *insists*, as a lane insists on a village (Eliot, 'East Coker' I [= 1944: 15]), is this, namely, *just what it is* that prevails upon Paul to come up with either, or both. Forgetting the *form*, or the *genre*, of what is being said here, what is the *content*? And what is it that has provoked him to come up with it? And, moreover, in what terms of *our* own is that to be stated, for which Paul found terms of *his* own? What language is available for the interpretation of Paul's language? If, by the hypothesis of the present chapter of the present essay, what has here found artistic form is art, what is the right method, what is *a* right method for getting hold of a content of such a kind?

Suppose, too, that the writer, and the reader, are operating in a logical space in which they partially know and partially do not know. And suppose that the words, 'transrational' (Seidlmayer 1960, s.v.: 'Nikolaus von Kues') and 'transcendental' (so von Balthasar on his aesthetic [1965: III.1, 21-29]) are words that Mackinnon would call 'inevitable' (*op. omn. passim*). But *evitable*, it seems, is what they are for this writer; to be avoided like Satan and Jerusalem. Paul is as ignorant of the register of Diotima (Plato, *Smp*. 201d1-212c3) in Plato's *Symposium* as he is ignorant of 'the things after the physics', on which physics depends (Aristotle). Paul is making, not a rational assumption, an assumption, by which he can reason, but an imaginative assumption, or *salto immortale*, on the

8.   'Das Unbeschreibliche einer Formenunendlichkeit, die sich jeder Festlegung zu versagen scheint, ist hier mit malerischen Mitteln bewältigt.'

basis of which he imagines a locution, imagines an audition, 'My grace...' And he produces, too, the summary of a transcendent and transrational travel narrative (diarized?): he has been 'caught up into Paradise' (ἡρπάγη εἰς τὸν παράδεισον, *herpage eis ton paradeison* [2 Cor. 11.3]), into the third 'sky-as-God's-space' (2 Cor. 11.2), by transport into trans-Appletonian space, to and from which (presumably) 'the way up and the way down are one and the same' (Heraclitus, in Diels 1906: I, 70 (*Fr.* 60), cit. Eliot 'Four Quartets' (= 1944: 6). From the standpoint of worldly wisdom and commonsense philosophy, this man is an idiot. He has lost the place and 'needs help'.

Enthusiasm and '[t]he pretending to extraordinary revelations and gifts of the Holy Ghost' (to put things in an English way [Butler, in Wesley n.d.: XIII, 500]), 'is a horrid thing, a very horrid thing'. Ecstasy and being taken out of oneself, having oneself taken out, is hardly less horrid. For either Paul has taken leave of Paul, or something must have got into him (Guthrie 1950: 149). The Apostle is, *prima facie* at least, sufficiently confused to allow either word ('ecstasy' or 'enthusiasm'), or both of them to be indifferently applied, though the prize must go to 'ecstasy'.

But it is by the former, the locution, not the latter, the travel, that Paul is himself impressed. To put the matter in blunt German, transcendental travel for Paul is 'sausage' (*Wurst*). Or in the more elevated language of Stoicism, ecstasy is an *adiaphoron*, a matter of indifference to him. What is *not* a matter of indifference is what enables him to soldier on. And here it is the locution and not the travel that acquires the weight. The locution, for a language user or letter writer like Paul, is linguistically fertile. It is a text that gives birth to texts. And the fertility that produced this fertile thing was fertile in formed speech (the chiasmus!). How does *this* text get *that* form? Who, or what, was the in*form*er? And the question is only the more complicated, in that the subject of a verb, which has none, can only be ambiguously inferred from the verse that precedes it: 'Three times I besought the Lord' (2 Cor. 12.8). With this itself ambiguous phrase (which 'Lord'? God? Jesus?) only a very temerarious person would dare to go further. If we should be reasoning with a deeper reason, what kind of reasoning would that be?

[T]he Beautiful, expelled from the realm of transcendence, has been restricted to what is within the world, where there can be caught only tensions and contradictions that are enclosed by clarity (von Balthasar 1965: III.1, 928).[9]

So how are we to move here?

Would we be much aided by adding to Paul's two outcrops from 'the other side' (Bultmann 1960a: 22 [= 1957: 10]) the figure of Satan on his 'bad errand' (Milton, *Paradise Lost* 10.41), one of Vaihinger's 'As if' fictions, if ever there was one (Collingwood 1967). But it is fiction, too, *in sensu bono*, if a bad character doing badly can have a good sense. For a nonentity is being employed nevertheless to say *something*. For the human animal is not incapable of having the wit to see that mills can be Satanic and Governments demonic. A vocabulary, by the deletion of 'Satan', for example, can only be impoverished at one's peril. There is too, also, a 'transcendentality' (to use von Balthasar's word) of evil, even if we have to put Lucifer back into heaven where he belongs, if, that is, with Jung (1954), we are (to speak carelessly) to make of the trinity a quaternity (1954). But perhaps, with Bultmann (1960a: 18 [= 1967: 5]), we should just switch on the light (sc. demytholo-gize) and take metheglin (mead), or, like Burns's 'Tam o' Shanter', his *usquebaugh*, or 'water of life', even though Tam was achieving 'his good at a price which only a fool would pay' (Collingwood 1942: 82).

But enough of Satan. Like Lazarus, the subject 'stinks' (Jn 11.39, cf. Bultmann 1976: 68). It leaves 'a smell as if a gun had been dis-charged' (Collingwood 1967: 174).

Is not all this to do no more than like a dog to urinate upon the tree, up which the squirrel has already disappeared? But of the deity it may be said that it has absconded, but not only. The deity also winks from the topmost branches. Is hidden 'in, with and under' the leaves. *Absconditus*, 'hidden', and *revelatus*, 'revealed', form a dialectical pair. But while it is easier to be sure of the for-mer, it requires Plato's and von Balthasar's μανία (*mania*: 'mad-ness') to become unsurely sure of the latter.

But vision is not far from any of us, that we should say, Where is

9.   '...das Schöne, aus der Transzendentalität vertrieben, ist ins Inner-weltliche eingeschränkt, wo nur von Eindeutigkeit umgriffene Spannungen und Widersprüche zu bändigen sind...'

it? And Hamann (von Balthasar 1962: II, 621-29) sees the connection between artistic and sexual creation'. (Is the mystery of sex to seek in Paul?)

Today
     I'll go to the moor again
to walk the dog
(one needs one's excuse
to be alone),
the village behind me
for a time,
     the clamour of people and their laws.

And here I see another law,
nature's law, being striving to be
and beautiful for the most part,
not touched by right or wrong.

     I always liked wild things,
     plants growing without asking,
     bracken and heather in flower,
     and you will certainly be on my mind
     and the law of the village, and the law of love,
     and I will try to come to a conclusion,
     to compare the two,
     and I will know that it is useless,

that you are beautiful and wild like nature,
growing on my feeling and sense,
merging with many an image
in the heart long since
and I will see you amidst the moor
co-existing with all weather,

and I will know that you are my law
my freedom and bind
my judge
     my life
        my beauty
who is my desire, my young secret love.

                      (Caimbeul 1987: 12-13)[10]

In a context of conflict with 'Hebrews', 'Israelites', 'descendants of Abraham', 'deacons of Christ' (2 Cor. 11.22-23), with ethnic Judaisers, lawyers, legalists, a poem, this poem, fits not the less well for being a poem on 'Laws', *Laghan*. And if the 'you' of the poem can be read by the reader, against the writing of the writer, as a pronoun that does not preclude *das ewig Weibliche*, 'the eternal feminine', nor does not go on not to preclude the anchoring of that notion in a pronoun that, by whatever route, is patient of being capitalized as 'You', is patient of being anchored in what metaphysicians and theologians call 'God', the fit (in every sense of that word!) will not be the less fitting here.

10.   *An-diugh*
　　　　thèid mi dhan a' mhonadh a-rithist
　　　　a choiseachd leis a' chù
　　　　(feumaidh neach a leisgeul
　　　　airson a bhith leis fhèin)
　　　　agus bidh am baile air mo chùlaibh
　　　　airson greis,
　　　　　　gleadhraich sluaigh agus a laghan.

　　　　Agus ann an seo chì mi lagh eile,
　　　　lagh nàduir, bith a' strì gus a bhith
　　　　agus bòidheach anns a' chuid as motha,
　　　　gun ceart no ceàrr a' bontainn ris.

　　　　　　Bu toigh leam riamh rudan fiadhaich,
　　　　　　lusan a' fàs gun faighneachd,
　　　　　　fraineach is fraoch le flùr,
　　　　　　agus gun teagamh bidh tusa air m'inntinn
　　　　　　agus lagh a' bhaile agus lagh a' ghràidh,
　　　　　　agus feuchaidh mi ri tighinn gu co-dhùnadh,
　　　　　　ri coimeas eadar na dhà,
　　　　　　agus bithidh fios agam gu bheil e gun fheum,

　　　　gu bheil thu brèagha agus fiadhaich mar nàdur,
　　　　a' fàs air m'fhaireachdainn 's mo rian,
　　　　a' measgachadh le iomadh ìomhaigh
　　　　a bha 'nam chridhe o chian,
　　　　is chì mi thu air feadh na mòintich
　　　　co-shìnte ris gach sian.

　　　　Agus bidh fios a'm gur tusa mo lagh
　　　　mo shaorsa is mo chuing
　　　　mo bhreitheamh
　　　　　　mo bheatha
　　　　　　　　mo bhòidhchead
　　　　thus' mo mhiann, mo chiall dìomhair òg.

And to see, or come to see, to have insight, or to get it, is to lose oneself in a *complicatio*, that calls for *explicatio* (Cusanus). And such insight is achievable, or receivable, by the following of the *explicatio* onwards, with no holds barred, a following onwards, that must sometimes be done with what is, or seems to be, a stance that is 'well endowed with the charisma of impiety' (Oakeshott 1983: 169).

But this can only be done by wandering on a good errand in strange places, where there rules the ἄλογον, *alogon*, 'that which is without *logos*', 'the trans-rational' (Aristotle, *Po*. 1460a29), where there rules the ἄτοπον, *atopon* (Aristotle, *Po*. 1460a35), the 'fantastic' (Aichele and Pippin 1992: 1). And '[t]he fantastic text is always a fictional text' (Aichele 1992: 53). Such texts find no place (*atopon*!), or introduce to a place (Corinth? Edinburgh?), from where a place may be discovered, that is no place (οὐ τόπος, *ou topos* [Utopia!]). But such discovery may produce a text, of which the discourse 'interrupts' (Aichele 1992: 53) that world of discourse, where this proposition constitutes the ruling paradigm, namely, that: 'This is a human hand', or that: 'There is a thing, and only one thing, of which it is true both that it is a human hand and that *this surface* is a part of its surface' (Moore 1959: 55).

Is Paul's audition a locution? Is this a place, to which he does (or does not) travel? 'Tzvetan Todorov has defined the literary fantastic as interruptions of reference within a story which result in narrative hesitation or indeterminacy between the genres of the marvellous and of the uncanny' (Aichele 1992: 53).

It is, however, high time to have left IAFA (the International Association for Fantasy in Art and Literature), for:

Every schoolboy, who has been told it, knows that the width of Piero's *Baptism* can be mathematically expressed as:

'116.2 ÷ 58.36 cm = 1.99'
= *damit* ('thereby') nearly 2

where 53.36 cm is the Florentine *braccio*, or standard measure. And she knows also (the schoolgirl), that 'the painted surface' is 'composed of two geometric shapes: a rectangle, 112.25 × 116.2 cm, and a semicircle with a diameter of 109.5 cm', where 'the total height (167 cm) is very nearly equal (within 0.6 cm) to half the width (58.1) added to the diameter of the semicircle'; and that

Figure 6. *Baptism of Christ*, c. 1442 by Piero della Francesca (c. 1419/21-92) (reproduced by courtesy of the Trustees, The National Gallery, London and the Yale University Press, for the overlay after B.A.R. Carter [1981])

[t]wo facts are immediately evident: the outstretched wings of the
dove align exactly with the top of the rectangle; the figure of Christ
coincides with a vertical line bisecting the panel. Using the top side
of the rectangle we construct an equilateral triangle, and we find
that its apex falls at the point where the central vertical axis passes
through the tip of Christ's right foot (Carter 1981: 150-51).

Thus far (if no further) art history and aesthetics are an exact
science.

Every student of Plato, moreover, knows that Plato (*Apology* 38a)
tells us that 'a life that is lived without the Research Assessment
Exercise is not worth living' (ὁ ἀνεξέταστος βίος οὐ βιωτὸς
ἀνθρώπῳ, *ho anexetastos bios ou biotos anthropo[i]*), and, not
only that, but that no student should enter the Academy 'without
geometry' (μηδεὶς ἀγεωμέτρητος εἰσίτω, *medeis ageometretos
eisito* [so Elias, on Aristotle's *Categories* 118.18]). And I dare say
the Lyceum (in the Athens of the South) was not much different.

The importance for the Greeks of the latter, of geometry, has
been known ever since by the Scots (Davie 1964: 127), its
importance for philosophy, for aesthetics and for life. The alleged
importance of the former, of Assessment, sadly, has been known to
the Scots only since 1979 (to give a rough and ready round figure, a
figure, that is, that is rough, for which the Scots are not, and never
will be, ready and are very willing to get round).

But, for Plato and for many after him, from Pico della Mirandola
through Marsilio Ficino to Fra Luca Pacioli (to say nothing of a kind
of thinking that ranges from the Kabbala through astrology to the
frankly bazaar), mathematics and geometry, while rooted for the
Scots (though not, despite his Scots extraction [Wallace 1882: 8-9],
for Kant) in the structure of the empirical world, are rooted also in
reality as such, in ontology, in transcendence, in that which is
beyond that which is (ἐπέκεινα τῆς οὐσίας, *epekeina tes ousias*
(Plato, *Republic* 509b).

That there is formal excellence in Paul's Catalogue of *Peristases*,
Aporias, his list of those 'difficulties', that impede his provision for
them, has already been shown. But his use of adverbial numbers
does not yet show that in geometry and mathematics he was the
peer of Piero. The exegesis, the interpretation, the criticism of the
Pauline epistles is not, for all that we might wish, an exact science
of this kind. His writing is wrenched rather by transcendence into

Cubism, or the Surreal. One day the Postmodernists will have their day of him.

One cannot simply in Paul draw a straight line through the Holy Spirit (or in Piero, either, for that matter [Lavin 1981: 107-48]). For Paul is being more than mathematical and geometrical, which latter Piero also is. But *à tâtons* is, 'gropingly' is the watchword. Sense and sensibility, criticism and scholarship, all of these are required. And that not without the Brahmsian warmth of the last of the Four Serious Songs, the one on 1 Corinthians 13 in the context of Solomon's lay, the one on ἔρως (*eros*), opposed by and re-affirmed by ἀγάπη (*agape*), erotic passion re-affirmed by *caritas*, or love.

Paul's quest, in this Second Corinthians Catalogue, his Quest for the Historical Paul, which, if selective and laconic, it very nearly is, is, for Paul, a Quest, too, for the Historical Jesus, being a quest for a kenotic life, that culminates in a death. More exactly, that culminates in one death for Jesus and many 'deaths' for Paul: 'in deaths oft' (2 Cor. 11.23 KJV). The historical Jesus is, as it were, the hidden presupposition of the piece. And Paul finds himself to have been sustained by a lapidary term, or rather two: 'grace' and 'strength', coordinated by chiasmic parallelism. The two nouns inter-play. I animadvert here to the first only.

'Grace' is lapidary and fundamental, is no erratic block, but a head of the corner, one of those words (but there are others, as: 'spirit'), by which *all* is sustained. How Feuerbach would have loved it, a word wrested from the earth and transposed to the sky. It is a root metaphor. But 'earth words', or literal words, are not the only words for which an ontology, perhaps a complex ontology, may be claimed. For a 'stroke of art', as this one is, has not only the ontology of a work of art, but has the ontology that a work of art implies: the emotion imaginatively expressed may be an emotion that is felt *in relation to something*, something that is for the most part, or is necessarily so (Collingwood and Aristotle [combined]). A stroke of art may imply a work of art; a fragment the whole, of which it is a part, together with that, about which they are.

In an aesthetic approach to a text, which is, sc. is here being taken to be, closer to poetry and fiction than it is to anything else, for all that other 'voices' (the historical, say) can also be overheard, it would be proper to consider 'grace' to be synonymous with 'beauty'. And in some texts, on some occasions, synonyms they actually are—

> All flesh is grass,
>> and all its beauty
>> is like the flower of the field.
>>> (Isa. 40.6 [RSV] [= *hasdo* (MT), δόξα (LXX)], *gloria* [vg])

But the basis in our (closed-canonical) documents is slim.

But if the basis in these documents, for the equation:

$$\text{grace} = \text{beauty}$$

is slim, so much the worse for these documents.

But the canon is a canon within a canon. The canon of biblical documents is a canon within the canon of Western literature (to name one compass point).

Or does the thesis halt on this stone? Does the thesis, that the New Testament is art and that the end of art is beauty, stumble against the fact that the evidential basis in the New Testament documents is lacking, or is vestigial?

But is, or is not, one asks (von Balthasar 1961: I, 9), the *pulchrum* (the beautiful) a *transcendentale*, a concept that might still cover what is needed? The question arises here, with this text, with *this* speech of *this* fool, whether 'beauty' can be an *onym*, a name, a term, a metaphor, not for this occasion only, but for all. And, if for all, then a concept, an image, a root metaphor for loss ('crucifixion') as well as gain ('resurrection'). Is 'grace' not a metaphor, that can indifferently cover tragedy as well as comedy?

For is not *Oedipus* beautiful? The question arises whether here, and everywhere, 'grace' is a kind, or genre, of beauty, which is rooted and planted in a transcendental aesthetic, or (Greek) *ana-aesthetic* (lit. 'upward aesthetic'), by which all ugliness and chastisement may be transfigured. Can tragedy, too, be beautiful? For does not Alexander say (1933: 82) that '[a]ny subject is available for beauty if it be treated beautifully'. And does not Paul write beautifully here, with his dyads, concatenation, climax and chiasmus?

To translate 'grace' by 'beauty', of course, is to prefer 'beauty' before 'glory', *Schönheit* before *Herrlichkeit* (von Balthasar). But the preference of a term is less important than the choice of a meaning; or the recognition, the creation of a meaning, of meaning.

Is not 'beauty' the secular translation of 'grace'? But more will follow below.

The task proposed now is to describe, or, like Scaliger, square, make a quadrature of the circle (Knight 1925: 71), an attempt to square the circle of grace as the circle of beauty, without the triangles, circles, squares, rectangles, pentagons and decapentagons of Piero (Carter 1981). It is a proposal to abandon, with the triangles, the trinity, and to retain, along with the memory of the pentagon and the proleptic five wounds of the Baptist's baptisand (Jesus), only the wounds of Paul, the wounds of Paul 'crucified'. It will also be to abandon further consideration of Piero's painting *more geometrico*. Although '[f]or the first three hundred years following his death, Piero was remembered as a mathematician rather than as a painter' (Carter 1981: 159 n. 2), further consideration of his geometry and mathematics *more pingendi* can be safely left to other co-adjutors in the field.

That Paul was conscious of Paul was not perhaps entirely Paul's fault, for people kept telling him not to be what he was. But Paul, on his own account, was what he was, because he had come to be what he was, namely (in his own words, or as his own words imply) 'a new creation' (2 Cor. 5.17). Now the ontology of anything should give cause of surprise, when we realize that, if we had to be dealing with the ontology of nothing at all, *we* could not, as not being, be dealing with *it*, non-being. The ontology of grace, however, invites ambage as being the occasion of texts, in terms of the Lukan litotes, 'not a few' (Acts 12.18). We do not speak here for the first time.

The locution of this very passage (2 Cor. 12.7) is cited by Paton (1955: 339). And it is a philosopher, who is citing it. With some philosophical confidence, Paton there (1955: 337) supplies three meanings for 'grace': 'beauty', 'favour' and 'gratitude'. The greatest of these is beauty. I concentrate on this. This translation is the most important for my present purposes.

This confidence of Paton may need to be complexified, made more diffident, jettisoned even, in the light of Brown, Driver and Briggs (s.v. *hesed* and *hen*) on the one hand and Botterweck and Ringgren (1982) on the other. Or roundly reasserted in despite of all of them.

But Paton, among other things, is citing the locution as cited by

Samuel Butler (Paton gives no reference). Butler chooses not beauty, favour and gratitude, but something like what, for the (non-Presbyterian) citizens of Edinburgh, must, in the first instance, be represented by a different triad, the Three Graces of Canova. Not inappropriate for the author of *The Way of All Flesh*.

As Butler puts it (somewhere):

> The waves came in one after another, the sea-gulls cried together after their kind, the wind rustled among the dried canes upon the sandbanks, and there came a voice from heaven saying 'Let My grace be sufficient for thee'. Whereon, failing of the thing itself, he [sc. Paul] stole the word and strove to crush its meaning to the measure of his own limitations. But the true grace, with her groves and high places, and troups of young men and maidens crowned with flowers, and singing of love and youth and wine—the true grace he drove out into the wilderness—high up, it may be, into Piora, and into such-like places. Happy they who harboured her in her ill-report (Butler, cit. Paton 1955: 339).

This quotation persuades Paton energetically to round on Butler: 'From a religious point of view this may be regarded as deplorable...' For Paul's grace as beauty *overlaps*, by philosophical analysis (Collingwood 1933), with Butler's. From Butler's grace Paul's is distinct and opposed to it, while re-affirming it, for '[w]e may even think that Pagan grace was too readily extruded from the Christian religion—that the snares of loveliness loomed too large in the minds of celibate priests' (Paton 1955: 339).

While only Paton's own eloquence can do justice to what he there takes time to say, his drift may be jaloused by some further phrases from the same place:

> 'Beauty...is to be found in the ritual and myth and language by which a religion is expressed...is surely to be found above all in...a life of unself-conscious service and kindness... Are we going beyond the empirical evidence if we say that what distinguishes the beauty of the saint is that it seems to be given and received rather than fought for and won?

And:

> Morality is an appeal for effort, an appeal to be strong; but religion can appeal also to those who feel that they have no strength in themselves, that they are incapable of effort and in need of help... The beauty of the religious life...contains within it elements of pain, and so is more akin to tragedy... A religious man [and a religious

woman]...has to be steady in affliction; but if he is not always
sustained by consciousness of divine help, perhaps he is always
assured of final victory (Paton 1955: 340).

But if beauty is as central as the *semeion*, or centre-point, that
is everywhere, within a circle, of which the circumference is
nowhere, a longer story needs to be told, a more extended philosophy proposed, more heuristic fictions found, more propositions founded, that shed light on the life of Paul: 'In the presence
of futility and flabbiness we have to remember that there is such
a virtue as courage [Paton 1955: 341-42]... This can be best
expressed in the language of poetry, which is also the language of
religion—in such an affirmation as "If thou wilt carry thy cross, thy
cross will carry thee" [342]... The gratitude of the religious man is
manifested in service to his fellows... [H]e [sc. the Christian] thinks
of God, at least in part, under the figure of a man in whom self-
surrender was complete [343]...[I]t is a pity that those who
explore the unconscious restrict themselves so much to abnormal
experiences' (345)—which, as we have seen, is as much as Paul
himself says of his journey to Paradise: 'On behalf of this man I will
boast, but on my own behalf I will not boast...so that no one may
think more of me than he sees in me or hears from me' (2 Cor.
12.5-6).

Can, then, tragedy be beautiful? Can grace be beauty and beauty
grace?

Beauty is a complex word, which covers more than the *fin-de-
siècle* aestheticism of the pedestrian in Piccadilly

> with a poppy and a lily
> in his mediaeval hand...
>
> (W.S. Gilbert, *Patience*)

or the pre-Raphaelite figures, that survive on thin gruel. And
Paton's analysis is supported by the Greeks. Does not Sophocles,
for example, operating on the assumption (ἀνάλημψις, *analemp-
sis*) of Heracles (on a *pelike*, 'pitcher', at Munich [Cook 1940: III,
512-13; Easterling 1982: 17-18]), put a question mark against the
finality of tragedy? Tragedy need not, that is, exclude the happy
end, however carefully the end must be crafted to fit the middle.
And if for the Greeks, why not for the Christians? Why should
beauty not cohere with Paul's pain?

And yet the middle is dire. It is the man who sees, says

Sophocles, in *Oedipus*, who does not see and the man who does not see, who sees. So says Teiresias, who *does* see, because he occupies an Olympian standpoint. He is the spokesman of Apollo, the spokesman, by audition, of a locution, mediated, it is true, by some Sibyl overcome by mephitic vapours, of which the result has been written down in ambiguous Greek.

> And be these juggling fiends no more believed,
> That palter with us in a double sense...
>
> (Shakespeare, *Macbeth* V.viii.20-21)

Or is Hopkins beautiful? Can the one writer write beautifully about and find beauty in a 'dappled' world, 'charged with the grandeur of God' and, both in sequence and at the same time, do the same for passion and crucifixion? Even 'God's Grandeur' (1970: 66) contains 'crushed',

> like the ooze of oil
> Crushed...

and 'Hurrahing in Harvest' contains 'glean' (1970: 70):

> I lift up heart, eyes,
> Down all that glory in the heavens to glean our Saviour...

For the bread that sustains is derived from the death of the grain.

And on 'The Windhover', on the three posssibilities of understanding 'Buckle' (l. 10), Gardner says (in Hopkins 1970: xxxiii, 267-69), that 'he still cannot read it without receiving the instress of a complex symbolism involving all three meanings', sc. (1) 'buckle in', 'draw together' (the discipline of the hawk's controlled flight, of the Christian soldier, of the Christ), (2) 'buckle to', 'engage the enemy' and (3) 'buckle under pressure', 'collapse'— 'with its anticipation of the falling embers of the second tercet'.

But, before all, what Hopkins 'spelt from Sibyl's leaves' was also the six sonnets that begin with 'Carrion Comfort', was not only the lyrically beautiful, but the terrible beauty, that makes all words pause.

Paul's better beauty, then, Paul's 'masterful' beauty (German *herrliche*) saves Paganism by including, by opposing and then reaffirming what in Paganism is good. 'Beauty' is a complex word and contains within itself affirmation, negation and reaffirmation. Or incarnation, crucifixion and resurrection (or ἀνάλημψις, *ana-lempsis*, 'taking up'). Beauty is a complex word and its *complicatio* may not, for him (though it does for Piero della Francesca), involve any decapentagonal explication. Paul's writing is not formal in this strictly geometrical sense.

But the word is sufficiently complex to require three, five, fifteen and more stories, if it is adequately to be apprehended. And while it may be said that the Apostle would hardly have been harmed either by a reading of Hopkins, or of Sanday and Headlam on the letter he was labouring over (Rom. 8 in particular), it should also more strongly be said that the reading of tragedy either by *charis* (beauty) or *to kalon* (the beautiful) can never be the *lectio facilior*, or 'easier reading'. Is there a reading of things (and a living of things) that, in Eliot's phrase, costs 'not less than everything' ('Little Gidding' V [= 1944: 44])? And can such a reading ever be called easy, or easier than other, more nameable alternatives?

Paul's *dos moi pou sto*, Paul's 'standpoint', his 'Give me where to stand', is expressed by him in a variety of places in a variety of letters in a variety of ways, as 'being crucified with Christ' (Gal. 2.19), or, as here (2 Cor. 12.9), 'Let my grace be sufficient for thee'. It is Paul's privilege to read *anything* as the expression of a loving God. And Hamann shares this privilege (*Golgatha und Sheblimini*: Gregor Smith 1960: 223-32). And von Balthasar puts his finger on this, when he says that

> for Hamann the act of aisthesis, when it is not reduced, is itself the originary religious act, since all things are God's word and his language, and therefore whoever grasps things hears God himself speak (1962: 606).[11]

For there is that (is there not?), which moves, to move the mind and the imagination.

---

11. '... für Hamann der Akt der Aisthesis, wenn er nicht verkürzt wird, der ursprüngliche religiöse Akt selber ist, weil alle Dinge Gottes Wort und Sprache sind, und deshalb, wer die Dinge auffasst, Gott selber reden hört.'

10

'History Is Now [sc. Then] and South of the Border': 'Little Gidding' in the Context of *Four Quartets* (T.S. Eliot: Critic, Philosopher, Poet. Historian?)

Plus ça change, plus c'est une autre chose

An Explicatory Incipit:

Where not everything can be, nor nothing ought to be, at least this can be said, that, whatever else may importantly be being said in the chapter below, there is also this importantly to be said, namely, that the word, or the thing, 'metaphysics', on the lips of a metaphysician is one thing, on the lips of a poet another. And it is another thing, too, even on the lips of a poet, who was also, or had been also, a metaphysician (as Eliot, when he was working on Bradley [Eliot 1964]). And when that which has to be changed has been commuted, the same applies, too, to the little word, 'history'. And the same, too, to the little words, 'literary criticism'.

Round these three words, these three disciplines, much of this book has been revolving, though history has been the silent partner, who has emerged from the shadows only punctually to emit the kind of locution that can make clear that the kinds of locution emitted by the other two disciplines are other (as each of these from one another). Each discipline has its modal peculiarities. Each discipline is dealing with truth, but with truth of different kinds, however unitary in the end they should prove to be.

Or to make all this beyond a peradventure clear, 'History', on the lips of Eliot, the poet, means what Eliot, the poet, chooses it to mean. The word, 'history', on the lips of Eliot is, in the first instance, of interest to the literary critic, though it may further, logically later, be of interest to the historian and the philosopher. And it is in this, in that Eliot's text is of interest not only to the literary critic, that Eliot's text is like the texts of the New Testament, or that they are like his. Many different people are interested in these texts for different reasons. And they are texts that can bear this multiple examination.

Just as, in a word, when dealing with Pentecost, one does not do well to summon the fire engine, or anxiously consult the morning isobars, even so, when dealing with 'History…' in Eliot, if one does well to summon the historian, one does better, first, to summon the literary critic.

Texts of the kind with which we are dealing are of the poetic kind. Such texts are of interest, of course, to other poets. They are also of interest to the historian, the literary critic and the philosopher. If the poet should happen to use in his poem a word that is borrowed from history, literary criticism, or philosophy, it is not likely to retain the meaning it had in the context from which it has been prised. Its meaning will now depend on the context in which it now finds itself.

The word 'history', importantly occurs here. What does T.S. Eliot mean by it?

And can such an examination be made by any of these practitioners without the necessity of 'taking arms', as is somewhere said, 'against a sea of troubles', or taking to the sea, as is elsewhere said (2 Cor. 11.25), from a troubled boat? Talk in this quarter is everywhere difficult.

An Obfuscatory Explicit:

> As we get older we do not get any younger.
> Seasons return, and today I am fifty-five,
> And this time last year I was fifty-four…
>
> T.S. Eliot, 'Chard Whitlow'

So Eliot. So Eliot almost. For Reed (in Macdonald 1964: 218) goes on:

> And this time next year I shall be sixty-two.

But if the proper voice is adopted from the right furniture, as in the liturgy from the pulpit, and 'sixty-two' taken as a textual corruption for, say, 'I meant fifty-six', one may, to be disabused, have to wait a little longer for Ramsey's 'penny' to drop (1967: *passim*), to disclose that the reader's leg is being pulled. One has to read on until, say:

> There are certain precautions—though none of them very reliable—
> Against the blast from bombs and the flying splinter,
> But not against the blast from heaven, *vento dei venti*,
> The wind within a wind unable to speak for wind;
> And the frigid burnings of purgatory will not be touched
> By any emollient...

The mere Latinist may wonder how '*vento dei venti*' is to be construed. And it is easy to make fun of Eliot, but Ricks (1988), despite his rigorous examination of and critical comments on Eliot's prejudices, runs nevertheless to the defence of Eliot (p. 267), the real Eliot's '*Erhebung*' (German: 'lifting up'(?), 'somehow being lifted over it all') in 'Burnt Norton' II (= 1944: 9), with its subtle Hegelian instress of *Aufhebung* (German 'sublation'). Good parody, wicked as Till Eulenspiegel, is good criticism. Good parody gets a writer right.

Eliot, like most of the writers in the New Testament, who steal from the old (so Strauss 1840 [1970: *passim*]) is a great pillager, a pillager of the Western European tradition—and, more sparingly, the Eastern as Arjuna ('The Dry Salvages' III), too, of course; and sometimes, indeed, almost a plagiarist, of the kind to make an examination board anxious. He plagiarized from the English mystics, for example:

> With the drawing of this Love and the voice of this Calling
> ('Little Gidding' V [= 1944: 43]):

'The beautiful line which puzzles you [sc. John Hayward, Eliot's friend and confidant during the gestation of the poem]...comes out of *The Cloud of Unknowing*' (Gardner 1978: 70). And, in D4 (= Draft 4), he plagiarizes even from himself: 'I think silence will have to stand, because I was using a line from the Family Reunion'—though this self-plagiarism was transitory, for 'silence' disappeared in D5 (p. 223).

And he pillages *Purgatory*, for example, and, indeed, the *Inferno*, and, indeed, the *Paradiso*, all three places. He pillages Mallarmé (for Eliot's 'purify the dialect of the tribe' ['Little Gidding' II (= 1944: 39)], Mallarmé has: *donner un sens plus pur aux mots de la tribu*).[1] He pillages Lady Julian ('Sin is Behovely': 'Little Gidding' III [= 1944: 41]; Julian 1950: 56). And thieves St Luke's

---

1.   Mallarmé, 'Le Tombeau d'Edgar Poe', cit. Gardner 1968: 179.

'wind', the 'wind' of Acts 2, the wind of Pentecost, but makes it 'windless' ('Little Gidding' I [= 1944: 35]). How many lines of Eliot, indeed, could not be underlined as the lines of others?

But this thief is a fence, engaged in reset. What he receives from Eliot, the thief, Eliot, the fence, makes his own and alters before resale. His voice is inseparable from the voice of Lady Julian, but distinguishable from it. The hands, from which he receives, are the hands of Lady Julian, but the voice is the voice of Eliot.

Something strange happens to tradition, when tradition is received. What is handed on is the same and *not* the same as what was received. Fiction is in this sense historical, in that it changes over time. *Plus c'est la même chose, plus ça change*, 'the more it is the same thing, the more it changes'.

'History', says Eliot, 'is now and England' ('Little Gidding' V [= 1944: 43]). But what Eliot means by 'history' is not impatient of fiction. If history is fact, all the fictive and fictional resources of the West are called in by Eliot to explain it. How about Heracles (the shirt of Nessus, 'The intolerable shirt of flame' ('Little Gidding' IV [= 1944: 42])? While new facts are added to old ones, fictions are added to facts, fictions to fictions, and old fictions repeated in a new context.

If Paul is a classical writer, Eliot was a canonical one. Each is an individual talent, operating on the basis of a tradition, the only difference being that Eliot is riding on the back of a longer tradition and that he has read more widely than Paul. This is probably true, even if Paul quotes Menander (1 Cor. 15.33 [*Thais*, fr. 218]), whom (*m.W.*, so far as I know) Eliot does not. And when each joins the tradition, the kaleidoscope is shaken and we see the tradition in a new way, even if it would be very hard to be determinate about what that new way is.

Is it that Paul has classically added 'justification', say, to the human vocabulary, the vocabulary of man (for since 4004 it had belonged already to the vocabulary of woman), by stealing it from his forebears, doctoring it with a spin and converting it (among other things) into a forensic paradox: 'God [the judge] acquits the guilty' (so [at any rate] Dodd 1932: 52)? While Eliot, for his part, finding *en passant* a right context for 'voluptuary' on the one hand ('the hedges...White again, in May, with voluptuary sweetness': 'Little Gidding' I [= 1944: 36]) and 'valid' on the other ('You are here to kneel / Where prayer has been valid'), has made of the Great Authour, who heals all our iniquities, a 'ruined millionaire' and has made of what he authorized, his creation, a trust 'hospital':

> The whole earth is our hospital
> Endowed by the ruined millionaire,
> Wherein, if we do well, we shall
> Die of the absolute paternal care
> That will not leave us, but prevents us everywhere.
>
> ('East Coker' IV [= 1944: 21])

But the words are wounded by their removal from the whole.

If the omission to take soundings in Paul's literary past can be justified by their familiarity, or by their ease of becoming familiar through commentary, monograph and encyclopaedia, it is clear, in Eliot, that, together also with the surds of life, a Collect from the *Book of Common Prayer* is waving to the reader through 'prevent': 'Prevent us, O Lord, in all our doings.'

Both Paul and Eliot are buoyed up by the past. Both are allusive writers. Both men steer by a providence and end that is beyond nature, Immanuel Kant might say (and de Wette with him), are saying that '[t]here is then indeed a certain presentiment of our Reason or a hint as it were given us by nature, that, by means of this concept of final causes [cf. 'purposiveness' there *passim*], we go beyond nature' (Kant 1914: 299 [= 1913: 254]),[2] if neither, perhaps not even Eliot *qua* Bradleyan philosopher, would have thought of saying it this way. In relation to winks and hints both men guess.

But (by way of parenthesis) I produce this sentence from Kant with great hesitation, partly as I am here, in Kantian studies, a postulant, not an initiate, and partly because to produce it may simply be the attempt to get chalk to throw light on cheese. But the question is relevant: What are these two artists doing here and against what environment do they think they are doing it? And if they thought not of it, of what is one to think that *they* did *not*? If Aquinas uses Aristotle in order to say what he, Aquinas, wants to say, and if de Wette makes use of Kant (and Fries) to get purchase

---

2. 'Es ist also wohl eine gewisse Ahnung unserer Vernunft oder ein von der Natur gegebener Wink, dass wir vermittelst jenes Begriffs von Endursachen [cf. Zweckmässigkeit] wohl gar über die Natur hinauslangen.'

on the Old Testament, and if Bultmann turns to Heidegger—how is the literary critic, how is the philosopher to make clarificatory inroads into Eliot? Why not use one's (would-be) philosophical mind on literature?

But Eliot, where Paul is not, is a poet's poet, a poet *sensu strictissimo*, in a sense (what sense?), in which Paul is not. All students of, or critics of, or simply readers, who enjoy Eliot, when they are not enjoying Paul (do verb and object here cohere?), are in the debt of Helen Gardner, *The Art of T.S. Eliot and The Making of Four Quartets*. Piero's *De prospectiva pingendi*, 'On Perspective in Painting', already provides one avenue to his painting and no doubt one who knew Eliot better could produce from the work of the poet *as critic* some keys that would open *his* poetry. To what extent is Eliot's poetry illuminated by his critical writings? And there is pictorial evidence from Ackroyd's 57th photograph in his Eliot album (1993: 256), which (Eliot's asymptotic approach to Piero) demonstrates beyond a peradventure that Eliot thought long and deeply about *structure* (but Paul no less [Weiss 1897]), the structure in this case of *The Cocktail Party*. But even the tyro who has got no further than the face of Eliot's *Quartets* can see how carefully the *Four* are each divided into five and how the music, the voice and the metre of each of the five reveal infinite variety. There is, for example, in the dramatic dialogue of 'Little Gidding' II (= 1944: 38: 'In the uncertain hour before the morning...'), the subtle translation of Dante's *terza rima* (Gardner 1968: 39)[3] into an English analogue or variant of the Italian prosody. This *techne* (craft), this *ars*, the craft of Horace that anchors, disciplines 'genius' (*ingenium*), is to seek in Paul, even if the temptation must remain strong to find concerning the *Carmen Christi* (Philippians 2) something pherecratean (sc. a Greek metre, a catalectic glyconic [they tell me]), namely (and with permissible variations):
‐‐‐‐∪∪‐‐ .

It is probable that Paul, in his head, drafted and redrafted, formulated and reformulated what he had to say in his ἀγρυπνίαι ('sleeplessnesses', 'many a sleepless night': 2 Cor. 11.27), as he anxiously feared, or hoped for Phoebe's knock:

---

3. Also Gardner (1978: 63-64) and her reference there to Eliot (1965: esp. 128-29).

> Between midnight and dawn, when the past is all deception,
> The future futureless, before the morning watch
> When time stops and time is never ending
>   (Eliot, 'The Dry Salvages' I [= 1944: 26])

But Eliot's prodigious transcriptions and retranscriptions, draftings and redraftings (there were 5 drafts [D1-5] and 13 manuscripts [M1-13]!), to say nothing of the correspondence and 'after the "Final Recension",...the alterations in proof' (Gardner 1978: 171) of 'the uncertain hour...'

> Near the ending of interminable night
> At the recurrent ending of the unending...

find in Paul no parallel, that fully persuades.

Or take again the epithet, de Wette's 'aesthetic-religious' (1817: 218)[4] (we have, I think, met it before). Eliot (clearly) and Paul (I am claiming) are writing work to which that epithet applies. But there is more of the miracle of aesthetic distance in Eliot, while Paul is embroiled with the recalcitrant. Paul's art is always for a strictly persuasive purpose.

It is not, of course, as if Eliot were talking, and wanting to talk, to no one but himself. It would be too much to say that he was making a poet's contribution to the war effort, because (what might be called) 4Q is not a didactic poem of that kind. But nevertheless, the Second World War is the context in which he is writing, and to which he is responding. He is doing something for *l'âme de l'Europe* (Aristotle's) *Anima*, or 'soul' of Europe. And Eliot's essay, the *Notes towards the Definition of Culture* (1962, but first published in 1948) confirms this, not least in view of an 'Appendix' there on 'The Unity of European Culture' (1962: 110-24).

But Paul's art is more closely controlled by the peculiarities and the particularities of a situation, or situations, which call forth from him almost as many voices as those that Eliot commands, or by which Eliot, like Paul, is commanded. The voices are voices they hear, their locutions are auditions. For Eliot is commanded, by his poetic vocation and Anglo-Catholic creed. He is commanded to harrow Hell and Purgatory. And he is commanded to be not only the maker, but the maker-recipient of 'hints and guesses' ('The Dry

---

4.   = 1821: 254, cit. Hartlich and Sachs 1952: 115.

Salvages' V [= 1944: 33]) about Paradise, where 'the fire and the rose are one' ('Little Gidding' V [= 1944: 44]).

But for both, 'humility is endless' ('East Coker' II [= 1944: 18]), despite the hint of stung pride in the one and the earlier prejudices (Ricks 1988) of the other.

Sex, the 'Greatest Mystery of All'

But if in a secular world, in a less Anglo-Catholic world than Eliot's and in a world less 'full of gods' (Thales ['perhaps'], cit. Aristotle, *de Anima* 411a7: πάντα πλήρη θεῶν, *panta plere theon*) than Paul's ('gods many and lords many' [1 Cor. 8.5]), we may not speak of mystery, except for the mysterious disappearance of one who was never quite clearly there, or quite clearly never there, we may nevertheless, perhaps, make an attempt to speak, not 'of the vulture's path through the air, the serpent's on the crag, the ship's through the sea', but of 'the greatest mystery of all—that of sex' (Robinson 1946: 6).

Paul does not wax lyrical ('You say I am repeating / Something I have said before. I shall say it again' ('East Coker' III [= 1944: 20]) about the 'voluptuary sweetness' of the Cilician hedges (the climate, I expect), or about the 'nightingale' of 'well-horsed Colonus'. But what is missing also from Paul (and this was the point of the *obiter dictum* of Mackinnon L.) is any but implicit lyricism about what the Greeks, what some Greeks called *eros*, 'erotic love', for all that it, erotic love, is finally sublated by the *agape*, or 'charity', of the finely crafted, lyrical encomium of 1 Corinthians 13.

Such a significant fact, or mystery, the mystery of passion, the mystery of the passion of erotic love, has somehow to be taken up into any account of human living that makes any attempt to be, even humanly speaking, exhaustive. And if you do not take it up into your account ('accompt' would be a better word), Collingwood and Euripides (to name but two) will tell you why (Collingwood 1940: 207-10; Euripides, *Hippolytus*).

St Jerome here can hardly be our guide, for it is Jerome's (not Jerome's view [1889]), that, if 'marriage replenishes the earth (Gen. 1.28)', it is 'virginity' that 'replenishes paradise' (*Nuptiae terram replent, virginitas paradisum* (Jerome, *Against Jovinian* 1.16, cit. Kelly 1975: 183). Paul has, of course, some humane remarks on the mutual accommodation of one sex to the other (if not of one to the same!): 'the wife does not rule over her own body...the husband does not rule over his own body' (1 Cor. 7.4). But there is none, for all Lawrence's rant (though to one who loved much, much may be forgiven), of Lawrence's 'rush of the sap in spring' (1949: 8, cf. 122-26), a phrase (choriamb and iamb) from a passage, where the distinction between poetry and prose breaks down. Erotic love, too, has its occupation at the edges of language.

It is no doubt a temerarious prank to draw swift inferences from the utterances of a poet to the poet's life. But there is something about Eliot that leads one to think, not only that he was not 'at the hot gates' ('Gerontion'), but that he said truly of himself that 'I shall wear the bottoms of my trousers rolled' ('The Love Song of J. Alfred Prufrock'). And yet the shades of Jane Harrison stalk, squawk and gibber behind his lines: the 'loam' and 'the weak pipe and the little drum' and 'the association of man and woman' and 'the time of the coupling of man and beast' ('East Coker I [= 1944: 16]) are there to show that the Lawrentian 'time of milking and the time of harvest' have made their mark, unless we are to put down the whole *topos* not to Eliot, but to Elyot (*The Governour* [Gardner 1968: 165 n. 1]). But, still, there is more to Eliot than just 'birth, copulation and death'. There is 'coupling'.

Who, however, can throw stones here? Or even the implication of a stone, if, indeed, 'humility is endless'? The world without either (Eliot, or Lawrence) would be the poorer. And poorer still, if we do not add the third: Paul is a great singer, and in 1 Corinthians 13 more excellently than anywhere else; Paul is no dispraiser of love (for 'dispraise' see Gow on Housman (1936: 46)[5] and love (*agape*) sublates love (*eros*). In some measure, it contradicts it. Nevertheless, it does not annihilate, it reaffirms it.

'History'

The Rainbow, yes (Mackinnon 1968: 51), belongs, with the *Quartets*, on the theologian's table. Yes, but why? Because fictions, the fictions of the novelist and the poetic fictions and fashionings of the poet, are *about reality*. The main question, here in this chapter, is only whether the word 'reality' can be exhausted by the

5.   'What for d'ye so dispraise the Scots?'

word 'history' and whether to suppose this, that reality can be so exhausted, is not to get 'history' to do so many jobs that it becomes, so to say, *begrifflich verschwommen*, conceptually confused.

For is not to use 'history' in this way, too broadly and confusingly, no better than to 'jump onto one's horse' (and Bucephalus it may be) and 'gallop off in all directions' (Leacock says this somewhere in *The Nonsense Novels*)? *Other* words are needed, too, and I am suggesting that these are, or that among these are, (1) reality, (2) literature and (3) metaphysics, the main problem being and remaining, for those of us who toil in this furrow and sweat over these thistles, how to get the rainbow to end on your table, how to realize one's eschatology, how to relate everything to everything else and remain a '*human being*' (Wittgenstein, in Malcolm 1967: 61) at the same time. The story that historians tell is a limited, and can only be a limited, story (and Aichele [1985] would surely agree, that novelists and poets are in the same perplexity).

M.a.W. (in other words), Bultmann and Strauss and de Wette would say, Paul in 1 Thessalonians (esp. 4.13-18) is not *broadcasting* from Corinth (Kümmel 1983: 232), as little as Welles, on Wells (1946), from New York (*The War of the Worlds*), when the dramatic fiction of Wells (as spoken by Welles) was mistakenly taken, by some members of the public, to be documentary fact. Or, *if* he is, it is *fact* in the form of *fiction*. And if the form is fiction, the public need to be told this. But much of the public much of the time manages very well easily to discriminate the one from the other. The Great Scottish Public does so everyday. We are meeting here, in Wells and Paul, not with fact *tout court*, not with history *yet*, but with fiction, in which, *it may be*, facts, or what will be facts, are very peculiarly embodied. The relation between fiction and fact is not a mirror image. The relation is elliptical. Is Eliot's relation with history less so?

When T.S. Eliot has the brass neck to say that:

> History is now and England.
>
>   ('Little Gidding, V [= 1944: 43])

(rather than saying 'is now and England and the United Kingdom of Great Britain and Northern Ireland') he means, that, whatever he is saying, when he says this ('I am talking about something real here'[?]), he cannot adequately say his *je ne sais quoi*, whatever it is, without having recourse:

to the *Purgatorio* ('Little Gidding' III [= 1944: 38-40]),
the *Inferno* ('What! are *you* here?' [Dante *Inferno* XV, *cit.* Gardner 1978: 64]),

and the *Paradiso*, for '[Eliot] returns to Dante again at the end of the poem…: to the image of the redeemed gathered together in the form of a pure white rose' (Gardner 1978: 59)

or without having recourse:

to Sophocles' *Trachiniae* (for Nessus' unlaundered shirt)
and to Mallarmé,
to say nothing of Lady Julian's

> Sin is Behovely, but
> All shall be well, and
> All manner of thing shall be well.

('Little Gidding III [= 1944: 41])

or

> Synne is behovabil, but al shal be wel
> & al shal be wel
> & al manner of thyng shal be wele.

(Julian 1950: 56)

And Lady Julian here is not so much doing history as talking about that which makes history possible.

'History', of course, *is* sometimes used in something like Eliot's manner, as Gregor Smith does, when he speaks of 'God's history with man' (1966: 21, but see Chapter 12 below).

But should not this way of using the word be called rather, with Collingwood, 'theocratic myth and history' (1946: 14-17)? When 'history' is autocephalous, a discipline by which all other disciplines are ruled, it can deal, it seems, also with the cephalophorous. But *ought it to*?

To put this point less enigmatically: a 'cephalophorous' person (Chadwick 1981: 54) is a person, who, after she, or preferably he (or v.v.) has been beheaded, walks off to church, where the head of the person sings the *Te Deum* (Van Harvey 1967: 81). Of such a person, and to pass, too hastily (I fear), over 'Porphyry's commentary on the *Harmonics* of Ptolemy (Chadwick 1981: 78), it has been observed, as I am kindly informed by private communication, 'by an 18th century, French lady', on hearing that one of these had walked a couple of miles': [*c'est*] *le premier pas qui coûte*, 'it is the first step that counts' (p. 43).

An 'autocephalous' person, a 'self-head', is *par excellence one* for whom the state is himself, '*l'état c'est moi*', one who is sole ruler. 'History', for this is the point, is not the sole ruler among the categories. Something less royalist, some more democratic deliverance of the 'democratic intellect' (Davie 1964) is required. My point is also that there is no need to recoil in horror from something that is *not* history, but a very great need to enjoy something that *is* fiction. And most people, certainly most children, crouched over those square caverns, out of which strange stories come (*The X-Files*, say), do not need to be told this. Long live the common man, the common child! They are very common, indeed.

'History' is not the sole category. 'Fiction' is another. If a term needs to be found that would cover both, an *Inbegriff* sought, by which both might be subsumed, 'reality' is better.

The *problem* is (if the iteration of the *italic* mode may be allowed to rival the usage of Holden Caulfield of *The Catcher in the Rye* [Salinger 1958]) to explain *what fiction is* and what is its proper *enjoyment* and what it is that is enjoyed in its enjoyment, especially if it is remembered that fiction can be a very serious business indeed, covering as it does *Macbeth* and *Oedipus* on the one hand and *The Frogs* of Aristophanes on the other.

What (to have recourse yet again to his generous parenthesis) does Paton mean by saying of the poet: '(if we may regard as also a thinker him who is so much more)' (1965: 19)? Eliot (like Paul? like Mark? like John?) is one of these '*so much more*' men (and women: Ms Eliot!). How does Eliot (and Ms Eliot) do it?

Eliot, of course, does not only know his Massinger (Eliot 1960: 123-43), but is *historically* well informed. Eliot knows his history. One recalls the 'and more' of 'Little Gidding' III [= 1944: 41]), where, punning like a Hebrew prophet (for example *qayits/qets*, 'summer-fruit'/'end': Amos 8.2), he manages to get 'and more' to refer not only to the co-adjutors of Strafford, Laud and Charles, but to the 'and More' himself (Thomas) and probably, too, by connotation, to the Great And More Himself, who was, historically speaking (if, at the same time, credally speaking) 'crucified under Pontius

Pilate'. The English Civil War is running along behind the back of all this, as well as a historical novel, or, as the author J.H. Shorthouse called it, a 'Philosophical Romance' (Gardner 1978: 60), *John Inglesant*, a novel about Nicholas Ferrar and the Little Gidding community. And there was, of course, Eliot's *own historical* visit to Little Gidding, for '[h]e went there, as he wrote to Mrs. Perkins, on a "really lovely day" at the end of May in 1936' (p. 58).

But the visit, in May 1936, of Eliot, the historian, to 'a secluded chapel' ('Little Gidding' V [= 1944: 43]) was also the visit of a poet (and more!).

For the poet, who was a historian, was also a metaphysician. Immersed in history, soaked in and baptised by literature—neither of these phrases exhaustively describes the confines of a mind and imagination that the Greeks (Euripides, anyway: *Iphigeneia in Tauris* 1149) have a word for: *polupoikilos* (πολυποίκιλος). And Shelley might say 'daedal' (but that is Greek, too [among others: Nonnus (again) *Dionysiaca* 5.391]).

The voice of the metaphysician is another of Eliot's voices:

> What might have been is an abstraction
> Remaining a perpetual possibility
> Only in a world of speculation...
>
> ('Burnt Norton' I [= 1944: 7])

And if the 'haruspicate and scry', the 'Biography from the wrinkles of the palm', of one of Eliot's astrological *topoi* ('The Dry Salvages' V [= 1944: 32]) can be decently omitted from an inquiry into metaphysics, one may compare another metaphysical phrase, from Movement II of the same Quartet (= 1944: 10):

> To be conscious is not to be in time

with a fragment from Eliot's thesis on Bradley: '...and the knower, *qua* knower, is not a part of the world which he knows: he does not exist' (1964: 154).

The *Four Quartets* sequence seems to be, no, quite certainly is interfused by quite sinewy reflection on the relation between time and eternity. In the actual, but

> impossible union
> Of spheres of existence
>
> ('The Dry Salvages' V [= 1944: 33])

Aristotle's *Metaphysics* Λ seems to be crossed with Aquinas's *Summa*. But, if this is metaphysics, or philosophy, it is metaphysics, or philosophy, as felt by a poet, who has interwoven it with his poetry. It is philosophy digested. It is philosophy along the veins. These are not stray incursions of foreign material. They are integrally a part of the poem, and that part, with the other parts, are parts of a whole. And the whole is a poem. Mereology and Mariology are combined. And the whole is a fiction. God is *not* a 'ruined millionaire'. He wins the lottery every time.

There are various ways in which the poet as 'hacker' can gain access to reality: the poetic imagination, for one, the scientific (*scientia*) intellect, for another. Eliot has not confused the modes, but has fused them and he is familiar with more than one.

So metaphysics is now and England. We have here, in the *Four Quartets*, the Bradleyan Eliot, if not the Bradleyan Eliot of his Oxford thesis: 'Aristotle is here betrayed by his representation theory' (1964: 184). But not only the Bradleyan Eliot. We also have metaphysics in terms of the symbolic system of Anglo-Catholicism, the mysticism, the philosophy of religion and the language of the rite. But this variety is comprehended within the unity of a poem.

And literature is now and England. Or now and Europe, its poems (Baudelaire), its novels (Dostoyevsky), the plays (Pirandello). And with literature literary criticism. And Eliot's alarming intelligence and his industry. We have the Eliot who has laboured 'to distil...to press and press the essence of each author, to apply exact measurement to our own sensations' (1960: 124).

If 'history is now', 'history' is a complex word, a complex word within a poem.

And history is 'now'. The word 'history' slips and slides, as words

> strain,
> Crack and sometimes break, under the burden,
> Under the tension...perish,
> Decay with imprecision, will not stay in place,
> Will not stay still...
>
> ('Burnt Norton' V [= 1944: 12])

'History' slips and slides, here, from a Collingwoodian inquiry into 'actions of human beings that have been done in the past' (1946: 9), or an Oakeshottian inquiry into an event as 'an occurrence or situation, inferred from surviving record, alleged to be what was actually happening, in a certain respect, then and there' (1983: 62). With Eliot 'history' becomes, not so much an 'event', as (what might be called) an *'evenient'*, not so much 'what has happened' (Aristotle, *Po.* 1451a37), as what is now happening. It is a happening that seems capable of giving way to 'what *may* happen' (οἷα ἂν γένοιτο, *boia an genoito*: 1451a38), where possibility takes, is taking shape as actuality, the actuality of a recipient (*Empfänglichkeit*, 'receptivity'!) in 'a secluded chapel'.

By saying, 'now', that 'History is now', Eliot moves, in fact, from history to the making of it. And the making of history is *why* Eliot, the historian, is interested in it. And yet that is still not exhaustively what he is writing *about*. For the history made by whom? By what? By God. But not by God only. Here an 'individual talent' (1950: 47-59) is himself making a contribution to the tradition in which he stands, a tradition, which he revises as he extends it.

But this individual's contribution is no solipsist one. This individual is spokesman for the society of which he is a part, for the body of which he is a member. Where Eliot is is where we all are, or where *mutatis mutandis* we all are, if the Westminster Confession has to be substituted for Gore, or Karl Marx's *Manifesto* for the rite of aspersion (the mutations must be taken seriously). Eliot, that is, is operating, as we all operate, within a certain ideology (a pejorative term), or within a certain system of ideas. Eliot was Anglo-Catholic in religion, in politics monarchist, conservative and aristocratic, while the determinants of the present writer belong, ideologically speaking, to the tradition of Geneva and Glasgow and to the kind of 'righteousness', or social justice, that 'comes to speech' in *Ane Satyre of the Thrie Estaitis*. Others think otherwise.

What Eliot is writing about is a *Konjunktur*, 'an economic situation', if and only if 'economic' is to be understood in the Patristic sense, not simply of the management of a household, or the finances of a state, but in the sense of the management of the human affairs of a world, from alpha to omega. This model, *oikonomia*, is given extended treatment in Ramsey (1973: 15-27).

But *poetice* is how he is writing about it. What he is writing is a poem. This poem is Eliot's own exploit as spokesman, the forming and fashioning of words, a 'fictioning', that draws widely, not only on a historical tradition and a philosophical and metaphysical one, but on fiction. Reality is now and England.

In 'Little Gidding' V (= 1944: 43) Eliot is using the word 'history' in a Pickwickian, or unparliamentary sense. 'History' is appearing here within a 'reach' of words that are not, or are not primarily, historical, nor philosophical, but literary. A change is occurring, the 'new' is occurring 'in a secluded chapel', a change that plays havoc with the English tongue. '(A) change', writes Oakeshott,

> may perhaps be recognised as 'miraculous' and, although it may be difficult to ascertain exactly what this means (and it may be a merely rhetorical expression [I would myself say 'literary']), it certainly attributes to an occurrence something other than the character of an historical event and the outcome of an assembled passage of antecedent historical events (1983: 116).

The word 'History', that is (is it not?), as it occurs for Eliot in 'Little Gidding', 'has something other than the character of an historical event'. 'Reality', in my submission, a reality that, while it includes history, includes more, is the juster term. This is *not*, however, to ask Eliot to rewrite, to add to his margin, as Bonhoeffer's schoolmaster to his 1923 essay on Catullus and Horace: *kommt sehr unerwartet* ('the word is unexpected here', or *Ausdruck verfehlt*, 'faulty in expression' [Bonhoeffer 1986: IX, 204]). It is simply to note what Eliot is doing, when he does it. Eliot's 'history' is neither Collingwood, nor Oakeshott (though very nearly Gregor Smith). And Gregor Smith's views, the views of that *doctor subtilis*, will be more or less directly encountered—and countered in The Complot (Chapter 12). But here with Eliot, to stick to him, we are dealing with the 'History' of Eliot, the poet. We reach here, not the zenith of Luke's prologue, but the nadir of Luke's history, whose history is 'history'.

But someone will say that the poet's history (Eliot's) differs from the historian's history only by being more profound; both more profound and more elevated. 'The way up and the way down,' says Eliot, 'is one and the same' (1944: the second of the two initial mottos: Heraclitus, *Fr.* 60 [Diels (*which* edition of Diels was Eliot using?) 1.89]). And what Eliot is doing is to go farther down than historians usually can go and further up than they cannot.

He goes down. He covers the experience of the traveller in the 'tube', who is apparently impatient for *très grande vitesse*:

> Or as, when an underground train, in the tube, stops too long
>   between stations
> And the conversation rises and slowly fades into silence
> And you see behind every face the mental emptiness deepen
> Leaving only the growing terror of nothing to think about…
>
>   ('East Coker' III [= 1944: 19])

He covers the experience of the senescent, worse, the senile:

> Do not let me hear
> Of the wisdom of old men, but rather of their folly,
> Their fear of fear and frenzy, their fear of possession,
> Of belonging to another, or to others, or to God.
>
>   ('East Coker' II [= 1944: 18])

He can, of course, remain, less catachthonically, on the terrene level, the level of the (Kelham) kingfisher:

> After the kingfisher's wing
> Has answered light to light, and is silent, the light is still
> At the still point of the turning world.

Or Heraclitus's ἄνω (*ano*), he goes up. He goes up, to something more than the 'zero summer'[6] of 'Little Gidding' (which is there, in any case, not enjoyed, but desiderated). He climbs, say, to the climax of the terminal unity of 'the fire and the rose' ('Little Gidding' V [= 1944: 44]). But again this is something hoped for rather than something enjoyed, though, historically speaking, people have hoped for something like this and formulated their hopes like this. But still:

> For most of us, there is only the unattended
> Moment, the moment in and out of time,
> The distraction fit…
>
>   ('The Dry Salvages' V [= 1944: 33])

Some kinds of horror, some kinds of ecstasy, are, beyond cavil, everywhere intercalated into the sequence of poems.

The Poet as Thinker

The distinction between fact and fiction, between poetry and history, is not an easy distinction to make (Kermode 1990). It is a

---

6.   Is Stevens's 'zero green' on the 'blue island': 'A green baked greener in the greenest sun' (1955: 393) the best exegetical parallel?

sliding scale, not easy to determine at which point one thing is turning, or has turned, into another. And yet, to the tradition of Scottish common sense and Scottish common sense philosophy, it seems obvious that some distinction can with some clarity be drawn.

For Collingwood, the development of mind can be hierarchically organized into sensation, imagination and thought, much as for Spinoza into imagination, reason and intuition. Eliot is a man of feeling, more or less successfully anchored in Hamann's 'senses and passions' (*Sinne und Leidenschaften*). And he is finding language to express his feelings. He is finding words, images. But Eliot is also a thinker, which means that his imagination is penetrated by thought. But what he is doing, if Collingwood is right and rightly interpreted, is to express not only what it is to have certain sensations, but to express, not thought, but what it *feels* like to *think* in a certain way (Collingwood 1938: 292-99).

And, in this very passage, Collingwood (1938), writing before the *Four Quartets* were written and referring mainly to 'The Waste Land', a poem that includes both other lines and these:

> That corpse you planted last year in your garden,
> Has it begun to sprout?
>   (Eliot, 'The Waste Land' I. The Burial of the Dead)

writes (1938: 295), in a passage that follows on from a discussion of how Donne 'expressed how it feels to live in a world full of shattered ideas, *disjecta membra* of old systems of life and thought':

> And Mr. Eliot, in the one great English poem of this century has expressed his idea (not his alone) of the decay of our civilisation, manifested outwardly as a break-down of social structures and inwardly as a drying-up of the emotional springs of life.

But by 1944 the corpse that Eliot had planted in the wilderness of the Muses had begun to sprout and had produced in the garden and glebe of the Muses, not 'orient wheat', yet at least a world, where 'hints and guesses' could, and did, occur. But the question remains, for the cultural historian, for the writer of a history of literature, for the historian of literary art, for the literary critic, for the philosopher of literature, How much, how little, what exactly, what as exactly as possible in matters of this kind, does Eliot mean

by the word 'history', and by what means (history? fiction?) does
he express what he means by it?

What is the difference between a poet's history and a historian's
history, in the case where 'a poet' is *the* poet, Eliot. And the over-
tones of a third area of inquiry may be overheard: What of the
philosopher's history, where the philosopher is Collingwood
(1946), Collingwood conjoined in some measure with Oakeshott
(1983)?

But let us first make what the French call a *déviation* (and the
English a 'deviation'), through Eliot's metaphysics and philosophy.
For the enquirer, interrogator, the torturer, must often, like the
writer of fiction, operate by stealth, or indirection. The question is
again transposed: What is the difference between a poet's
metaphysics and a philosopher's metaphysics, in the case where
Eliot, as the author of *Knowledge and Experience in the philosophy of F.H. Bradley* and Eliot as the author of the *Four Quartets*,
is the author of metaphysics of both kinds.

Metaphysics, it may be added, may be equated with theology, if
and only if the termination -logy, of the word 'theology', be given
the kind of force that the word 'word' (*logos*), has in Plato and
Aristotle, but may not be so equated, when theology is applied to
the New Testament, where we have rather the deliverances of ink-
ling. We have the deliverances of de Wette's *Ahnung*, Kant's
'presentiment' (through Fries). In New Testament 'theology', in
New Testament 'thought', in New Testament religion, religious
poetry, we have, not a 'ballet of bloodless categories', but rather a
ballet, sometimes *strictissimo sensu*, of bloody metaphors, as:

> The bloody flesh our only food
> ('East Coker' IV [= 1944: 21])

The word 'right' is much misused by Ministers of the Crown ('It
is, in my view, right…'), but I think nevertheless the equation right
of theology and metaphysics. Theology is a branch of metaphysics.
Such a theistic metaphysic, if you will, is the attempt, not only to
account for human behaviour (Leach 1954: 13), but also to account
for the *context* in which humans behave, especially if theology, or
metaphysics, or theistic metaphysics, can be taken to be, not 'a
contraption of silk and metal or what not, which shelters a certain
space from the rain, the space in question moving as the thing that

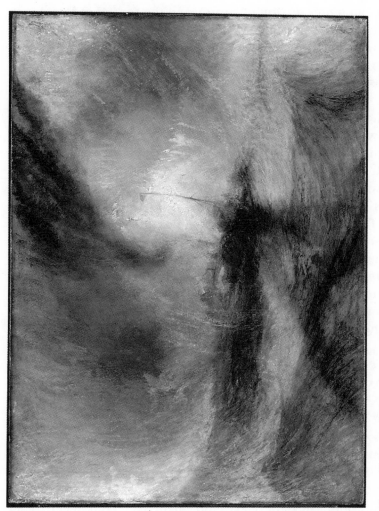

Figure 7. *Snow Storm: Steamboat off a Harbour's Mouth*, 1842, by J.MW. Turner (1775–1851) (reproduced by courtesy of the Trustees, The Tate Gallery, London)

shelters it is carried forward' (Collingwood 1942: 135), but Turner, *tied to a mast and a storm*.

The discipline of metaphysics, in a word, is not a device for protection from the weather, but a licence that allows exposure to the elements; not a prop for illusions but a meeting with reality. These metaphors, umbrella and mast, are not simply idle, but depend, the first on an *obiter dictum* of Heaton and the second of Mackinnon, on the fact of the binding of Turner, if fact it was. For it was repeated from *recollection* by the Revd William Kingslake to Ruskin.

Those metaphors raise, that fact raises, two important questions: (1) In what context can theology properly be done? And: (2) How can theology properly be done and can it always be done in the same way?

Turner's picture was 'Snow Storm: Steamboat off a Harbour's Mouth making Signals in Shallow Water, and going by the Lead. The Author was in this Storm on the Night the Ariel left Harwich'. It was based on the experience of being lashed to a mast at the time. The picture was greeted by the derision of the critics. It was 'soapsuds and whitewash'. The *Art Union* (1 June 1842) wrote: 'Through the driving snow there are just perceptible portions of a steam-boat labouring on a rolling sea; but before any further account of the vessel can be given, it will be necessary to wait until the storm is cleared off a little.'

Turner's own response is worth recalling too:

> I did not paint it to be understood, but I wished to show what such a scene was like... I was lashed for four hours and I did not expect to escape, but I felt bound to record it if I did... What would they [sc. the critics] have? I wonder what they think the sea's like? I wish they'd been in it (Butlin, Wilton and Gage 1974: 140).[7]

In *Colour in Turner*, Gage (1969: 39) calls it 'one of the darkest and least chromatic' of his oils. Gage's subtitle is apt: *Poetry and Truth*. But we hardly need to be reminded that the conjunction of the two words is as valid as the conjunction of man and storm on this occasion. They are (Oakeshott might say) 'contingent'. They are touching one another. Man and storm here are distinguishable, but not separable. Even the metaphysician's ballet need not be bloodless, cannot be.

7. Cf. Finberg 1939: 390; Reynolds 1969: 190.

Bradley is a difficult philosopher. And Eliot on Bradley hardly less so. But it is clear that Eliot's obscure remarks in the 'Conclusion' to his Bradley book (1964: 153-69) and his strictures, there, on 'objects', 'half-objects' and 'double half-objects' (p. 163 n. **), might well have impressed Piero (are we to think of the geometrical diagrams of the *De prospectiva pingendi*?), Turner in a storm (are we to think of how things may be seen, when it is difficult to see them?). However that may be, and however Eliot may be said to have benefited from 'the discipline of a close study of the Greek text of the *Posterior Analytics*' (p. 9) with Harold Joachim, 'the disciple of Bradley who was closest to the master' (p. 9), and from a study of Joachim's own *Nature of Truth* (1906: 113, cit. Eliot 1964: 166 n. *), Eliot's 'Conclusion' contains the following important quotation.

It is only the last sentence, on which I wish to fasten, but that sentence makes somewhat more sense, if (as Joachim seems to be recommending [1906: 113] and Collingwood [1939: 29-43] seems to be suggesting [the two were colleagues]), some idea is given of some of the context, in which this last sentence occurs:

> we feel that there are truths valid for this world, though we do not know what these truths are; and it is with this sort that the refined and subtilized common sense which is Critical Taste occupies itself. The true critic is a scrupulous avoider of formulae; he refrains from statements which pretend to be literally true; he finds fact nowhere and approximation always. His truths are truths of experience rather than of calculation.
>
> Even these lived truths are partial and fragmentary, for the finest tact after all can give us only an interpretation, and every interpretation, along perhaps with some utterly contradictory interpretation, has to be taken up and reinterpreted by every thinking mind and by every civilization. This is the significance of the late Samuel Butler's epigram to the effect that the whole duty of man was to serve God and Mammon: for both God and Mammon are interpretations of the world and have to be reinterpreted. It is this sort of interpretation (which formally consists I believe in transformations of object-type) that *the historian, the literary critic and the metaphysician* are engaged with (1964: 164).

I have first to apologize to the reader for producing a passage, which very nearly passes as intelligible. This makes the passage unrepresentative. The phrase italicized shows that Eliot *himself* there recognizes that the activities of historian, literary critic and metaphysician are three distinguishable (though they may not be separable) activities. And if, by implication from his 'objects of fiction, which have a reality [like 'mental images' and 'hallucinations'] in their own space and time, and a different reality in our space and time' (1964: 162-63), the poet and writer of fiction be added to these, we have not three 'distincts', but four: poet, historian, literary critic and metaphysician.

But the main point is this, that between the poet as metaphysician and the metaphysician's metaphysics there is a distinction. Eliot's 'Conclusion' to the Bradley essay gives very little hint of Eliot, the poet, except for his remark, that 'Truth on our level is a different thing from truth for the jellyfish' (1964: 166). But his own mouth betrays him as one who did not think, his own mouth confirms that he himself did not think the distinction vacuous: 'Forty-six years after my academic philosophizing came to an end, I find myself unable to think in the terminology of this essay' (1964: 10). His next sentence re-assures: 'Indeed, I do not pretend to understand it.'

All this is to argue, not by the production of a syllogism, but by the provision of an example. It is an appeal to the reader to read Eliot's 'Conclusion' and compare it with one of the only three great poems in English of the twentieth century. It is also an appeal to the reader to think.

There is a distinction, then, between the philosopher as metaphysician and the poet as metaphysician. And the distinction is similar between the poet as historian and the historian's history. There is no one who will not feel here that Eliot is doing more for history than the historian usually does. What is important to the poet is what the historian leaves out.

Take Conzelmann. Take his classic article, 'Jesus Christus' (1973). Take Morgan, or be about to take Morgan, more briefly, in *The Oxford Dictionary of the Christian Church* (forthcoming [no longer: 1997). And note what they include, but note what they leave out. What is left out, what is *almost* left out is the thing itself. What is to be taken is not there for the taking.

Take Walls's objects (1995) in *Vom Jordan nach Jerusalem*. When an earlier article of the same writer appeared in France, it was observed by him, 'When it was translated into French, I almost

believed it myself'. The *libellus* that demands our present credulity
is in German and treats of Baptism, Temptation, Transfiguration,
the Entry into Jerusalem and the Institution of the Last Supper
(1995). But if these are there in Conzelmann and Morgan, are they
there *at all*, and, if so, *how* are they there? And if they are not
there, where are they? Does the place thereof know them at all?
Are we dealing here with an hissing and a desolation? This is the
deepest source of Hamann's quarrel with Michaelis, that what matters is either omitted, or suppressed, or distorted. Like Macdonald
on fiction (1954), the historian is asking the kind of question that
precludes an answer. Macdonald seems (to the present writer) to
be struggling to ask the kind of questions, that her kind of philosophy does not allow her to answer. The progress of science
depends (does it?) on the resolute asking of the wrong questions.

The historian is, of course, right, right to give the right answers
to historical questions. The further question is only whether historical questions are the only right questions to ask. And the more
important question is whether the most important question is
being asked? On Hamann's assumption, that 'poetry is the mother-
tongue of the human race' (1950: 197)[8] and that Jesus and his early
successors *spoke* the mother-tongue, literary questions are also
right. They give promise.

For when the gospel writers write history, if that is what they are
doing, if that is what they ever do, they cannot do so without
telling lies, not (as Hesiod) 'lies like the truth' (ψεύδεα...ἐτύμοισιν
ὁμοῖα, *pseudea...etumoisin homoia: Theogony* 27), but *un*like it.
They cannot do so without telling tales. And tales are for children.
But unless we become as little children, we may not be able to
enter the mind, or the imagination, of the New Testament writers.
Gregor Smith speaks (1969: 133-34) of 'the historical and literary
imagination': do we not need both? And do we not now need the
second more?

But again the question remains: Rather than the introduction of a
neoteric category, 'literary' (and 'literature'), why not expand the
old, why not expand 'history'? If 'history' is a portmanteau word,
why not pack more into it? And is it not simply this that Eliot has
done? Can we not produce a more adequate category for the production of a more adequate history? Is the right history to write a

8.   = Gregor Smith 1960: 196; Crick, in Nisbet 1985: 141.

'theocratic history' (Collingwood 1946: 14-17)? Or why should not the historian delve more fully into the 'senses and passions' (like Renan into Jesus' ass, 'that favourite riding-animal of the East, which is so docile and sure-footed and whose great dark eyes, shaded by long lashes, are full of gentleness' [cit. Schweitzer 1911: 184])? Or why should we not permit the subjective engagement of the historian to get conflated with his history, the present of the historian with the past of his history, of the kind that makes Gibbon a historian, not of the *Decline and Fall of the Roman Empire*, but of the decline and rise of the eighteenth century?

What Collingwood, sanguine about King Arthur, does with *Roman Britain*, is not the kind of thing that Eliot is doing in the *Four Quartets*. What Collingwood says there is that '[t]he place which the name of Arthur occupies in Celtic legend is easiest to explain on the hypothesis that he really lived' (1937: 321). But Eliot would have been more interested in the stories of the Arthurian cycle than the facts around whom they were cycling. For Eliot is speaking, and knows that he is speaking, 'the mother-tongue'. And it would be interesting to know what either Collingwood, or Oake-shott, would do, if they were offered the *Four Quartets* as historical evidence for a historiographical exploit. There are, of course, two questions: (1) Was Eliot a historiographer? And (2) what historical inferences can be drawn from whatever it was that Eliot was doing?

If we want to know *if*, and, if so, *when*, Eliot visited 'Little Gidding', even if we might cautiously infer *from the poem* that he did so, we must, for the evidence, turn, rather than to *Four Quartets*, to *The Composition of the Four Quartets* (Gardner 1978). Or we must turn to (one of) his biographer(s), for example, Ackroyd (1993). Similarly for Eliot's Air Raid Post duties. And if we want to know, not this time about the 'dove' that 'breaks' Mark's air ('Little Gidding' IV [= 1944: 42]), but about the 'dove' of the Second Movement of 'Little Gidding':

> After the dark dove with the flickering tongue
> Had passed below the horizon of his homing...
> ('Little Gidding' II [= 1944: 38])

we must turn elsewhere. For this 'dove' is a *Taube*, a German aircraft. This dove is not 'wise as a serpent and harmless', but harm-*ful* (contra Mt. 10.16) as a serpent, constructed by devilish ingenuity. The gunner's fire of the departing aircraft 'flickers' like a serpent's tongue (Ricks 1988: 254, and, with Brown's assistance [see Acknowledgments], Matthiesson and Flint, in Bergonzi 1969: 100, 117). We must study what historians have said about the Blitz and what his biographers have said about this point of Eliot's biography. And we might want to check up on Eliot's medical history for 'The wounded surgeon plies the steel' ('East Coker' IV [= 1944: 20]). And what history books had he read? Should we read them too?

Is Eliot an apt subject for the historian's inquiries? Can the historian draw historical inferences from the *Quartets*? It is for the cultural historian, for the art historian, the literary historian, the student of the history of Christian symbolism to draw inferences, or make some observations here. The history of European culture and art, from Piero to Haydn's *Seven Last Words from the Cross*, demonstrates how artists have responded to art, how 1 Corinthians 13 [again] turns into the last of Brahms's *Four Serious Songs*. The echoes have answered. But in art (and in religion) the echo may itself be a voice.

Eliot, in a word, but the New Testament also, belongs not to the history of history *tout court*, but rather to the history of art, the history of *literary* art, and so to the history of literature. The *Quartets*, in a word, are incantations in reponse to incantations, to the incantations of the New Testament (Loisy 1923: 405-39 *passim*), and, indifferently (the incantations do not end with the end of the New Testament), to the incantations that follow it. Writing succeeds writing. Scripture succeeds scripture.

If this means that there is a sense of the word 'history', the history of literature, say, which can include fiction, then it is as fiction that fiction is included in it.

The quotidian historian, who looks at the *Four Quartets*, can do something with the history of Mr Eliot. And that might well be a higher and a deeper something than is attainable in most historical inquiries. For the historian as biographer (Knowles 1963) Eliot is a high task. But we should need a great deal more: his Travel Diary, a passenger list of the men (and women) on the Little Gidding omnibus (not, of course, as now after privatization, the Little Gidding nemini) and a great deal more of the kind of intelligence that has been patiently exhumed by Ackroyd and Gardner. But it is the one, by vocation, art historian, or literary historian, to whom 'the voice of this Calling' ('Little Gidding' V [= 1944: 43]) here most properly is coming.

The End of This Chapter

'History' in 'Little Gidding' is a large word in a large poem.

Students of *Tom A Lincoln* will recall the larger word, 'metagrabolizde' (Proudfoot 1992: 57, l.2071). It may well, or may well not, mean 'excogitating', *excogitare* (so Jonson, 'in a marginal gloss in the British Library copy (given by Ben Jonson to Thomas Skinner in 1628)' (Proudfoot 1992: xxxi). The 'metagrabolizing', or 'excogitating' of the meaning of the Lincolnshire terms *phraises* (sc. dishes of eggs and butter), and *kadumbeld* (sc. tipsy), which are discussed by Proudfoot there, are, for all their difficulty, easier terms (in my submission) for the literary historian to contend with than the little word 'history' in 'Little Gidding'.

For on this word converges not only the whole of 'Little Gidding', and the whole sequence of poems and, together with the past, 'the organisation of the totality of experience *sub specie praeteritorum*' (Oakeshott 1933: 111), the present and the future as well, all conspiring to make a moment of plenitude.

'The study of human thought', writes Isenberg (1973: 199) 'embraces at least these three kinds of work: (a) interpretation, (b) explanation, and (c) criticism or evaluation'. A 'still point', in Eliot (and in Maxwell [1943], for that matter) may take, may demand the emission of a deal of critical noise, before we can begin to know something about where such a 'still point' is to be found. Even the sub-Erasmian paraphrast must either despair, or write, not a paragraph, or a chapter, but a book. So it is, too, with the word 'history'.

Any definition, or steps towards a defining, of this very loose-textured word in a poet's mouth must, in the first instance, depend on the precision (but are we always dealing with precision?) of the poet's language. Collingwood's *'principle of the limited objective'* (1942: 253) is important, too: 'Limit your objective. Take time seriously. Aim at interpreting not, as the Greeks did, any and every fact...but only those which you think need be interpreted' (254). Nor is it unimportant to recall his remarks in the *Essay on Philosophical Method*, where he is speaking about the languages of art on the one hand and of philosophy on the other: 'the philosophical writer...follows the trade not of a jeweller but of a lens-grinder' (1933: 214).

In order, then, to avoid saying nothing at all, the following may be hazarded: the little word 'History', allows Eliot, despite history's excoriations, the sarcasm of God, to affirm the experience of life and the paradoxical notion of a non-terminal end of life:

> to make an end is to make a beginning...
>
> We are born with the dead...
>
> ('Little Gidding' V [= 1944: 42-43])

It allows Eliot to assert *poetice*, that history for this poet- historian does not end with what he is studying, or (better) *contemplating*. It allows him, in view of what Paul, in 2 Cor. 12.7, means by δύναμις (*dunamis*, 'power', Mr Alexander Guinness's 'the Force', *la forza del destino*), to assert that he, the writer, and he or she, the well-disposed reader, may say that meaning, the meaning of experience and its context, both for human- and non-human beings, is *meant* by that which is neither the former nor the latter.

'For a metaphysics to be accepted, good-will is essential' (Eliot 1964: 168).

But, if a servant is not above a master, neither is a critic above a poem.

T.S. Eliot is not exhaustively named, when he is called a poet. He was also a tramper through the waste land of the *Posterior Analytics*, though it was a 'waste land', in which and through which Joachim was the psychagogue. Eliot had his Virgil here. Eliot was philosopher and poet. Moreover, like Horace before him, and more than Horace before him, Eliot was literary critic, a critic of immense industry, and that not only within his critical writing, but also within his creative, *creational* writing:

> The word neither diffident nor ostentatious
> An easy commerce of the old and the new,
> The common word exact without vulgarity,
> The formal word precise but not pedantic,
> The complete word dancing together...
>
> ('Little Gidding', V [= 1944: 42-43])

And Eliot was, moreover, a man, whose 'authorial self' (Cohen 1994: *passim*) was capable of *Notes towards the Definition of*

Culture, reader of *The British in Asia* (1948: 91 n. 1), who
'would...read to his wife at the end of the day—from Boswell's
Life of Johnson' (Ackroyd 1993: 322), who had been 'encouraged'
by his mother to read Macaulay's *History of England* (p. 20), was
at least not unacquainted with what historians do; though cultural
history, rather than history *tout court*, was much more his field,
such works, for example, as *The Symbolist Movement in Literature* of Arthur Symons (p. 34). Eliot's awareness of the historical
past, as it surfaces in the *Four Quartets*, is patent.

In 'The Humanism of the Twelfth Century', Knowles (1963: 17)
speaks of 'the year in which Dante, waking in the hillside forest,
passed in imagination through the realms beyond the grave'.
Changing what must be changed, and exchanging for Dante's
'hillside forest' the *selva oscura* (dark wood) of war-time London
(Eliot, 'East Coker' II [= 1944: 18] Gardner 1978: 103), these, too,
and even in Dante's own metre, are the realms to which Eliot
passed ('Little Gidding' II [= 1944: 38-40]).

There abide, then, these three: history, literature and metaphysics. Coordinate among these is literature. And, with literature,
fiction. This is not to say that only these three are required; it is
only to say, at least these three. But terms, that may be coordinate
within the economy of a human life, or may gain, within a human
life, now more, now less emphasis, may not be co-equal, when we
look at the *Four Quartets*. In these poems, in this poem, metaphysics and history are transmuted into images, symbols and
allusions. In the *Four Quartets*, the greater one, the one that is
greater than either history, or metaphysics, is literature. The
greatest is literature.

'Jerome Begat the Tubas': Notes towards 'Notes towards a Supreme Fiction': Imagination and Reality in a Poem by Wallace Stevens

> The final belief is to believe in a fiction, which you know to be a fiction, there being nothing else. The exquisite truth is to know that it is a fiction and that you believe in it willingly.
>
> (W. Stevens, *Opus Posthumous*)

The first thing to be said about Stevens is that he is a very difficult poet. He has acquired a tongue of his own. If that is true of every poet, of some of them it is more true than others. There is no reader that will not note some difficulty.

And does Stevens do theology? Has Stevens a language for God? If so, how does he do it and what is his language? And would we be assisted in our understanding of the New Testament, if we were to regard *it* as a fiction, and perhaps as supreme among fictions? And what would make a fiction 'supreme'? How would it differ from other fictions? And what would it be to believe in a fiction *as a fiction*?

And what is the proper physiognomy of a modern believer? What is, not that which, but that *by which* the believer believes, not (as the Latins say) the *fides quae creditur*, but the *fides qua*?

No student of Stevens's 'Notes towards a Supreme Fiction', who is going to see Naples and die, can spend more profitably the terminal moments than by thumbing through the *Annali dell' Instituto Universitario Orientale*, Sezione Germanica (Naples), or be more delighted to find there the Commentary on the 'Notes... of Kermode (1961). It precedes Kermode's Edinburgh book, *Wallace Stevens* (1960), which precedes it, for the one that comes after it (in publication) is the one that comes before it (in writing), for it was before it (in importance).

This is a way of putting it, a formulation, that echoes the religious genius of John's enigmatic utterance to the 'religious genius',

Jesus (Ashton 1991: 126), an utterance by prosopopoea given by the religious genius of John to John, the evangelist to the baptist: 'This was he of whom I said, He that cometh after me is become before me: for he was before me' (Jn 1.15). For John, the evangelist, too, is a difficult writer. What he has made the Baptist say is difficult and is not, surely, what the Baptist said. The evangelist here has made use of Lowth's second type of prosopopoea, or personification, 'when a probable but fictitious speech is assigned to a real character' (Lowth 1839: 136). And its 'probability' here is literary, not historical. Its probability is a plausibility, a literary plausibility, something that 'makes sense' in its context.

Stevens's 'Notes...' is a triadic, or trinitarian, poem, each of its three parts being divided into ten (or x), segments, of seven (or vii) three-line stanzas. The whole is prefixed by a prologue of eight lines; and suffixed by a coda, that consists of one segment of vii three-line stanzas—on war, the soldier and the poet. The three parts have, severally, three headings:

It Must Be Abstract,
It Must Change, and
It Must Give Pleasure.

Change and *Pleasure* speak for themselves, but by *Abstract* Stevens means, not the withdrawing of attention from particulars and the turn to generalities, but the selection of particulars from among particulars.

Stevens (1960: 118, cit. Kermode 1960: 111) speaks of 'a rhetoric in which the feeling of one man is communicated to another in words of the exquisite appropriateness that takes away all their verbality'. 'Comment', Kermode there adds, 'puts the "verbality" back in; the clearer the explanations, the falser they are likely to be', to which he adds Stevens's aphorism (1959: 171): 'Poetry must resist the intelligence almost successfully.' But what, if 'almost' be omitted?

Eliot's bird (or one of them) says: 'Go, go, go' ('Burnt Norton' I [= 1944: 8]). Stevens's birds come up, also in 'Notes...', with a variety of noises: 'Bethou me...', for 'the sparrow' (1955: 393 [= II.vi]), 'Ah, ké!', for 'the bloody wren, the felon jay', and 'Ké-ké' for 'the jug-throated robin' (394 [= II.vi])—which *does* bring another Eliot noise, or call, to mind ('The Waste Land' II [= 1936: 64]). But before Kermode goes on to the 'squawk and clatter', he says this, that 'the final poem is a fact not before realised, a contribution to reality'. As with Eliot's *Quartets*, we have here, Kermode seems to be thinking, an addition by an individual talent to the tradition, that, like John or Paul, has every chance of remaining permanent, of entering the canon. Moreover, Kermode goes on (1960: 112), the poem 'is true; it deals not with myth but with fact, the fact not realised before. The fiction is the ever-changing truth'. Like myth, too, Bultmann, and all of us, would add. In Stevens's categories, imagination is about reality. And reality is the truly real.

But the question is, *how* myth, *how* fiction, *how* imagination are about it, about reality. But there are more questions. For example, *in what terms* does Stevens state 'the fact not realised before'? And how do his terms relate to the historian's terms? And the philosopher's terms? The literary critic's terms? What are the terms for the fact, terms for the facts, of which 'the clearer the explanations, the falser they are likely to be'? What kind of facts are *they*?

The word 'fiction' used of the New Testament has a polemical edge to it. What *is* fiction is *not* history. The question, raised by Stevens, is whether that polemical edge can be turned by calling it 'supreme', by calling the New Testament a supreme fiction. That would raise the further question, how Stevens 'Notes towards a Supreme Fiction' relate to the 'Supreme Fiction', towards which they are the 'Notes'. And the further question, how they relate to the Supreme Fiction, which is the New Testament, or towards which the New Testament constitutes the notes. And further questions will readily spring to mind.

'Garlic and sapphires in the mud...' ('Burnt Norton' II [= 1944: 8]) is not the easiest passage in Eliot's *Four Quartets*. Eliot is not always, not ever, an easy poet. Solomon's Song is easier:

> Thy temples are like a piece of a pomegranate
> Behind thy veil (Cant. 4.3).

And Stevens, here, is Eliot's competitor. And he confesses himself, by implication, to be a difficult poet, when he speaks of 'the poet's gibberish' (1955: 396), though he may astound the common man, and perhaps St Jerome, by going on to speak of 'the gibberish of the vulgate', though, even when the poet is not at the breakfast table, even at the common breakfast table, there is very commonly much talk that could go straight on to the pages of Beckett, of

Ionesco. Gibberish is not far from any one of us, that we should say, 'Where is it?'

The history of European art is a history of iconographic change. Language changes over time. Languages have to be learnt. There are styles, fashions, conventions. The kaleidoscope is shaken and in every moment (Faculty Meetings?) new and startling revelations. The imagination, like thought, has a history. Bosch (Rowlands 1975) differs from Dürer (Panofsky 1971) and both from Turner (Finberg 1939; Reynolds 1969). Idiosyncratic idiolects all.

Are there sometimes things that cannot be said? Or that are not said, because no one is interested in saying them? Or because there are more interesting things that clamour for speech, that out-shout other topics, make some topics into utopics, 'not-topics'?

The history of the iconography of God is subject to the same fate, or destiny. No less the verbal icon than the pictorial image. Add tones, clay and the literate computer.

God is subject to the same historical forces, gets obliterated, disappears (Miller 1978), has a non-teaching sabbatical.

Now poets, by and large, are as great fools, as the rest of us, if Eliot and Lady Julian are right to say that 'Sin is Behovely' (Eliot, 'Little Gidding' III [= 1944: 41]; Lady Julian 1950: 56 n. 1). But, if there is anything in what Stevens said, was earlier quoted as saying, in a Memorandum addressed to the Henry Church, to whom the prologue of 'Notes…' is also addressed (1959: xv), his proposition, that '[t]he major poetic idea in the world is and always has been the idea of God', then are we to 'adapt it to our different intelligence, or create a substitute for it, or make it unnecessary'?

What does Stevens do? Which of these alternatives is his chosen one? And whatever Stevens, the fool, does, what are we fools to do? Or (to say it again), if the choice is 'not a choice / Between excluding things…not a choice / Between, but of' (1955: 403 [= III.vi]), what are we *bound* to choose? And are we (not *pace*, but *bello* Thatcher) sure, by what we here are bound? Are we bound as captives of cupidity? As citizens of the *civitas cupiditatis* (Oakeshott 1983: 176), where '[t]hey find a man's dignity in the way in which he is different from other men, whereas his real dignity consists in the way in which he can be like God' (Henderson 1948: 68), where the citizens rejoice in a *lex* without *jus* (Oakeshott 1983: 160)? Or are we bound as free, bound to the one, 'whom [or which] to serve is to rule', 'whose service is perfect freedom' (*cui servire est regnare*)? Is there now a language for God?

Stevens's barbarian 'gibberish' continues (1955: 381):

> The death of one god is the death of all.
> Let purple Phoebus lie in umber harvest,
> Let Phoebus slumber and die in autumn umber,
>
> Phoebus is dead, ephebe.

And, if we are to take the course of resurrecting the gods of the one, whom Longinus calls simply 'the poet' (sc. Homer), can we call a halt before the repristination of the garden gnome? Why should we call a halt? Or shall we return to the 'angels', ask them into our gardens to 'expel nature with a fork' (Horace, *Ep.* 1.10.24: *naturam expellas furca*, though he goes on: *tamen usque recurret*: 'it will always come back'). Homer had a *necessary* speech, speech that he was *bound* to utter. What is Stevens's necessary speech?

What is Stevens's doctrine of God?

Mackinnon (1968: 50) speaks of 'the devotedly religious man, who tends to speak and act as if there were no *revelations* (I have chosen that word deliberately) concerning the human situation to be obtained from writers of the stature of Sophocles and of Shakespeare'. And he goes on to ask (51) whether 'we reach for such works as *Anna Karenina, Middlemarch, Nostromo, The Wings of the Dove, The Rainbow* for relaxation'. And whether Waismann did not 'speak often of the need of a "logic of poetry"' (now in Waismann 1977: 104-21). And if Mackinnon's word, 'revelations', is right, then they are not only 'revelations concerning the human situation', but revelations, too, concerning that which reveals it. They are revelations concerning the divine.

What are Stevens's revelations?

Such writers as Tolstoy, George Eliot, Conrad, James and Lawrence, such poets as Sophocles and Shakespeare, T.S. Eliot and Stevens, are in the business of anagnorisis ('recognition' [Aristotle, *Po.* 1452a29]), and that not just in Aristotle's sense ('if the footprints are that size, it must be my brother'), but in the sense in which tragedy can be recognized as a moment in the divine comedy, but comedy not without the waste, the surds, the anfractuous follies, the annihilations. But the *futile* is not final, conjoined as it is with 'useful' and 'pleasant' (Horace, *Ars Poetica* 343). Comedy on its own is not enough.

Any exegete knows, or anyone who has to read what exegetes write, knows of 'the celestial ennui of apartments' (Stevens 1955: 381), of the interminable, but not infinite, corridors, almost blocked by apocalyptic furniture. And any theologian, who knows that 'the use of theology is that it enables one to speak to other theologians' (as an Angolan once put it to me), knows that, if the 'model theory' of religious language (Ramsey [1967], say) is true, or the 'metaphor theory' (Ricoeur [1978], say) is veridical, that (have I said it before? shall I say it again?) 'a more or less elderly person in a tweed suit living somewhere out of sight overhead' (Collingwood 1924: 124) easily becomes 'The hermit in a poet's metaphors' (Stevens 1955: 381 [= I.ii]). Metaphor, imagination can as well lose reality as find it.

What is Stevens's doctrine of God?

But is that question possible? Is it right to be direct with Stevens' indirection?

The hermit, the eremite, lives off the beaten track. How are we, as Phoebe to Paul, to beat our way to Phoebus's door? How is the hermit's home to be found, the tones to be caught? How is the exegete to find his way into the *eremos*, 'the wilderness'? How is he to capture the hidden decibels of the *vox clamantis*, 'the voice of one crying' (Mk 1.3; Isa. 40.3), especially when the poet, unlike the academic grammarian, is free, as Mark here is free, to get his quotations wrong? For Mark's voice is in the wilderness and Isaiah's wilderness is what the voice cries, that that is where the highway is to be made straight.

Metaphor, imaginative speech can lose reality. And this is why Stevens so often turns from 'my green, my fluent *mundo*' (1955: 407 [= III.x]), turns away from his summer world of luxuriance and colour, to a winter world without metaphor, as one might turn from the roseate amplitudes of Rubens to the geometrical stringencies of Mondrian, or from the transcendental, ideal world of Plato to the 'half-', or 'double half-objects' (Eliot 1964: 163 n. **) of Lucretius's *De rerum natura*, his atomism *un peu scientiste*.

Necessary speech is essentially dialectical. Spring returns. And sex, like spring, returns. Neither winter on its own, nor summer on its own, but both. For:

Two things of opposite natures seem to depend
On one another, as a man depends
On a woman, day on night, the imagined

On the real. This is the origin of change.
Winter and spring, cold copulars, embrace
And forth the particulars of rapture come.

Music falls on the silence like a sense,
A passion that we feel, not understand.
Morning and afternoon are clasped together

And North and South are an intrinsic couple
And sun and rain a plural, like two lovers
That walk away as one in the greenest body.

(Stevens 1955: 392 [= II.iv])

The characteristic register of theology is stupefaction; 'the heavenly silt' (so Gregor Smith, in a student journal, *Skandalon*) 'accumulates'. But Stevens is not a characteristic theologian. He is not a simple one.

'Imagination' and 'reality' ('the imagined [depends] / On the real') are two of Stevens's fundamental categories. The vice of the imagination is to obfuscate the real and fight shy of it. The somnolent 'Canon Aspirin' (Stevens 1955: 401) does theology; eponymously he takes them: Aspirin takes aspirins. His theology is more than a placebo, but less than a cure for the headache of the world; an opiate, merely, an anodyne. Kermode (1961: 22) calls him 'an expert in sedation'. He cannot stand winter, probably; understands the cross as a tree, I expect: as a tree, before it has become beams, the beams of the cross, or as a tree, after it has been a cross, as a magic tree, the magic tree of a fairy-tale, that sprouts; not a corpse planted in a garden, but a seed.

In a dream, 'When at long midnight the Canon came to sleep' (Stevens 1955: 402), the Canon's mind bifurcates. The Canon is a learned cove, can clothe the nudity of nothingness, can progress beyond fact, especially beyond the loss of fact, the loss of all of them. The Canon, *this* Canon, proceeds by fiction. But he proceeds by fiction, if fiction means the lie. For he:

conceived
Once more night's pale illuminations, gold

> Beneath, far underneath, the surface of
> His eye and audible in the mountain of
> His ear, the very material of his mind.
>
> So that he was the ascending wings he saw
> And moved on them in orbits' outer stars...

But angels, if that is what the Canon sees and what the Canon was, bifurcate into bringers of light, like Michael, and bringers of darkness, like Lucifer:

> Forth then with huge pathetic force
> Straight to the utmost crown of night he flew.
>
> (Stevens 1955: 402-403)

Angels, like apostles, as Paul knew, are ambiguous entities, 'for even Satan fashioneth himself into an angel of light' (2 Cor. 11.14). And it is very hard to be clear about angelology and very hard to be clear about the angelology of Stevens. But the Miltonic echoes of the lines above seem to me unmistakable. And it seems reasonable to hazard, that Stevens has in mind here the real hero of *Paradise Lost*: Satan. Satan, the '*Auld Clootie*' of Burns's 'Tam o' Shanter', has here penetrated into the Canon's heaven, as Satan into Paradise:

> and this high seat your Heav'n
> Ill fenc't for Heav'n to keep out such a foe
> As now is enterd...
>
> (Milton, *Paradise Lost* iv.371-73,
> cit. Kermode 1963: 97)

But the Canon, by calling on some Cusanian analogue of the *coincidentia oppositorum*, resolves the whole, in a passage both ironic and sympathetic, by including:

> the things
> That in each other are included, the whole,
> The complicate, the amassing harmony.
>
> (Stevens 1955: 403)

Canon Aspirin's is not the 'supreme fiction'. His is fiction *in sensu malo*.

But what is the *right* angelology? Or what is the *right* doctrine of God?

But 'doctrine' is as curious a word to use of Stevens's poem, as to use of the New Testament. But doctrine, if doctrine it is, is found (in both?) in the form of 'gibberish'. But *what* gibberish? The gibberish of the poet, or the gibberish of the common woman, the common man? Stevens is clear about what the poet is after:

> It is the gibberish of the vulgate that he seeks.
> He tries by a peculiar speech to speak
>
> The peculiar potency of the general,
> To compound the imagination's Latin with
> The lingua franca and jocundissima.
>
> (Stevens 1955: 396 [= II.ix])

But doctrinal doctrine, the quotidian humdrum of the liturgy, crouches, like Collingwood's 'black animal' in a corner (1938: 181), at the confines of this strange 'Latin'. For compare:

> Now the God of peace, that brought again from the dead our Lord Jesus, that great Shepherd of the sheep, through the blood of the everlasting covenant (Heb. 13.20)

and the 'imagination's Latin' of the Vulgate:

> *Deus autem pacis,*
> *qui eduxit de mortuis*
> *pastorem magnum ovium*
> *in sanguine testamenti aeterni*
> *Dominum nostrum Jesum*

with the following lines, preceded, as they are, by some sort of a descant on some sort of an image of a dead deity (is it?) in rose-red stone, 'An effulgence faded', which 'might have been' and 'might and might have been':

> But as it was,
> A dead shepherd brought tremendous chords from
> hell
>
> And bade the sheep carouse…
>
> (Stevens 1955: 400)

though Stevens goes on:

> Or so they said.

But 'God', asymptotically approachable by Stevens, for 'Phoebus', if Phoebus is anything to go on, 'was / A name for something that never could be named' (1955: 381 [= I.i]), is joined by a further, asymptotically approachable *terminus technicus* from the vocabulary of religion. It is again 'angel', only not, this time, the 'angel' of

Canon Aspirin. The angel, this time, is *for real*. A detour around
this figure *s'impose*, for 'detour', 'deviation', 'indirection' name the
mode, in which to speak about the mode, by which the text
speaks, if text-level and interpretation-level are to correspond.
Kermode (1960: 85-91; 1961: *passim*) will be our guide.

The title of Stevens's *Essays on Reality and the Imagination* is
The Necessary Angel.

What is Stevens's doctrine of angels? What is Stevens's doctrine
of the one angel necessary, the *unus necessarius*?

The angel's genesis was as follows: Stevens had received a pic-
ture (30 September 1949) by Tal Coat, a still-life of 'a Venetian glass
bowl on the left', surrounded 'by terrines, bottles and...glasses'
(Stevens 1967: 650). To this picture, as he recounts, in a letter of 5
October 1949, Stevens gave the title: *Angel Surrounded by
Peasants*. A poem with this title (1955: 496-97), first published in
Poetry London 17 (January 1950) was sent to the son of G.E. Moore
(Stevens 1967: letter of 13 October 1949).

Stevens's angelology can be as easily deduced from that poem as
the metaphysical position of St John the Divine from the Prologue
to the Fourth Gospel. But where everything cannot be said, this
can at least be said, that the angel for Stevens belongs as substantially to the earth as Antaeus for Bonhoeffer.

The figure of Antaeus, who lost his force when lifted from the
earth, was sufficiently important for Bonhoeffer to make use of it,
not only *before* Tegel, when Bonhoeffer was writing as ethical
thinker (1992: 344-45), but also *in* Tegel as author of dramatic
fiction (1994: 69-70). For Stevens, by prosopopoea:

> ...I am the necessary angel of earth,
> Since, in my sight, you see the earth again...
>
> (Stevens 1955: 496)

This angel, this 'necessary angel', is in the business of imagining
and what the angel is in the business of imagining is the real. This
is an earthy task and more, just as the agent that undertakes it is of
the earth *and more*.

Why is Stevens's 'angel' 'necessary'? Why this relapse into *Bor-
ghettosprache*, 'the language of the theological ghetto'?

Some Jews found angels necessary. And gave them necessary
names: 'Michael', by etymology: 'Who is like God?', 'Raphael': 'the
Strength of God', 'The Force' of *Star Wars* (1977), of *Revelation*

(0096 [or n.d.], a Force redolent of the military and olfactory figure, who is 'perfumed', 'anointed', who is 'christ' (1 Cor. 15.20-28). For such a Force has the right *smell*, if, and only if, *power* is understood as *weakness*. Or the word we want is not 'power', but 'influence' (Henderson *obiter dictum*, but see *Power without Glory* [Henderson 1967: xi ('love')]. *Nur der leidende Gott helfen kann*, 'only the suffering God can help' (Bonhoeffer 1971: 361). The only right opinion is patripassian.

And now drop 'Raphael' and retain the 'strength'. And do you yet have a name for 'something that never could be named' (Stevens 1955: 381 [= I.i])?

Fiction, for Stevens, is parasitic on fact, imagination on reality, just as Eliot's history (in the proper sense), too, is left behind in 'a secluded chapel' ('Little Gidding' V [= 1944: 43]). Linked with a locality that can be named by the historian and geographer, Eliot's fictive imagination names what the historian and geographer cannot. But it is an imagination that, nonetheless, may be and may be claimed to be parasitic on fact, parasitic on reality. Not historical and geographical fact only, but metaphysical fact, if such facts there be.

And why should there not be such?

But can the fact be named? Can the reality be named?

Shall we call it 'Absolute'? But 'Absolute' only tells us that we have to do with what is on its own: *absolvo*: 'I loose off from everything else', *absolutus*: 'I have been so loosed off'.

But we cannot remain silent. Perhaps it is necessary to break silence sufficiently so as to retain an 'angel'—and make the angel into a thoroughgoing hesychast, a figure that will make publishing impossible:

> To find the real,
> To be stripped of every fiction except one,
>
> The fiction of an absolute—Angel,
> Be silent in your luminous cloud and hear
> The luminous melody of proper sound.
>
> (Stevens 1955: 404)

'What has Athens', cries Tertullian (the ancient world was full of his aphorismic cries), 'to do with Jerusalem?' (*Quid Athenae Hierosolymis?*)

Everything. Stevens's 'gibberish' (there is no end to the idiosyncrasies of his idiolects [Blackmur 1954: 221-49]) goes to Athens for the word 'ephebe' (Stevens 1960: 39-67, and *passim*), for the warrior, the athlete, the dialectician, the companion of Socrates—and Socrates himself:

> Well then, Phaedrus, this is how it was. I was walking on the very edge of the sea. I was following an endless shore... This is not a dream I am telling you. I was going I know not whither, over flowing with life, half-intoxicated by my youth. The air, deliciously rude and pure, pressing against my face and limbs, confronted me— an impalpable hero that I must vanquish in order to advance. And this resistance, ever overcome, made of me, too, at every step an imaginary hero, victorious over the wind, and rich in energies that were ever reborn, ever equal to the power of the invisible adversary... That is just what youth is. I trod firmly the winding beach, beaten and hardened by the waves. All things around me were simple and pure: the sky, the sand, the water (Valéry 1960: 116, cit. Stevens, in Valéry 1958: ix-x).[1]

And Valéry (and Stevens) goes on:

> O coeternal with me in death, faultless friend, and diamond of sincerity, hear then:
> It served no purpose, I fear, to seek this God, whom I have tried all my life to discover, by pursuing him through the realms of thought alone; by demanding him of that more variable and most ignoble sense of the just and the unjust, and by urging him to surrender to the solicitings of the most refined dialectic. The God that one so finds is but a word born of words, and returns to the word. For the reply we make to ourselves is assuredly never anything other than the question itself; and every question put by the mind to the mind is only, and can only be, a piece of simplicity. But on the contrary, it is in acts, and in the combination of acts, that we ought

---

1.   'Eh bien, Phèdre, voici ce qu'il en fut: je marchais sur le bord même de la mer, je suivais une plage sans fin...Ce n'est pas un rêve que je te raconte. J'allais je ne sais où, trop plein de vie, à demi enivré par ma jeunesse. L'air, délicieusement rude et pur, pesant sur mon visage et sur mes membres, m'opposait un héros impalpable qu'il fallait vaincre pour avancer. Et cette résistance toujours repoussée faisait de moi-même, à chaque pas, un héros imaginaire, victorieux du vent, et riche de forces toujours renaissantes, toujours égales à la puissance de l'invisible adversaire... C'est là précisément la jeunesse. Je foulais fortement le bord sinueux, durci et rebattu par le flot. Toutes choses, autour de moi, étaient simples et pures: le ciel, le sable, l'eau.'

to find the most immediate feeling of the divine, and the best use for that part of our strength that is unnecessary for living, and seems to be reserved for the pursuits of an indefinable object that infinitely transcends us (Valéry 1960: 142-43, cit. Stevens, in Valéry 1958: x).[2]

Sire, remember the Scots and the wind from the Rounded Hill of Cheese and *An Teallach*.

And Stevens's 'Two Prefaces' (in Valéry 1958: 9-28) conclude with the words: 'Man has many ways to attain the divine, and the way of Eupalinos [sc. architecture] and the way of Athikte [sc. the dance] and the various ways of Paul Valéry are only a few of them.' The title of the second, *Chose légère, ailée, sacrée* (= κοῦφον γὰρ χρῆμα ποιητής ἐστιν καὶ πτηνὸν καὶ ἱερόν, *kouphon gar chrema poietes estin kai ptenon kai hieron*, 'a poet is a light thing and winged and sacred' [Plato, *Ion* 534b3-4] is the summation of the ways, not only of Valéry, but of Stevens.

But there are words and there are things. As a bible is not a god, so a poem is not a plum. There is *das In-der-Welt-sein der Pflaume*, the 'being-in-the-world of the plum', and 'poems of plums', as for Crispin, confronted, in 'The Comedian as the Letter C' (Stevens 1955: 27-46, cit. Kermode 1960: 46) by the reality of the sea:

> The imagination here could not evade,
> In poems of plums, the strict austerity
> Of one vast, subjugating, final tone.
>
> (Stevens 1955: 30)

Stevens is *after* reality, in hot, *and* cold, pursuit of it. But he is after reality by means of the imagination; or, more strictly, by means of it, when he can, *and without it, when he cannot*. For the

2.   'O mort coéternel, ami sans défauts, et diamant de sincérité, voici:
Ce ne fut pas utilement, je le crains, chercher ce Dieu que j'ai essayé de découvrir toute ma vie, que de le poursuivre à travers les seules pensées; de le demander au sentiment très variable, et très ignoble, du juste et de l'injuste, et que le presser de se rendre à la sollicitation de la dialectique la plus raffinée. Ce Dieu que l'on trouve ainsi n'est que parole née de parole, et retourne à la parole. Car la réponse que nous nous faisons n'est jamais assurément que la question elle-même; et toute question de l'esprit à l'esprit même, n'est, et ne peut être, qu'une naïveté. Mais au contraire, c'est dans les actes, et dans la combinaison des actes, que nous devons trouver le sentiment le plus immédiat de la présence du divin, et le meilleur emploi de cette partie de nos forces qui est inutile à la vie, et qui semble réservée à la poursuite d'un object indéfinissable qui nous passe infiniment.'

Figure 8. *An Teallach range from west slope of Carn Bhreabadair, Allt Gleann Chaorachain in fore* (22 May 1925) by R.M. Adam (1885–1967) (reproduced by courtesy of the University of St Andrews Library)

imagination is involved in dialectical play, through the demythologizing of myths, the deconstruction of constructions, the de-imag-
ining of accretions, down to the bedrock of 'winter'. Whence,
abjuring thought, abjuring Bergson, Whitehead, Santayana, Stevens
turns to reality as accessible to *re-imagining*, to reality as accessible, not to the philosopher, but to the poet. After winter spring.
After spring summer, 'my green, my fluent mundo' (1955: 407).
And winter again follows the auroras of autumn. There is a seasonal
cycle of the poet's mind.

Says Blackmur (1985: 218),

> Wanting, as we all do, a supreme fiction, wanting that is to con-
> ceive, to imagine, to make a supreme being, wanting, in short, to
> discover and objectify a sense of such a being, he [Stevens] sets up
> three phases through which it must pass. It must be abstract; it must
> change; it must give pleasure.

But *is* this theology? Is it metaphysics? Or history? Or a mixture of
all these? Or if it is *none* of these, if it is *poetry*, how is it *related* to
all of these? Or, whatever it is, why does it have to be done in such
a mode, as makes Romans 9–11 (an imperspicuous passage) look
like the less inaccessible pericopes of *Winnie Ille Pu* (Milne 1961)?
Stevens himself speaks in his poem, in his poems, in the several,
decadic poems of which 'Notes...' is constructed, of 'difficultest
rigour'.

And tells us that 'Jerome begat the tubas' (1955: 398 [= III.i]).

Does this help?

Language is being subjected to strain. But this is not surprising, if
Stevens is, if *one* is, if *you* are after a '*supreme* fiction'. Discussing
a translation of 'Disillusionment of Ten O'Clock' (1955: 66) with
the Henry Church of the prologue to 'Notes...' (Stevens 1967:
letter of 1 June 1939) he makes the admission: 'Personally, I like
words to sound wrong.'

They *do*, Mr Stevens, they *do*.

This is the gratuitous love (the epithet is analytic) of strange
words and the the love of putting strange words to strange uses.
'The most striking if not the most important thing about Mr.
Stevens' verse is its vocabulary' (Blackmur 1954: 221). More importantly, it is the desire to find 'faithful speech' (1955: 408 [= the
epilogue]). For, if the soldier, if the man of action is to 'live on the
bread[!] of faithful speech', someone, the poet, is required to

produce the bread. You cannot eat it, if no one bakes it. But, if the bread, if the speech is to be 'faithful', it may need, it does need to be subjected to strain, to 'more than rational distortion':

> That's it: the more than rational distortion,
> The fiction that results from feeling. Yes, that.
>
> (Stevens 1955: 406 [= III. 10],
> cit. Blackmur 1985: 219)

And the dry denizen of the academy should be alert to what follows:

> They will get it straight one day at the Sorbonne.
> We shall return at twilight from the lecture
> Pleased that the irrational is rational,
>
> Until flicked by feeling, in a gildered street,
> I call you by name, my green, my fluent mundo.
> You will have stopped revolving except in crystal.

'Jerome begat the tubas...'?

Stevens (and Jerome, virginally begetting) goes on: '...and the fire-wind strings' (how St Luke would have loved that epithet!). But the *post*-context of 'fire-wind strings' has a *pre*-context, or *pre*-text (Carroll 1992):

> To sing jubilas at exact accustomed times,
> To be crested and wear the mane of a multitude
> And so, as part, to exult with its great throat,
>
> To speak of joy and to sing of it, borne on
> The shoulders of joyous men, to feel the heart
> That is the common, the bravest fundament...

So far, so good: we are in the cloister—for the passionless passion of Solesmes, its ordered expression, at Christmas, of Athos at Easter. But not (strictly) Athos. It is Jerome, and the Vulgate, and the Latin mass; the *requiems*, *jubilates*, *laudates*. It is the *floruit* of Western monasticism, the *tuba mirum spargens sonum*, the last trump rousing the torpor, awakening the sleeper, 'bidding the sheep carouse'.

But then:

> This is a facile exercise. Jerome begat... etc.

Kermode, in his commentary (1961: 191) glosses: 'The ritual enactment of joy is easy and unsatisfactory compared with the true new perception of reality, not falsified by fixed myth and exact repetition.'

Does this exhaust what Stevens is saying here? Does this exhaust what Stevens says everywhere about the relation between the present and tradition? But at least we are discovering that Stevens is (also) parasitic on Aristotle's 'what people say'.

If *something* has now been said about Stevens's doctrine of God, via the 'necessary angel' and inquisitive ephebe of Valéry, not *much* has been said. For what is one to make of the adage, ignored so far: 'God and the imagination are one' (1959: 178)? And something, not much, about his attitude to tradition, to the past. But what is to be made of his Christology, his anthropology? What does he say about Man-and-Woman?

Take the clansman, 'MacCullough' (1955: 386 [= I.viii] *et seq.*). What are we to make of *him*? Stevens, himself, was asked the question and begins with the helpful reply (Stevens 1967: letter of 12 January 1943):[3] 'the MacCullough is MacCullough'.

He continues: 'MacCullough is any name, any man.' And further:

> The trouble with humanism is that man as God remains man, but there is an extension of man, the leaner being, in fiction, a possibly more than human human, a composite human. The act of recognising him is the act of this leaner being moving in on us.

MacCullough? MacTavish? Smith? Jones? And a *more than human* Jones?

Then, in a letter to Henry Church (Stevens 1967: letter of 18 May 1943):

> Your 'Supreme Court Justice' is the MacCullough of the NOTES. They say that in Ireland, God is a member of the family and that they treat Him as one of them. For the mass of people, it is certain that humanism would do just as well as anything else. If God made a progress [2 Cor. 2.14(!)] through the streets of Moscow in a carriage drawn by twelve horses, ornamented with red pom-poms, and preceded by the massed bands of the Red Army, I don't believe that he would cut any more ice than Stalin would, even if Stalin followed Him barefoot: in fact, sensation for sensation, Stalin would probably be the more thrilling one. But if you and I were looking on, you would say that God did not need all that livery, or any, and I would

3.   To Hi Simons, 'a critic and publisher of medical textbooks, who was preparing a Stevens bibliography' (Stevens 1967: 257).

say of Stalin that I could never be sure of him until he was dead. The chief defect of humanism is that it concerns human beings. Between humanism and something else, it might be possible to create an acceptable fiction

'Between humanism and something else...'?

And, if the quotation, on MacCullough, may continue, on Stevens (even poets are human):

Every now and then we have a perfect day. But spring is always rainy here [Hartford, Connecticut] and, for me, a restless and dissatisfied time. My imagination starts to move round and the more it moves the clearer it becomes that I don't move with it, and that I, and you, and all of us live in a monotony which would be all right except for the horrid disturbances that come chiefly from within ourselves

Would not this letter, even to the extension on Stevens's 'horrid disturbances', have recommended itself both to Paul of Tarsus and Johann Georg (Hamann) of Königsberg, to the first as undertaker, as author, or underwriter, of the *Carmen Christi* (Phil. 2.6-11: 'he emptied himself') and of θριαμβεύοντι (*thriambeuonti*, '[God, who] leads us in triumph' [2 Cor. 2.14]); to the second, as author of *Golgatha und Sheblimini*, 'Golgatha and "Sit thou at my right hand"' (Ps. 110.1)?

By what is Stevens persuaded that by fiction he is dealing with reality? What is it that makes him think that it is by *un*reality that he can approach the real? There is nothing unreal about language, of course. It is just that there may be nothing to babble, to bar-bar (to 'be barbarian') about. But *is* 'angel', *is MacCullough* to babble about nothing at all?

When is language used to good effect? How does one speak, how does a work go about 'saying the words of the world that are the life of the world' (Kermode 1960: 119)? What is it that makes MacCullough a 'beau linguist'? And what sort of a metaphysical poem is this one, that follows? A prologue to a Fifth Gospel? Stevens babbles:

> The first idea is an imagined thing
> The pensive giant prone in violet space
> May be the MacCullough, an expedient,

Logos and logic, crystal hypothesis,
Incipit and a form to speak the word
And every latent double in the word,

Beau linguist...
(Stevens 1955: 387 [= I.viii])

Having, with 'Jerome' and the 'tubas', been taken into the history of Western monasticism, we now seem to have plunged into the Prologue of the Fourth Gospel: 'first', 'Logos', 'Incipit', 'word', only to be hurried past Jehovah and Jesus to MacCullough, *the* MacCullough.

Come, come, Mr Stevens, you can be clearer than this!

How is one to resort to 'reason's click-clack' (1955: 387 [= I.ix])? How is one to 'reason of these things with later reason' (1955: 401 [= III.iv])?

'There are several things in the NOTES', says Stevens helpfully (in Stevens 1967: letter to Hi Simons of 1 December 1943), 'that would stand a little annotating.'

'Life is always new; it is always beginning', Stevens goes on there. And he has just said above: 'The abstract does not exist, but it is certainly as immanent: that is to say, the fictive abstract is as immanent in the mind of the poet, as the idea of God is immanent in the mind of the theologian.'

It is as difficult to be determinate about 'NOTES' as it is for Turner to be determinate about a storm. But it is not *really* more difficult to be determinate about them than it is to be determinate about the Prologue to the Fourth Gospel, if one is not simply to hang up one's coat and one's brains in the church porch. But it *is* difficult. And that not only for the critic, but for the author, in this respect not differing from Hamann (I think), when Hamann came to read what he had written.

'I don't actually recall what I had in mind', says Stevens, re-assuringly, if not helpfully (in Stevens 1967: 1 December 1943), on 'obvious acid' (Stevens 1955: 390 [= II.i]), 'but it is clear that the meaning is visible change'. There is obscurity, which does not repay examination, but there is also obscurity that does.

If Plato is right to say that poetry is confused cognition, *cognitio confusa*, then it is right to *attempt* to think non-confusedly about it. There are relevant acts posterior to the act of creation; after *tohuwabohu*, 'chaos and void', there come ordering, science, system. Stevens's words, here, and elsewhere, suffer, not from a lack, but from an *excess* of substance. Can we disambiguate, explicate, say something determinate, something sensible on the subject of this excess?

Stevens, the 'beau linguist', has produced a text, that contains, among his words, the word 'word', or rather 'word-in-Greek', *logos*, which, standing at the beginning, or the Beginning, of a line, is not 'logos', but 'Logos'. And, if as theologians, or as readers of theological texts, we do not know what happens to a word, when it begins with a capital, then we need to go to a theological school, where they produce these things. And where they produce such phrases, or the analogues of such phrases, as 'a pensive giant prone in violet space', a giant like Rodin's *Penseur*, but stretched out flat, like John's, in and with (and perhaps under) a giant bosom. And then John's words, with Plato's words and Wisdom's words and Heraclitus's words get transmitted. And get transmitted by writers, by writers in a world of writers, by writers in a world *tout court*. And why a world?

A world is a *locus* of events, events sometimes of the following kind:

> Perhaps there are times of inherent excellence,
>
> As when the cock crows on the left and all
> Is well, incalculable balances,
> At which a kind of Swiss perfection comes
>
> And a familiar music of the machine
> Sets up its Schwärmerei, not balances
> That we achieve but balances that happen,
>
> As a man and woman meet and love forthwith.
> Perhaps there are moments of awakening,
> Extreme, fortuitous, personal, in which
>
> We more than awaken, sit on the edge of sleep,
> As on an elevation, and behold
> The academies like structures in a mist.

'I say not this', writes Hobbes (1946: 8), 'as disproving the use of universities; but because I am to speak hereafter of their office in a commonwealth, I must let you see on all occasions by the way, what things would be amended in them; amongst which the frequency of insignificant speech is one'.

But what is the ontology of 'balances that happen'? Is this, is this not what words like 'grace' and 'beauty' are after? We may wonder, but what is the *cause* of wonder?

Stevens is a poet, not a philosopher. But neither is he innocent of philosophy, at least to the extent that his contributions, in the *Necessary Angel*, were 'intended to be contributions to the theory of poetry' (1960: vii). But, if not a philosopher, nevertheless a philosophical, a metaphysical poet. What is his gist? What is the gist of the 'Notes...'? To summarize Blackmur's summary (1985: 218-19), not of Stevens's system, but of his 'NOTES' towards one, the abstract idea of being, symbolized by the sun, is 'blooded', finds concretion in a world of change, where the fresh eye of the poet can prehend it. But the furniture of the mind is always new. Not unrelated to the old, but always new. For *ostraka* give way to Louis Quatorze, *le roi soleil*, the 'sun-king', to Charles Rennie Mackintosh.

'The world of Wallace Stevens' poetry has always been two, "things as they are" and "things imagined"' (Heringman 1949: 325). Imagination and reality are the two poles, between which Stevens moves and 'fiction' is the concept, and 'angel' the image, that bridges them. As he said, in 'A High-Toned Old Christian Woman' (1955: 59), right at the outset of his poetic career:

> Poetry is the supreme fiction, Madame.

'Richness and secularity', the 'essential qualities' of 'Esthétique du Mal' (Stevens 1955: 313-26 [Pearce 1951: 579]) fairly characterize, too, the 'Notes...', and with these two, Stevens's work as a whole. The sound and fury of the academic critic, the poverty of his splitting hairs rather ('[o]ne hears the lecturing voice' [Collingwood 1938: 264]), Pearce continues:

> can only indicate propositions, lines of argument, and conclusions—and so moves too far away from these essential qualities. What makes the argument stick, the poetry, is perhaps lost; but this is a chance we must take. I think it is worth taking. For such a (temporary) cutting down of the poems to the critic's size allows one to see them in all their richness and secularity... What emerges in 'Notes towards a Supreme Fiction' and 'Esthétique du Mal' is the possibility of belief in a world in which the conditions and forms of belief are themselves products of the interaction of the believer and his world, of the conjoining of imagination and reality (Pearce 1951: 579-80).

But even the rich, secular poetry of Stevens's 'strongly indi-
vidualistic antitraditionalism' (for '[u]nlike an Eliot, he has refused
to move out of our culture into another' [Pearce 1951: 581, 562])
finds him unable to dispense with the angel, be it an 'angel of
earth', nor with 'MacCullough, *the* MacCullough', that vulgarian
name, by which the *conatus* of the poetic *penseur* makes for a
humanism, not where 'man as God remains man', but where 'there
is an extension of man, the leaner being, in fiction, a possibly more
than human human, a composite human' (Stevens, in Stevens 1967:
letter of 1 December 1943).

We are all poets, at least in this sense, that we are men and
women of imagination; mostly obstructed, it may be, yet not
always without insight. Insights occur. We have access to language.
Even the dumb—to gesture, gesticulation, the dance.

That is not to say that we are not poets under a curse, for: 'I, and
you, and all of us live in a monotony which would be all right
except for the horrid disturbances that come chiefly from within
ourselves…' (Stevens, in Stevens 1967: letter of 18 May 1943). And
these 'disturbances' receive classical exegesis in 'Esthétique du Mal'
(Stevens 1955: 313-26). In the old tongue, which the old learned to
speak, 'Sin is Behovely' (Julian 1950: 56, cit. Eliot, 'Little Gidding'
III (= 1944: 41). Hamann's Adam has his 'rhapsody of fig-leaves'
(1950: 198 [= Crick, in Nisbet 1985: 141]).

But melancholy, monotony, lobotomy, their like and worse than
their like—are *they* the sum? Not without 'balances that happen',
surely, 'times of inherent excellence'.

'Fate, or destiny?' one may ask. And ask it in a world where the
question is valid: 'Who am I? I am just another of those same
obscure people who like everyone else is more or less conscious of
the futility of his existence, and of how it is rushing towards death'
(Gregor Smith 1969: 136).

But what has the last word?
What has the last Word?

If a final *explicit* (crude conclusion!) be permitted, it must be
confessed, that this chapter is less a chapter than the raw material
of which a chapter might have been composed. If the present
writer has failed to show that Stevens is worth reading, he has
failed. But it should nevertheless have become clear that Stevens,

no less than Eliot in the *Four Quartets*, and, interestingly enough, almost exactly coeval with 'Notes...', is not only a poet *tout court*, but a poet-metaphysician. But it is no more easy to move from 'Notes...' to apodeictic metaphysics (is there, are there such?) than it is to do so from John's prologue, with which the MacCullough as 'beau linguist' so remarkably overlaps.

There is no short cut even to a modest comprehension of Stevens's poem other than with 'difficultest rigour' to examine his 'accurate songs'. But at least it *ought* to be clear that Stevens is a theologian. This is demonstrated, not only by the extent to which his secularity is nevertheless soaked, if idiosyncratically and elliptically soaked, in the religious terminology of the past, for Stevens is clearly in the theological tradition of Homer (Phoebus) and Jerome (the Vulgate). More centrally, it is demonstrated by the word 'angel'. In a heuristically suggestive essay, 'Bridging Ambiguities' (1994: 71-89), Ashton has importantly suggested, even *shown*, that 'angel' may be a fundamental key to the understanding of the Fourth Gospel, a key that is fundamentally transcendental, while fundamentally ambiguous, not to say loose. And 'angel', for Stevens, too, is an image of this kind, which mediates between the opposites, in particular the opposites of imagination and reality. This angel sends messages (and is sent?) to Stevens. And 'MacCullough', '*the* MacCullough' seems indifferently to be both man and God, if Stevens is right (and why should he not be?) to say, as we have seen above, with the very greatest caution and qualification, that there is 'a possibly more than human human' (in Stevens 1967: letter of 12 January 1943) and if Kermode is right, in his commentary (1961: 183) to say, (again) with the very greatest caution and qualification, that '[t]he MacCullough is a chance name for some modern equivalent of God'. But, before all other things, '[t]he major poetic idea in the world', Stevens is recorded as thinking, 'is and always has been the idea of God' (1959: xv).

But what *necessary* speech can any *necessary* angel *now* provide? Only it must be remembered, that Stevens is *not* and by his own admission is not, a philosopher. He is philosopher-poet, or poet-philosopher, it may be, but if he wrote a thesis on Bradley, or Santayana (Stevens 1955: 508; 1960: 147-48, cit. Kermode 1960: 124), this has not come down to us.

In his Journal entry for 2 June 1900 (Stevens 1967: 34, cit. Doyle 1985: 471),[4] Stevens writes:

> I want my powers to be put to their fullest use—to be exhausted when I am done with them. On the other hand I do not want to make a petty struggle for existence—physical or literary. I must try not to be dilettante—half dream, half deed. I must be all dream or all deed.

Let Stevens have the last Word. But now we must act.

4.   What Doyle there cites is an unsigned review ([Roy Fuller?] *TLS* 30 March 1967).

⌂L⌐ÓⴱⵎL ⴲⵌⴳⴐL⌂ⴱL ⴱⵙⴱⵌⵌⵛ
⌐ⴱⴲ⌽ⴱⴳⵌⵌⴱ ⴶⴱL ⴱⴲⴱⵟ

Ronaldo Gregorio Smith

nescienti quo iret

12

The Complot: Literature versus History: Ronald Gregor Smith and History Reconsidered

Ronaldo Gregorio Smith

exiit nesciens quo iret
and he went out, not knowing whither he went

Heb. 11.8

an clamhan air chaithris 'na rìoghachd
ag èisdeachd ri beul-aithris na gaoithe
[the buzzard wakeful in his kingdom
listening to the oral tradition of the wind]

Caimbeul, '*An Clamhan*' (The Buzzard).

De Peregrinatione Utopiensium

Of their iourneyenge or trauaylynge a brode, with dyuers other matters cunnyngly reasoned and wittilie discussed

Sir Thomas More, *Utopia* (1518)

Sunrise in the Alps is a beauty of nature. Sunrise at Delphi is Apollo's theophany: the apparition of the god who was not merely light but enlightenment; the god whose terrible command 'know thyself' men have been trying to obey ever since it was given. Unless you can look at the scenery of Delphi with some sense of that command, and of the inexorability which makes it divine to you, whatever religion you profess, you are not seeing Delphi.

R.G. Collingwood, *The First Mate's Log*

In this chapter, the attempt is made to summarize the position reached, though not the evidence for reaching it. That, the evidence, is taken as read, in this book, or in other, more scientific treatises, as W.G. Kümmel, *Einleitung in das Neue Testament*, (*Introduction to the New Testament*) (21st edn [new and expanded] 1983) and (by the same author), *Das Neue Testament: Geschichte der Erforschung seiner Probleme* (*The New Testament: A History of Research into its Problems*) (1958). Both are translated (though, not [so far as I know] the 21st edition of the first of these). These two works show that people in our trade have worked on these problems and have not, for the most part, just come up with the first thing they have thought of, though there are exceptions to this rule. But *de mortuis et vivis nil nisi bonum*.

Gregor Smith was less the buzzard (of Caimbeul, above) and more the blackbird of *Still Point* (Maxwell 1943: 9):

> A blackbird hops across my lawn before me...

And yet his view is the panoramic view, seen

> turning and turning in the widening gyre
> (Yeats, 'The Second Coming' [1950: 210])

And it was less 'the oral tradition of the wind', to which he listened. It was the wind, the wind *tout court*.

For Gregor Smith was not so much dealing with *tradita*, 'that which has been', as with *tradenda*, 'that which is to be transmitted'. Latin embarrasses by the absence of a present participle passive. The Greek is better: he was not so much dealing with παραδοθέντα, *paradothenta*, 'what has been handed down', as with παραδιδόμενα, *paradidomena*, 'what is being handed over'. 'That, which is *now* coming into my hands, I am *now* handing over.' He was dealing not so much with what the wind had said to human kind, though the wind had a history, but with what the wind was saying.

If an autobiographical note be permitted, with no better than Pauline anachronism (how well did Paul remember what happened in Antioch [Gal. 2]?), I received, while writing for Gregor Smith a doctoral thesis, a summer exhortation from a Sienese villa, after two years of work and 35 pages of script (they were dense). This epistle, not much longer than the one to Philemon, was, as I recall, to the following effect:

(1)   All jokes must go.

(2)   *Eppur si muove* does *not* mean: 'It is pure, if it moves.'

(3)   οἷα ἂν γένοιτο (*hoia an genoito*): expand!

This last phrase, to recall, is one half of Aristotle's famous distinction (*Po.* 1451b5) between the poet and the historian, the one being concerned with 'what has happened', the other with 'what may happen', a distinction perhaps clearer in the mind of

Aristotle than in the New Testament. Supervisors, while often to be ignored, are not always to be so. This book, this essay, is that expansion.

But Gregor Smith, under the feet of whom in Glasgow I had gone to sit, because Frau Professor Gregor Smith knew how to make coffee (by contingencies of this kind is one's fate, or one's destiny, decided and an invitation extended to one's freedom and responsibility), had almost immediately driven me, frightened and hotfoot, to Germany and, first, to Gerhard Gloege of Jena, to engage with *die phänomenal-ontologische Analyse der Zeitlichkeit*, 'the phenomenological and ontological analysis of temporality'. 'Herr Templeton', said Herr Gloege, 'we do not understand it either'.

Gerhard Gloege's book, *Aller Tage Tag (Day of All Days)*, had fallen foul of the post-Prussian censorship of Walter Ulbricht's régime. Gloege, in exploring the antecedents of the life of Christ, had been too eloquent about the bureaucracy of Alexandrian Egypt. Examples nearer to hand could have been found, had he known of the British university since 1979. For the situation of Alexandrian Egypt has remained quite without parallel until the recent intrusion of this [late] Conservative administration into the dogmatic slumbers of the Great Bed of Ware, to which these British centres of excellence had been so drastically reduced.

I was sent, second, to Hans Conzelmann in Göttingen. Had I known then that Lowth had got an honorary doctorate there, the intelligence (in Ms Austen's sense) would then have flowed off me like water off a coot's back, when it returns to the surface of the Edinburgh Canal, that leads to the city of Glasgow, where they combine theology with thought. It was said of Conzelmann (with what truth I do not know), that he had spent the Second World War shooting down British aircraft and was spending peace-time shooting down British theologians.

Conzelmann's Seminar was on the Resurrection. The Seminar had started, of course (this was Germany) with *Sterbende u. auferstehende Götter* (Dying and Rising Gods) and was now going through *everything else*. It was *gründlich* (it probed to the postulates), *rigorös (und wie!!!)*, it was rigorous (and how!!!) and *wissenschaftlich sauber* (scientifically clean and clinical). The student members of the Seminar sat there, as if (as Donald Mackinnon once said of conducting a supervisory tutorial) they had been left alone with an axewielding-madman, in a room where the walls had been lined with axes. Conzelmann's Seminar was taking place, as it were, in one of those revolving rooms in a fairground, where the floor suddenly falls away, to leave the occupants 'in the air' (1 Thess. 4.17). It was clear, from the line of questioning followed, that further questions had been raised, prior to my arrival, and that further questions were to be. Conzelmann was gadfly, no, the Highland Midge of the State.

But if, I would now ask, you put together Ashton's 'fairy-tale atmosphere of the resurrection' (1991: 511) with Aristotle's οἷα ἂν γένοιτο, 'what may happen' (*Po.* 1451b5), what do you get? A fairy-tale that *says something*, I would now answer, though it might not be right to drop Ashton's 'atmosphere'. For an atmosphere is something in which you can breathe. Or not, as the case may be.

With what is called in German an *Empfehlungsbrief*, in Greek an ἐπιστολὴ συστατικὴ, *epistole sustatike*, and in English a 'letter of reference' (so the scholars, interminably), I had been sent, by Gregor Smith to his friend Rudolf Bultmann in Marburg, to Bultmann's home in the *Calvinstrasse*, which (as was pointed out to me), had *Calvin* known, he (Calvin) would have turned in his (Calvin's) grave. But it was *all* the Orthodox that were turning in their graves.

Fear and a rushing, mighty wind round Bultmann's patio made it difficult for me to light my pipe, but as the conversation turned from Fielding (whom I had not read) and Dickens (whom I had) to Fontane (whom I would), I plucked up sufficient courage to ask Bultmann whether Black Mallory (a gift from Gregor Smith and the City of Perth) was sufficiently in stirling condition and whether thought was detectible in the New Testament. 'Did not Paul think?' he asked.

This was the Previous Visit.

In my bodily presence, on the Second Visit a year later, after the Conzelmann Seminar, a green young man asked Bultmann the following question:

> *Glauben Sie oder denken Sie, dass die Leichnam Christi*
> *in Palästina liegt?*
> [Do you think, or do you believe, that the corpse of Jesus
> lies in Palestine?]
> *Ja.*
> [Yes.]

Bultmann's answer was brief.

This was the Severe Question. And that was the Severe Answer. As Paul Ricoeur would say about myth in *The Symbolism of Evil*, it 'gave rise to thought' (*donner à penser*).

But does *thought* occur in the New Testament? Is not de Wette, rather, right to talk, not about thought, but about *Ahnung/ Ahndung*, 'intimation' (1831: 8-19), or, if about thought, about thought as 'occulted' (Collingwood 1924: 133), as 'half-concealed in the torrent of sensation' (p. 292)?

In Glasgow Gregor Smith, assisted by the mythical pioneer, Ian Henderson (1952), was producing a *capiteux*, or 'heady', mixture of Kierkegaard, Buber, Bonhoeffer and Bultmann. ('The *magus* of the North', Hamann, came in a little later.) There, in Glasgow, the students in Purgatory (to put it so) were introduced to Bultmann's axial essay, 'The New Testament and Mythology', in which (as we have seen above) Bultmann pointed out to the Confessing Church, that to counter Nazism with Christianity was to counter a *myth* with a *myth*, one of these being translatable into a thinkable philosophy (so Jüngel, in Bultmann 1988: 7-8).

For what is a myth, if it is not a story? And if it is a story, is 'story' not also a *literary* category? And is it not literary criticism that a literary category requires? And if it is, why should one necessarily resort to anthropology, or *Religionsgeschichte*, 'the history of religion'? And why turn, or why turn now, why turn immediately to philosophy? Why not stay with the story and, in Whitehead's term, 'enjoyment', or in the term, *jouïssance*, of Barthes, why not *enjoy* it? There are these other approaches, but they do not stand alone. And each of them deserves attention. And the first first. What is logically first has the prior claim.

Bultmann's 'programme' involved the opening (if one could) and the closing (which one could) of Heidegger's *Being and Time*. It involved, for Bultmann, the *turn* to philosophy. This, too, is legitimate, but *at what point* should it be undertaken? Is there not an argument for dallying with *literary* criticism, in the sense in which *literary* critics (and not scholars [Blackmur 1954: 394-96]) do it.

Bultmann (*passim*) shows his own literary knowledge and sensitivity by his extensive quotations from the Greek classics, his essay, *Zur Geschichte der Lichtsymbolik im Altertum*, 'On the History of the Symbolism of Light in the Ancient World' (1967: 323-55), and

Figure 9. *Kreuzzüge des Philologen* [*Crusades of the Philologist*] (title page of the volume in which the Aesthaetica was included) 1762 by J.G. Hamann (reproduced by courtesy of the Niedersächsische Staats- und Universitätsbibliotek, Göttingen)

his parodies of German poetry, extant (so Gregor Smith) in manuscripts, that I dare say are now included in the Bultmann archive. But Bultmann moved, *m.E.* (in my view), too quickly here, though one must remember that he was writing in a context in which, if you did not move quickly, you might not long be there to move at all (Bethge on Bonhoeffer [1967 (= 1970)] *passim*). This was a night, when all cats were carnivores.

It is never easy, as Ian Henderson (in lectures) pointed out, to move over territory that Bultmann has mined. But it is at least fair to raise the question, whether Bultmann is not historian and philosopher, *before* he is literary critic. The question imposes itself, whether Farrer, Kermode, Blackmur and Eliot (*qua* critic) do not do something, or do not do something more thoroughly, which Bultmann does not do. 'What are analogies,' asks Farrer (1948: 62), 'but sober and criticised images?' It is analogy to which Bultmann has given his attention (1953: 197), though only in a concessive clause with a brief, causal supplement.

And it is Bultmann's 'analogy' that I wish to retro-translate into Farrer's 'images'. And I wish to pursue it, then, further still into the literary field, the field where Lowth's *Sacred Poesy* (1770 [= 1829]) is at home. It is, to speak paradoxically, as a philosopher that Bultmann is a literary critic. It is *literary criticism* that needs more work. And this will then lead further to a different philosophy, or to a philosophy *differently* 'nuanced' (*anders nuanciert*).

There were problems with the move to Heidegger. What are Bultmann's 'translation rules'? By what criterion, for example, does Bultmann get *that* bit of Heidegger out of *that* bit of Paul? And Bultmann's theory of myth, in the Confessing Church essay, was not fully worked out—'the other side in terms of this side' (in a footnote [1953: 10 n. 2]) with some other merely antepenumbral adumbrations. And there are some other more minor problems, such as the one to do with nineteenth-century individualism, which were not always quite fair to Bultmann. But, then, there were those who were desperate. And when theologians are desperate, all hell is let loose.

But there was another angle of approach to all this, which stemmed from Wittgenstein and the British school of linguistic empiricism. And all this reflected very hardly on another area of Bultmann's complex thought: the *Erbe*, the 'inheritance', that derived from Luther and Lutheran scholasticism, that derived from dogmatics *in sensu malo*, dogmatics controlled by the *WA* (the *Weimarer Ausgabe*, the Weimar Edition of Luther's *Works*), as Scots are controlled by the WC (the Westminster Confession).

What, in other words, was linguistic empiricism, linguistic analysis to make of the Westminster and the Augsburg Confessions and of the Calvinist and Lutheran thinking that depended on them? What is the difference between dogmatics and *bad* philosophy? Was not the dogmatics paradigmatically found in, or implied by, Collingwood's 'Quicunque Vult' (1940a: 213-27) a far better thing? Was there here not something more than assertions merely asserted?

For shibboleths from the Lutheran and Calvinist quarters floated through talk about the New Testament and the concomitant Heideggerian components like large lumps through rather thick porridge. 'We may regard Wittgenstein, I suggest', said Ian Ramsey at the Church Leaders' Conference in the Selly Oak Colleges, Birmingham, on Tuesday, 12 September 1972 p. 9 (unpublished[?]), but made available to Edinburgh by H. Smith), 'as he who represents the development of logical empiricism over some thirty years, as, in the providence of God, the Cyrus of our time'.

But, once confront Luther and the Lutherans (or Calvin and the Calvinists) with Ramsey's 'Cyrus' (and his myrmidons), and many questions arose. For much of that Reformed tradition was the assertion with a straight face of impossible things. Accordingly, with some caution, for 'weakness', if unqualified, is always the wrong, and never the right word to use of Bultmann, there is need to follow out Fergusson's apodeictic comment (1992: 127): 'A central weakness in his [sc. Bultmann's] theology concerns the nature of religious language.' But it was hardly possible for Bultmann to combine potency with omnipotence. One man cannot do everything. Nor can he answer the questions that will only subsequently arise.

And if you conflate these problems of the Bultmannian settlement with the tradition of a *radical* historical criticism, that runs through the taciturn Reimarus, who had the good fortune, not to fail to find a publisher, but not to look for one, through Strauss and Renan to Bultmann, a tradition trenchantly continued by the pugilistic Käsemann (is von Balthasar well versed here?), then we have the sparks *and* the fuel *and* the cylinders for a turn to literary study. Literary study is 'enabled' (ἱκανοω, *hikanoo*, with ἱκανός, *hikanos*, 'able', and ἱκανότης, *hikanotes*, 'ability'), to note *en passant* Paul's playing the texts (2 Cor. 3.5-6).

Literary sensitivity is something that Gregor Smith shares with Bultmann, the Johnsonian word, the discreet (and discrete) selection, as the blackbird the worm:

> The common word exact without vulgarity,
> The formal word precise but not pedantic…
> (Eliot, 'Little Gidding' V [= 1944: 43])

Here, by way of example, is one signal passage from that seminal work, *The New Man* (Gregor Smith 1956: 59):

> What we are concerned with, therefore, is the search for a new anthropology, a view of man, which will pay proper respect both to the insights of the Renaissance about man and the insights of Christianity about God in relation to man. In this search I do not believe that it can be fruitful, or even legitimate, to attempt to take our stand on the old battle-fields, where the corpses of decaying categories are locked in meaningless embrace, where revelation lies stricken beside reason, where the supernatural lies dead beside the natural, where the trumpet of the Lord, borrowed by the dying dogmatist, lies tarnished by the side of the deaf and also dying secular hero, captain of his fate no longer. The knight of faith, as Kierkegaard called him in a beautiful image, can no longer come prancing into the tournament in the panoply of absolute assurance. Absolute solicitude, yes; and absolute resignation. For he comes not from another world but in the new hope and strength which he is given in this world because of what has been done in and for this world. Like his master, he is the servant, so far as he may be, of men.

The present essay finds its support in Gregor Smith's bold *Doctrine of God* (1970), much as the mind in health finds its support in what Hamann calls 'the senses and passions' (Hamann 1950: 197 [= Lumpp 1970: 205]), where there is no 'lie in the soul', where emotion is truly, with poetic accuracy, expressed (Plato, *Rep.* 382a-c, cit. Collingwood 1938: 219 n. 1).

But before I operate against the background of the posthumous Doctrine of (a posthumous) *God* (Altizer 1967), I will first cite, or *re*-cite, a phrase from *The Free Man*, before going on to explain why I do so, or to insist that I *a m* doing so. And I say insist, because, although I do not think I have managed to demonstrate it to the philosopher, I have nevertheless, in earlier pages, attempted, by the production of bizarre and far-flung evidence, not only to say, but to *show*, that the words 'poetry' and 'fiction' are words that apply to the texts of the New Testament.

In 'The Resurrection of Christ' (Gregor Smith 1969: 133-34), there occurs the bifurcation, 'historical *and literary* imagination' (my italics). All I am saying in this chapter is that *both* adjectives are demanded by the texts, and that reflection on the second leads through literary criticism to aesthetic philosophy, to ontology, to the 'about-what', to an aesthetic philosophy within the body of philosophy and metaphysics. And I would like to think that even the student of the New Testament should make an amateur's attempt not to fight shy of raising these questions for the philosophers to pursue.

But '[t]he task of this concluding chapter is merely to weave together the conclusions of the other chapters and present them if possible as a coherent whole; and to touch as well upon certain consequences which have not as yet appeared'. So far Eliot, in the conclusion to his Bradley book (1964: 153). In the present Conclusion, a preliminary account is first required of the doctrines that have been put forward earlier.

These doctrines, opinions, are specifications of the Christian doctrine of literature. And if the epithet is otiose, they are specifications of a doctrine of literature *tout court*. What they are should already be apparent to anyone who has been patient enough to sink a ploughshare in the 'scaupie grund...amang thrissles' (Mk 4.16, 18 [Lorimer 1983: 67]), over which my reader may (or may not) have travelled. 'The coulter rusts', one might put it so, 'that should deracinate such savagery' (Shakespeare, *King Henry* V.ii.46-47).

They were perhaps crude specifications.

They were stochastic.

They were these:

The Christian doctrine of literature is anterior to the question of the Christian doctrine of Christian literature, to the question, whether there is, or should be, a list of books that qualify for inclusion as Christian and an index (the *mot juste*!) of those that do not.

But I do not think the division helpful. And, if it is not, then we do not want a Christian doctrine of Christian literature, or a Christian doctrine of literature, but only a doctrine of literature as such, though Jesus of Nazareth, *qua* author, as much as *qua* actor, belongs somewhere. And 'oral literature', that oxymoron, must be included, too.

But I do not mind: Jesus is *my* MacCullough (see Chapter 11). And a Christian doctrine of *Christian* literature will do very well, provided that 'Christian' is understood to mean: (1) that there is a *theistic* metaphysic that finds its centre somehow in what is usually called a *theos*, or real entity (or real nonentity, for one does after all have to keep Cusanus in the conversation), and (2) that this metaphysic is somehow centred on Jesus of Nazareth (or elsewhere), these two propositions being correlated *by* and goes under the name *of* a good deal of hot air, there being no other way of accounting for the emission of it.

Literature differs from history as fiction differs from fact. We see from the historical novel that fact and fiction can occur in combination. The study of extant literature is a historical study, but not a historical study of historiography, except where, and to the extent that, fiction is combined with fact. There can be no study of literature that is not yet extant, but it is a probable fact (we might call it certain) that more literature will come to be added to the extant corpus. History and literature are equally modes of dealing with, of finding language for, *reality*. What already exists is actual; there is also what is possible. What does not yet exist is not yet real. There are more deeds to be done and more books to be written. More to be read (legend)—and more to be unreadable.

The historical study of fiction, the historical study of fiction in the New Testament, is a study of the radically contingent. *That* then and there is how they said what they said. *Those* were the styles and conventions that they followed. The styles and conventions of Stevens and Eliot differ from Mark, John and Paul. But difference is connected with sameness, discontinuity with continuity. We do not write like them, but we can read them. Or what *we* write is not identical with what *they* wrote. There is no reason why we should not hold fast to the New Testament, but there is no reason why we should not *do something different*; and hold to that, too. Perhaps something better, something in some ways better.

Bonhoeffer, on 'The Right to Bodily Life', for instance (1955: 112-22)[1] is better than Paul on the same subject. It will not, at any rate, be very difficult to do something worse. But what will that something be? The production of facts, or the production, the construction of fictions? Both? A better historiography? A better literature? Or, not better, but different? And what about the production of those conditions, without which there cannot be facts? The production, or recognition, or both, that is, of philosophy, or metaphysics.

This book has been concerned with three types of writing: poetry, history and philosophy. New Testament research has recently been dominantly concerned with history, though it is more often concerned less with these than with tautology, with insignificant tautology. It is easier to let the questions go by default. There are some modes of scholarship that are modes of evading the questions. It is easier to eat, drink and write a monograph.

But a dominant concern with history is *beside* the point, if the New Testament is dominantly concerned with poetry. It hits the *target*. It does not slay the bull. Many of the realities of which the New Testament speaks are simply not accessible to the historian. What we have in the New Testament is the language of the human heart, the language of emotion, the language of the 'senses and passions' (Hamann 1950: 197 [= Gregor Smith 1960: 196]).[2]

But this is only what Lowth says (1847: 51):

> Poetry, in this its rude origin and commencement, being derived from nature, was in time improved by art, and applied to the purposes of utility and delight. For, as it [sc. poetry] owed its birth to the affections of the mind, and had availed itself of the assistance of harmony, it was found, on account of the exact and vivid delineation of the objects which it described, to be excellently adapted to the exciting of every internal emotion, and making a more forcible impression upon the mind than abstract reasoning could possibly effect: it was found capable of interesting and affecting the senses and passions, of captivating the ear, of directing the perception to the minutest circumstances, and of assisting the memory in the retention of them.[3]

1. Bonhoeffer 1992: 179-91 (Das Recht auf das leibliche Leben)—the analogue of de Chardin's 'noosphere' ('somatosphere'?) is to seek.
2. Lumpp 1970: 205 (*facsimile* 163); Crick, in Nisbet 1985: 141.
3. But this is not quite identical with Lowth, who spoke no English, but

But Gregory's happy coincidence, in his translation of Lowth, with the *Sinne und Leidenschaften*, the 'senses and passions' of Hamann, *who had Lowth before him, too* (e.g. Hamann 1950: 214 n. 58),[4] is justified by more than one phrase of the Latin Lowth. The translation of Lowth coincides verbally with Hamann, Lowth himself materially.

That the Gospels are not histories has been amply (I hope) shown and no attempt will be made here to re-adduce what has been adduced above. But to offer the name of one link from a concatenation that stretches out (almost) to the crack of doom, the fact has been paradigmatically shown by Eliot's Strauss (1840). That history can be derived from the Gospels has likewise been amply shown, but the history that has been shown has not been ample, if Conzelmann (1973) and Morgan (1997) are reliable guides, to say nothing of the famous paragraph of Bultmann, that begins: 'With some caution, then...Jesus drank a glass of wine' (1967: 451-52). The major concern of the Gospel writers and of the New Testament is something different, is some other thing.

What the Gospel writers have done is much better expressed by saying that they have been writing, not history, but literature. For they are writing not just about the past, but about past, present and future. And what historian, writing as a historian, is allowed to do that? And they are writing not just about the past, but about a past that never was. The fairy-tale is included. And not just about the future, but about a future, that may, or will never be. Are clouds sufficiently substantial to carry the living, or even the dead?

And that means that they are writing about a present that is then poised between what never was and what may or will never be and about their own present experience conceived as part of a

---

with Gregory, his translator. For Lowth's actual words are these (1770: I, 69): 'Poeticam, hoc modo, ut videtur, rudi quodam initio ab natura fusam, mature excepit ars, atque ad delectationem et utilitatem transtulit. Nam quemadmodum ex affectibus mentis suam originem duxerat, numerosque etiam sibi adsciverat, ita ad omnem animi motum concitandum, seque ei penitus infigendum egregie erat comparata; cum rerum omnium imagines in animo eminenter expressas signaret et effingeret, sensus percelleret, delectaret aures, efficeretque, ut mens attente singula perciperet, nec percepta facile elabi pateretur.'

4. Lumpp 1970: 231 (facsimile 214 [*]), Crick, in Nisbet 1985: 149 n. [fff].

larger and longer story. And *story* (*myth*, if you prefer) is what the story is.

They are writing—surely it is better to put it this way—not about history, but about reality. And they are writing about reality as imagined by poets, about imagined reality, which *includes* history, but it is history *with the superaddition of*, history *transfused by* imagination.

And for a theistic metaphysic, history without imagination, without the transfigurations of the poet's mind, without the transmutations and transpositions of story tellers of genius, is fruitless. For:

> unless we do these things to reality, the damned thing closes in us, walls us up and buries us alive... Reality is the footing from which we leap after what we do not have and on which everything depends (Stevens, in Stevens 1967: 599-600).

And what if that, 'on which everything depends', if that, which is not itself history, is to be found in history, is part of reality, finds its embodiment there, as a necessary or probable truth is found in a work of art?

But 'reality' is a slippery word (which only makes it more adequate for including what is excluded by the historian). And Stevens (above) means something more like Zola and less like the 'magical realism' of García Márquez (1994), something more, in Stevens's terms, like his 'winter' reality and not the reality of the 'green, my fluent *mundo*' (1955: 407 [= III.x]). For that, too, is real, is it not so?

By 'reality as imagined by poets' I mean to conjoin summer with winter. I mean to include what is included by the historian, as defined by Collingwood (1946) and Oakeshott (1983). I mean, in a word, to include the 'winter' of what is included by the rhetoric of St Luke's Prologue (Lk. 1.1-4) and to include the 'summer' of his practice, the former as history and the latter as literature.

I want, moreover, to concede, that poets, philosophers, historians and those, too, who are none of these, are incarnate. But the question would still arise, how that can be said? Is 'God's history with man' (Gregor Smith 1966: 21) best expressed, or only expressible, by the historiographer? Or by the poet, or the philosopher? Surely, and indifferently, but *differently*, by all three. These are three ways of telling the truth.

But (again) into what category, or categories, do the New Testament writers fall? Here we must speak, not of, or not only of 'God's history with man', but of God's *literature* with man, of God's *literature* with woman and (especially) with God's *literature* with child. For 'Mencius tells of the tendency in humans as they move out of childhood to throw away their minds. Thereafter the whole of life is to recover the lost mind of the child' (Swimme and Berry 1992: 189). We must, Swimme and Berry are saying, learn to re-adopt the pathological gullibility of the child. We must become as little children. For only so can one of the sores of theology be healed.

In a word, if in 'The Resurrection of Christ' (Gregor Smith 1969: 133-34), there occurs the bifurcation, 'historical *and literary* imagination', then both adjectives need nouns. Literature deserves a place with history. And it is the former that most nearly names the nature of the New Testament. Historical literature, some of it (but how much?), but literature all the same. Lowth has shown this (1829 [= 1821]). But he has shown it for the *Auld* Alliance.

From Lowth, of course, those after Lowth must sometimes differ. Not just in holding that the Song Solomon had written and sung for him was really the song the young men sang as they returned in spring from their late night roistering, though the allegorical reading (God and Israel, Christ and the Church) has, within the relaxes of postmodernism, its legitimate place, if sexuality is part of incarnation. But we must (we certainly *may*) differ from him in being able ourselves to hold to fewer historical facts than in Lowth's day was possible. Science has now gone further. But what Lowth, with these qualifications, did to the Old Testament must be done to the New.

This is this essay. This we must essay. ''Tis time to seek a newer world.'

We must 'do a Lowth', just as we must 'do' a more (thoroughgoing, *konsequent*) de Wette. Nor must we resile, as Strauss seems to resile, or to resile too quickly, from his very reasonable findings and hasten, or hasten too quickly, to metaphysics. We must hasten to metaphysics, but hasten slowly.

Such haste in the critic is, of course, easy to comprehend. For there is a natural inclination in the critic, when reading poetry, to 'disconfuse' the confused cognition of the childhood of the human race. There is a natural *nisus*, or appetition, not only in the Common Sense of the Democratic Intellect (Davie 1964), but in the Uncommon Sense of the disert Strauss to hurry on from the poet's way of knowing. And if there is a difference, not only between the philosopher and the poet, but between the scholar and the literary critic, there is all too often a difference, in some quarters, between the literary critic with poetic sensibility and the literary critic with none. And this is to say nothing of the critic, who is dealing with poetry, but escapes her own notice that she is doing so. So Michaelis, in his preface to Lowth (1770: XV [= 1821: 396]):

> For though all those may be sensible of poetic beauty, who are well acquainted with the poet's tongue, yet few make judgements about it that are just and discriminating, and almost those only, who themselves are by nature poets: not critics, not grammarians' (1770: XV [= 1821: 396] [my trans.]).[5]

If there is one thing clear from these tentative lucubrations, this going about and about, it is that an act of interpolation may have to be made, the interpolation, into the task of interpretation, not of historical, but of literary criticism. Literary criticism, logically, comes *after* literature and *before* philosophy.

But has *Bultmann* already done this? Has *he* carried this out?

Philological acumen, yes. His beautiful essay on 'Die Symbolik des Lichtes im Alterthum', 'The Symbolism of Light in the Ancient World', yes. But his work on myth needs to be continued with the kind of analysis into its component parts, the rhetorical, poetic parts, so lucidly distinguished by Lowth in his praelections to the *Academici* of the Oxford of his day. Damn tropes, yes; the vortices, the epicycles. Lowth damns them, too. But Lowth's careful divisions of the figurative and his conscientious attention to genre were a real and axial exploit. So that we need from Bultmann, not only a 'de-mythologizing' debate, but a de-metaphorizing, a de-imagizing, a de-comparisonizing, a de-prosopopoeizing (or de-personificationizing) debate also.

Or do we?

We do not, or not only.

That debate, *that de*-construction, we need complemented—by

5. 'Poeticam enim pulchritudinem licet omnes sentiant, qui linguam poetae callent, pauci tamen de ea recte et acute judicant, ac fere hi soli, qui ipsi a natura poetae sunt: non critici, non grammatici.'

the disquisitions of the literary critic. What we need is an affirmation by the literary mind of literature. We need the enjoyment of
literature, to revel in 'anthropopathy', the emotions of the human
animal as a symbolic scheme (Lowth 1847: 340). We need, not the
dismissal of legend, but the enjoyment of what should be read.
Lowth's poets lied well. Jesus (and Jesus' poets—Matthew, Mark,
Luke and the rest) lied better. Heracles had a father. Jesus had a
father. Jehovah and Zeus are anthropopathic fathers. Let fiction
flourish.

And then, if *they* wrote, we must write. We must leave the
poets—for our own poetry. The task is not yet finished.

In a radically contingent world, where things touch for a time
(Oakeshott 1975: 101-107), in the terror of, in the exhilarating
theme park, of history, we badly need the renaissance of the Christian lie, the 'difficultest rigor' (Stevens 1955: 398 [III.i]) of a
contemporary poetic. But we need a poetic that does not despise
the past, that does not despise the millennia of poetry that have
produced us (and the New Testament). But we need a poetic that
does not need to be convinced that all that has been said leaves us
with nothing to say.

Read it. Leave it. Write.

Not (with Forster): Only collect.

But: write something, too.

Go out 'not knowing whither'. Go out, as Gregor Smith went out
nesciens quo iret, unless, for ourselves, for myself, we are to go
out, not knowing whether...

For why should we take history, or why, rather, should we take
reality to be dumb? For either there is, or there is not, 'the creative
power which constitutes the inward essence of all things' (Collingwood 1934: 265). The occurrence of 'the new' in history has to be
explained. The occurrence of new literature has to be explained.
The creation of reality, by the poet, by the historian, by the philosopher, has to be explained.

The senses and passions give rise to speech. The emotions find in
speech their imaginative expression. And then it is the task of the
literary critic to interpret, explain and criticize. But literary criticism is different from scholarship. It is at the point where scholarship breaks down, comes to its end, that the literary critic begins.
It is in the interstices between scholarship and the text, where the

critic belongs. The scholar is the anatomist, but the text is not a corpse. It is the critic's profession, the critic's art, to invite the reader to meet the living text. It is the critic's profession to re-animate, re-awaken the text that the scholar has killed; or to rescue the reader (and the critic as reader) from the scholar; or to point the reader to what 'shows itself', *zeigt sich* (Wittgenstein 1960: 82 [= 6.522]) in the text. The text, for the scholar, is all that the scholar says it is. But the text, if the text is worth reading, is all this *and more*. The text is also what the scholar has not said and also what the critic cannot finally say. Else criticism would be a substitute for the text. Scholarship is what you say before you reach the mystery (this a variant on an *obiter dictum* of O'Donoghue [1993]), that 'theology is what you do, before you reach mystery'). It is to the mystery that the critic is bound to point. The text transcends scholar and critic and both are bound to concede it.

But none of this would be worth saying, no distinction between literary scholarship and literary criticism, like the distinction between art history and art criticism (Kemal and Gaskell 1991: 1), would be worth making, if it were not sometimes the case that something more comes to be said than has been said, and if it were not always the case that it could be. There are genuine advances. The point is rather that it is possible to make advances on advances. It is always possible to advance further and never necessary only to have advanced thus far. But we can legitimately rest, can pause...

But (unresting and unhasting) the watch-word is *Unverfügbarkeit*, 'unmanageability' (Bultmann 1984: 55; also *das... Unverfügbare*, 'that which one does not have at one's disposal' [1960: 29]).[6] And that demands our modesty. And does not foreclose the future.

And even our old texts have a future, after the scholars have done their worst. And even new texts have a future, because they are not yet written.

But why write histories only? And why assert that only histories have been written? Why assert the worthlessness of fictions? Why insist that fictions are histories? Why fear that fictions are false? To assert that fictions are false is only to say that fictions are not histories. But to assert that they are true is to say that they are other than, and, it may be, more than, not less than, histories. Of course,

---

6.   Bultmann 1953: 19 (ET has 'intangible').

it is hard to un-confuse confused cognition. Cleave, then, to triangles, if you will, to non-Euclidean triangles, if you must. But why
not sing ? *C'est l'air* [may I say it again?] *qui fait la chanson, et nos
évangiles se chantent,* 'It is the melody that makes the song and it
is a song our gospels sing' (Loisy 1923: 439). Why not enter into
the 'logic' of the song, be it the *Carmina Burana*, the *Cumha
Mhic Crioman* ('MacCrimmon's Lament' [Stewart, see Acknowl-
edgments]), or the *Carmen Christi? Solvitur non ambulando, nec
interloquendo* (*contra* Collingwood 1938: 251), *sed cantando,*
'The matter is solved, not by perambulation, nor by interlocution,
but by song'.

But how should literary criticism be done?

God knows.

Kermode knows.

It is unfashionable, or has never yet become the fashion, where
scripture is concerned (though the only literature anywhere that is
not scripture is oral (*scribo*: I 'write', 'I am a scribe')), to engage full-
bloodedly in comparative literature, to bring about the synizesis,
for example, of the Fourth Gospel with *The Hitch-Hiker's Guide to
the Galaxy*. But there will be a time for such things. But fashions
may change, fashions, styles, conventions. But one fashion is the
analogue of another, for the human animal is never so totally other
from what the animal has been. Comparisons can be heuristic. And
what is so unlike as to be totally different?

And comparative literature, the comparing of one writing with
another, can be complemented by the comparison of one art with
another, of painting with literature, or sculpture with literature. Or
music. The problems of the artist in one art are analogous to the
problems in another. Only Piero, or the Phigaleian Frieze, can
clarify beyond a peradventure, that Paul paints and sculpts; has a
circumcising knife in his palette. Hence, too, Kermode is co-
implicated with Wölfflin, the art critic with the literary critic. Let
inter-disciplinarity rule. Let the Glasgow School flourish in the
Edinburgh *Kindergarten*.

In history some of the people some of the time pay attention to
what is not history. To the future, for example; to writing fiction,
for example; to the expression of their 'senses and passions'. They
use other people's pictures and find more for themselves. They
write stories, or rewrite stories. They engage in actions, that consist

in finding words. They dance to a tune, flourish a brush, see the unseen. Visionaries, dreamers. They find metaphors, develop metaphors into stories: *Abba* is a father, an *Abba* had two sons. And one of them went off with his share of the money... They write whole histories, not 'The Economic Influence of the Developments in Shipbuilding Techniques, 1450-1485' (Amis 1961: 15), but *The History of Tom Jones* (Fielding 1959).

Religion would not make much headway in the world, to the gallows, to freedom, or to both, if it were not anchored in passion. Humankind can only bear reality. And religion, and the literature, which religion produces, enables one to know one's passions, not as someone else's, but as one's own. But 'humankind cannot bear very much reality' (Eliot, 'Burnt Norton' I [= 1944: 8]). And 'passible' (Doway 1633: 680 (Jas 5.17)[7] men and women are often happier to identify the splinters in the eyes of another. But, in the last analysis, humankind can only bear reality. And religion, not never their ally, has at its best, like pyscho-analysis at its best, 'already won a great place in the history of man's warfare with the powers of darkness' (Collingwood 1938: 221). But if religion is anchored in passion, as theology in the academy, then religion is, like art, 'the mother-tongue of the human race' (Hamann 1950: 197, trans. Gregor Smith 1960: 196).[8]

Religion is, like poetry, anchored in sense and sensuality, in feeling, appetite, hunger and love, in passion and desire (Collingwood 1942: 18-82). But religion (so 'Golgatha and Sheblimini' [Hamann, in Gregor Smith 1960: 224-32]),[9] anchored, rooted in the earth, is rooted, anchored in the sky, or like 'a tree... which grows from the birds down' (Templeton 1988: 289). In both of these together. The Hamann of the *Aesthetica in nuce* (1950 [= 1985]) is an aesthete. But Hamann is no *lily-livered* aesthete. Religion is no idle and etiolated sport. Poetry is not the perquisite, the exquisite perquisite of a coterie,

> cut off not only from the ordinary world of common people; but even from the corresponding worlds of other artists. Thus Burne-Jones lived in a world whose contents weere ungraciously defined by a journalist as 'green light and gawky girls'; Leighton in a world

7.   Cit. Knowles 1963: 19 (Inaugural Lecture 1955).
8.   Lumpp (facsimile) 1970: 205, cf. Unger 1925: 245-47.
9.   Hamann 1956: 46-163.

of sham Hellenism; and it was the call of practical life that rescued Yeats from the sham world of his Celtic twilight, forced him into the clear air of real Celtic life, and made him a great poet (Collingwood 1938: 120).

Take *Oedipus*. Take *Macbeth*. Take Jesus, making a point in a parable, a point aimed at the heart of a 'law', which 'grace' has not sublated. He was a Jew after all. Take Paul, describing love as love (1 Cor. 13), re-describing law as 'death' (2 Cor. 3.7)—and so engineering his own? And take More, author of a Utopian fiction, 'cunnyngly reasoned and wittilie discussed' (Robynson, in Lupton [More 1895: 167]), before turning, in the Tower, to *A Dialogue of Comfort* (1847). As flies are we to the wanton *Abba*.

Are we? It is reasonable, we are told by Kant (1914: 362-429 [= 1915: 306-61]), by Davidovich (1993), and by Paton (1965: 188), to come up with an idea of God, but not always easy to come up with a God that is reasonable. For there are occasions when this can only be done, as Livingstone found, in the teeth of the evidence (a lion):

> The shake annihilated fear, and allowed no sense of horror in looking round at the beast. This peculiar state is probably produced in all animals killed by the carnivora, and, if so, is a merciful provision by our benevolent Creator for lessening the pain of death (Livingstone 1858: 21 [with thanks to A.C. Ross]).

There are occasions when one desiderates that the grin would disappear with the cat.

But the reasonable animal feels. And, here, the figure that mediates between de Wette and Kant is Fries. For Fries, the concept, or conviction, that mediates between understanding and reason is 'presentiment': *Ahndung ist eine nothwendige Überzeugung aus blossem Gefühl*, 'presentiment is a necessary conviction based on mere feeling' (Fries 1805: 64). And this 'presentiment', this 'intimation', this *Ahndung* mediates between the necessities of nature and the freedom of *homo risibilis*, the laughing animal, by inviting from him the kind of contemplative judgment about *the world as purposeful* that one makes about a work of art as intentional and as beautiful.

But how is Grünewald's crucifixion to be contemplated? As beautiful?

> Perhaps poetry, instead of being the rather meaningless transmutation of reality, is a combat with it; and perhaps the thing to do when one keeps saying that life is a dull life is to pick a fight with reality (Stevens, in Stevens 1967: 620-21).

Job shakes his fist. 'Only the suffering God can help' (Bonhoeffer 1971: 361).

But with 'Golgatha' also 'Scheblimini', 'Sit thou at my right hand':[10]

> in everything, One Note of immeasurable height and depth. A demonstration of the most lordly majesty and emptiest abandonment (Hamann 1950: 204)![11]

This, in a nutshell, is Hamann's aesthetic standpoint. It is in standing here, that he makes the kind of contemplative judgment about the world as purposeful that one makes about a work of art. It is in standing here, that he moves the world. It is in standing here, that he:

> remains a 'humorist'; there is for him no religious stage beyond that of humour. That is to say, his faith includes, and never gives up, scepticism. He combines believing and not believing within the conditions of this world (Gregor Smith 1960: 19).

But for Hamann to move Hamann's world is different from us to move ours. Each world needs its classical texts. A classical text can be cited in a new world, as Hamann cites Manilius and Paul, Persius and John. But contingency must be caught, new classics written. The occurrence of the *new* needs *new* speech.

Take the words of Grotius, his *etsi deus non daretur*, 'even if God were not being given', his *etiamsi daremus deum non esse*, 'even were we to grant that there is no God'. This *obiter dictum*, this parenthesis, this counter-factual protasis on hypothetical crime, this occasion for the charge of atheism, signals, perhaps against his will, that new facts, a world of new facts, need new fictions, new texts that articulate new emotions. For to say that the Gospels are fictions is to say that they are transcripts of the inner life of their authors (and their readers) in an outer form, which they wrote in response to what they had received. But not inner

10. Hamann 1956: 46-163.
11. '...in allen Ein Ton von unermässlicher Höhe und Tiefe. Ein Beweis der herrlichsten Majestät und leersten Entäusserung!'

life only, but the life of subjects in relation to objects.

Inner facts and inner fictions, outer facts and outer fictions, styles of the productive and reproductive imagination, change over time. And even when the old styles reoccur, are made to re-occur, they do so in a new context. 'Secularity', for Gregor Smith, gives the new context its name. What is named by the name? And how is the Hebrew name to be renamed ('I will be what I will be' [Exod. 3.14]). How is the Hebrew joke to be re-told? What fictions are now demanded of the Christian, free and responsible, claudicant towards Zion, busy in Babylon? What is demanded of the envoy, the tramp?

> 'The man
> In that old coat, those sagging pantaloons,
>
> It is of him, ephebe, to make, to confect
> The final elegance, not to console
> Nor sanctify, but plainly to propound.
>   (Stevens 1955: 389 [I.x.])

'The daring nature of Christianity consists...in its philosophical stance: it takes the bull of impermanence by the horns and shakes it into permanence' (Gregor Smith 1970: 171).

How are we to do this?

If '[t]he bland conviction that the old traditions are *as such* normative must be rejected', if 'there can be no theology that is not in some sense philosophical' (p. 175), if 'historicity is not fully self-explanatory' (Gregor Smith 1970: 177); and if literature and fiction, as 'confused cognition', are not self-explanatory either, and if the symbol, *qua symbolizans*, *qua* symbolizing, is incomplete without what is symbolized by it; if, in a word, neither nature, nor history, nor any science of either, is self-explanatory, then we either accept the axiom that there is an explanation, of a kind that is partly, but not wholly known (1 Cor. 13.12), or we do not accept it. The explanatory axiom, that grants that God is given, that grasps, with Grotius, that his protasis is counter-factual, offers at least a Pickwickian explanation of why the human animal moves, or is moved, or is moved to move.

But 'poetry tends to express the universal' (Aristotle, *Po.* 1451a6). If Aristotle's 'universal' (τὰ καθόλου, *ta katholou*) can be pushed as far as the making of philosophical statements (and even if it cannot!), a philosophical axiom, a metaphysical axiom can be expressed imaginatively by poetry and fiction, by metaphor and symbol, in the literary mode. If philosophy can be stated *as* philosophy, philosophy can also be stated as *literature*. And the 'right' science for investigating the literary mode is literary criticism. The question, What is literary criticism? is answered, or is investigated, by aesthetics—though all this within the limits of necessary ignorance. *Learned* ignorance, it may be, but *ignorance* all the same.

We then have three tasks to fulfil, three opportunities to take: the writing of poetry and fiction (and the other arts), the criticism of these and philosophical reflection on both. The making of art, the criticism of art and reflection upon it are no less pressing than the writing, and belong to the making, of history.

But if we are to make art, we must make it ours, must make it for an age of secularity. But this does not mean, to use Gregor Smith's distinction between 'secularism' and 'secularity' (1966: 172), that we must make it as modern secularism, which 'wishes to have direct and unmediated enjoyment of its primary insight that man "now runs his own life" (to use Gabriel Marcel's phrase for describing modern man's autonomy)' (Gregor Smith 1966: 172). (And as Gregor Smith believed 'that footnotes were a sign of indiscipline' [*obiter dictum*] Marcel's phrase is given no reference). Why should we confidently reduce novelty by misdescribing its source? This would be tantamount to creating no religious works of art at all. Or should we restrict ourselves to the repetition of a requiem from the past about the past and to the 'tubas' that 'Jerome begat' (Stevens 1955: 398 [III.i])?

In dealing with the datable documents (that bald word) of the datable events of Christian origins, we are dealing with poetry and imagination, with the fictive imagination. Even the historian (Chadwick 1985: 191) has to recognize that

> the events which were so dated came clothed in garments that were not so historical; of poetry and saga, of the nation's hymnody, of legends about the making of the world, and of the patriarchs, prophets and martyrs, a treasure-house of a people's faith.

And so the word 'literature', and the word 'fiction', in both its positive and its negative senses (but its positive sense especially) must move more into the centre of inquiry than for Gregor Smith it had done, though the seeds are there in his work. 'God's February' (Craig, in Templeton 1991: vi) is the harbinger of spring:

> There is a time of the year in Scotland—it is about the middle of
> February—when you will see a dream in the eye of the garden-lover;
> a dream which is not the bastard of wishful thinking, but the lawful
> offspring of the garden-lover's knowledge of sun and soil and seed.

But imagination, the artistic imagination, is parasitic on reality,
fiction parasitic on fact.

But this is to equate neither with the other.

But it connects each.

Fiction is a valid approach to fact. But, more importantly, fiction
is a valid approach to what is going to be factual, to what we hope
is going to be factual. Fiction is an approach, not to facts, or not to
facts only, but to *facienda, nondum facta*, to those things that are
to be done, but have not yet been done. It is an approach, not to
ontology, the study of being, but (so to speak) to 'genesiology', the
study of becoming. This gelastic term, for the 'friend and lover of
laughter' (Kierkegaard 1939: 125) does more justice, does more
righteousness to the Hebrew background of the Greek of Exod.
3.14 (ὁ ὤν, *ho on*, 'he, who is') and to the extended discussion of
The Doctrine of God (Gregor Smith 1970: 92-99).

But in what sense valid? For the writer of fiction approaches fact
by diverging from fact. The writer of fiction depicts what is not,
what has never been and will never be. Centaurs and angels! How
is fact approached by these?

There are times, 'hypocrite lecteur' (Eliot 1936: 63 [= 'The Waste
Land' I]), there are times, Rider in the Chariot (Stevens 1960: 3-36),
there are times, Knight of Faith (Kierkegaard 1941: 52), when you
and the horse are one, when men become animals *in sensu malo*,
when a character, that might have been and might still become
angelic, has become a nature that might have been otherwise than
bestial? And are there not times, when insights occur, some of
them good? Centaurs and angels are an asymptotic transcript of
experience. And add Circe's pigs. Must Friedrich Waismann (1977)
make such heavy weather?

This is, after all, Pascal's anthropology (1950: 90 [187]): 'Man is
neither angel nor beast, and the mischief is that he who would play
the angel plays the beast.'[12] The combination of man with horse is
surely an analogue of the collocation of angel with beast. The

---

12. 'L'homme n'est ni ange ni bête, et le malheur veut que qui fait l'ange
fait la bête.'

figure of the centaur is translatable. It shows to human animals their bestial possibilities.

See the *words* of the Lord. All pictures, and the pictorial world of the New Testament, belong to a contingent world, were painted *then* and *there*, were painted *tunc et illinc*. The right pictures have to be devised for each contingency, by Sophocles, Shakespeare, Scott, by *Four Quartets*, by 'Notes...'. The New Testament is not so much there to provide us with our pictures, as to provide us with the stimulus to *finding our own*. By history made we are emancipated for the making of it—if the book is read aright.

But where would we be, if we needed evidence for what we say? For then we could say nothing about the future, except by cautious extrapolation from the past. But what kind of a policy is caution? Prudence, *Besonnenheit*, Common Sense are virtues. But fortitude, too. But, then, even these, prudence and fortitude, with justice and temperance, are sublated, surely, by a confidence, a hope, and a love, that have *everything* (Gk πάντα [*panta*]) for their object:

> πάντα πιστεύει,
> πάντα ἐλπίζει,
> (love) believeth all things,
>   hopeth all things (1 Cor.13.7),

and, he might add:

> πάντα ἀγαπᾷ
> loveth all things.

It is only by such stumbling steps that an approach can be made, not just to 'God's history with man', but to a Doctrine of Literature. If 'writing in the New Testament is poetry rather than prose' (Mackinnon, in Mackinnon and Flew 1955: 175), then a doctrine of poetry is required, a doctrine not only of what was then written, but of how it came to be written; and then a doctrine of what was subsequently written; and then of what will come to be written. For a doctrine is required, not just of the written, but of *writing as such*.

To use Spinoza's curious, but scholastic, distinction between *natura naturans* and *natura naturata* (1843: I, 210) (= *Ethica* I, *prop.* XXIX, *schol.*), we need (as it were) a *literatura literaturans*. We need, that is, literature, not as 'the system of what is created... an established system', but literature 'actively creating herself and deploying her essential powers in her infinite attributes'

(Hampshire 1988: 46-47). The doctrine of creation is also a doctrine of creativity. Sublunary woman, 'men under the sun' (Mackinnon and Flew 1955: 183) aim higher than both sun and moon together, for:

> a man's reach must exceed his grasp
> Or what's a heaven for?
>   (Browning, cit. Collingwood 1924: 132)

The future comes last. And the study of the last is eschatology. How does eschatology affect the written and the writing? Our studies are not complete, when we have studied the past, or even when we have scrutinized the present. For we must form a view of the future.

For the stochastic belongs to the nature of philosophy and theology, if philosophy and theology are only aptly done when 'touched by the longing for newness, for revolution, for the unpredictable powers of the spirit to engage man in society in ever new ventures of historical existence' (Gregor Smith 1970: 117).

And Gregor Smith goes on, importantly, if not intelligibly, to add: 'Do I mean the spirit with a capital "S", or "merely" human spirit? Both.' But both upper and lower case 'spirit' ('case', too, being a *mot juste*) need more talk. *Sonst bleiben wir bei einem blossen Vokabel*, 'More talk is needed, if the word "spirit" is not to remain a mere word'.

The topic I am after here is, in the *patois* of the schools, what eschatology *does* to history and what it *does* to literature. And it is here, as so often, that Gregor Smith's lambent and fastidious mind gives a hint in a subject area, 'apocalyptic eschatology', 'Messianism', of which, for the early Christians, the importance is paramount. And for us, later Humans, also.

SF? Is that an analogue of their earlier apocalypses? Gregor Smith, again (he is writing in 1970):

> The place of so-called science fiction in this state of affairs, both as an expression and as a cause of this forward-looking interest, deserves a study for itself. Even though a lot of what is written in this *genre* is just twaddle, and boring twaddle at that, there is other writing which has more to it.
>
> There are the whirling swirling fantasies of Ray Bradbury, especially *The Illustrated Man*, there are the straightforward projections

of technical mastery, with a strong allegorical infusion, in the stories of Brian Aldiss, and there are the immensely moving problem stories of James Blish, who has written in *A Case of Conscience* a theological novel which far outstrips the more popular but too preciously mythological stories of C.S. Lewis, *Perelandra, That Hideous Strength* and *Out of the Silent Planet* (1970: 121).

And, after citing Jules Verne and Jonathan Swift, and evaluating the formations and deformations of the *genre*, he concludes:

> Possibly the degraded forms will prevail; which is another way of saying that possibly the autonomy of present-day society will bring about its doom. But there is another hope, and it is that *the new, what comes out of the future*, may be accepted in a more solid and comprehensive context than that of individual fantasy and angst (1970: 123 [my italics]).

Here, too, is the place for More's *Utopia* (1895) (why did he not write *Uchronia* ['No Time']?), and *Erewhon* (Butler 1934) and *Rasselas* (Johnson 1968) and *Brave New World* (Huxley 1932) and *1984* (Orwell [on Jura] 1984), 'the classic description of [manipulation] for our time' (Gregor Smith 1966: 173) and *The Hitch-Hiker's Guide to the Galaxy* (Adams 1979), with that condign companion piece of New Testament criticism, 'The Man from Heaven in Johannine Sectarianism' (Meeks 1972, also in Ashton 1986: 141-73).

For is 'Messianism' really different from these (Schürer 1979: 488-554)? In what ways?

And does the question of truth not arise for these works of fiction and their like? It arises, patently enough, for Gregor Smith (above). And are there not Isenberg's tasks to be done, the tasks of '(a) interpretation, (b) explanation, and (c) criticism' (1973: 199)? Is there not a task here for the aesthetic philosopher? We remember well what has been imagined well. We remember good fictions well, supreme fictions best of all.

History is not the only kind of writing. Poetry, fiction, the poetic fashioning of poetry and prose, is also a kind of writing. And the good poet, the good writer of fiction may have more insight into history than a bad historian, more insight into history than any historian can ever have. But the poet and the writer of fiction may also have insights into *nature*, as well as history. And not only that, but they may also have insights into the conditions that make both of these possible, insights not into 'how the world is, but *that* it is'

(Wittgenstein 1960: 81 [= 6.44]), insights into 'absolute presuppositions' (Collingwood 1940), insights that change and 'develope' over time (Tennant 1928–30), insights that can, or may occur to anyone, who takes a look at nature and history. History is not the only theme, the historian's not the only trade. Paton's repeatable (and repeated) parenthesis on the artist (1965: 19) is palmary: '(if we may regard as also a thinker him who is so much more)'.

The fact that literature has a history, that there is a history of fiction, does not convert that history into a history of facts, a history of historiographies. Fictions are broader (*Rehoboth*, εὐρυχωρία: 'Broad Rooms' [Gen. 26.22]), more ample, more free than histories and, if parasitic on fact, on reality, then parasitic on fact in myriad ways. But the history of fiction makes abundantly clear (a new, a post-Cambrian, insight this), that changes in the language of fiction are due to the clocking up of the millennia, to the 'turn' towards language, to that turn stimulated by Wittgenstein, de Saussure and the Enlightenment. More models, now, are available, instantly available by depression, the depression of a key.

All this suggests that St Anselm, 'the last Archbishop of Canterbury to be a theologian' (Gregor Smith *obiter dictum* [Lowth declined on grounds of health]) did not go far enough in his definition, his 'infinition' one might call it, of God as:

> *id quo nil maius cogitari possit*
> [that than which nothing greater can be thought].

In view of the gap between what we want to say and that about which we want to say it; in view of the fact that no one definition of the infinite is likely to be sustainable over time (though Anselm was cunning enough to offer form without content); in view of the fact that his *dictum* implies, or may be understood as implying, that the unattainable can be attained, then *accordingly* his definition of the infinite might be complexified *one stage further* by an addition, so as to read, not simply: *id quo nil maius…*, 'that than which nothing greater…', but:

> *id eo maius, quo nil maius cogitari possit*
> [that greater than that than which nothing greater can be thought].

But when the topic is fiction, is *Fielding's* (1959) 'history', in the sense of the novel, is the poem, is the metaphor, is the production of *ingenium* and *ars* (Horace, in Brink 1963–82), is the production of artistic genius and, in particular here, the genius that creates *religious* art (but what kind of epithet is that?), Anselm's formula might be further modified:

> *id eo pulchrius, quo nil pulchrius ex imaginatione fingi possit*
> [that more beautiful than that than which nothing
> more beautiful can be imagined].

A further anthropological implicate would then follow:

> *id eo melius sperandum esse, quo nil melius sperari possit*

which means, being interpreted, that for humankind, but not just for humankind, but, in this '*Ecozoic era*', for the '*United Species*' (Swimme and Berry 1994: 4):

> there is that better thing to be hoped for than that than which noth-
> ing better can be hoped for.

For it must be insufficient to say of Jesus of Nazareth, or of anyone else for that matter, that, after he died, he was dead. For you cannot nail a good man down. Or a good woman either. Or bad ones of either.

And this may still be to say nothing of the *apokatastasis*, the 'renewal', not just of 'the temple cell of the goddess Artemis at Magnesia' (Dittenberger, *Syll.* 552 [Moulton and Milligan 1929, s.v.]), but the *apokatastasis panton* (Acts 3.21), (the times) 'whan *aa things* is to be restored' (Lorimer 1983: 205). We are to think of the renewal of *everything*.

This, or something like this, is how Anselm, the philosopher, and how reflection on Anselm, the philosopher, can deal, might deal with the fairy tale of the resurrection: the waking up, the getting up, the standing up, the walking about for 40 days, the going up, the meeting in the air. This is how the philosopher might reflect on fiction, might reflect, that fiction is parasitic upon reality, might reflect on future fact. This is how we can get above it all. And if we will get above it all, it is not unreasonable that we should now, now and then, get, like Longinus, 'overheated' (Brink 1971: 76).

But before the philosopher reflects on tales, the literary critic can tell the philosopher that these discrete tales, these 15-line peri-copes, these metaphorical abridgements, are parts of a great cycle of tales, are chapters in a uchronian utopia, the story of a timeless time and a placeless place. And how Samuel Alexander (1920) would love that! *Space, Time and Deity*!

If you prefer, we are engaged on the history of literature, the history of 'the language of Christian symbolism' (Oakeshott 1983: 50), the 'magical realism' of the Early Christians, their García Márquez (1994) in a different key. And this history of writing, of literature, may be complemented by a study of what musicians and painters, what artists have done with the same material, the discovery of new iconographies, new transpositions, new variations on a theme. But if this is history, it is the study, not of '*res gestae*: actions of human beings that have been done in the past' (Collingwood 1946: 9), but of their artistic imagination, their contemplation, their aesthetic judgment: Here is beauty, the beauty of *whatever it is* that is called 'holiness', a beauty than which nothing more beautiful can be imagined.

Literature, literary criticism, a philosophy of literary criticism: these three, but the greatest of these is literature. While history is part of the whole that is science, aesthetics, too, is a moment. But aesthetics must take account of what I have called 'the gap'. All these (somewhat tortured) reformulations (above) of Anselm's famous words are an attempt to take account (to recall) of the *gap* between what we want to say and that about which we want to say it. It emerges with special force in this essay, when we note that the gap here is the gap between literature and reality and when we note that the relation between literature and reality is, in divers manners and modes, elliptical and indirect.

The present essay has gone so far, but there are points, however, where it needs to go further.

More needs to be said to clarify the distinction between literature in general and religious literature in particular; more on the distinction between high art and the literature of the people. For *what* are the peculiar excellencies, and limitations, of *folk-literature* and *then* what kind of discrimination is to be made between the synoptics, Paul and John? For the bench-marks here, from Sophocles, Shakespeare and Scott, through Eliot and Stevens, to Jacobson and Adams, are too narrowly restricted, to constitute an adequate list of comparators. And is it possible and desirable to give a more determinate answer to the question, What is literary criticism? Kermode, Blackmur and Ricks, say, are critics, Aristotle a philosopher-critic,

Horace and Eliot poet-critics (with Eliot, by early training, a philosopher); and Lowth, of course, too, a classical critic of an eighteenth-century, and Graeco-Roman, sort. But there are more. And are there more, that are *more* to the point?

It is sometimes tempting to think, that the greatest disaster that ever befell the Christian Church was the invention of pen and paper. For it is *persons*, says St Paul (2 Cor. 3.3), that take priority. And while it is reasonable that persons should take time to weep, it is also reasonable that they should, from time to time, give way to hilarity. For hilarity, too, belongs to the ethical life, life *convenienter cum natura*, life in *ac*-cordance and *con*-cordance with nature, a life where ethics cohere with ontology, with 'genesiology', with 'the study of becoming'.

'The virtues required in an heroic poem,' writes Hobbes, 'and indeed in all writings published, are comprehended all in this one word—*discretion*' (1844: iii). I cannot follow Hobbes here, though I must accede, when he goes on to say there of 'profit' to the reader, that

> by profit, I intend not any accession of wealth, but accession of prudence, justice, and fortitude, by the example of such great and noble persons as he introduceth speaking, or describeth acting. For all men love to behold, though not to practise virtue. So that at last the work of an heroic poet is no more but to furnish an ingenuous reader, when his leisure abounds, with the diversion of an honest and delightful story, whether true or feigned.

Hobbes is no cynic, but he is a realist. But does he 'come too short' (*zu kurz kommen*) on the aesthetic? Can the O.T. (the *Oedipus Tyrannus*) be best understood as a 'diversion'? Or, if that example be faulted as too 'élitist' for the man on the Clapham *omnibus*, or the Portobello *nonnullis* (for not *all*, but only *some* can travel there), let us take a different example from 'folk art', a Border ballad, say. But, give or take some differences, as the difference between virtues that are cardinal and virtues that are theological, and speaking more generally than is altogether warranted, it is the intention, I believe, of the New Testament writers to delight the reader with joy and profit the reader with love. And it is their intention to do so by a story that is at the same time both true and feigned, seeing that (in Origen's great phrase, in his *Commentary on St John's Gospel* [x.4], cit. Nineham [1958: 248-49]) 'the true spiritual meaning being often preserved in what at the corporeal level might be called a falsehood'. 'Aesthetic-religious' (*ästhetisch-religiös*: de Wette): it is by the conjunction of profit and delight that the compound epithet is justified.

The task here, the *attempt* here, in this *essay*, in these chapters, has been, not to look for the facts within the fiction (that has recently often been done), but to look for the fiction *within* and *around* the facts. The attempt has been to uncover, with Mackinnon, yet again (1955: 175), the fact that 'writing in the New Testament is poetry rather than prose'. But that fact has implications. And the attempt has been made to follow out some of them.

If the social anthropologist, in his attempt to do justice to the facts, has to turn to fiction (Cohen 1994: 180-92), if the poet, in his attempt to do justice to history, has to turn to poetry (Eliot, 'Little Gidding' V [= 1944: 43]), if Jesus of Nazareth, in his attempt (a failure?) to get his contemporaries to do justice in history, had to turn to the short story, why should we attempt to deny that the Gospel writers did so, too, *about* Jesus, that others have done so, and that we could do so?

To lose the Bible as history is not to *lose truth*, but to lose *one kind of it and find another*. But we have not lost it and do not lose it. We change the question merely. This essay does not ask the historical question, except for the purposes of making use of history as a 'control' discipline, that might shed some light on where the disciplines divide and even inextricably overlap. The question here is *literature* and the attempt to answer *that*. If the reader has marked, let the reader judge: How is that question to be rightly answered? And how is that question to be *beautifully* answered?

But a parting word to Gregor Smith.

In a fine passage the philosopher, Spinoza, writes (*Ethica*, IV, *prop*. XLV, schol. II):

> It is, I say, the part of a wise man to feed himself with moderate, pleasant food and drink, and to take pleasure with perfumes, with the beauty of growing plants, dress, music, sports, and theatres, and other places of this kind which man may use without any hurt to his fellows. For the human body is composed of many parts of different nature which continuously stand in need of new and varied nourishment, so that the body as a whole may be equally apt for performing those things which can follow from its nature, and consequently so

THE NEW TESTAMENT AS TRUE FICTION

that the mind also may be equally apt for understanding many things
at the same time. This manner of living agrees best with our
principles and the general manner of life: from which it follows that
this manner of life is the best of all, and in all ways to be com-
mended, nor is there any need for us to be more clear or more
detailed on this subject (Spinoza 1843: 353 [=1959: 174]).[13]

It used to be said by his students, in a saying that contained as
much truth as such slanders usually do, that the only conversion,
for which Gregor Smith in Glasgow was responsible, was conversion to the London Wine Society. There are many places, in this
essay, where there was need to have been both more clear and
more detailed. But it cannot be concluded without being clear on
this, that it was the privilege of his students to sit at the feet of one
who was both fearless in speculation and faithful to his convictions.

In his *Essay on Metaphysics* (1940: 172), Collingwood cites
Wordsworth:

> The Child is father of the Man;
> And I could wish my days to be
> Bound each to each by natural piety,

and recalls how Samuel Alexander 'said that natural piety should
be the clue to metaphysical thinking'. Metaphysics 'were revealed
to any babe who would accept them as the child Wordsworth
accepted the rainbow'. For 'The Son of the Child', '[t]he rainbow is
a rainbow still, and the man who knows it for an effect of refrac-
tion looks at it with the same eyes with which he saw it as a child,
before he had ever heard of the spectrum and the prism' (Collingwood 1940: 174).

Gregor Smith went out *nesciens quo iret*, 'tuik the gate

---

13. 'Viri, inquam, sapientis est, moderato et suavi cibo et potu se reficere et
recreare, ut et odoribus, plantarum virentium amoenitate, ornatu, musica,
ludis exercitatoriis, theatris et aliis huiusmodi, quibus unusquisque absque ullo
alterius damno uti potest. Corpus namque humanum ex plurimis diversae
naturae partibus componitur, quae continuo novo alimento indigent et vario,
ut totum corpus ad omnia, quae ex ipsius natura sequi possunt, aeque aptum
sit, et consequenter ut mens etiam aeque apta sit ad plura simul intelligendum.
Hoc itaque vivendi institutum et cum nostris principiis et cum communi praxi
optime convenit; quare si quae alia, haec vivendi ratio optima est et omnibus
modis commendanda, nec opus est, de his clarius, neque prolixius agere.'

onkennin whaur he wis gaein til' (Heb. 11.8, Lorimer 1983: 386).
Anchored in the tradition, but ready to innovate, he left his followers signposts. We must, then, follow them and go on, listening
not only to 'the oral tradition of the wind', but to the wind.

And to the wind alone.

Coda to the Canon: The Plot Thickens (The Song of Solomon and the Sublation of Law: Canticle 2.4)

Thy teeth *are* like a flock *of sheep*
that are even shorn,
which came up from the washing;
whereof every one bear twins,
and none *is* barren among them.

Orlandoni Furioso:

τί δ᾽ ἄρα περὶ πράγματος;
[What about thing, then?]
(Walls *frequenter dictum*)

The problem here in this Coda is this: How do the 'teeth' of the first stich of Cant. 4.2 relate to the 'twins' of the fourth? What is the 'logic', Waismann's 'logic of poetry' (1977), here? What, here, is happening in and outside the mind, or the imagination, of the oriental poet? And then (again) the content: What is to be made of *this*? And how does this kind of 'love' relate to all other kinds? And to law (or *torah*)? Or (classically): How does *agape*, 'Christian love', relate to *eros*, 'passionate love'? And, further, how important are *words* here? And *texts* here? What is the relation between *words* and *things*?

How does the *academy* relate to *life*?

But some further levity may be allowed in what, after all, is the *concluding*, or *deluding* section. *Alea jacta est*, 'the die is cast'.

How aleatory can you get?

Pro-oemium:

'Once upon a time...'
'[T]he story says that...' (Collingwood 1940: 56).

This all began (did it?) with Donald, my dog, trying to replicate the Quorn and the Pytchley in Stockbridge, Edinburgh (we have more foxes *here*, you know, more 'vermin', my Aunt Dahlia would say, than those hunters have). Cant. 2.4 reads:

and his banner over me was...

When Donald gets excited by foxes (last night in Inverleith Park, Donald and a fox were both eating out of the same dustbin [doubly exciting]),

his banner over him is tail.

His tail wags furiously. His tail wags the dog. Donald thinks it, for dogs think (Aristotle's *De anima*, of course), an interesting symbiosis. Or as St Jerome would have put this:

VEXILLUM SUPER EUM EST CAUDA

And if *CAUDA* is *CODA*, 'Bob's your uncle'.

Central Section:

Now, then (but which? 'now', or 'then'?), let us take up 'thing', which 'as a thing is something of a thing, probably' (as one of my old teachers [Griffith (1979)] would add and as another of my old teachers [Deas (1931)]), a tacit Scot, would not, but would look out instead at the chimneys on the Senate House roof.

Deas had in his room a picture of Macbeth, the one by James Martin (1789 [a good year]–1854). The picture hangs in the National Gallery of Scotland, for it is the other one (London), which has Piero's *Baptism*. Is Martin's Macbeth there for the history's sake, the history of the kings and queens of Scotland (Adam 1957: 381-87)? Or is it here for the Scottish play's sake, for Macbeth seems to be having a discussion about promotion on a blasted heath with three, thinly dressed, female companions, who have stopped his way to offer 'strange intelligence' (*Macbeth* I.iii.76)?

But begin we must, so long as nothing, either now, or then, is said that is 'inappropriate in tone and substance' (Weir 1996: vi). I think it has been said: 'One cannot be theological about cows.' And *mutatis mutandis* this should apply, too, to dogs. So we cannot properly begin *there*, we cannot begin with *them*. But I think it has also been said (perhaps the Heaton, who supplied Ramsey [1966] with Heaton [1949]): 'Some people like their religion red-hot on Sundays. I like mine lukewarm throughout the week.' (Was this to neglect St Paul?) Heaton was trying, if I remember right to be rude about Dissenters. So we will now begin properly:

Beginning of The Coda:

The Beginning is this:

> *ET VEXILLUM EIUS SUPER EUM EST CARMEN*
> [and the banner over him is song]

Which means, being interpreted, what?

> Hang out our banners on the outward walls

says Macbeth (V.v.1). But this is not much to the point. I think that we must concentrate on Carmen (not the Spanish one), but on 'song'.

Someone somewhere, in Scandinavia, I think (but I cannot now track it down), says: *canto ergo sum*. Has it something to do with the music of evangelical propositions? Do we not recall from the prolegomena to the Coda (above), the Gregor Smith section, do we not recall the *Journal de psychologie* of 1923, where M. Loisy says (1923: 439): *Mais c'est l'air qui fait la chanson, et nos évangiles se chantent* ('But it is the air [my word-processor is trying to write: *aor*, which is (is not it?) the Hebrew for 'light'?] that makes the song and it is a song our gospels sing')? Or is Loisy using here, not the *passivum divinum*, the 'divine passive', but the 'divine reflexive'?

Does the Canticles text (2.4), the 'banner' one, not mean, that a song rings gladly over him, as a tail waves cheerfully over the tail end of a cheerful dog?

Dogs? Yes (*pace* Heaton). For it is part of *The Universe Story*, after all (Swimme and Berry 1992), that God's life made the Dog's life, too, and that, 12,000 years ago in the Neolithic Village (Stockbridge again, I suppose), the dog became the companion of the human being (274).

But is this the right textual reading? Does the text *actually* read: *CAUDA* (or: *CODA*)?

St Jerome (again) is no help to us here. His Hebrew, perhaps, let him down. Anyway, so far as can be ascertained from the *Biblia Sacra juxta Latinam vulgatam versionem ad codicum fidem (jussu PII PP. XII) cura et studio monachorum Abbatiae Pontificae Sancti Hieronymi in Urbe Ordinis Sancti Benedicti edita... MDCCCCLVII* (how they *do* go on!), beginning from: *In principio*...and ending with the *Undecimum Volumen*, the nearest thing to 'and his banner over me was...' is:

introduxit me in cellam vinariam

Now that's all right. That's a bit of all right. For, though it literally means 'he introduced me to a vinous cell/oenological trial-chamber', it very nearly means:

He introduced me to the London Wine Society

And that would be Gregor Smith again (see above). And, with the right locative addition, *Londinio* (or some such [did the Romans *have* London?]), that is what it *would* mean.

But, for that verse (Cant., or Song 2.4a), St Jerome's disciple, King James, comes up here with:

He brought me to the banqueting house

which again makes one think of London, Chancellor Brown's fine clothes, and 'silken dalliance'. And then, if one is taking the allegorical reading of the *Song of Songs*, that would make God (for the Jews) and Jesus (for the Christians) into something like a 'glorified' Lord Mayor (von Balthasar for 'glorified' [!]). And would make the occasion a Lord Mayor's Banquet, with a lot of fictional, if not fictive, speeches (depends on the Government of the day, I suppose).

Well, the Jews and the Christians can do what they like with a collection of young men's drinking songs, but we must recall Bonhoeffer's letter of 2 June 1944, where (to say it so) it 'stands written' that:

> I must say I should prefer to read it as an ordinary love song, and that is probably the best 'Christological' exposition (Bonhoeffer 1971: 315).

But I should have thought that, rather than 'banqueting house', Luther's Weinkeller, 'wine-cellar', or *Gasthaus* (Song 2.4a [1565: I, 342]) was much nearer to the Hebrew *beth yayyin*, 'house of wine', or to the Greek of the LXX (εἰς τὸν οἶκον τοῦ οἴνου, *eis ton oikon tou oinou*). And what, had he got round to it, would Lorimer's *Old Testament in Scots* have said? Or Hugh MacDiarmid? *A Drunk Man Looks at the Song of Songs*? Or (to relapse into learning again) another *Paraphrase*, more *Dionysiaka*, by the well-known Nonnus?

And then, at Song 2.4b, we have:

> *ORDINAVIT IN ME CARITATEM*
> [he ordained in me charity]

But one is seeing the invisible, even after ploughing through 'The Application of Thought to Textual Criticism' (Housman 1961: 131-50), if one is seeing, how it is possible, in an impossible subject (textual criticism), to move from *ORDINAVIT* to *VEXILLUM*. And, even less, how it is possible to get:

> *ET VEXILLUM EIUS SUPER EUM EST CARMEN*
> [his banner over him is song]

Then after ploughing, but not very thoroughly, through the *Appendix* of the *Undecimum Volumen*, the eleventh volume of the Vulgate, the *MDCCCCLVII* one, the one on the *de codice Sangallensi rescripto 194 (m)* (is that 'metres'?), I have, like Jerome, and the 'men in the boat' with him, caught nothing, though, by dint of searching about, I *have* managed to find the following *variae lectiones*, variant readings. There are three.

I begin with two:

> *ET VEXILLUM EIUS SUPER EUM EST CODA*
> [and his banner over him is a coda]

(A coda waves cheerfully over the end of a book?)

> *ET VEXILLUM EIUS SUPER EUM EST FABULA*
> [and his banner over him is a fable]

The source of this last reading, *FABULA*, a *Roman* source, is the *Nova Vulgata* of the:

> *Sacros. Oecum. Concilii Vaticani II Ratione Habita jussu PAULI*
> *PP. VI RECOGNITA auctoritate IOANNIS PAULI PP.II promulgata*

Permit me to diverge, for a moment, into the last word there: *promulgata*, 'promulge'.

This word has the authority of the copy of the *Shorter Oxford*, that I got, by grace (from you), where, and when other rivers than *Allt*s (Gaelic 'streams') flowed.

And Murray's *Dictionary*, too, permits it, of course (*vide* s.v.). You will recall:

> 1495 *Act* II *Hen.* VII, c.59 *Preamble*, An utlarie upon him [is]
> therupon *promulged*.

And even Butler's *Analogy* (1736) has it. And Blackstone (1766). And even 'Mrs Jay', in *Holden with Cords* (1874), or, rather (so the British Library Catalogue [but which is right?]): *Holden with the Cords*. And (this you may have forgotten) 'Mrs. Jay's' work was a pseudepigraphon (like *George Eliot*), W.M.L.J. being, in fact, J.M.L. W(oodruff). It was a 'Tale', or *FABULA* (fable, story), which went through at least two further editions, appearing in 1883 *twice*, both in London, once with Ward, Lock & Co., and once with Griffith & Farran. It seems likely that the 1874 edition was in the Home Treasure Library.

Now that that has been clarified (did you want it clear?), I conclude with the intelligence that, for 'promulge', the *Shorter Oxford* (s.v.) has: '...2...to bring before the public, to publish (a book, etc.).' And one might almost say 'placard'. Quite relevant, you see, though not all of it, of course.

Beginning, then, now, with the first of these variants, the following, I think, we are 'licensed' (Ramsey's word [*passim*]) to say:

'Coda' cannot be right.

Though there *is* a 'coda', or 'end' to everything, I suppose. 'Who am I?' to cite again that sentence from Gregor Smith, on 'The Resurrection' (1969: 136), 'I am just another of those same obscure people who like everyone else is more or less conscious of the futility of his existence, and of how it is rushing towards death'.

This quotation comes towards the middle of the end of his 'Resurrection' essay, which itself comes towards the end of the end of his *Essay* (his name for a book) on *The Free Man*. For Gregor Smith a collection of essays is itself an Essay, *un ballon d'essai*, 'a small balloon for determining the direction of the wind'.

For his books (to use an Aristotelean word, 'what the poet should aim at' [*Po.* 1452b28]), were 'stochastic', were 'guessing', were 'feeling their way', though the next word after 'stochastic', in the *Shorter Oxford*, I hasten to add, should also be taken into account: 'stoccado': '*Obs. exc. arch.* 1569. [Corruptly a. It. *stoccata*, f. *stocco* point of sword, dagger...] A thrust or stab with a pointed weapon.'

For this word, 'stoccado', recalls '*inevitably*' (Mackinnon's word *passim*) Burckhardt's *History of the Renaissance in Italy*, and the passage in that book, where, after some remarks on the family of

Sforza del Destino, the following is said of a Renaissance gentleman of the family of Malatesta:

> Unscrupulousness, impiety, military skill, and high culture have been seldom combined in one individual as in Sigismondo Malatesta...the accumulated crimes of such a family must at last outweigh all talent, however great, and drag the tyrant into the abyss (1955: 21; contra Dom David [Knowles 1963: 16-30]).

Can one, then, make a stab at a problem (fiction, say) without faction as the result? Or better, can one, like (and unlike) 'the wounded surgeon', '[plie] the steel' (Eliot, 'East Coker' IV [= 1944: 20])?

What if fictions can be *true* fictions? What if more or less historical fictions (less? more?) can be *true* fictions? What if 'Baptism, Temptation, Transfiguration, the Entry into Jerusalem, the Institution of the Eucharist' (Walls 1995: 9) are *true fictions* of this kind? What if each is, within a work of art (*Kunstwerk*: Walls 1995: 7), a work of art? What if each, appearing as an 'icon' (1995: 9), is one of these, is a little work of art within a greater? What if they are little *drams*, I mean *dramas* (aren't word-processors marvellous?)? And what *is* drama? And (you say) what *is* Theo-drama (von Balthasar 1988)? *What about that 'thing', then, now?*

This returns us to '*FABULA*', the 'middle' reading above (as Aristotle might call it [*Po.* 1450b27]):

The middle reading, *FABULA*, 'fable', 'story', is the one that should *have* one, a middle, that is. And should have, too, a beginning and an end.

But the end, as we all know, as we all *can* know, is an end with a 'to be continued...' at the end. The end is an end, with *The Sense of an Ending* (Kermode 1967) it may be, but is, too, an end with the sense of a beginning. And, Bultmann would add, as he added in Edinburgh (I say it, advisedly, again) in his Giffords (1955, published in 1957: 155), is an end even in the middle:

> In every moment slumbers the possibility of being the eschatological moment. You must awaken it.

This is the *end* of Maxwell (1943), of Gregor Smith's (1943), of T.S. Eliot. It is 'Burnt Norton's' *Still Point*, 'the still point of the turning world' (1944: 9 [= 'Burnt Norton' II]).

A story (all the 'incorrigible plurality' of me has been trying to maintain) is a true fiction.

Or all stories are true, but some are truer than others. Even Spinoza thinks that there is a sense (what?) in which all stories are true, in which all that the 'imagination', a Spinozan, or Benedictine(!) *t.t.* (*terminus technicus*), tells is true. But Spinoza thinks also that they must be distinguished from the kind of 'stories', that (*t.t.* again) *reason* tells, and that these are different again from the kind told by 'intuition' (is *that* like, or something like, *metaphysical* reason?).

But what Spinoza is saying is only that the 'concatenation of the modifications of the human body' (my God!) are to be distinguished from 'that concatenation of ideas which takes place according to the order of the intellect through which the mind perceives things through their first causes' (1959: 56 (= *Ethica* II, *prop*. XVIII, *not*.).

Or, more simply, that art is to be distinguished from philosophy. Or, more strongly, not with Spinoza, but with Paton, with the *Patonian parenthesis* (1965: 19), that the artist, compared with the philosopher, can do 'much more' (see above, in the body of the book, for the whole of Paton there; it's a *Leitmotiv*, really).

The Sense of a Beginning

But to come to the tale end, the 'to be continued', of the reading of the processing of the word, we reach, not Jerome (King James we must think about 'with a later reason' [Stevens 1955: 399 (= III. i)]), but the reading of the *Nova Vulgata*:

> ET VEXILLUM EIUS SUPER ME EST CARITAS
> [And his banner over me is love].

and, 'with a later reason', King James:

> And his banner over me was love.

But how does the New Vulgate get '*is*'? Or how did those Jacobaeans, those Jacobites, get '*was*'? 'Was' is not what we find in the Hebrew, nor, for that matter, neither is 'is' in the Latin.

But big texts, with big words (*CARITAS*? von Balthasar 1977?), are baffling. Would it not be better to turn to Solomons fong (*sic.* 1611) ['Christ sheweth the graces of the Church'] 6.2a, 6.2b, 6.2c and to d?:

Thy teeth *are* as a flocke of sheepe
which goe vp from the washing,
wherof euery one beareth twinnes,
and there is not one barren among them.

Now I remember asking once, whether 'beareth twinnes' meant 'double-teeth' and your reply was: 'Come to Little Gidding.'
We went to Little Gidding:

If you came this way,
Taking the route you would be likely to take
From the place you would be likely to come from,
If you came this way in may time, you would find the hedges...
(Eliot 1944: 35 [= 'Little Gidding' I])

But I do not remember the hedges—and neither did Eliot, I suspect, the old poetic fraud. But then they are all frauds, these poets, aren't they?

But the *real* question is: What *kind* of frauds are they? It is all (to recall) in the fraud, Hesiod (*Th*. 27), who got it from the fraud, Homer (*Od*. 19.203). What we find there is: 'lies like the truth'

ψεύδεα...ἐτύμοισιν ὁμοῖα
[*pseudea...etumoisin homoia*]

We know, Hesiod says, or (even worse) the Muses say (and the Muses are simply divine), how to tell lies:

ἴδμεν ψεύδεα πολλὰ λέγειν ἐτύμοισιν ὁμοῖα.
[*idmen pseudea polla legein etumoisin homoia*]
[we know how to tell many lies like the truth]

You will recall, too, that we have been enjoined 'to incline our minds like reflectors to catch the light of the early Plato and the whole Montaigne' (Blackmur 1954: 375). But even the early Plato, philosopher *and* poet, was highly suspicious of poetry (Murdoch 1978). And Collingwood, in his lucid exposition of the Platonic position (1925b) shows that (quite rightly, in my opinion, though I don't think I have always held this, that, even for the early Plato (and the whole Montaigne?), poetry, in the end is *cognitio confusa* and that the critic needs not only to *read* poetry, but to *think* about it.

But 'humankind' (as the poet truly says) 'cannot bear very much thinking'. And especially (one might be forgiven for thinking), humankind of the presbyterian sort.

But to this present Essay (you would say), to this confused study of confused cognition (I am afraid), there should be added Lady Julian and Carl Gustav Jung (and [I would now add] Aichele and Pippin on phantasy in the New Testament [1992]). And (*you* would now add)—to Collingwood's *Speculum Mentis* (1924a), to Collingwood's 'through a glass in an enigma' (1924a *ad init.*, in Paul's Greek [1 Cor. 13.12]), to Collingwood's *Autobiography* (1939) and to Newman's *Essay on the Development of Christian Doctrine* (1846), there should be added *An Essay on the Development of Christian Ethics*. Oh? What would *that* look like? Tell us.

And we would both add, too, these specially excerpted words of Collingwood, which come from *Speculum Mentis* (1924a: 151):

> God is not known, he is adored. We cannot think him, we can only love and fear him.

And, indeed, this Essay, the present book, is no more than an attempt at a kind of a specification of the Collingwoodian quincunx of art, religion, science, history and philosophy, if (1) you omit the science, (2) keep the history as a 'control' discipline and (3) forgive the philosophy. Gregor Smith did the history by making history porous to 'the transcendent', while I have tried to do something with art: with tragedy, with comedy, with beauty. For with both of the former, the latter must come.

But texts, as you point out von Balthasar pointing out, in *Love Alone: The Way of Revelation* (1977), as Paul pointed out before him: 'the fleshlie tablets o the hairt' (2 Cor. 3.3 [Lorimer 1983: 308]), are not worth the stone they are chiselled on. We must turn rather to the Cartland coefficient (or do I mean Proust?).

Ms Cartland, to take her, has written some 300 texts, 21 of these in 1976, 24 in 1977 (it is at this kind of productivity that the Research Assessment Exercise is aimed, though the mark is sometimes missed).

But I wish to cite here only the Brent Housebound Library Services copy (stamped 'Withdrawn') of *Love and the Marquis*, and only to the first page of that historical novel and there only to lines 13-16, where we find the Bultmannian toast and the register of Heideggerian *Zukünftigkeit* (futurity):

> He [the Earl of Kingsclere] drank deeply as if he was in need of it, and then with what appeared almost a reckless gesture he raised his glass and said aloud: 'To the future!' (Cartland 1982: 7).

Cartland, here, should be taken together with Bultmann (1953: 32 [= 1960a: 39]): 'Only those who are loved are capable of loving.' And should be taken (again) with the following also:

> If, as St. Paul believed, law is given for the better ordering of life, and grace is something of the same general kind but a higher term in the same scale, it is no paradox that grace should perform exactly what law promised to perform but did not (Collingwood 1933: 89).

And it is in this context (shall I say it again?), where 'grace', or its synonym, *CARITAS*, *sublates* law (it is a philosophical *'overlap'* [Collingwood 1933]), that, though 'Synne is behovabil', the twin assertions become possible, that (1) you can't nail a good man down (resurrection! awakening!) and (2), more broadly, as broadly as you like, that:

> Al shall be wel
> & al shall be wel
> & al manner of thyng shal be wele
> (Julian 1950: 56 (cf. Eliot, 'Little Gidding' III [= 1944: 41]

But, I know very well, that, when you get this thing, which is something of a thing, when you get this Coda, and when you get what the Coda comes after, the tribute to our friend, Gregor Smith, and *The Preceding Notes towards Some of the Literature, Some of the Literary Criticism and Some of the Aesthetics, that Fill Full Some of the Interstices between Abraham and Wittgenstein*—I know very well, that you will say, at the end, as you said at the beginning:

> τί δ' ἄρα περὶ πραγματος;
> [What about thing, then?]

Well, anyway:
Feci. (Fake he?)
Taceo.
This Coda and this Essay has here an end, that begins again with your question (better than a question mark?),...

Glenadale,
Southend,
By Campbeltown,
Argyll.

'Washing Day', 24 September 1995
(contra 'AT SEA' [Templeton 1905: 80])

PS 1 (I am quoting from memory as I do not have the Folios here, and the dog has a 'banner over him'):

Dun.   This cottage hath a pleasant seat; the spirit
        Nimbly and sweetly recommends itself
        Unto our gentle senses.

Ban.   This guest of summer,
        The temple-haunting martlet, does approve
        By his lov'd mansionry that the heaven's breath
        Smells wooingly here; no jutty, frieze,
        Buttress, nor coign of vantage, but this bird
        Hath made her pendent bed and procreant cradle.
        Where they most breed and haunt, I have observ'd
        The air is delicate...

(Shakespeare, *Macbeth* I.vi.1-10)

PS 2: It seems, too, that the rainbow ends here, in the glen. And it seems to be the home of Hopkins's pittock. Farmer John's wheat is not 'orient' just now, for we have 'autumn umber', but it will be... (Gosh, what a lot of texts and people there are, to live and die and live by!)...

PS 3: From Kettridge's *French and English Military Dictionary* (1940), it appears that the French for 'manpower' (s.v.) is: *les effectifs*. What is the French for the opposite?

Bibliography

Ackroyd, P.
1993   *T.S. Eliot* (London: Penguin Books).
Adam, R.J.
1957   'The Real Macbeth: King of Scots, 1040–1054', *History Today* 7: 381-
            87.
Adams, D.
1979   *The Hitch-Hiker's Guide to the Galaxy* (London: Pan Books).
1992   *The Hitch-Hiker's Guide to the Galaxy: A Trilogy in Four Parts*
            (London: Pan Books).
1995   *The Hitch-Hiker's Guide to the Galaxy: A Trilogy in Five Parts*
            (London: Heinemann).
Addis, W.E.
1914   'Elijah', in T.K. Cheyne and J.S. Black, *Encyclopaedia Biblica*
            (London: A. & C. Black).
Aichele, G., Jr
1985   *The Limits of Story* (Chico, CA: Scholars Press).
1992   'The Fantastic in the Discourse of Jesus', *Semeia* 60: 53-66.
1996   *Jesus Framed* (London: Routledge).
Aichele, G., and T. Pippin
1992   'Introduction: Why the Fantastic?', *Semeia* 60: 1-6.
?Ailred of Rievaulx?
1165   *De situ Albanie, que in se figuram hominis habet, quomodo fuit
            primitus in septem regionibus divisa, quibusque nominibus
            antiquitus sit vocata, et a quibus inhabitata* (Paris: MS Colb. Bib.
            Imp. 4126, fol. 26 verso; also in Skene 1867).
Alexander, S.
1920   *Space, Time, and Deity* (2 vols.; London: Macmillan).
1933   *Beauty and Other Forms of Value* (London: Macmillan).
Allegro, J.M.
1970   *The Sacred Mushroom and the Cross: A Study of the Nature and
            Origins of Christianity within the Fertility Cults of the Ancient
            Near East* (London: Hodder & Stoughton).
Allingham, W.
1865   *The Ballad Book* (London: Macmillan).
Alter, R.
1981   *The Art of Biblical Narrative* (New York: Basic Books).
Altizer, T.J.J.
1967   *The Gospel of Christian Atheism* (London: Collins).
Amis, K.
1961   *Lucky Jim* (London: Penguin Books).
Anderson, J.
1981   *Sir Walter Scott and History* (Edinburgh: Edina).

Anselm
1965   *St. Anselm's Proslogion* (ed. M.J. Charlesworth; Oxford: Oxford
            University Press).
Aristotle,
1907a   *De Anima* (ed. R.D. Hicks; Cambridge: Cambridge University Press).
1907b   *The Poetics of Aristotle* (ed. S.H. Butcher; London: Macmillan, 4th
            edn).
1909   *Aristotle on the Art of Poetry* (ed. I. Bywater; Oxford: Clarendon
            Press).
1924   'Rhetorica', in W.R. Roberts (ed.), *The Works of Aristotle*, XI (ed.
            W.D. Ross; Oxford: Oxford University Press).
1925a   'Ethica Nicomachea', in W.R. Roberts (ed.), *The Works of Aristotle*,
            XI (ed. W.D. Ross; Oxford: Oxford University Press).
1968   *Aristotle: Poetics* (ed. D.W. Lucas; Oxford: Clarendon Press).
Ashton, J.
1986a   *The Interpretation of John* (London: SPCK; Philadelphia: Fortress
            Press).
1986b   'The Transformation of Wisdom', *New Testament Studies* 32: 161-86.
1991   *Understanding the Fourth Gospel* (Oxford: Clarendon Press).
1994   *Studying John* (Oxford: Clarendon Press).
Auerbach, E.
1953   *Mimesis: The Representation of Reality in Western Literature*
            (trans. W.R. Trask; Princeton, NJ: Princeton University Press).
Auld, A.G. (ed.)
1993   *Understanding Poets and Prophets: Essays in Honour of George
            Wishart Anderson* (JSOTSup, 152; Sheffield: JSOT Press).
Austin, J.L.
1962   *How to Do Things with Words* (Oxford: Clarendon Press).
Bacon, F.
1858   *Works*, I (ed. J. Spedding, R.L. Ellis and D.D. Heath; London: Long-
            mans).
1870   *Works*, IV (ed. J. Spedding, R.L. Ellis and D.D. Heath; London: Long-
            mans, new edn).
Baillie, D.M.
1957   *The Theology of the Sacraments and Other Papers* (London: Faber
            & Faber).
Balthasar, H.U. von
1961   *Herrlichkeit: Eine theologische Ästhetik*, I (Einsiedeln: Johannes
            Verlag).
1962   *Herrlichkeit: Eine theologische Äesthetik*, II.1, II.2 (Einsiedeln:
            Johannes Verlag).
1965   *Herrlichkeit: Eine theologische Äesthetik*, III.1.i, III.1.ii (Einsiedeln:
            Johannes Verlag).
1967   *Herrlichkeit: Eine theologische Äesthetik*, III.2.i (Einsiedeln: Johannes
            Verlag).
1969   *Herrlichkeit: Eine theologische Äesthetik*, III.2.ii, III.2.iii (Einsiedeln:
            Johannes Verlag).

1977   *Love Alone: The Way of Revelation* (ed. A. Dru; London: Sheed & Ward).

1988   *Theo-Drama: Theological Dramatic Theory* (3 vols.; San Francisco: Ignatius Press).

Barry P.

1904   'On Luke xv.25, *symphonia*: Bagpipe', *Journal of Biblical Literature* 23: 180-90.

Beer, F.

1978   *Julian of Norwich's Revelations of Divine Love, The Shorter Version ed. from B.L. Add. MS 37790* (Heidelberg: Carl Winter Universitätsverlag).

Berenson, B.

1952   *The Italian Painters of the Renaissance* (London: Phaidon).

1954   *Piero della Francesca, or the Ineloquent in Art* (London: Chapman & Hall).

Bergonzi B.

1969   *T.S. Eliot: Four Quartets: A Casebook* (London: Macmillan).

Bernstein, J.M.

1984   *The Philosophy of the Novel* (Brighton: Harvester).

Bethge, E.

1967   *Dietrich Bonhoeffer: Theologe—Christ—Zeitgenosse* (Munich: Chr. Kaiser Verlag).

1970   *Dietrich Bonhoeffer: Theologian—Christian—Contemporary* (London: Collins).

Bevan, E.

1962   *Symbolism and Belief* (London: Collins).

Biblia Sacra

1957   *Biblia Sacra juxta Latinam Vulgatam Versionem*, XI (Libri Salomonis; Vatican City: Libreria Editrice Vaticana).

Black, M.

1954   *An Aramaic Approach to the Gospels and Acts* (Oxford: Clarendon Press, 2nd edn).

Black, M.

1962   'Metaphor', in *Models and Metaphors* (Ithaca, NY: Cornell University Press): 25-47.

1979   'More about Metaphor', in *Metaphor and Thought* (Cambridge: Cambridge University Press): 19-43.

Black, M.H.

1963   'The Printed Bible', in S.L. Greenslade (ed.), *The Cambridge History of the Bible* (Cambridge: Cambridge University Press).

Blackmur, R.P.

1954   *Language as Gesture* (London: George Allen & Unwin).

1985   'An Abstraction Blooded', in C. Doyle (ed.), *Wallace Stevens: The Critical Heritage* (London: Routledge & Kegan Paul): 217-22 (also 1943: *Partisan Review* 10: 297-301).

Blaikie, W.G.

1905   *The Life of David Livingstone* (London: John Murray).

Boler, J.F.
1963   *Charles Peirce and Scholastic Realism: A Study of Peirce's Relation to John Duns Scotus* (Seattle: University of Washington).
Bonaventura
1754   *Itinerarium mentis in Deum, in Opera Sixti V. Pont. Max. jussu diligentissime emendata* (5 vols.; Venice: Joan Baptistae Albritii Hier. F.).
Bonhoeffer, D.
1951   *Widerstand und Ergebung* (Munich: Chr. Kaiser Verlag).
1955a   *Ethics* (ed. E. Bethge; London: SCM Press).
1955   *Schöpfung und Fall* (Munich: Chr. Kaiser Verlag).
1959   *Creation and Fall* (ET; London: SCM Press).
1971   *Letters and Papers from Prison* (London: SCM Press, enlarged edn).
1986   *Werke. IX. Jugend und Studium 1918-1927* (Munich: Chr. Kaiser Verlag).
1991   *Werke. X. Barcelona, Berlin, Amerika* (Munich: Chr. Kaiser Verlag).
1992   *Werke. VI. Ethik* (Munich: Chr. Kaiser Verlag).
1994   *Werke. VII. Fragmente aus Tegel* (Munich: Chr. Kaiser Verlag).
1998   *Werke. VIII. Widerstand und Ergebung* (Munich: Chr. Kaiser Verlag).
Botterweck, G.J., and H. Ringgren
1982   *Theologisches Wörterbuch zum Alten Testament*, III (Stuttgart: W. Kohlhammer).
Bowra, M.
1938   *Early Greek Elegists* (Oxford: Oxford University Press).
1949   'Mimnermus', in *The Oxford Classical Dictionary* (Oxford: Oxford University Press).
Boyle, A.
1959   *Spinoza's Ethics* (London: Dent).
Briggs, C.A.
1900   'The Use of *ruach* in the Old Testament', *Journal of Biblical Literature* 19.2: 132-45.
Brink, C.O.
1963   *Horace on Poetry: Prolegomena to the Literary Epistles* (Cambridge: Cambridge University Press).
1971   *Horace on Poetry: The 'Ars Poetica'* (Cambridge: Cambridge University Press).
1982   *Horace on Poetry: Epistles Book II: The Letters to Augustus and Florus* (Cambridge: Cambridge University Press).
Broneer, O.T.
1930   *Results of the Excavations Conducted by the American School of Classical Studies at Athens. IV, Part II. Terracotta Lamps* (Cambridge, MA: Harvard University Press).
1962   'The Apostle Paul and the Isthmian Games', *Biblical Archaeologist* 25: 2-31.
1977   *Isthmia Excavations by the University of Chicago under the Auspices of the American School of Classical Studies at Athens. III. Terracotta Lamps* (Princeton: American School of Classical Studies at Athens).

Brown, C.
1998   ' "A Huge Burden of Guilt": Christianity and Nature', *Expository Times* 109: 139-42.
Brown, G.M.
1995   'The Road to Emmaus', in *idem*, *Winter Tales* (London: John Murray).
Buchan, D.
1985   *A Book of Scottish Ballads* (London: Routledge & Kegan Paul).
Bultmann, R.
1950   *Das Evangelium des Johannes* (Göttingen: Vandenhoeck & Ruprecht).
1952a   'Das Problem der Hermeneutik', in *Glauben und Verstehen*, II (Tübingen: J.C.B. Mohr [Paul Siebeck]): 211-35.
1952b   *Theology of the New Testament*, I (London: SCM Press, 4th edn).
1953   'New Testament and Mythology', in *idem*, *Kerygma and Myth* (trans. R.H. Fuller; London: SPCK).
1957   *History and Eschatology* (Edinburgh: Edinburgh University Press).
1958   *Geschichte der synoptischen Tradition* (Göttingen: Vandenhoeck and Ruprecht, 4th edn).
1960a   'Neues Testament und Mythologie', in H-W. Bartsch and H. Reich (eds.), *Kerygma und Mythos* (Hamburg: Herbert Reich, 4th edn).
1960b   *Die Erforschung der synoptischen Evangelien* (Berlin: Alfred Töpelmann, 3rd edn).
1961   *Theologie des Neuen Testaments* (Tübingen: J.C.B. Mohr [Paul Siebeck]).
1965   *Glauben und Verstehen*, IV (Tübingen: J.C.B. Mohr [Paul Siebeck]).
1967   *Exegetica* (Tübingen: J.C.B. Mohr [Paul Siebeck]).
1971   *The Gospel of John: A Commentary* (Philadelphia: Westminster Press, 11th edn).
1972   *History of the Synoptic Tradition* (Oxford: Basil Blackwell).
1984   *Theologische Enzyklopädie* (Tübingen: J.C.B. Mohr [Paul Siebeck]).
1988   *Neues Testament und Mythologie: Das Problem der Entmythologisierung der neutestamentlichen Verkündigung* ([with introduction by] E. Jüngel; Munich: Chr. Kaiser Verlag).
Burckhardt, J.
1955   *The Civilisation of the Renaissance in Italy* (trans. S.G.C. Middlemore; London: Phaidon, 2nd edn).
Burke, K.
1945   *A Grammar of Motives* (Englewood Cliffs, NJ: Prentice-Hall).
1966   *Language as Symbolic Action* (Berkeley: University of California Press).
1970   *The Rhetoric of Religion: Studies in Logology* (Berkeley: University of California Press).
Burney, C.F.
1925   *The Poetry of our Lord* (Oxford: Oxford University Press).
Burton, R.W.B.
1962   *Pindar's Pythian Odes* (Oxford: Oxford University Press).

Butler, S.
1934   *Erewhon* (revised edn, with introduction by A.L. Huxley; New York: Pynson Printers for the members of the Limited Editions Club).
n.d.   *Nehwon* (Erewhon: Ydobon).
Butlin, M., A. Wilton and J. Gage
1974   *Turner, 1775-1851* (London: Tate Gallery).
Caimbeul, M.M.
1987   *Bailtean* [Villages/Towns] (Glaschu [Glasgow]): Gairm Publications).
1990   *Bailtean* (Mull Recordings [Quinish, Isle of Mull]: MR1018).
Cam, H.
1961   *Historical Novels* (General Series, 48; London: Historical Association Pamphlets).
Campbell, D.A.
1967   *Greek Lyric Poetry* (London: Macmillan).
Campbell, G.
1988   *The Philosophy of Rhetoric* (ed. L.F. Bitzer; Carbondale, IL: Southern Illinois University Press).
Carroll, L.
1929   *Alice in Wonderland* (London: J.M. Dent).
Carroll, R.P. (ed.)
1992   *Text as Pretext: Essays in Honour of Robert Davidson* (JSOTSup, 138; Sheffield: JSOT Press).
Carter, B.A.R.
1981   'A Mathematical Interpretation of Piero della Francesca's *Baptism of Christ*', in Lavin 1981: 149-63.
Cartland, B.
1982   *Love and the Marquis* (London: Pan Books).
Cassirer, H.W.
1988   *Grace and Law: St. Paul, Kant, and the Hebrew Prophets* (Edinburgh: Handsel Press; Grand Rapids: Eerdmans).
Chadwick, H.
1981   *Boethius: The Consolations of Music, Logic, Theology, and Philosophy* (Oxford: Clarendon Press).
Chadwick, O.
1985   *The Secularization of the European Mind in the Nineteenth Century* (Cambridge: Cambridge University Press).
Clark K.
1969   *Piero della Francesca* (London: Phaidon, 2nd edn)
Clarke, W.K.L.
1929   *New Testament Problems* (London: SPCK; London: Macmillan).
Clines, D.J.A.
1976   *I, He, We, and They: A Literary Approach to Isaiah 53* (JSOTSup, 1; Sheffield: JSOT Press).
Cohen, A.P.
1985   *The Symbolic Construction of Community* (London: Routledge).
1987   *Whalsay: Symbol, Segment and Boundary in a Shetland Island Community* (Manchester: Manchester University Press).

1994   *Self Consciousness: An Alternative Anthropology of Identity* (London: Routledge).

Coleridge, S.T.

1863   *Confessions of an Enquiring Spirit* (ed. H.N. Coleridge; London: Edward Moxon, 4th edn).

Collingwood R.G.

1916   *Religion and Philosophy* (London: Macmillan).

1924   *Speculum Mentis* (Oxford: Clarendon Press).

1925a   *Outlines of a Philosophy of Art* (London: Oxford University Press).

1925b   'Plato's Philosophy of Art', *Mind* 34: 154-72.

1926   'The Place of Art in Education', *Hibbert Journal* 24: 424-48.

1927a   'Aesthetic', in J.S. McDowall (ed.), *The Mind* (London: Longmans).

1927b   'Reason Is Faith Cultivating Itself', *Hibbert Journal* 26: 3-14.

1927c   B. Croce, *An Autobiography* (trans. R.G. Collingwood; Oxford: Clarendon Press).

1928a   Review of S. Alexander, *Art and Instinct*, *Journal of Philosophical Studies* 3: 370-73.

1928b   Review of L.R. Farnell, *Hedonism and Art*, *Journal of Philosophical Studies* 3: 547-48.

1928c   B. Croce, 'Aesthetic' (trans. R.G. Collingwood, *Encyclopaedia Britannica*, 14th edn).

1929   'Form and Content in Art', *Journal of Philosophical Studies* 4: 332-45.

1930   Review of W.T. Stace, *The Meaning of Beauty: A Theory of Aesthetics*, *JPS* 5: 460-63.

1931   Review of C.J. Ducasse, *The Philosophy of Art*, *Philosophy* 6: 383-86.

1932   Review of L.A. Reid, *A Study in Aesthetics*, *Philosophy* 7: 335-37.

1933   *An Essay on Philosophical Method* (Oxford: Clarendon Press).

1934   'The Present Need of a Philosophy', *Philosophy* 9: 262-65.

1938   *The Principles of Art* (Oxford: Clarendon Press).

1939   *An Autobiography* (Oxford: Oxford University Press).

1940a   *An Essay on Metaphysics* (Oxford: Oxford University Press).

1940b   *The First Mate's Log* (Oxford: Oxford University Press).

1942   *The New Leviathan* (Oxford: Clarendon Press).

1945   *The Idea of Nature* (ed. T.M. Knox; Oxford: Clarendon Press).

1946   *The Idea of History* (ed. T.M. Knox; Oxford: Clarendon Press).

1967   'The Devil', in D.Z. Phillips (ed.), *Religion and Understanding* (Oxford: Basil Blackwell): 171-89.

Collingwood, R.G., and J.N.L. Myres

1937   *Roman Britain and the English Settlements* (Oxford: Clarendon Press, 2nd edn).

Conzelmann, H.

1959   'Jesus Christus', in K. Galling *et al.* (eds.), *Die Religion in Geschichte und Gegenwart: Handwörterbuch für Theologie und Religionswissenschaft* (Tübingen: J.C.B. Mohr [Paul Siebeck], 3rd edn, 1957-62).

1973   *Jesus* (Philadelphia: Fortress Press).

Cook, A.B.
1940   *Zeus: A Study in Ancient Religion*, III.1 (Cambridge: Cambridge University Press).
Crane, R.S.
1953   *The Languages of Criticism and the Structure of Poetry* (Toronto: Toronto University Press).
Croce, B.
1922   *Aesthetic as Science of Expression and General Linguistic* (London: Macmillan, 2nd edn).
1927   *An Autobiography* (trans. R.G. Collingwood; Oxford: Clarendon Press).
1928   'Aesthetic' (trans. R.G. Collingwood, *Encyclopaedia Britannica*, 14th edn).
Cromwell, O.
1904   *Letters and Speeches, with Elucidations by T. Carlyle* (3 vols.; London: Methuen).
Crossan, J.D.
1975   *The Dark Interval: Towards a Theology of Story* (Niles, IL: Argus Communications).
cummings, e.e.
1926   *Is 5* (New York: Boni & Liveright).
1954   *Poems 1923-1954* (New York: Harcourt, Brace & Company).
Cupitt, D.
1990   *Creation out of Nothing* (London: SCM Press).
Cusanus, N.
1954   Of Learned Ignorance (trans. G. Heron; introduction by D.J.B. Hawkins; London: Routledge & Kegan Paul).
Dahood, M.
1965-70   *Psalms I, II, III* (Garden City, NY: Doubleday).
Dante, Alighieri
1950   *The Divine Comedy*. I. *Hell* (trans. D.L. Sayers; London: Penguin Books).
Darling, F.F.
1937   *A Herd of Red Deer* (London: Oxford University Press).
Davidovich, A.
1993   *Religion as a Province of Meaning* (Minneapolis: Fortress Press).
Davidson, G.R.
1952   *Results of the Excavations Conducted by the American School of Classical Studies at Athens*. XII. *The Minor Objects* (Princeton: American School of Classical Studies at Athens).
Davie, G.E.
1964   *The Democratic Intellect* (Edinburgh: Edinburgh University Press, 2nd edn).
1991   *The Scottish Enlightenment and Other Essays* (Edinburgh: Polygon).
1996   'The Philosophy of J.F. Ferrier (1808-1964)' (unpublished paper).
Davies, W.D.
1948   *Paul and Rabbinic Judaism: Some Rabbinic Elements in Pauline Theology* (London: SPCK).

Davis, C.
1982   'The Theological Career of Historical Criticism of the Bible', *Cross Currents* 32: 267-84.
1986   *What Is Living, What Is Dead in Christianity Today?* (San Francisco: Harper & Row).
1994   *Religion and the Making of Society: Essays in Social Theology* (Cambridge: Cambridge University Press).
Deas, H.T.
1931   'The Scholia Vetera to Pindar', *Harvard Studies in Classical Philology* 42: 1-78.
Denniston, J.D.
1954   *The Greek Particles* (Oxford: Clarendon Press, 2nd edn).
Dibelius, M.
1929   'Die Formgeschichte des Evangeliums', *Theologische Rundschau*, NF 1: 185-216.
Dickie, M.W.
1995   'A New Epigram by Poseidippus on an Irritable Dead Cretan', *Bulletin of the American Society of Papyrologists* 32: 5-12.
Dickinson, E.
1955   *The Poems of Emily Dickinson* (Cambridge, MA: Harvard University Press).
Diderot, D.
1821-34   *Oeuvres* (ed. J.A. Naigeon; 3 vols.; Paris: J.L.J. Brière).
Diehl E.
1925   *Anthologia Lyrica Graeca*, I (Leipzig: Teubner).
Diels, H.
1906   *Fragmente der Vorsokratiker* (Berlin: Weidmann, 2nd edn).
Dinsmoor, W.B.
1933   'The Temple of Apollo at Bassae', *Metropolitan Museum Studies* 4: 204-27.
1956   'The Sculptured Frieze from Bassae (a Revised Sequence)', *American Journal of Archaeology* 60: 401-52.
Dittenberger, W.
1915-24   *Sylloge Inscriptionum Graecarum* (Leipzig: S. Hirzel, 4th edn).
Dodd, C.H.
1932   *The Epistle of Paul to the Romans* (London: Hodder & Stoughton).
1953   *The Interpretation of the Fourth Gospel* (Cambridge: Cambridge University Press).
Doway
1633   *The New Testament of Jesus Christ faithfully translated out of the authentical Latin, diligently conferred with the Greek and other Editions in divers languages* (Rheims: Ioan. Cousturier, 4th edn).
Doyle, C. (ed.)
1985   *Wallace Stevens: The Critical Heritage* (London: Routledge & Kegan Paul).
Dryden, J.
1962   *Of Dramatic Poesy and Other Critical Essays* (2 vols.; London: J.M. Dent).

Ducasse C.J.
1931   *The Philosophy of Art* (London: George Allen & Unwin).
Dufrenne, M.
1973   *The Phenomenology of Aesthetic Experience* (trans. E.S. Casey; Evanston, IL: Northwestern University Press).
Easterling, P.E. (ed.)
1982   *Sophocles: Trachiniae* (Cambridge: Cambridge University Press).
Eliade, M.
1954   *The Myth of the Eternal Return* (London: Routledge & Kegan Paul).
Eliot, G. (M. Evans) see Strauss 1970.
Eliot, T.S.
1936   *Collected Poems 1909-1935* (London: Faber & Faber).
1944   *Four Quartets* (London: Faber & Faber).
1960   *The Sacred Wood: Essays on Poetry and Criticism* (London: Methuen, 7th edn).
1962   *Notes towards the Definition of Culture* (London: Faber & Faber).
1964   *Knowledge and Experience in the Philosophy of F.H. Bradley* (London: Faber & Faber).
1974   *Collected Poems* (London: Faber & Faber).
Erasmus, D.
1984   *Collected Works of Erasmus* (ed. R.D. Sider; 42 vols.; Toronto: University of Toronto).
Euclid
1482   *Praeclarissimus liber elementorum Euclidis perspicacissimi: in artem Geometrie incipit quam foelicissime* (Venetiis: Erhardus Ratdolt).
1955   *The First Book of Euclidis Elementa* (ed. E.J. Dijksterhuis; Leiden: E.J. Brill).
Farrer, A.
1948   *The Glass of Vision* (London: Westminster Press).
1949   *A Rebirth of Images* (London: Dacre Press).
1951   *A Study in St. Mark* (London: Dacre Press).
1972   'Poetic Truth', in C.C. Conti (ed.), *Reflective Faith* (London: SPCK): 24-38.
1976   *Interpretation and Belief* (London: SPCK).
Fergusson, D.A.
1992   *Bultmann* (London: Geoffrey Chapman).
Fielding, H.
1959   *The History of Tom Jones* (London: The Folio Society).
Finberg, A.J.
1939   *The Life of J.M.W. Turner, R.A.* (Oxford: Clarendon Press).
Fish S.
1980   *Is There a Text in This Class?* (Cambridge, MA: Harvard University Press).
Fitzmyer J.A.
1985   *The Gospel According to Luke*, II (Garden City, NY: Doubleday).
Forbes, C.
1986   'Comparison, Self-praise and Irony', *New Testament Studies* 32: 1-30.

Foster, M.B.
1957   *Mystery and Philosophy* (London: SCM Press).
France, A.
1891   'Le Procurateur de Judée', in *Le Temps* (25 December 1891) (also 1892 in *L'Etui de Nacre* (Paris: Calmann-Levy).
1947   'The Procurator of Judea', in *The World's Greatest Short Stories* (repr.; London: Odhams Press, n.d.).
Frankenberg, L.
1949   *Pleasure Dome: On Reading Modern Poetry* (Boston: Houghton Mifflin; Cambridge, MA: Riverside Press).
Friedländer, M.J.
1942   *On Art and Connoisseurship* (London: Bruno Cassirer).
Fries, J.F.
1805   *Wissen, Glauben und Ahndung* (Jena: J.C.G. Göpferdt) (also ed. L.C. Nelson [Göttingen: Vandenhoeck und Ruprecht, 1905]).
Fry, C.
1950   *The Lady's Not for Burning* (Oxford: Oxford University Press, 2nd edn).
Frye, N.
1964   *The Educated Imagination* (Bloomington: Indiana University Press).
Fuller, R.C.
1984   *Alexander Geddes, 1737–1802: A Pioneer of Biblical Criticism* (Sheffield: The Almond Press).
Funk, R.W.
1978   'The Form of the New Testament Healing Story', *Semeia* 12: 57-96.
1982   *Parables and Presence* (Philadelphia: Fortress Press).
1988   *The Poetics of Biblical Narrative* (Sonoma, CA: Polebridge Press).
Gabel, J.B., and C.B. Wheeler
1986   *The Bible as Literature* (Oxford: Oxford University Press).
Gage, J.
1969   *Colour in Turner: Poetry and Truth* (London: Studio Vista).
García Márquez, G.
1994   *Strange Pilgrims* (London: Penguin Books).
Gardner, H.
1963   *The Business of Criticism* (Oxford: Oxford University Press).
1968   *The Art of T.S. Eliot* (London: Faber & Faber).
1978   *The Composition of Four Quartets* (London: Faber & Faber).
Gilbert, W.S.
1923   *Original Plays: Third Series* (London: Chatto & Windus).
Gillies, H.C.
1906   *The Place-Names of Argyll* (London: David Nutt).
Gombrich, E.H.
1968   *Art and Illusion: A Study in the Psychology of Pictorial Representation* (London: Phaidon, 3rd edn).
Gow, A.S.F.
1936   *A.E. Housman: A Sketch together with a List of his Writings and Indexes to his Classical Papers* (Cambridge: Cambridge University Press).

1952   *Theocritus.* I. *Text*; II. *Commentary* (Cambridge: Cambridge University Press, 2nd edn).

Griffith, G.T.
1979   'The Reign of Philip the Second', in N.G.L. Hammond and G.T. Griffith (eds.), *A History of Macedonia*, II, Chs. 5-19, 21 (Oxford: Clarendon Press).

Griffith, G.T., and M.J. Oakeshott
1936   *A Guide to the Classics* (London: Faber & Faber).

Grimm. J.L.C., and W.C. Grimm
1954   *Fairy Tales* (London: Collins).
1975   *The Complete Grimms' Fairy Tales* (London: Routledge & Kegan Paul).

Grotius, H.
1646   *Annotationum in Novum Testamentum Tomus Secundus* (Paris: G. Pelé and I. Duval).
1853   *Hugonis Grotii: de jure belli et pacis* (trans. W. Whewell; Cambridge: Cambridge University Press).

Gulley, N.
1979   'Aristotle on the Purposes of Literature', in J. Barnes, M. Schofield and R. Sorabji (eds.), *Articles on Aristotle*. IV. *Psychology and Aesthetics* (London: Gerald Duckworth).

Guthrie, W.K.C.
1950   *The Greeks and their Gods* (London: Methuen).
1981   *A History of Greek Philosophy: Aristotle: An Encounter*, VI (Cambridge: Cambridge University Press).

Halliwell, S.
1986   *Aristotle's Poetics* (London: Gerald Duckworth).

Hamann, J.G.
1950   *Aesthetica in nuce*, in *idem*, *Sämtliche Werke*, II (ed. Gerald Nadler; Vienna: Herder): 195-217 (see also: Lumpp 1970: 203-34 [facsimile]).
1952   *Sämtliche Werke*, III (ed. Gerald Nadler; Vienna: Herder).
1956   *Golgatha und Scheblimini* (ed. L. Schreiner; Gütersloh: Carl Bertelsmann Verlag).
1960   'Aesthetica in nuce' (select texts), in Smith 1960: 195-200.
1985   *Aesthetica in nuce* (trans. J.P. Crick), in Nisbet 1985: 139-50.

Hamilton, W.
1993   *A Quest for the Post-Historical Jesus* (London: SCM Press).

Hammond, N.G.L., and G.T. Griffith
1979   *A History of Macedonia* (2 vols.; Oxford: Oxford University Press).

Hampshire, S.
1988   *Spinoza* (London: Penguin Books).

Harris, E.E.
1978   'Is There an Esoteric Doctrine in the Tractatus Theologico politicus?', in *Mededelingen XXXVIII vanwege het Spinozahuis* (Leiden: E.J. Brill).

Harris, H.A.
1964   *Greek Athletes and Athletics* (London: Hutchinson).

Harris, R.
1995   *Enigma* (London: Hutchinson).
Hartlich, C., and W. Sachs
1952   *Der Ursprung des Mythosbegriffes in der modernen Bibelwissen-schaft* (Tübingen: J.C.B. Mohr [Paul Siebeck]).
Harvey, V.A.
1967   *The Historian and the Believer: The Morality of Historical Knowl-ege and Christian Belief* (London: SCM Press).
Hauser, A.
1959   *The Philosophy of Art History* (London: Routledge & Kegan Paul).
Hawkes, T.
1972   *Metaphor* (London: Methuen).
Heath, M.
1989   'Aristotelian Comedy', *Classical Quarterly* 39: 344-54.
1991   'The Universality of Poetry in Aristotle's Poetics', *Classical Quarterly* 41: 389-402.
Heaton, E.W.
1949   *His Servants the Prophets* (London: SCM Press) (*The Old Testament Prophets* [Harmondsworth: Pelican Books, rev. edn, 1958]).
1994   *The School Tradition of the Old Testament* (Oxford: Clarendon Press).
Heidegger, M.
1927   'Sein und Zeit', *Jahrbuch für Phänomenologie und phänome-nologische Forschung* 8 (ed. E. Husserl).
1962   *Being and Time* (trans. J. Macquarrie and E. Robinson; London: SCM Press).
Heliodorus
1935-60   *Les Ethiopiques* (ed. R.M. Rattenbury and T.W. Lumb; trans. J. Maillon; 3 vols.; Paris: Collection des Universités de France).
Henderson, I.
1948   *Can Two Walk Together: The Quest for a Secular Morality* (London: Nisbet).
1952   *Myth in the New Testament* (London: SCM Press).
1967   *Power without Glory: A Study in Ecumenical Politics* (London: Hutchinson Press).
1969   *Scotland: Kirk and People* (London: Lutterworth Press).
Henry (of Huntingdon)
1596   *Henrici Archidiaconi Huntindoniensis Historiarum lib. VIII*, in H. Savile, *Rerum Anglicarum Scriptores post Bedam praecipui, ex vetustissimis codicibus manuscriptis nunc primum in lucem editi* (London: G. Bishop, R. Nuberie, R. Barker).
1853   *The Chronicle of Henry of Huntingdon* (London: Henry G. Bohn).
Henry, P.
1950   'Kénose', in *Supplément au Dictionnaire de la Bible*, Fasc. xxiv (Paris: Librairie Letouzey et Ané): 7-161.
Hepburn, R.W.
1984   *'Wonder' and Other Essays* (Edinburgh: Edinburgh University Press).

1990 'Art, Truth and the Education of Subjectivity', *Journal of Philosophy of Education*, 24.2: 185-98.

Heringman, B.
1949 'Wallace Stevens: The Use of Poetry', *Journal of English Literary History* 16: 325-36.

Hess, H.
1975 *Pictures as Arguments* (London: Chatto & Windus).

Higgs, P.W.
1964a 'Broken Symmetries, Massless Particles and Gauge Fields', *Physical Review Letters* 12.2: 132-33.
1964b 'Broken Symmetries and the Masses of Gauge Bosons', *Physical Review Letters* 13.16: 508-509.
1966 'Spontaneous Symmetry Breakdown without Massless Bosons', *The Physical Review* 145.4: 1156-63.

Hobbes, T.
1844 '*The Iliads and Odysses of Homer*', in W. Molesworth (ed.), *The English Works of Thomas Hobbes*, X (London: Longman, Brown, Green & Longmans).
1946 *Leviathan* (ed. M. Oakeshott; Oxford: Basil Blackwell).

Hodgson L.
1957 *For Faith and Freedom* (2 vols.; Oxford: Basil Blackwell).

Hoff, B.
1984 *The Tao of Pooh* (London: Methuen).

Hopkins, G.M.
1970 *The Poems of Gerard Manley Hopkins* (ed. W.H. Gardner and N.H. MacKenzie; Oxford: Oxford University Press).

Housmann, A.E.
1903-31 *M. Manilii Astronomicon* (5 vols.; London: Grant Richards).
1961 *Selected Prose* (Cambridge: Cambridge University Press).

Hügel, Baron Freiherr F. von
1921 *Essays and Addresses on the Philosophy of Religion* (London: Dent).
1926 *Essays and Addresses on the Philosophy of Religion: Second Series* (London: Dent).

Hunt, W.
1893 'Lowth or Louth Robert 1710-1787', *Dictionary of National Biography* (London: Smith Elder).

Hunter, G.K.
1967 *Macbeth* (Harmondsworth: Penguin Books).

Hunter, J.
1966 *Gerard Manley Hopkins* (London: Evans Brothers).

Huxley, A.L.
1932 *Brave New World: A Novel* (London: Chatto & Windus).

Ingarden, R.
1985a 'Uwagi na marginesie *Poetyki* Arystotelesa' and 'O tak zwanej "prawdzie" w literaturze', in *Studia z estetyki*, I (Warsaw: Państwowe Wydawn. Naukowe).

1985b   'A Marginal Commentary on Aristotle's Poetics', and 'On So-called "Truth" in Literature', in *Selected Papers in Aesthetics* (Washington: The Catholic University of America Press; Vienna: Philosophia Verlag).

Isenberg, A.
1973   *Aesthetics and the Theory of Criticism* (Chicago: University of Chicago Press).

Jacobson, D.
1970   *The Rape of Tamar* (London: Weidenfeld & Nicolson).
1982   *The Story of the Stories* (New York: Harper & Row).
1987   *Her Story* (London: Deutsch).
1989   'Biblical Narratives and Novelists' Narratives' (Ethel M. Wood Trust Lecture; London).

Jaeger, W.
1934   *Aristotle* (trans. R. Robinson; Oxford: Clarendon Press).

James, H.
1962   *The Art of the Novel* (New York: Charles Scribner's Sons).

James, M.R.
1924   *The Apocryphal New Testament* (Oxford: Clarendon Press).

Jasper, D.
1989   *The New Testament and the Literary Imagination* (London: Macmillan).
1992   *The Study of Literature and Religion* (London: Macmillan, 2nd edn).

Jerome
1854   'Epistolae', Migne, *Patrologia Latina*, XXII.

Jerome, Jerome K.
1889   *In cumba tres viri* (Bristol: J.W. Arrowsmith).

Joachim, H.H.
1901   *A Study of the Ethics of Spinoza* (Oxford: Clarendon Press).
1906   *The Nature of Truth* (Oxford: Clarendon Press).

Johnson, A.H.
1962   *Whitehead's Philosophy of Civilisation* (New York: Dover Publications).

Johnson, S.
1805   *A Dictionary of the English Language* (London: Longman, Hurst, Rees & Orme, 9th edn).
1906   *Lives of the English Poets* (2 vols.; Oxford: Oxford University Press).
1968   *Rasselas: Prince of Abissinia* (ed. J.P. Hardy; London: Oxford University Press).

Jonas, H.
1964–66   *Gnosis und spätantiker Geist*, (Göttingen: Vandenhoeck & Ruprecht; Part 1: 3rd edn; Part 2.1: 2nd edn).
1971   'Philosophical Meditation on the Seventh Chapter of Paul's Epistle to the Romans', in *The Future of our Religious Past: Essays in Honour of Rudolf Bultmann* (London: SCM Press).

Joyce, J.
1922   *Ulysses* (Paris: Shakespeare).
1975   *Finnegans Wake* (London: Faber & Faber).

1979   *Epiphanies* (Philadelphia: Richard West).
Julian of Norwich
1950   *Revelations of Divine Love* (ed. G. Warrack; London: Methuen, 13th edn) (see also Beer 1978).
Jung, C.G.
1954   *Answer to Job* (London: Routledge & Kegan Paul).
Kant, I.
1914   *Kant's Critique of Judgement* (trans. J.H. Bernard; London: Macmillan, 2nd edn).
1915   *Kritik der Urteilskraft* (ed. K. Vorländer; Leipzig: Felix Meiner), in *Sämtliche Werke*, II (ed. O. Buek, P. Gedan, W. Kinkel, J.H.V. Kirchmann, K. Vorländer, F.M. Schiele, Th. Valentiner; Leipzig: Felix Meiner).
Käsemann, E.
1960   'Kritische Analyse von Phil. 2,5-11', and 'Begründet der neutestamentliche Kanon die Einheit der Kirche?', in *Exegetische Versuche und Besinnungen*. I. (Göttingen: Vandenhoeck und Ruprecht).
1964   'The Canon of the New Testament and the Unity of the Church', in *Essays on New Testament Themes* (London: SCM Press).
Kazantzakis, N.
1958   *The Odyssey* (London: Secker & Warburg).
Kelly, J.N.D.
1975   *Jerome: His Life, Writings and Controversies* (London: Gerald Duckworth).
Kemal, S.
1986   *Kant and Fine Art: An Essay on Kant and the Philosophy of Fine Art and Culture* (Oxford: Clarendon Press).
1992   *Kant's Aesthetic Theory: An Introduction* (London: Macmillan).
Kemal, S., and I. Gaskell
1991   *The Language of Art History* (Cambridge: Cambridge University Press).
Kermode, F.
1960   *Wallace Stevens* (Edinburgh: Oliver & Boyd).
1961   'Notes toward a Supreme Fiction: A Commentary', *Annali dell' Instituto Universitario Orientale*, Sezione Germanica (Naples) 4: 173-201.
1963   *The Living Milton: Essays by Various Hands* (London: Routledge & Kegan Paul).
1967   *The Sense of an Ending* (New York: Oxford University Press).
1979   *The Genesis of Secrecy: On the Interpretation of Narrative* (Cambridge, MA: Harvard University Press).
1986   'St. John as Poet', *Journal for the Study of the New Testament* 28: 3-16.
1990   *Poetry, Narrative, History* (Oxford: Basil Blackwell).
Kermode, F., and R. Alter
1987   *The Literary Guide to the Bible* (Cambridge, MA: The Belknap Press of Harvard University Press).

Kerr, C.
1993   *the mud is quiet* (Edinburgh: Chapman).
Kerr, J.
1989   *Fiction against History: Scott as Storyteller* (Cambridge: Cambridge University Press).
Kettridge, J.O.
1940   *Kettridge's French and English Military Dictionary* (London: George Routledge & Sons).
Kierkegaard, S.
1939   *The Point of View for my Work as an Author, etc.* (trans. W. Lowrie; London: Oxford University Press).
1941   *Fear and Trembling: A Dialectical Lyric* (trans. W. Lowrie; Princeton, NJ: Princeton University Press).
1955   *On Authority and Revelation: The Book on Adler, or a Cycle of Ethico-Religious Essays* (trans. W. Lowrie; Princeton, NJ: Princeton University Press).
Kirk, G.S., J.E. Raven and M. Schofield
1983   *The Presocratic Philosophers: A Critical History with a Selection of Texts* (Cambridge: Cambridge University Press, 2nd edn).
Knight, W.S.M.
1925   *The Life and Works of Hugo Grotius* (London: Sweet & Maxwell).
Knowles, D.
1963   'The Historian and Character', 'The Humanism of the Twelfth Century' and 'The Censured Opinions of Uthred of Boldon', in *The Historian and Character and Other Essays* (Cambridge: Cambridge University Press).
Kromer, M.L.
1989   'World, Metaphor, Text: Contributions to the Interpretation of 2 Corinthians 3' (unpublished thesis, University of Edinburgh).
Kümmel, W.G.
1983   *Einleitung in das Neue Testament* (Heidelberg: Quelle und Meyer, 21st edn).
Kundera, M.
1988   *The Art of the Novel* (London: Faber & Faber).
Lakoff, G., and M. Johnson
1980   *Metaphors We Live By* (Chicago: University of Chicago Press).
Lavin, M.A.
1981   *Piero della Francesca's Baptism of Christ* (New Haven: Yale University Press).
Lawrence, D.H.
1949   *The Rainbow* (Harmondsworth: Penguin Books).
Leach, E.R.
1954   *Political Systems of Highland Burma: A Study of Kachin Social Structure* (London: London School of Economics and Political Science).
Leavis, F.R.
1969   *English Literature in our Time and the University* (London: Chatto & Windus; Toronto: Clarke, Irwin).

Lee, R.S.
1955   *Psychology and Worship* (London: SCM Press).
Lentricchia, F.
1980   *After the New Criticism* (London: Athlone Press).
Levinas, E.
1985   *Ethics and Infinity* (Pittsburgh: Duquesne University Press).
Lewis, C.T., C. Short, E.A. Andrews and W. Freund
1951   *A Latin Dictionary Founded on Andrews' Edition of Freund's Latin Dictionary: Revised, Enlarged and in Great Part Rewritten by Charles T. Lewis and Charles Short* (Oxford: Clarendon Press).
Lightbrown, R.
1992   *Piero della Francesca* (New York: Abbeville).
Lightfoot, R.H.
1935   *History and Interpretation in the Gospels* (London: Hodder & Stoughton).
1962   *The Gospel Message of St. Mark* (Oxford: Oxford University Press).
Livingstone, D.
1858   *Livingstone's Travels and Researches in South Africa* (Philadelphia: J.W. Bradley).
Locke, J.
1894   *An Essay Concerning Human Understanding* (ed. A.C. Fraser; 2 vols.; Oxford: Clarendon Press).
Lohmeyer, E.
1928   *Kyrios Jesus* (Heidelberg: Carl Winter Universitätsbuchhandlung).
Loisy, A.F.
1920   *Les Actes des Apôtres* (Paris: Emile Nourry).
1922   *Les Livres du Nouveau Testament* (Paris: Émile Nourry).
1923   'Le style rythmé du Nouveau Testament', *Journal de Psychologie* 20: 405-39.
1924   *My Duel with the Vatican* (New York: E.P. Dutton).
1933   *La naissance du christianisme* (Paris: Emile Nourry).
1948   *The Birth of the Christian Religion* (trans. L.P. Jacks; London: George Allen & Unwin).
Longinus
1899   *Longinus on the Sublime* (ed. W.R. Roberts; Cambridge: Cambridge University Press).
Lorimer, W.L.
1983   *The New Testament in Scots* (Edinburgh: Southside).
Lowth, R.
1770   *De Sacra Poesi Hebraeorum Praelectiones Academicae Oxonii habitae: subjicitur Metricae Harianae brevis confutatio: et Oratio Crewiana.—Notas et epimetra adiecit Ioannes David Michaelis* (Göttingen: Ioan. Christ. Dieterich, 2nd edn).
1787   *Memoirs of the Life and Writings of the Late Right Reverend Robert Lowth, D.D.* (London: W. Bent; repr. from the *Universal Magazine*, November 1786).
1821   *De Sacra Poesi Hebraeorum Praelectiones Academicae...*, etc. (Oxford: Clarendon Press, 2nd edn).

1839   *Lectures on the Sacred Poesy of the Hebrews* (London: Thomas Tegg).

1847   *Lectures on the Sacred Poesy of the Hebrews* (London: S. Chadwick).

Lucas, J.R.

1992   'Is my Article Really Necessary?', *The Oxford Magazine* (Second Week, Trinity Term): 2-3.

Lucretius

1922   *De rerum natura* (ed. C. Bailey; Oxford: Clarendon Press).

Lukács, G.

1989   *The Historical Novel* (trans. H. and S. Mitchell; London: Merlin Press).

Lumpp, H.-M.

1970   *Philologia Crucis: Zu Johann Georg Hamanns Auffassung von der Dichtkunst mit einem Kommentar zur 'Aesthetica in nuce' 1762* (Tübingen: Max Niemeyer).

Lupton, J.H.

1895   *The Utopia of Sir Thomas More in Latin from the Edition of March 1518, and in English from the First Edition of Ralph Robynson's Translation in 1551* (Oxford: Clarendon Press).

Luther, M.

1565   *Biblia: Das ist: Die gantze heilige Schrifft: Deudsch*, I (Wittemberg: Hans Lufft).

Lynch, M.

1992   *Scotland: A New History* (London: Pimlico).

Macdonald, D.

1964   *Parodies: An Anthology from Chaucer to Beerbohm—and After* (London: Faber & Faber).

Macdonald, D.B.

1933   *The Hebrew Literary Genius* (Princeton, NJ: Princeton University Press).

1936   *The Hebrew Philosophical Genius* (Princeton, NJ: Princeton University Press).

McDonald, L.M.

1995   *The Formation of the Christian Biblical Canon, Revised and Expanded Edn* (Peabody, MA: Hendrickson).

MacDonald, M.

1954   'The Language of Fiction', *Proceedings of the Aristotelian Society* 28: 165-84 (also in Margolis 1978).

McGuinness, B.

1990   *Wittgenstein: A Life. Young Ludwig, 1889-1921* (Harmondsworth: Penguin Books).

Machiavelli, N.

1961   *The Prince* (Harmondsworth: Penguin Books).

McIntyre, J.

1987   *Faith, Theology and Imagination* (Edinburgh: Handsel).

Mack, B.L.

1988   *A Myth of Innocence* (Philadelphia: Fortress Press).

Mackenzie, I.
1966   'Science Fiction: Sublimation or Prophecy?', *Student World* 4: 399-
            405.
1993   *Tunes of Glory* (Carberry: Handsel).
1995   *Work in Progress* (unpublished).
Mackey, J.P.
1973   'Theology 20: Grace', *The Furrow* 24: 338-52.
Mackey, J.P. (ed.)
1986   *Religious Imagination* (Edinburgh: Edinburgh University Press).
Mackinnon, D.M.
1957   *A Study in Ethical Theory* (London: A. & C. Black).
1968   *Borderlands of Theology and Other Essays* (London: Lutterworth).
1974   *The Problem of Metaphysics* (Cambridge: Cambridge University
            Press).
1986   'Some Reflections on Hans Urs von Balthasar's Christology with
            Special Reference to Theodramatik II/2, III and IV', in J. Riches (ed.),
            The Analogy of Beauty (Edinburgh: T. & T. Clark).
1992   'Collingwood on the Philosophy of Religion', *The Scottish Journal of
            Religious Studies* 13: 73-83.
Mackinnon, D.M., and A. Flew
1955   'Creation', in A. Flew and A. MacIntyre (eds.), *New Essays in
            Philosophical Theology* (London: SCM Press): 170-86.
Macmurray, J.
1957   *The Self as Agent* (London: Faber & Faber).
1961   *Persons in Relation* (London: Faber & Faber).
Macquarrie, J.
1955   *An Existentialist Theology* (London: SCM Press).
1963   *Twentieth-Century Religious Thought* (London: SCM Press).
MacVicar, A.
1971   *Salt in my Porridge: Confessions of a Minister's Son* (London:
            Jarrolds).
Malcolm, N.
1967   *Ludwig Wittgenstein: A Memoir, with a Biographical Sketch by
            Georg Henrik von Wright* (London: Oxford University Press).
Malevez, L.
1958   *The Christian Message and Myth: The Theology of Rudolf Bult-
            mann* (London: SCM Press).
Manilius, M.
1903-30   *Astronomicon* (ed. A.E. Housman; 4 vols.; London: Grant Richards).
Manson, T.W.
1949   *The Sayings of Jesus: As Recorded in the Gospels According to St.
            Matthew and St. Luke* (London: SCM Press).
Margolis J.
1978   *Philosophy Looks at Art: Contemporary Readings in Aesthetics*
            (Philadelphia: Temple University).
Martin G.D.
1975   *Language Truth and Poetry* (Edinburgh: Edinburgh University
            Press).

1990   *Shadows in the Cave: Mapping the Conscious Universe* (London: Arkana).

Martin, R.P.
1967   *Carmen Christi* (Cambridge: Cambridge University Press).

Martyn, J.L.
1979   *History and Theology in the Fourth Gospel* (Nashville: Abingdon Press, 2nd edn).

Maxwell, R.
1943   *Still Point* (London: Nisbet).

Meeks, W.A.
1972   'The Man from Heaven in Johannine Sectarianism', *Journal of Biblical Literature* 91: 44-72 (also in Ashton 1986).
1983   *The First Urban Christians: The Social World of the Apostle Paul* (New Haven: Yale University Press).

Meiss, M.
1978   *The Painter's Choice: Problems in the Interpretation of Renaissance Art* (New York: Harper & Row).

Merritt, B.D.
1931   *Results of the Excavations Conducted by the American School of Classical Studies at Athens*. VIII, Part I. *The Greek Inscriptions, 1896-1927* (Cambridge, MA: Harvard University Press).

Miller, J. Hillis
c. 1975   *The Disappearance of God: Five Nineteenth Century Writers* (Cambridge, MA: The Belknap Press of Harvard University Press).

Milne, A.A.
1926   *Winnie the Pooh* (London: Methuen).
1961   *Winnie Ille Pu* (London: Methuen; New York: Dutton).

Miscall, P.D.
1993   *Isaiah* (Sheffield: Sheffield Academic Press).

Mitchison, R.M.
1982   *A History of Scotland* (London: Methuen, 2nd edn).

Moore, G.E.
1959   'A Defence of Common Sense', in *Philosophical Papers* (London: George Allen & Unwin): 32-59.

Moore, G.F.
1905   'Symphonia not a Bagpipe', *Journal of Biblical Literature* 24: 166-75.

Moore, S.D.
1989   *Literary Criticism and the Gospels* (New Haven: Yale University Press).
1994   *Poststructuralism and the New Testament: Derrida and Foucault at the Foot of the Cross* (Minneapolis: Fortress Press).

More, T.
1847   *A Dialogue of Comfort against Tribulation* (London: Thomas Baker).
1895   *The Utopia of Sir Thomas More, in Latin* (Edn 1518) and English (ed. J.H. Lupton; trans. R. Robynson (1551); Oxford: Clarendon Press).

Morgan, J.R., and R. Stoneman
1994   *Greek Fiction: The Greek Novel in Context* (London: Routledge).
Morgan, R.
1997   'Jesus Christ', in *The Oxford Dictionary of the Christian Church* (ed.
            F.L. Cross and E.A. Livingstone; London: Oxford University Press, 3rd
            edn).
Morgan R., with J. Barton
1988   *Biblical Interpretation* (Oxford: Oxford University Press).
Morse, S.F.
1958   'The Native Element', *The Kenyon Review* 20: 446-65.
Moulton, J.H., and G. Milligan
1929   'ἀποκαταστασις', in *The Vocabulary of the Greek New Testament*
            (London: Hodder & Stoughton).
Murdoch, I.
1978   *The Fire and the Sun: Why Plato Banished the Artists* (Oxford:
            Oxford University Press).
Murphy, J.
1978   *The Worst Witch* (Harmondsworth: Puffin Books).
Murphy-O'Connor, J.
1976   'Christological Anthropology in Phil. II, 6-11', *Revue biblique* 83: 25-
            50.
1980   'Sex and Logic in 1 Cor. 11.2-16', *Catholic Biblical Quarterly* 42:
            482-500.
1983a   *St. Paul's Corinth* (Wilmington, DE: Michael Glazier).
1983b   'Corinthian Bronze', *Revue biblique* 90: 23-26.
1991   *The Theology of the Second Letter to the Corinthians* (Cambridge:
            Cambridge University Press).
1996   *Paul: A Critical Life* (Oxford: Clarendon Press).
Murray, J.A.H.
1888-1933   *A New English Dictionary on Historical Principles; Founded
            Mainly on the Materials Collected by the Philological Society*
            (Oxford: Clarendon Press).
Nash, O.
1959   *Collected Verse from 1929 on* (London: Dent).
Newman, J.H.
1846   *An Essay on the Development of Christian Doctrine* (London:
            J. Toovey, 2nd edn).
Nicetas Paphlago
1862   *Laudatio magni Gregorii, Constantinopolitanae urbis archiepis-
            copi, cognomento Theologi*, Migne, *Patrologia Graeca*, 105.
Nineham, D.E.
1958   'Eyewitness Testimony and the Gospel Tradition, II', *Journal of
            Theological Studies* NS 9: 243-52.
1967   '... *et hoc genus omne*—An Examination of Dr A.T. Hanson's Stric-
            tures on Some Recent Gospel Studies', in *Christian History and
            Interpretation: Studies Presented to John Knox* (Cambridge: Cam-
            bridge University Press): 199-222.

Nisbet, H.B.
1985   *German Aesthetic and Literary Criticism: Winckelmann, Lessing,*
              Hamann, Herder, Schiller, Goethe (Cambridge: Cambridge Univer-
              sity Press).
Norman, C. (ed.)
1965   *Poets on Poetry* (Glencoe: Free Press).
Noth, M.
1960   *History of Israel* (London: A. & C. Black, 2nd edn).
Nova Vulgata
1979   ed. E. Schick (Vatican City: Libreria Editrice Vaticana).
Novum Testamentum Latine
1911   ed. J. Wordsworth and H.J. White (Oxford: Oxford University Press).
Nowottny, W.
1965   *The Language Poets Use* (London: Athlone Press).
Nupela Testamen bilong Bikpela Jisas Kraist
1974   *The New Testament in New Guinea Pidgin (Neo-Melanesian)*
              (Hong Kong: British and Foreign Bible Society).
Oakeshott, M.
1933   *Experience and its Modes* (Cambridge: Cambridge University Press).
1975   *On Human Conduct* (Oxford: Clarendon Press).
1983   *On History and Other Essays* (Oxford: Basil Blackwell).
1989   *The Voice of Liberal Learning* (ed. T. Fuller; New Haven: Yale Uni-
              versity Press).
1993   *Religion, Politics and the Moral Life* (ed. T. Fuller; New Haven: Yale
              University Press).
Odeberg, H.
1928   *3 Enoch, or The Hebrew Book of Enoch* (Cambridge: Cambridge
              University Press).
O'Donoghue, N.D.
c1993   *The Mountain behind the Mountain: Aspects of the Celtic Tradition*
              (Edinburgh: T. & T. Clark).
O'Donovan, O.
1978   *Marriage and Permanence* (Bramcote: Grove Books).
Oman, J.
1960   *Grace and Personality* (London: Collins).
O'Neill, J.C.
1988   'Hoover on Harpagmos Reviewed, with a Modest Proposal Con-
              cerning Philippians 2.6', *Harvard Theological Review* 81: 445-49.
Orwell, G.
1984   *Nineteen Eighty-Four* (London: Secker & Warburg).
Pack, R.
1958   *Wallace Stevens: An Approach to his Poetry and Thought* (New
              Brunswick, NJ: Rutgers University Press).
Panofsky, E.
1971   *The Life and Art of Albrecht Dürer* (Princeton, NJ: Princeton Univer-
              sity Press, 4th edn).
Pascal, B.
1950   *Pascal's Pensées* (ed. H.F. Stewart; London: Routledge & Kegan Paul).

Paton, H.J.
1922   'Plato's Theory of ΕΙΚΑΣΙΑ', *Proceedings of the Aristotelian Society*
            22: 69-104 (also in Paton 1951: 255-82).
1951   *In Defence of Reason* (University Library London: Hutchinson).
1955   *The Modern Predicament* (London: George Allen; New York: Mac-
            millan).
1965   *The Categorical Imperative* (London: Hutchinson, 5th edn).
Pattison, G.L.
1992   *Kierkegaard: The Aesthetic and the Religious. From the Magic
            Theatre to the Crucifixion of the Image* (London: Macmillan).
Pearce, R.H.
1951   'Wallace Stevens: The Life of the Imagination', *Proceedings of the
            Modern Language Association* 66: 561-82.
Pearson, H.
1948   *The Smith of Smiths, Being the Life, Wit and Humour of Sydney
            Smith* (Harmondsworth: Penguin Books).
Persius
1845   *The Satires of Persius and Juvenal* (ed. C.W. Stocker; London: Long-
            man, Brown, 3rd edn).
1987   *The Satires of Persius* (ed. W. Barr; trans. G. Lee; Liverpool: Francis
            Cairns).
Petersen N.R.
1978   *Literary Criticism for New Testament Critics* (Philadelphia: Fortress
            Press).
1985   *Rediscovering Paul: Philemon and the Sociology of Paul's Narra-
            tive World* (Philadelphia: Fortress Press).
Peterson, E.
1926   ΕΙΣ ΘΕΟΣ (Göttingen: Vandenhoeck & Ruprecht).
Piero della Francesca
1984   *De prospectiva pingendi* (ed. G. Nicco-Fasola; Firenze: Casa Editrice
            le Lettere).
Potier, J.-P.
1991   *Piero Sraffa—Unorthodox Economist (1898-1983): A Biographical
            Essay* (London: Routledge).
Powell, J.E.
1977   *Wrestling with the Angel* (London: Sheldon).
Preziosi, D.
1989   *Rethinking Art History: Meditations on a Coy Science* (New Haven:
            Yale University Press).
Prickett, S.
1986   *Words and the Word: Language, Poetics and Biblical Interpretation*
            (Cambridge: Cambridge University Press).
Pritchard, J.B.
1954   *The Ancient Near East in Pictures Relating to the Old Testament*
            (Princeton, NJ: Princeton University Press).
Protevangelium of James
1963   in E. Hennecke, *New Testament Apocrypha* (ed. W. Schneemelcher;
            London: Lutterworth).

Proudfoot, G.W.
1992   *Tom a Lincoln* (Oxford: Oxford University Press).
Quinton, A.M., and R. Meager
1960   'Tragedy', *Proceedings of the Aristotelian Society* 34: 145-86.
Rad, G. von
1949   *Das erste Buch Mose: Genesis Kapitel 1-12,9* (Göttingen: Vanden-
              hoeck & Ruprecht).
1972   *Genesis* (trans. J.H. Marks; London: SCM Press, 3rd edn).
Ramsey, I.T.
1964   *Models and Mystery* (London: Oxford University Press).
1966   'Talking about God', in F.W. Dillistone (ed.), *Myth and Symbol*
              (London: SPCK).
1967   *Religious Language* (London: SCM Press).
1972   'The Crisis of Faith' (Lecture to the Church Leaders' Conference,
              Selly Oak Colleges, Birmingham, 12 September 1972).
1973   *Models for Divine Activity* (London: SCM Press).
Ranke, L. von
1874   *Geschichte der romanischen und germanischen Völker*, in *Sämmt-
              liche Werke*, XXXIII–XXXIV (Leipzig: Duncker und Humblot).
Reid, L.A.
1931   *A Study in Aesthetics* (London: George Allen & Unwin).
Reimarus, H.S.
1971   *Fragments* (London: SCM Press).
Renan, E.
n.d.   *Vie de Jésus* (Paris: Calmann-Lévy, 13th edn).
1864   *The Life of Jesus* (London: Trübner).
Reynolds, G.
1969   *Turner* (London: Thames & Hudson).
Richardson, J.S.
1995   'The Roman Mind and the Power of Fiction', in L. Ayres (ed.), *The
              Passionate Intellect: Essays on the Transformation of Classical
              Traditions* (New Brunswick: Transaction Publishers).
Riches, J. (ed.)
1986   *The Analogy of Beauty* (Edinburgh: T. & T. Clark).
Ricks, C.
1988   *T.S. Eliot and Prejudice* (London: Faber).
Ricoeur, P.
1969   *The Symbolism of Evil* (Boston: Beacon Press).
1975   *La metaphore vive* (Paris: Editions du Seuil).
1976   *Interpretation Theory: Discourse and the Surplus of Meaning* (Fort
              Worth: Texas Christian University Press).
1978   *The Rule of Metaphor* (trans. R. Czerny with K. McLaughlin and
              J. Costello; London: Routledge & Kegan Paul).
Rimmon-Kenan, S.
1983   *Narrative Fiction: Contemporary Poetics* (London: Methuen).
Roberts, C.H., and T.C. Skeat
1983   *The Birth of the Codex* (London: Oxford University Press).

Robinson, H.W.
1946   *Inspiration and Revelation in the Old Testament* (Oxford: Claren-
            don Press).
Robinson, J.A.T.
1963   *Honest to God* (London: SCM Press).
Robinson, J.M.
1957   *The Problem of History in Mark* (London: SCM Press).
Rogerson, J.W.
1992   *W.M.L. de Wette: Founder of Modern Biblical Criticism* (Sheffield:
            Sheffield Academic Press).
Roscommon, Earl of: see Wentworth 1971.
Rose, H.J.
1953   *A Handbook of Greek Mythology* (London: Methuen, 5th edn).
Ross, W.D.
1964   *Aristotle* (London: Methuen, 5th edn).
Rowlands, J.
1975   *Bosch* (London: Phaidon).
Ruskin, J.
1886   *Praeterita* (London: George Allen).
1904   *Modern Painters*, I (London: George Allen, 2nd edn).
Salinger, J.D.
1958   *The Catcher in the Rye* (Harmondsworth: Penguin Books).
Salyer, G., and R. Detweiler
1995   *Literature and Theology at Century's End* (Atlanta: Scholars Press).
Sanday, W., and A.C. Headlam
1902   *The Epistle to the Romans* (Edinburgh: T. & T. Clark, 5th edn).
Santayana, G.
1953   *My Host the World* (London: Cresset Press).
1988   *The Sense of Beauty* (Cambridge, MA; London: MIT Press).
1990   *Interpretations of Poetry and Religion* (Cambridge, MA; MIT Press).
Saussure, F. de
1960   *Course in General Linguistics* (London: Peter Owen).
Scaltsas, T.
1990   'Is a Whole Identical to its Parts', *Mind* 99: 583-98.
Schick, E. (ed.)
1979   *Nova Vulgata* (Vatican City: Libreria Editrice Vaticana).
Schlegel, F. von
1956   *Kritische Schriften* (ed. W. Rasch; Munich: Carl Hanser).
Schürer, E.
1979   *The History of the Jewish People in the Age of Jesus Christ (175
            B.C.-A.D. 135)*, II (rev. and ed. G. Vermes, F. Millar and M. Black;
            Edinburgh: T.& T. Clark).
Schütz, J.H.
1975   *Paul and the Anatomy of Apostolic Authority* (Cambridge: Cam-
            bridge University Press).
Schweitzer, A.
1911   *The Quest of the Historical Jesus* (trans. W. Montgomery; London: A.
            & C. Black, 2nd edn).

1913   *Eine Geschichte der Leben-Jesu-Forschung* (Tübingen: J.C.B. Mohr [Paul Siebeck], 2nd edn).

Scott, W.
1814   *Waverley* (Edinburgh).
1877–82   *Poetical Works* (12 vols.), *Waverley Novels* (48 vols.), *Prose Works* (30 vols.; London: A. & C. Black).
1972   *Waverley* (Harmondsworth: Penguin Books).

Scruton, R.
1990   *The Philosopher on Dover Beach* (Manchester: Carcanet).

Seidlmayer, M.
1960   'Nikolaus von Kues', in *Die Religion in Geschichte und Gegenwart* (Tübingen: J.C.B. Mohr [Paul Siebeck], 3rd edn).

Shaffer, E.S.
1975   *'Kubla Khan' and The Fall of Jerusalem: The Mythological School in Biblical Criticism and Secular Literature, 1770–1880* (Cambridge: Cambridge University Press).

Shakespeare, W.
1951   *William Shakespeare: The Complete Works* (ed. P. Alexander; London: Collins).
1959   *Macbeth* (ed. K. Muir, with minor corrections and new appendix; London: Methuen, 8th edn).
1972   *King Lear* (ed. K. Muir; London: Methuen, 9th edn).

Sharpe, C.K.
1888   *Letters from and to Charles Kirkpatrick Sharpe* (2 vols.; Edinburgh: W. Blackwood).

Sigountos, J.G.
1994   'The Genre of 1 Corinthians 13', *New Testament Studies* 40: 246-60.

Skene, W.F.
1867   *Chronicles of the Picts, Chronicles of the Scots, and Other Early Memorials of Scottish History* (Edinburgh: H.M. General Register House).

Smend, R.
1958   *Wilhelm Martin Leberecht de Wettes Arbeit am Alten und am Neuen Testament* (Basel: Helbing & Lichtenhahn).

Smith, N.C.
1953   *The Letters of Sydney Smith* (2 vols.; Oxford: Clarendon Press).

Smith, R. Gregor
1956   *The New Man: Christianity and Man's Coming of Age* (London: SCM Press).
1960   *J.G. Hamann 1730-1788: A Study in Christian Existence* (London: SCM Press).
1966   *Secular Christianity* (London: SCM Press).
1969   *The Free Man: Studies in Christian Anthropology* (London: SCM Press).
1970   *The Doctrine of God* (London: SCM Press).
1996   'Notes on Penmanship', in *Ministers Forum* 186 (September): 2.

Sophocles
1889   *The Oedipus Coloneus* (ed. R.C. Jebb; Cambridge: Cambridge University Press, 2nd edn).
1893   *The Oedipus Tyrannus* (ed. R.C. Jebb; Cambridge: Cambridge University Press, 3rd edn).
1982a   *Sophocles: Oedipus Rex* (ed. R.D. Dawe; Cambridge: Cambridge University Press).
1982b   *Trachiniae* (ed. P.E. Easterling; Cambridge: Cambridge University Press).

Spinoza, B. de
1843   *Opera*, I-III (ed. C.H. Bruder; Leipzig: B. Tauchnitz).
1862   *Tractatus Theologico-Politicus: A Critical Inquiry into the History, Purpose and Authenticity of the Hebrew Scriptures: with the Right to Free Thought and Free Discussion Asserted, and Shown to Be Not Only Consistent but Necessarily Bound up with True Piety and Good Government* (London: Trubner).
1959   *Spinoza's Ethics and On the Correction of the Understanding* (London: Dent).

Sprigge, T.L.S.
1984   *Theories of Existence* (Harmondsworth: Penguin Books).
1993   'Spinoza and Santayana: Religion without the Supernatural', in *Mededelingen vanwege het Spinozahuis* 69.

Stanford, W.B.
1936   *Greek Metaphor: Studies in Theory and Practice* (Oxford: Basil Blackwell).

Ste Croix, G.E.M. de
1975   'Aristotle on History and Poetry', in B. Levick (ed.), *The Ancient Historian and his Materials* (Westmead: Gregg International).

Stevens, H. (ed.)
1967   *Letters of Wallace Stevens* (London: Faber & Faber).
1977   *Souvenirs and Prophecies: The Young Wallace Stevens* (New York: Knopf).

Stevens, W.
1955   *The Collected Poems of Wallace Stevens* (London: Faber & Faber).
1959   *Opus Posthumous* (ed. S.F. Morse; London: Faber & Faber).
1960   *The Necessary Angel: Essays on Reality and the Imagination* (London: Faber & Faber).

Strack, H.L., and P. Billerbeck
1956   'Das Evangelium nach Matthäus', in *Kommentar zum Neuen Testament aus Talmud und Midrasch*, I (Munich: C.H. Beck'sche Verlagsbuchhandlung).

Strauss, D.F.
1840   *Das Leben Jesu* (Tübingen: C.F. Osiander, 4th edn).
1970   *The Life of Jesus* (trans. M. Evans [George Eliot]; 2 vols.; Michigan: Scholarly Press).

Sutherland, S.
1990   'History, Truth, and Narrative', in M. Warner (ed.), *The Bible as Rhetoric* (London: Routledge).

Swann, D.
1968   *The Space between the Bars: A Book of Reflections* (London: Hodder
            & Stoughton).
Swimme, B., and T. Berry
1992   *The Universe Story: From the Primordial Flaring Forth to the Eco-
            zoic Era: A Celebration of the Unfolding of the Cosmos* (London:
            Penguin Books).
Tabraham, A.J.
1996   'Why Jesus Was Killed: The Scandal of Universality' (unpublished
            MS).
Tanvir, N.R., A. Aragon-Salamanca and J.V. Wall (eds.)
c. 1997   *The Hubble Space Telescope and the High Redshift Universe* (Singa-
            pore and London: World Scientific).
Templeton, E.A.
1991   *God's February: A Life of Archie Craig 1888-1985* (London: British
            Council of Churches).
1988   'Response by Mrs Elizabeth Templeton, Theologian, Church of
            Scotland,' in *The Truth Shall Make You Free: The Lambeth Con-
            ference 1988* (published for the Anglican Consultative Council;
            London: Church House Publishing): 289-92.
1993   *The Strangeness of God: Essays in Contemporary Theology* (Lon-
            don: Arthur James).
Templeton, J.S.
1905   *A Tentative New Creed with Notes: Also A Layman's Thoughts on
            the Church and its Ministry* (Glasgow: printed for private use).
Tennant, F.R.
1928-30   *Philosophical Theology*. I. *The Soul and its Faculties*; II. *The World,
            the Soul and God* (Cambridge: Cambridge University Press).
Theocritus
1952   *Theocritus* (ed. A.S.F. Gow; Cambridge: Cambridge University Press,
            2nd edn).
Thiering, B.
1967   'The Acts of the Apostles as Early Christian Art', in E.C.B. MacLaurin
            (ed.), *Essays in Honour of Griffithes Wheeler Thatcher 1863-1950*
            (Sydney: Sydney University Press).
Thomas, D.
1971   *Collected Poems 1934-1952* (London: Dent).
Thompson, A., and J.O. Thompson
1987   *Shakespeare: Meaning and Metaphor* (Brighton: Harvester).
Thorpe Davie, C.
1953   *Musical Structure and Design* (London: Dennis Dobson).
Thrall, M.E.
1994   *A Critical and Exegetical Commentary on the Second Epistle to the
            Corinthians*, I (Edinburgh: T. & T. Clark).
Tillich, P.
1953-64   *Systematic Theology*, III (London: Nisbet).

Tindall, W.Y.
1959   *A Reader's Guide to James Joyce* (New York: Farrar, Straus &
            Giroux).
Tinsley, J.
1983   'Tell It Slant', *Theology* 83: 163-70.
Tovey, D.F.
1935   *Essays in Musical Analysis*. I. *Symphonies* (London: Oxford Uni-
            versity Press).
Toynbee, A.
1956   *An Historian's Approach to Religion* (London: Oxford University
            Press).
Tracy, D.
1979   'Metaphor and Religion: The Test Case of Christian Texts', in *idem*,
            On Metaphor (ed. S. Sacks; Chicago: University of Chicago Press): 89-
            104.
Traherne, T.
1908   *Centuries of Meditations* (ed. B. Dobell; London: B. Dobell).
Tristram, H.B.
1885   *The Survey of Western Palestine: The Fauna and Flora of Palestine*
            (London: Committee of the Palestine Exploration Fund).
Trocmé, E.
1957   *Le 'Livre des Actes' et l'histoire* (Paris: Presses universitaires de
            France).
1992   'Un Christianisme sans Jésus-Christ?', *New Testament Studies* 38:
            321-36.
Trollope, A.
1980   *An Autobiography* (ed. M. Sadleir and F. Page; Oxford: Oxford
            University Press).
Tulloch, J., and H. Jenkins
1995   *Science Fiction Audiences: Watching Dr. Who and Star Trek* (Lon-
            don: Routledge).
Unger, R.
1925   *Hamann und die Aufklärung: Studien zur Vorgeschichte des
            romantischen Geistes im 18. Jahrhundert* (2 vols.; Halle: Max
            Niemeyer, 2nd edn).
Vaihinger, H.
1920   *Die Philosophie des Als Ob: System der theoretischen, praktischen
            und religiösen Fiktionen der Menschheit auf Grund eines idealis-
            tischen Positivismus* (Leipzig: Felix Meiner, 5th and 6th edns).
1924   *The Philosophy of 'As if': A System of the Theoretical, Practical and
            Religious Fictions of Mankind* (trans. C.K. Ogden [revised by the
            author]; London: Kegan Paul, Trench, Trubner & Co.; New York:
            Harcourt, Brace & Company, 6th edn).
Valéry, P.
1958   *The Collected Works of Paul Valéry*, IV (trans. W.M. Stewart, with
            'Two Prefaces' by Wallace Stevens: 'Gloire du long Désir, Idées' and
            'Chose légère, ailée, sacrée'); and VII (with 'Introduction' by T.S.
            Eliot; London: Routledge & Kegan Paul).

1960   *Oeuvres de Paul Valéry*, II (Paris: Gallimard).
Van Buren, P.M.
1972   *The Edges of Language: An Essay in the Logic of Religion* (London: SCM Press).
Vries, P. de
1958   *The Mackerel Plaza* (London: Gollancz).
Waddell, H.
1947   *Peter Abelard* (New York: Henry Hold).
Waismann, F.
1977   'Fiction', in B. McGuinness (ed.), *Philosophical Papers* (Dordrecht: D. Reidel).
Walker, K.
1942   *Diagnosis of Man* (London: Jonathan Cape).
Wallace, W.
1882   *Kant* (Edinburgh: William Blackwood & Sons).
Walls, R.C.
1995   *Vom Jordan nach Jerusalem* (Düsseldorf: Selbstverlag des Kommissariats des Heiligen Landes).
Walsh, T.F.
1963   *Concordance to the Poetry of Wallace Stevens* (University Park: Pennsylvania State University Press).
Warner, M. (ed.)
1990   *The Bible as Rhetoric* (London: Routledge).
Weir, J.A.
1996   *Casebook on Tort* (Andover: Sweet & Maxwell, 8th edn).
Weiss, J.
1897   *Beiträge zur Paulinischen Rhetorik* (Göttingen: Vandenhoeck & Ruprecht).
Weitz, M.
1955   'Truth in Literature', in *Revue internationale de philosophie* 9: 116-29.
1965   *Hamlet and the Philosophy of Literary Criticism* (London: Faber & Faber).
Wells, G.A.
1988   *Religious Postures* (La Salle: Open Court).
Wells, H.G.
1946   *The War of the Worlds* (Harmondsworth: Penguin Books).
Welsh, I.
1995   *Marabou Stork Nightmares* (London: Cape).
Wentworth, D.
1971   *An Essay on Translated Verse* (1685, 2nd edn), and *Horace's Art of Poetry made English* (1684) (Menson: Scolar Press [facsimiles]).
Wesley, J.
n.d.   *The Works of the Rev. John Wesley, A.M.*, XIII (London: Wesleyan-Methodist Book-Room).
Wette, W.M.L. de
1806-1807   *Beiträge zur Einleitung in das Alte Testament* (2 vols.; Halle: Schimmelpfennig).

1817   *Ueber Religion und Theologie: Erläuterungen zu seinem Lehrbuche der Dogmatik* (Berlin: G. Reimer).

1821   *Ueber Religion und Theologie: Erläuterungen zu seinem Lehrbuche der Dogmatik* (Berlin: G. Reimer, 2nd edn).

1831   *Biblische Dogmatik Alten und Neuen Testaments: Oder kritische Darstellung der Religionslehre des Hebraismus, des Judenthums und Urchristenthums* (Berlin: G. Reimer, 3rd edn).

1855   *Kurzgefasstes exegetisches Handbuch zum Neuen Testament. I.2. Kurze Erklärung der Briefe an die Corinther* (Leipzig: Weidmann, 3rd edn).

Whitehead, A.N.
1956   *Modes of Thought* (Cambridge: Cambridge University Press).

Wieacker, F.
1967   *Privatrechtsgeschichte der Neuzeit* (Göttingen: Vandenhoeck & Ruprecht, 2nd edn).

1995   *A History of Private Law in Europe, with particular reference to Germany* (trans. J.A. Weir; Oxford: Clarendon Press).

Wilder, A.N.
1976   *Theopoetic: Theology and the Religious Imagination* (Philadelphia: Fortress Press).

1982   *Jesus' Parables and the War of Myths: Essays in Imagination in the Scriptures* (London: SPCK).

Wiles, A.
1995   'Modular Elliptic Curves and Fermat's Last Theorem', *Annals of Mathematics* 142: 443-551.

Wiles, M.
1993   'Japanese Military Codes', in F.H. Hinsley and A. Stripp (eds.), *Codebreakers: The Inside Story of Bletchley Park* (Oxford: Oxford University Press).

Winnington-Ingram, R.P.
1980   *Sophocles: An Interpretation* (Cambridge: Cambridge University Press).

Wiseman, D.J.
1958   *Illustrations from Biblical Archaeology* (London: Tyndale Press).

Wittgenstein, L.
1949   *Tractatus logico-philosophicus* (London: Routledge & Kegan Paul).

1960   *Schriften: Tractatus logico-philosophicus, Tagebücher 1914-1915, Philosophische Untersuchungen* (Frankfurt on Main: Suhrkamp).

1977   *Vermischte Bemerkungen* (Frankfurt: Suhrkamp).

1980   *Culture and Value* (ed. G.H. von Wright; trans. P. Winch; Oxford: Basil Blackwell, 2nd edn).

Wodehouse, P.G.
1957   *The Mating Season* (Harmondsworth: Penguin Books).

Wölfflin, H.
1917   *Kunstgeschichtliche Grundbegriffe* (Münich: Hugo Bruckmann, 2nd edn).

1932   *Principles of Art History* (trans. M.D. Hottinger from the 7th German edn; London: G. Bell and Sons).

Woods, G.F.
    1958   *Theological Explanation* (Welwyn: James Nisbet).
Wordsworth, J., and H.J. White
    1911   *Novum Testamentum Latine* (Oxford: Oxford University Press).
Wright, D.F.
    1988   *The Bible in Scottish Life and Literature* (Edinburgh: St Andrew
                Press).
Wyatt, N.
    1996a   *Myths of Power: A Study of Royal Myth and Ideology in Ugaritic
                and Biblical Tradition* (Münster: Ugarit-Verlag).
    1996b   *Ugarit, Religion and Culture: Proceedings of the International
                Colloquium on Ugarit, Religion and Culture: Essays Presented in
                Honour of J.C.L. Gibson* (ed. N. Wyatt, W.G.E. Watson and J.B.
                Lloyd; Münster: Ugarit-Verlag).
Yeats, W.B.
    1950   *The Collected Poems of W.B. Yeats* (London: Macmillan, 2nd edn).
Young, E.
    1773   *The Complaint: or Night-Thoughts on Life, Death, and Immortality*
                (Edinburgh: J. Balfour and W. Creech).
    1989   *Night Thoughts* (ed. S. Cornford; Cambridge: Cambridge University
                Press).
Zeller, E.
    1874   *David Friedrich Strauss in his Life and Writings* (London: Smith,
                Elder).
Zzuurdeeg, W.F.
    1959   *An Analytical Philosophy of Religion* (London: George Allen &
                Unwin).

O all ye exorcisers come and exorcise now, and ye clergymen draw
nigh and clerge...

(Ogden Nash)

Index of References

1. Now published in G. Bastianini and C. Gallazzi, 'Il poeta ritrovato: Scoperti gli epigrammi di Posidippo in un pettorale di mummia', Ca' de Sass 121 (1993), pp. 34-39 (see Dickie 1995: 5-12).

Index Scotorum

Ap-Index

DATE DUE

DEMCO 13829810

προέκειτο γὰρ αὐτοῖς ὅπου μὲν ἐνεχώρει ἀληθεύειν πνευματικῶς ἅμα καὶ σωματικῶς, ὅπου δὲ μὴ ἐνεδέχετο ἀμφοτέρως, προκρίνειν τὸ πνευματικὸν τοῦ σωματικοῦ, σωζομένου πολλάκις τοῦ ἀληθοῦς πνευματικοῦ ἐν τῷ σωματικῷ ὡς ἂν εἴποι τις, ψεύδει.

[It was their [sc. the Evangelists'] purpose to give the truth where possible at once spiritually and corporeally [or outwardly], but where this was not possible, to prefer the spiritual to the corporeal, the true spiritual meaning being often preserved in what at the corporeal level might be called a falsehood.]

Origen, *Commentary on John*

3 5282 00468 7045